Problems and Issues in the Education of Exceptional Children

Edited by

Reginald L. Jones
University of California, Riverside

HOUGHTON MIFFLIN COMPANY · BOSTON
New York · Atlanta · Geneva, Illinois · Dallas · Palo Alto

Library of Congress Catalog Card Number: 74–142329

ISBN: 0–395–11228–1

This volume has been compiled to bring into focus certain problems and issues in the psychology and education of exceptional children. With emphasis on divergence as opposed to convergence, it represents a marked departure from current textbooks and collections of readings in this area: most contemporary writing has focused largely on points of agreement among authorities, while areas of disagreement have often been neglected. The concern with areas of agreement is understandable, given the large body of literature to be covered. Most textbooks would be unwieldy if they attempted to cover all the issues and problems of the areas with which they deal. Yet, it is these very areas of conflict which represent the reality confronting special educators. It is important, therefore, for practitioners and students to be aware of these divergencies and of the arguments and data surrounding them.

The book is seen as a supplement to survey textbooks in the psychology and education of exceptional children; and as well, as a source for advanced courses or seminars, where it is assumed that students have some familiarity with basic special educational facts and principles.

The first six sections deal with issues and problems related to the education of gifted, mentally retarded, speech and hearing handicapped, learning disabled, visually handicapped, and emotionally disturbed children. A final section addresses problems and issues in professional special education. It has seemed important to introduce the prospective practitioner and even those now in service to concerns unique to special education as a field and to several provocative issues and pressing problems. Writings dealing with diagnostic categories and labelling practices, those considering fractional practices in educational assessment and remediation, and articles about the validity of special education for mentally retarded and for minority children are taken up in this final section.

The volume includes several noteworthy features. It treats issues of diagnosis and identification—problems, as it turns out, which are unresolved for many exceptionalities. Educational issues and controversies are highlighted. Appropriately, several exchanges between specialists in the field are reprinted, thus giving the reader direct exposure to a number of very live issues and controversies as represented by their spokesmen. A third feature is the consideration of the multiply handicapped. Here too is an area frequently omitted in textbooks on the psychology and education of exceptional children. Where it is appropriate (as in the areas of the mentally retarded, deaf, blind, and orthopedically disabled), the reader will be introduced to some of the basic concerns involving multiple exceptionality.

As with any volume, the editor has had to be selective in his coverage. No claim is made for comprehensiveness. However, the editor has sought to touch both the theoretical and the applied bases, and to be representative in his coverage of the area. Final judgments of the extent to which these objectives have been met rest with the reader.

A number of my colleagues have facilitated my development and completion of the volume, and I am pleased to be able to publicly record my indebtedness to them. I am especially grateful for the assistance provided by Samuel Kirk, advisory editor to Houghton Mifflin, who guided me in important directions and helped in a variety of important ways in the overall production of the manuscript. This is certainly a better volume because of his counsel. I am also happy to acknowledge my indebtedness to a number of colleagues across the country who have provided helpful comments on various drafts of the materials and helped in other ways: Oris C. Amos, The Ohio State University; Bruce Balow, University of Minnesota; William Carriker, University of Virginia; Louis A. Fliegler, Kent State University; Clifford Howe, State University of Iowa; Frank Hewett, University of California, Los Angeles; Francis Lord, University of Arizona; Robert McIntyre, University of Southern California; Donald Moores, University of Minnesota; Max Mueller, U.S. Office of Education; Carson Nolan, American Printing House for the Blind; Harold Phelps, Illinois State Normal University; Melvyn I. Semmel, Indiana University; Thomas Stephens, University of Pittsburgh; Glenn Vergason, Georgia State College; and Harry Wall, California State College, Los Angeles. The comments and reactions of these specialists have certainly improved the quality of the manuscript, but I must, of course, accept responsibility for the flaws and omissions that remain.

Miss Valarie Bennett cheerfully typed various drafts of the manuscript, helped with bibliographic and library work, and communications with authors and editors. I am grateful to her for these services.

Finally, I acknowledge my continuous indebtedness to Johnette, my wife, who created the environment which made the meeting of the publication deadline and, indeed, the conception of this volume possible.

Reginald L. Jones

* CONTENTS

PART ONE

Gifted

There is no universally agreed upon definition of giftedness. Definitions range from the purely psychometric (giftedness defined by a score on an intelligence test) to the comprehensive one of Havighurst (1958) who wrote:

> The talented or gifted person is one who shows consistently remarkable performance in any worthwhile line of endeavor. Thus we shall include not only the intellectually gifted but also those who show promise in music, the graphic arts, creative writing, dramatics, mechanical skills, and social leadership. (p. 19)

Lucito (1963), in noting that "there is considerable confusion as to the meaning of the term gifted," presents five classes of definitions of giftedness. The first are ex post facto definitions (i.e., the gifted were those who had achieved outstanding stature in one of the professions). Second are the IQ definitions still persisting: gifted children are defined as those who score at or above some point on an intelligence scale. The dropping of the IQ from some definitions and broadening of the term to include individuals who excelled in such areas as music and art—the talented—led to a third class of social definitions.

The identification of the gifted as comprising some percentage of the population has given rise to a fourth class—percentage definitions. And finally, under the stimulation of work by Guilford on the structure of the intellect, definitions of a fifth class—creativity definitions—have arisen.

Small wonder, with the plethora of definitions, that problems of identification of the gifted exist! One study of methods used for identifying gifted children in a midwestern state (Gloss and Jones, 1968) revealed that of 159 school districts reporting educational programs for gifted children, 7 per cent considered as gifted those with IQs below 114, while another 7 per cent classified as gifted those with IQs between 114 and 119. At the upper end of the continuum, only one district set the cutoff as high as IQ 140, but 4 per cent of the districts set the lower limit at IQ 130. Thirty-seven per cent of the districts had no absolute IQ cutoffs, and no districts considered as gifted those with other than above average scholastic aptitude/intelligence and academic achievement. Thus, for more than half the districts, the operational definitions used in identification bear little relationship to past psychometric or current broadened definitions of giftedness (i.e. extension to include high creativity, unusual talent, etc.).

It is clear that problems exist in the identification of gifted children. Why? Martinson in the first article reprinted in this volume takes up a variety of concerns which inhibit identification of the gifted: (1) inadequacy of existing measures; (2) variability of intelligence (i.e., the age-old constancy of the IQ question); (3) cost of identification and special programs, and (4) establishment of a meritocracy or an elite by identifying and labelling individuals gifted.

Expansion of the concept of giftedness beyond purely psychometric considerations is a relatively recent development. Particular attention has been given to creativity as one form of giftedness (Lucito's fifth class of definitions of giftedness). A lively literature has resulted from this inclusion among categories of giftedness. Two of the more provocative articles from the literature are reprinted here. The first by White and Williams ("Identification of Creativity and the Criterion Problem") touches upon the range of definitions of the term creativity, and it also deals with the problem of the criterion of creativity—what are its referents?

Yamamoto in a third article in this section ("Creativity—A Blind Man's Report on the Elephant") presents an analysis of various writings on creativity with a view toward resolution of differences with regard to its nature and measurement.

Gifted individuals are often identified for special educational purposes, the objective, frequently, being to remove them from less endowed peers for purposes of providing a more concentrated and/or diversified educational program. Acceleration, ability grouping, and enrichment are commonly used administrative vehicles for educating gifted children. These practices are not without their critics, however, and the student of educational programs for the gifted will want to be acquainted with the controversies surrounding these plans. Three articles, reprinted here, are appropriate. Pressey ("Educational Acceleration: Occasional Procedure or Major Issue?") presents major arguments supporting the practice of accelerating high ability students; Passow, ("The Maze of the Research on Ability Grouping") analyzes the research on ability grouping and summarizes reasons that may account for difficulties in generalizing from the research; Newland ("Programs for the Superior: Happenstansical or Conceptual?") takes on a variety of problems of programs for the gifted, with special attention given to the practice of enrichment.

Taken together the writings reprinted in this section point up problems— and in some instances prospects—of acceleration, ability grouping, and enrichment as administrative arrangements for the education of gifted children.

REFERENCES

Gloss, G. and R. L. Jones, *Correlates of School District Provisions for Gifted Children: A Statewide Study,* paper presented at the Annual Meeting of the Council for Exceptional Children (New York, April 1968).

Havighurst, R. (ed.), *Education for the Gifted. Fifty-seventh Yearbook of the National Society for the Study of Education,* Part II (Chicago: University of Chicago Press, 1958), p. 19.

Lucito, L. J., "Gifted Children," in L. M. Dunn (ed.), *Exceptional Children in Schools* (New York: Holt, Rinehart and Winston, 1963), pp. 183–184.

Issues in the Identification of the Gifted

RUTH A. MARTINSON

In the field of education, we occasionally indulge in curiously anomalous behavior. We subscribe to the belief that education of children with exceptional learning needs must be based upon complete knowledge of their capabilities. Then we insist on complete case studies and individual examinations in the identification of all children with special learning needs except for one group: the gifted. Within the latter group, we somehow have not accepted the necessity for careful and complete individual tests and case studies. The trend has been, instead, to use shortcuts, group measures of dubious value, teacher nomination, and an almost frenetic effort to include sundry unvalidated measures in the hope that they will add to our understanding of all of the unknown dimensions of the intellect.

The literature on identification of the gifted appears in frequent pronouncements which seem to sort themselves into four general categories of concern. These are (a) concern about the inadequacy of existing measures; (b) concern about the variability, or assumed variability, of intelligence; (c) concern about the high cost of identification and programs; and (d) concern about the establishment of a meritocracy.

INADEQUATE MEASURES

The criticisms of IQ measures rather typically refer to the limitations of a single measure. The critics have by implication equated the single IQ derived from group tests with the broader types of information which are available to us through the combined use of appropriate individual tests and case studies. The assumption seems to be that, even when we use individual examinations and the case study, we identify a person who performs narrowly in the direction of academic excellence. This assumption persists, despite the fact that any large scale study provides ample evidence to the contrary. The point that is made by those who criticize tests

* From *Exceptional Children* 1966, *33*, pp. 13–16. Reprinted by permission of the author and the publisher.

on the basis of the narrowness of the IQ lies in the convergent nature of their own thinking, namely, that the test (meaning the group test, rather than the individual test) identifies only verbal and mathematical abilities. The view is then held that these are only two limited abilities among a potentially wide spectrum, instead of the plausible alternate view that the identification of verbal and mathematical abilities provides the basis for assessment of skills which reach into many, many academic subjects and many areas of human learning.

Criticisms have also been leveled at those who purport to measure intelligence but whose instruments do not include adequate assessment of creativity. Studies have been done in which various tasks grouped together have been labeled measures of creativity. On the basis of these studies, the authors have claimed that the measures of creativity provide information of value beyond the narrowness of intelligence tests. Persons who have conducted studies to measure creativity have been critical of the narrow concept of intelligence held by those who use intelligence tests which have been with us for some years, but which, to them, are no longer of value.

With the studies of Getzels and Jackson, Torrance, and others, a great swell of reaction against intelligence tests as a means for designating gifted children arose, and much of this reaction is still with us. After the thorough and systematic evaluations of these studies by persons like de Mille and Merrifield and Robert Thorndike, in which numerous necessary questions were raised, initial enthusiasm was replaced with more sober consideration.

A recent book of Wallach and Kogan (1965) starts with a summary of evaluative studies on the question of intelligence and/or creativity, which is a substantial contribution to a final state of sobriety and augurs well for more careful reporting in future studies of human abilities. In their evaluation, Wallach and Kogan point out that the indices of creativity possess little relationship to one another. They point out further that no evidence exists for a single unified dimension labeled creativity, similar to the concept of *g* or general intelligence. The analysis of a number of studies has shown consistently and without exception that the creativity tests relate more strongly to a standard intelligence index than they relate to one another.

The assumption that creativity is not related to intelligence is unwarranted on the basis of all evidence to date. Much controversy has occurred because of premature claims that certain tests were measures of creativity and by the implication that these measures, unvalidated though they may be, should replace the measures we now have.

A third criticism of existing measures has been raised regarding the failure of intelligence tests to identify the culturally disadvantaged. This has largely been the result of the use of group measures, rather than of individual tests. As Goslin (1963) points out, individual tests such as the Stanford-Binet have had extremely limited use with relatively few children in our school systems, despite the fact that it is considered by many to be the most accurate available measure. The criticisms which are made, then, are of *group* tests, which fail to assess the abilities of various lower strata socioeconomic groups and certain bilingual groups.

We thus find articles such as one in the January, 1966, Newsletter of the Council of State Directors of Programs for the Gifted which complain that there are no known measures to assess ability of children who speak Hawaiian pidgin, and that children are given intelligence tests involving reading on which they do poorly and thus fail to qualify for remedial help, although they have the potential for improvement. A typical and oft quoted comment of Allison Davis is that half the ability of this country goes down the drain because of the failure of intelligence tests to measure the real mental ability of children from the lower socioeconomic groups and because of the failure of the schools to recognize and train this ability (Sexton, 1961).

We all accept the validity of this charge. It is probable that Davis's criticism is conservative and that the loss is even higher than 50 percent. In the California state study, if group tests had been used instead of individual tests, over half of the gifted population would have been lost. Some of the gifted had group IQ's as low as 100, because group tests, as demonstrated elsewhere, lack items which are appropriate for the identification of gifted young people (Martinson and Lessinger, 1962). If thorough studies and continuing search utilizing individual tests and complete study could be the rule among the disadvantaged, we would find, as has been found in several studies, that the disadvantaged population also includes large numbers of gifted children.

VARIABILITY OF INTELLIGENCE

The second general issue frequently mentioned in connection with the identification of the gifted is the variability of intelligence. In much of the literature which has its grandparenthood really in the nature-nurture controversy, we read of individuals who have grown up in impoverished environments and who have been given certain educational advantages which have resulted in dramatic changes in intelligence. The Iowa studies of an earlier day were the precursors of present day studies, such as the Higher Horizons project and similar efforts dealing with younger children. In cases of extreme environmental deprivation and severe language impoverishment, these differences do exist and should be accounted for by any skilled school psychologist.

Longitudinal studies sometimes are cited to demonstrate the mutability of intelligence from early childhood to adulthood. Variability does exist, but the basic reasons usually are not made clear. Bloom (1964) has pointed out that intelligence measured at age one does have a zero correlation with intelligence measured at age 17. However, by age 2 the correlation is .41, by age 4 the correlation with the measurement at age 17 has increased to .71, and by age 11 it has increased to .92. The reason for the variance is that the tests which are used in the study of infant development are largely motor and physical development tests, and these differ markedly in content from the tests based on cognitive skills and verbal abilities which are used at later ages. The differences at the two extremes are not particularly surprising when we realize that the measures differ.

Bloom (1964) points out in his text that, in the major longitudinal studies such as the Berkeley Study, the Brush Study in Cleveland, and the Fels Study, the data are consistently comparable in a way which suggests that general intelligence develops in an exceedingly lawful way. Intelligence is regarded as developmental and as increasingly stable from birth to young adulthood. By age 4, 50 percent of the variation in intelligence at age 17 is accounted for; and, barring extremes, the environment has relatively little effect on IQ change after the early school years.

HIGH COST OF IDENTIFICATION

The third issue which is raised is the high cost for identification and for differentiated programs for the gifted. At the present time, very few states provide funds for excess costs incurred by programs in this area. In one of the states where support is given, the funds are roughly one-fifth the amount recommended in a comprehensive study. In California, the current expenditure on the gifted amounts to less than five percent of the total expended on exceptional children in the state (California State Department of Education, 1966). It is less than two percent of the annual revenue from tobacco and alcohol taxes and about six percent of the annual tax on horse racing (Report of the Legislative Analyst, 1966).

The question in every state has too long been whether the adult population actually is interested in education of the high quality which should be available for gifted young people. The real question is whether these people are as entitled to appropriate education as are other youth with unusual learning needs.

THE ISSUE OF MERITOCRACY

The fourth issue is probably basic to difficulties which those persons interested in the gifted have encountered in their efforts to get adequate educational programs within the public schools. This issue is based on the question of whether the gifted should be identified for special consideration at all. The fear is expressed that special programs or provisions create a meritocracy or an elite within the school population.

It is extremely difficult to convince people of the need to provide adequate educational opportunities for those who do better than they do anyway. Despite abundant research evidence, it is also extremely difficult to convince people that appropriate opportunity for intellectual growth serves to produce better human beings. Persons who are given the opportunity to grow optimally live better with other human beings. The waste of human talent which comes from apathy is understood by very few among us. The loss from wasted talent suffered by all of humanity is understood by still fewer.

The four issues arise because of a basic lack of willingness by many to accept the real meaning of individual differences and to assume the obligations based on such recognition. The notion that some individuals are brighter than others is unpalatable, and the notion that some persons are more capable of successful performance than others is rejected. The rejection of intelligence tests and the view of intelligence as environmentally developed is more acceptable to many. Thus the conclusion is that tests are not necessary and that, given the same environment, all persons have an equal opportunity to win. Such an idea has wide appeal. It falls flat, however, when we observe wide variations of ability within single families where opportunities presumably are highly similar.

More constructive than the elimination of tests is the use of individual tests and case studies to find and understand the educational needs of all gifted children, whatever their circumstances. Complete study should lead, in turn, to appropriate programs. A point of view (Hunt, 1961) often cited in reference to the disadvantaged but seldom cited in relation to the gifted is peculiarly appropriate as a fundamental premise:

> It is highly unlikely that any society has developed a system of child-rearing and education that maximizes the potential of the individuals who compose it. Probably no individual has ever lived whose full potential for happy, intellectual interest and growth has been achieved (p. 346).

If we could adopt this point of view and offer consistent, appropriate opportunities to the gifted people whom we identify, each child's potential for intellectual development would be maximized and untold benefits would accrue to both the individuals and to the society with which they have contact.

REFERENCES

Bloom, B. S., *Stability and Change in Human Characteristics* (New York: John Wiley and Sons, 1964).

California State Department of Education, *The State School Fund and Educational Statistics* (Sacramento, Calif.: Ruth A. Martinson, 1966).

Goslin, D. A., *The Search for Ability* (New York: Russell Sage Foundation, 1963).

Hunt, J. M., *Intelligence and Experience* (New York: Ronald Press, 1961).

Martinson, Ruth, and L. Lessinger, "Problems in the identification of intellectually gifted pupils," *Exceptional Children*, 26 (1962) pp. 227–231.

Report of the Legislative Analyst, *Analysis of the budget bill of the state of California, 1966–67.* (Sacramento, Calif.: California State Printing House).

Sexton, Patricia, *Education and Income* (New York: Viking, 1961).

Wallach, M. E., and N. Kogan, *Modes of Thinking in Young Children* (New York: Holt, Rinehart and Winston, 1965).

** 2 **

Identification of Creativity and the Criterion Problem

WILLIAM F. WHITE AND ROBERT E. WILLIAMS

Although "creativity" was a topic for discussion many years ago in Sigmund Freud's *Interpretation of Dreams* (1938), in E. L. Thorndike's *Psychology of Arithmetic* (1922), and in John Dewey's *How We Think* (1910), it has been only in the last decade that the identification and measurement of creativity has developed into one of the most volatile inquiries of educational consideration. The focus of theory and research has converged on the challenging query of what is creativity, in what situations can it be found, and in whom does creative ability exist.

Since the early part of the twentieth cenutry, differences in cognitive ability have been defined by the traditional concept of intelligence and have been measured by the critical metric of the IQ. Performances on one or more of the many well-known intelligence tests have been the accepted norms for interpreting individual differences in productive thinking. About the mid-point of this century many authors, such as Barron, Guilford, Thurstone, Patrick, Holland, McClelland, Getzels and Jackson, Taylor, MacKinnon, Parnes, Torrance, et al., have cited empirical evidence stating a significant difference in the measurement of intelligence and what is called "creativity." Torrance (1962) chooses to define creative thinking as the "process of sensing gaps, or disturbing missing elements; forming ideas concerning them, testing these hypotheses; and communicating the results, possibly modifying and retesting the hypotheses." Guilford (1952) defines creative thinking as "divergent thinking which

* From *Journal of Secondary Education* 1965, *40*, pp. 275–281. Reprinted by permission of the senior author and the publisher.

pertains to less structured situations in which the individual's thinking is free to take different directions." Sir Frederick Bartlett (1959) defines imaginative thinking as "adventurous thinking, or getting away from the main track out of the mold, being open to experience, and permitting one thing to lead to another." Ghiselin (1955), of the University of Utah, has stated: "The measure of a creative act should be the extent to which it restructures our universe of understanding." In a related definition, Robert Lackland (1955) of the National Aeronautical and Space Administration has verbalized that "a measure of creativity of a contribution may be made in terms of the extent of the area of science which it underlies. The more basic a contribution, the wider its effect." These two definitions may be considered as very nearly equivalent in meaning. The incorporation of a basic contribution will require a more extensive restructuring of our universe of understanding that will a less fundamental proposition. Both these definitions involve the "ideas," rather than concrete products.

The advancement of civilization down through the centuries has been produced by creative thinking. All inventions and discoveries in literature, music, painting, sculpture, drama, and other forms must point to creativity as the basic process. We have all wondered and marveled at a certain work of art, or an invention, and asked ourselves the question, "What is it that produced this magnus opus?" Present theories of creativity infer that creative performance is dependent upon a large number of relatively separate variables, each one of which accounts generally for only a small unique part of the total variation in the creative performance. Presently, no one predictor, no one instrument, could be considered a panacea, adequately identifying the creative potential. Currently used (and more traditional) methods of identifying giftedness are inadequate for identifying creative potential.

If we could identify and predict creative ability from school grades, our problem would be a very easy one. Research, however, has shown that school grades have little or no validity in the identification of the creative individual. At the adult level, several studies have demonstrated that there is no relationship between school performance (as measured by school grades) and later success in scientific research work.

In order to identify creative talent and creative products, it would be advisable to have some concepts about the creative process. Patrick (1955) characterizes creative thought processes into four stages: preparation, incubation, illumination, and verification. In the preparatory stage, the subject seeks to find out all he can about the particular problem. In a sense, the creative personality desires to collect all data on a particular problem. He is entirely curious in his behavior. As John Dewey (1910) stated: "This bringing forth of inventions, solution, and discoveries rarely occurs except to a mind that has previously steeped itself consciously in material relating to its question." The period of incubation is apparently characterized by a recurrence of the chief idea. The subject frequently has turned to other matters, e.g., relaxation, physical exercise, other mental gymnastics, but the central idea (or hypothesis) is growing and modifying. Other ideas may accompany it, but the main idea is more clearly defined than it was at the beginning. Within a period of illumination, the idea assumes a definite form. It is the time when lines of a picture are first sketched; it is the stage when a model is first designed. Verification is the final stage in the creating process, according to Patrick (1955), Claparede (1934) and Wallas (1926). The idea that has been obtained in the illuminative period is now made to conform to the criteria of art or science. It adopts the discipline, the technical application, the conformity of the logical world. Those authors who hold a four-step process in the creation of productive thinking state an overlapping in each of these stages. From descriptions by these authors of the particular stages, it seems a little "too logical" for many psychologists and educators. The important fact, perhaps, is found in the unfulfilled want of the organism which is induced by a particular problem. It is an irritating tension. A disturbance of the equilibrium in the nervous system is established (a lack of homeostasis). The problem, brought forward in the consciousness, presents an intolerable state that consistently and tyrannically demands a solution of the unknown.

Getzels and Jackson (1962) in their book *Creativity and Intelligence*, bring forth the major issues of the Freudian approach to creative activity in the following outline:

(1) Creativity has its genesis in conflict, and the unconscious forces motivating the creative 'solution' are parallel to the unconscious forces motivating the neurotic 'solution'; (2) the psychic function and effect of creative behavior is the discharge of pent-up emotion resulting from conflict until a tolerable level is reached; (3) creative thought derives from the elaboration of the 'freely rising' fantasies and ideas related to childhood, and day dreaming; (4) the creative person accepts these 'freely rising' ideas, the non-creative person suppresses them.

Whether we read in Freud's writings, or any psychologist since his time, whether we consult the modern pedagogies of the "creative thinking movement," we still know very little about the process and development of creativity.

Most of the authors of recent years state the criterion problem as the most serious object of study. They define the criterion problem as the difficulty of identifying individuals who have positively and clearly demonstrated a characteristic of creativity. During the past seventy years, a variety of tests have been devised to give some insight into the recognition of creative thinking in people from preschool to higher education. Early measurements were taken from Rorschach or analogies; modern trends have been developing a large variety of types of stimuli, materials, responses, in an attempt to measure a great diversity of mental abilities.

The famous work of the great American psychologist, Terman (1916), confirmed and strengthened the work of the Binet tests and brought about the prestigious value and respect for Intelligence Tests, or IQ Tests. The Wechsler tests gained enormous popularity and apparently confirmed the validity of the measurement of mental growth. So strongly were these IQ tests accepted in the American culture and schools that few even questioned the tests as complete measures of the intellectual ability in the scholastic curriculum. Moreover, hardly a voice of protest rose in art, music, or scientific discovery as to the validity of these tests as true criteria of intellectual talent and giftedness. It was not until the 1950s that the work of Thurstone (1952), Guilford (1950), Getzels and Jackson (1958–1962), and Torrance (1960) began to tear down the elaborate image of the intelligence tests. They were demonstrating that the IQ was not measuring other needful components of intellectual ability and skill. It was not that no one had dared, up to this time, to raise voices of skepticism regarding validity of the tests, etc., but it was the collective empirical evidence of the 1950s that was thrown line ram-rods against the palisades of the traditional impregnable castle and has formed a breach in the wall.

The Stanford-Binet and Wechsler tests were criticized gravely on the basis of convergent-divergent thinking. These tests were measuring the logical use of facts and data, but were they measuring the "either-or" complex of ideational fluency? Calvin Taylor (1957) argues that intelligence tests "essentially concern themselves with how fast relatively unimportant problems can be solved without making errors."

In 1960 Calvin Taylor spoke his criticism at a summer conference in Utah:

> To me it is highly inconsistent to conceive of the mind as being represented by a single score or even by only the handful of scores or dimensions present in our current intelligence tests. The brain which underlies the mind is far too complex for us to hope that all of its intellectual activities can be represented by only a single score or by a handful of dimensions. To seriously utilize such an oversimplified picture might be considered as an insult to the brain, to the human mind, and to the human being.

It was Guilford, however, who has made the most serious attacks on the typical intelligence tests. Since they represent a narrow measure of intellectual tasks, or what Guilford calls "convergent thinking," they neglect those tasks requiring "divergent thinking." In 1950 Guilford declared in an address before the American Psychological Association: "Examination of the content of intelligence tests reveals very little that is of an obviously creative nature."

Guilford suggests about fifty known factors of the intellect. In order to make the various factors understandable, it is necessary to identify two basic intellectual modes of these many factors. One vector tends toward recapturing the known, searching with exploration, and developing a new mode previously unknown. Various terms have been used to describe these directions: Guilford speaks about the "convergent" and the "divergent"; Rogers uses "defensive" and "openness"; Maslow calls them

"safety" and "growth." One mode is describing the acquired, the conformed; the other reaches out to an innovation. Guilford and Merrifield
(1960) summarized the creative thinking abilities within a framework of
Guilford's "structure of the intellect." There is no doubt that some components of convergent thinking such as memory, cognition, judgment, and
evaluation are important to creativity. It may be that divergent thinking
abilities are even more so. It is the area of divergent thinking abilities that
has been largely overlooked. The high level aptitude factors which may be
involved in creative performance are: originality, adaptive flexibility,
spontaneous flexibility, ideational fluency, expressional fluency, associational
fluency, word fluency, sensitivity to problems, visualization, judgment, and
redefinition.

Guilford and Merrifield found a large number of significant correlations
between non-aptitude traits and the measured component of ideational
fluency. Holland (1958) stresses a relationship between aggression, self-
confidence, ascendance, and originality. There has been a large amount
of study concerned with the relationship of originality, creativity, or inven-
tiveness with personality variables. A striking point brought out by
Guilford, Christensen, Frick, and Merrifield (1957) is that "those having
higher originality scores tend to be more interested in aesthetic expression,
in meditative or reflective thinking, and appear to be more tolerant of
ambiguity, and to feel less need for discipline and orderliness." Stein and
Heinze (1960) have shown relationships between individuals, identified as
highly creative, with personality measures from such tests as Minnesota
Multiphasic Personality Inventory, Thematic Apperception Test, Rorschach, and others. Torrance (1962) found eighty-four characteristics
differentiating highly creative personalities from less creative ones. Mac-
Kinnon (1961, 1962a, 1962b) posited significant perceptual differences
among architects of differing creativity. Contrasted with less creative
producers, creative architects conceived themselves more often as inventive, determined, independent, individualistic, enthusiastic, and industri-
ous.

Although most authors stress that present instruments of measuring personality characteristics are not suitable for identifying and developing
creativity in young people, nevertheless, such devices as the Strong Vocational Interest Blank, the Allport-Vernon-Lindzey Study of values, and the
Minnesota Multiphasic Personality Inventory, are able to provide some
satisfactory results for counseling and advisement. MacKinnon (1961) in-
terprets some interesting conclusions from measures of creative individuals
with the Allport-Vernon-Lindzey Values test. He states that creative
people are much more interested in the Theoretical and Aesthetical,
demonstrating a greater concern for symbolic relationships, meanings,
implications than any interest in small details and concrete finite data.
Furthermore, MacKinnon declares a surprising result in the examination
of creative personalities, for they score high on both the Theoretical
and Aesthetical Scales. Since many authors point to a conflict between

these two scales, it is notable to see the toleration for the tension and conflict in both these areas and the capacity to reconcile this dichotomy with some form of integration. Palm (1959) found that the highly creative persons in comparison with high scorers on the Miller Analogies Test had significantly stronger needs in the matters of deference, exhibition, succorance, abasement, and change. This need for change and exhibitionism is a most interesting factor and correlates highly with other studies showing the need for new and different things.

Torrance (1962), taking a cue from Tumin (1954) hypothesized five motivations that stunt creative productivity: "an excessive quest for certainty, power, meaning, and social relations, and pathological rejection of social relations." Perhaps one of the most interesting experimental papers relative to identifying creative talent is found in the study by Torrance, Rush, Kohn, and Doughty (1959) with American jet aces.

From the thirty-six fighter pilots (jet aces) interviewed, one of the most salient characteristics of each ace was his ability and desire to take calculated risks. Each pilot throughout his own life experiences has:

> Tested the limits—the limits of his own abilities, the limits of his equipment or material resources, the limits of the situation. He was willing to diverge from the behavioral norms, whether rules of flying safety, or classroom rules as a school boy, and to take calculated risks.

Although Atkinson (1957) proffered a theoretical model of need achievement and fear of failure to risk taking, and Scodel et al. (1959) utilized the Atkinson model in gambling behavior, Kogan and Wallach (1964) employed personality variables in a markedly different way by casting them into a moderator role. The authors declare that they can:

> specify some of the forces that determine the direction of their highly generalized decision making toward risk or conservatism. Similarly, for those subjects who exhibit lesser degrees of generality in the risk-taking domain, we are now able to pinpoint some of the personality determinants contributing to risk taking or conservatism in particular situational contexts.

Curiosity seems to be a central impulse of the creative personality, yet the conformity of society continually stifles this risk-taking endeavor. If conformity completely dominates and rigidly determines the way words are spelled, the way grammar is constructed, the way thoughts are originated, the way problems are solved, it could stultify original thinking. Under the guise of prudence, good manners, or reasonableness, teachers in private, public, and parochial schools frequently devaluate or restrict the "wild" or "silly" ideas of children. Often such rejection has moralistic overtones and may lead to an interpretation on the part of the child of the impropriety of using deferred judgment, or preconscious material. Along this same idea Wertheimer (1945) emphasizes: "Training in traditional logic is not to be disparaged: it leads to stringency and rigor in each step, it contributes to critical-mindedness; but it does not of itself seem to give rise to productive thinking."

Holland (1961) in his studies of the National Merit Scholarship Corporation suggests that creative performances at the secondary level occur more frequently among students who are "independent, expressive, asocial, consciously original, and who aspire for future achievement." He feels we must use "non-intellectual" criteria in selecting students for scholarships and fellowships.

Perhaps one of the most striking investigations of the identification and comparison of creative adolescents was published by Getzels and Jackson (1962). In comparing highly intelligent adolescent students with highly creative adolescent subjects, three specific areas were studied: scholastic achievement, need for achievement, and perception by teachers.

It was found that the high IQ and high creative students in the study were superior to their school population. An educational implication of the surprising result was that the highly creative group, although lower in IQ, were, nevertheless, superior in scholastic achievement. The apparent "overachievement" was unaccountable from tests of need achievement.

Teachers were reported to favor high achievers who were high IQ's but not to favor the high achievers who were high creatives. However, deMille and Merrifield (1962) cautioned the unjustified procedure and consequent erroneous findings of the Getzels and Jackson (1962) study.

Literature has abounded in studies that have attempted to pinpoint the creative function in terms of four orientations: (a) the nature and quality of the product created; (b) the actual expression and on-going process during the creation; (c) the nature of the creator; and (d) environmental factors that fostered creativity. While results of varying degrees of validity and reliability were reported, a singular lack of empirical research grounded in personality theory has been observed.

There has been much spoken and written on the subject of the identification of creativity. Enough has been presented to give room for the differential in intellectual make-up. Vast segments of our social order, especially our schools, are structured to legislate against and penalize the creative individual. Conformity to standards and ideals, rules and methods, can strangle the very life from creative talent. It is paradoxical—the one student who seems most capable of coping with our age of revolutions—the creative youth, the true revolutionary, the student who can tolerate psychic tensions, who will risk anything to solve or change an attitude, a method, or a problem, is our pedagogical misfit.

** 3 **

"Creativity"—A Blind Man's Report on the Elephant

KAORU YAMAMOTO

Something people call an elephant is there—this much is sure. And all of us, blind men, have been touching it, feeling it, figuring it out and describing it to each other. On some facts, we agree among ourselves; on others, we cannot even understand what each is trying to tell the other. But, it is precisely this amorphousness which *is* the elephant—the elephant of creativity.

So, we agree on certain things about creativity. We agree, without knowing exactly what, that creativity is an essential element in self-renewing man and society (Gardner, 1962) and that giving "a fair chance to potential creativity is a matter of life and death for any society" (Toynbee, 1964, p. 4). Most of us agree that the definitional and criterial problems must somehow be resolved, that theoretical formulation or model building is desirable, that refinement of measuring techniques and instruments is necessary, and that coordinated research efforts are essential (Gallagher, 1964; Stein, 1962; Yamamoto, 1964). But, alas, that about exhausts our happy agreement on the elephant.

Why the limitation in mutual understanding? Not that people have neglected to converse with each other—indeed not! To begin with, look at the number of published conference proceedings on this topic, including Anderson (1959), Gruber, Terrell and Wertheimer (1963), MacKinnon (1961), Street (1963; 1964), Taylor (1964a), Taylor and Barron (1963) and Torrance (1959; 1960; 1961). Also remember the efforts to present an overview of the field (Gallagher, 1964; Getzels, 1964; Guilford, 1950; Mackworth, 1965; Taylor, 1964b; Taylor & Holland, 1962) and to compile a list of reference sources (Gowan, 1965; Stein, 1962; Stein & Heinze, 1960).

Neither is it because we have not explored the elephant extensively and

* From *Journal of Counseling Psychology* 1965, *12*, pp. 428–434. Reprinted by permission of the author and the publisher, The American Psychological Association.

I acknowledge my debt to a lucid paper by Martindale (1965). Martindale applied the ontological (holism vs. elementarism)—epistemological (positivism vs. antipositivism) classification scheme to sociological theories in his analysis of functionalism.

intensively within the practical limits of time, resources and personnel, in the current "revival of American interest in creativity" (Burt, 1962, p. 293). Some among us tried to reach the general public (Osborn, 1957), while others have chosen to address mainly teachers (Lowenfeld, 1952; Marksbury, 1963; Mearns, 1958; Torrance, 1962; Torrance, 1963; Torrance, 1965b; Zirbes, 1959). Some concentrated upon investigation of children and adolescents (Getzels & Jackson, 1962; Torrance, 1965a) and others studied adults (Barron, 1963; MacKinnon, 1962; MacKinnon, 1965). There have been formulations based upon clinical experiences (Kubie, 1958; Rogers, 1961a) and those derived from logical analyses (Kneller, 1965; Rugg, 1963). The person, press, process and product of creativity (Rhodes, 1961) have been approached structurally (Guilford, 1959a; Guilford, 1959b), typologically (Stein, 1963), experimentally (Maltzman, 1960) and descriptively (Flanagan, 1965).

And, finally, it is not that the self-corrective measures of professional critique have been absent. Indeed, such criticisms have ranged from historical analyses (Joncich, 1964) to technical exhortations (Cureton, 1964). Some are general, and others are specific; some are mellow and scholarly, while others are harsh and abusive; some come from workers active in research and others from mere critics (Bram, 1962; Brown, 1964a; Brown, 1964b; Burt, 1962; Christensen, 1964; Coffman, 1963; Cronbach, 1962; deMille & Merrifield, 1962; Faris, 1962; Gallagher, 1965; McNemar, 1964; Merrifield, 1964; Michael, 1964; Thorndike, 1963a; Thorndike, 1963b; Vernon, 1964; Wodtke, 1964). One thing is clear in any case: this is not a one, big family in which peace and togetherness prevail!

HOLISTIC APPROACHES

Why, after all these efforts, have we not reached any kind of consensus about the elephant we are feeling? My thesis is that the reason may be found in the basic philosophical differences among workers in this area, and *not* in mere over-abundance of different techniques and methods nor in the wide variation in the degree of sophistication among investigators. In other words, I submit here that the confused and out-of-focus picture of the elephant drawn by the blind men is a result not so much of the restricted nature of their exploratory activities as of the radically different expectations with which explorations are initiated. Men might come to the same conclusion even if one touches the elephant's ears while another feels its tail—but not when the former started out with a clear intention of finding a rabbit and the latter a snake.

Non-Positivistic Holism

To begin with, it should be recognized that there are many people, especially artists of one kind or another, who firmly and sincerely believe that creative acts cannot and should not be analyzed because doing so will destroy the very essence of the process of creation. When lightning strikes, they insist, no one can or should try to catch it—the best thing to do is to observe it and appreciate it.

The holistic and non-positivistic (i.e., non-analytic or non-empirical) orientation of this group has its counterparts in educational-psychological spheres. For example, MacLeod (1963) declares: "The psychologist who insists that creativity can be studied scientifically must bear the burden of proof in the face of centuries of testimony from mystics and artists, and even from ordinary people, who claim that at least in his moments of inspiration man is not subject to the laws of nature" (p. 178).

Another example comes from Rogers (1961a) who enumerates three conditions for a "potentially constructive act" as (1) openness to experience, (2) an internal locus of evaluation, and (3) the ability to toy with elements and concepts. Rogers further speculates that, "When these three conditions obtain, constructive creativity will occur." However, he hastens to add, "But we cannot expect an accurate description of the creative act, for by its very nature it is indescribable" (p. 355).

Mooney (1963a) also proposes that "it is only by daring to take part in creation that one can consciously help himself to become a vitalized part of it" (p. 340). To him, the study of creativity has a meaning only as "a cue to creation-underway in the human being" (Mooney, 1963b, p. 45). The study of creativity thus leads to a study of creation-under-way or of reality which is represented in his OITC (open, integral, transactional, and creative) model of existence of an organism.

Actually, what is implied in these remarks by the existentially-oriented workers is a re-examination of the current trends in Anglo-American psychology, or of its scientism (after Rogers). Rogers himself paraphrases this implication, saying, "This tunnel vision of behavior is *not* adequate to the whole range of *human* phenomena" (Rogers, 1961b, p. 87). The same recognition of "the limits of verbal, analytic, conceptual rationality" is shared by Maslow (1961, p. 58) who emphasizes also the crucial role the future time plays in the presently existing personality. "Only the flexibly creative person can really manage future, *only* the one who can face novelty with confidence and without fear" (Maslow, 1961, p. 59).

To these people, description and explanation of creativity are more or less synonymous with a direct experience which is peculiarly human and defies any objective analyses based upon causal laws. Instead, such acts should be grasped through subjective and empathic understanding of the experience and interpreted in purposive terms. By definition, then, any communication between this group and those who believe in positivistic approaches is severely limited.

Nevertheless, some among the non-positivistic holists would answer in the affirmative to the question, "Can we have a science of creative thinking?" It should be clearly recognized, however, that what is meant by "science" here is principally "an attitude—an attitude of disciplined curiosity" (MacLeod, 1963, p. 179), rather than the rules of public inquiry and verification of knowledge claims which are based wholly upon deterministic presuppositions.

Positivistic Holism

Not all those who focus their attention on the "whole man" insist upon non-positivistic orientations. There are many who "aim to differentiate, yet to retain the whole" (Allport, 1957, p. 9), through observation of regularity and dependability of events and their relations.

Although still emphasizing the immediate, "organic" experiences and phenomenological viewpoints, the Gestaltist school "recognized that analysis is at the very heart of science" (Marx & Hillix, 1963, p. 185). They are against the reductionistic method of analysis employed by association psychologists and they tended to regard strict quantification premature. Nevertheless, Wertheimer, in his stimulating analysis of productive thinking (1945), shows how the human mind works in simple but novel problem-solving situations. His formulations are often subjective and largely qualitative, but his analysis is certainly insightful, heuristic and amenable to more rigorous studies than possible with the "existential" picture of creative processes.

Having the whole and analyzing it too—this orientation is also seen in the work of Lowenfeld (1952) who tries to analyze both "emotional and mental" aspects of the technique, topic and material of arts to provide teaching and evaluation principles not entirely dependent upon intuition. Thus, he states:

> In this book an attempt has been made to show methods of approach in art education based upon psychological relationships between creation and creator on the different age levels. Since these relationships cannot be bound by strict rules, the methods must necessarily be flexible. It is, however, the author's belief that as long as art is taught merely intuitively, art education is either the special province of a few privileged educators or a source of failure for the general classroom teacher. (Lowenfeld, 1952, pp. vii–viii)

Through his observations Lowenfeld detects different approaches to creative arts revealed by creators and feels strongly that such variations should not be ignored and disrupted since these are not merely superficial differences in technique but, instead, they are deeply rooted in the creators' thinking. For example, in his discussion of clay modeling, he describes two different modes of expression, the "pulling out from the whole" or analytic method and the "putting single representative symbols together into a whole" or synthetic method. The former is interpreted as dependent upon visually-minded thinking processes, while nonvisual experiences are regarded to underlie the latter approach. Similar observations are made by Blatt and Stein (1959) in their study of different styles of problem solving. Obviously, "there are different ways of achieving the same criterion" and "there is no single profile of *the* successful student, just as there is no profile of *the* creative individual" (Stein, 1963, p. 282).

The holistic emphases or the efforts to preserve the complexity of personality in analytical processes are also apparent in studies by MacKinnon (1962; 1963; 1965). Recently, Sanford (1965) clearly delineated the position of the positivistic holists in the following words:

> Just as complex phenomena are to be explained in part in terms of the activities of constituent processes, so simple processes have to be understood as partly determined by the larger structures in which they have place. Truth may be discovered by abstracting parts from the whole and studying them intensively, but the whole truth can never be discovered in this way. It is the whole truth, and particularly the truth about wholes, that is needed for parctice. (Sanford, 1965, p. 194)

Studies of creative behavior would indeed profit from systematic observation and analysis of the creative process *in situ*. For the purposes of articulating the whole personality systems with social systems, it may be that we need more of what Barker (1965) called "transducer data" than traditional "operator data." In other words, we may have to "carve nature at her joints," rather than establish synthetic laboratory models of creativity.

ELEMENTARISTIC APPROACHES

In spite of the perennial swinging of the pendulum, the overall picture in current American behavioral-social sciences seems to be characterized by elementarism (reductionism) and analytic attitudes.

Non-Positivistic Elementarism

Possibly because of his highly practical preoccupation, Osborn (1957) reveals much non-empirical orientation in his writings. He speaks, on the one hand, of the process of problem-solving in elementaristic terms (i.e., the seven steps beginning with orientation and ending in evaluation) and delineates what he calls the "detailed procedures of brainstorming." On the other hand, his data language is non-operational and his evidence is largely anecdotal and somewhat speculative. His intuitive argument runs like this:

> Our thinking mind is mainly two-fold: (1) *a judicial mind* which analyzes, compares and chooses. (2) *a creative mind* which visualizes, foresees, and generates ideas. . . . Judicial effort and creative effort are alike in that both call for analysis and synthesis . . . In the average person, judgment grows automatically with years, while creativity dwindles unless consciously kept up. . . . The right mood for judicial thinking is largely negative. . . . In contrast, our creative thinking calls for a positive attitude. We have to be hopeful. We need enthusiasm. (Osborn, 1957, pp. 26–27)

The workers of this orientation seem to share the conviction that it is possible not only to identify creative talent but also to promote it by applying certain definite methods (Mearns, 1958; Wilt, 1959; Zirbes, 1959). However, the description of the specific procedures by which creativity is supposedly nourished tends to be abstract and speculative. Hughes (1961) offers a typical statement: "All children possess creativity. It is a part of their inheritance as human beings. Creativity, like other aspects of an individual's potential, must be nurtured" (p. 80).

It should be understood here that such statements are articles of faith and pronouncements of personal belief which are not readily amenable to empirical verifications. In this context, "creativity" becomes an omnibus term. It connotes many psychological states and response tendencies, none of them clearly and unambiguously. No wonder, then, that published analyses of creativity tend to be at once high-sounding and unspecific, as exemplified by the following quotation.

> The media to be manipulated in teaching seem to be time, space, things, and the people, including the teacher himself, from whom the individual or group may learn. The teacher can manipulate the bearers of the culture, that is, he can arrange an environment that either includes or excludes certain people and things and that extends certain invitations to search and to experiment. The teacher also can vary the character of his mediation between the children and the culture at several points—when goals are being set, when information is being processed, when human interaction is going on, when evaluation is in progress. Creativity in teaching can thus be judged by the quality of opportunities actually provided by a teacher for young people to have educative experiences. (Miel, 1961, pp. 8–9)

It is very likely that, until and unless our knowledge and understanding of instructional processes are refined and more precisely formulated, the practical principles which are given to teachers and others for fostering creativity in children will remain quite general and grossly outlined as in the six rules described by Torrance (1965a, p. 315), namely, (1) respect for children's questions, (2) respect for imaginative and unusual ideas, (3) teaching self appreciation of ideas, (4) opportunities for experimentation without external evaluation, (5) encouragement and evaluation of self-initiated learning and (6) cause-consequent orientation in evaluation.

Positivistic Elementarism

It is not difficult to find examples of studies belonging to this category. These may be found to divide generally into Cronbach's "two disciplines of scientific psychology" (Cronbach, 1963), namely, experimenters and correlators.

Experimental psychology with its emphasis upon studies of variance among treatments is represented in the work of Maltzman (1960), Mednick (1962) and Staats and Staats (1963), among others. As a rule, such writers make a distinction between originality (the formation of new combinations of associative elements) and creativity (original problem-solving behavior which meets the additional requirement of social usefulness). "Thus a new pattern of response is produced; the responses are old, but the combination is new" (Dollard & Miller, 1950, p. 37) and "the more mutually remote the elements of the new combination," the more original the solution (Mednick & Mednick, 1964, p. 55).

Note here that the *newness* of the combination which is embraced by these definitions as the criterion for originality implies appraisal of an individual's present behavior against his own past behavior. Contrast this with Maltzman's definition that originality represents "behavior which occurs relatively infrequently, is uncommon under given conditions, and is relevant to those conditions" (Maltzman, 1960, p. 229). The latter, with its emphasis on infrequency and uncommonness, clearly implies a social criterion, or normative judgment of an individual's behavior with reference to the behavior of other members of his group (institution, society, etc.). Thus, even the seemingly monolithic definition employed by the association psychologists has not resolved the social-individual, or nomotheticidiographic, dilemma in studies of creativity (cf., e.g., Wilson, 1958).

In most of the experimental studies (e.g., Maltzman, Simon, Raskin, & Licht, 1960), the word association technique has been one of the standard methods and the results are interpreted as supporting the hypothesis that "originality can be learned and that the same principles of conditioning hold as in other forms of operant behavior" (Maltzman, 1960, p. 230) and that the shape and type of the associative hierarchy of responses determine the frequency and nature of creative behaviors (Mednick, 1962).

In sharp contrast, the correlational psychologists, notably Guilford, have openly rejected such associative interpretation of creativity (and of learning). Guilford (1963a, p. 106) points out that, "Traditionally, learning has been accounted for on the basis of the principle of association, whether of ideas, of stimuli, or of stimuli and responses." However, he then proceeds to challenge the appropriateness of the single concept of association for explaining learning in different realms of human behavior and he proposes the adoption of his structural model of intellect (more specifically, of the six product categories or concepts in the model) in lieu of the single associative principle (Guilford, 1964, p. 263).

The correlational psychologists' concern with the variation among organisms (individual differences) is revealed in their preferential application of multivariate methods and, specifically, of factor analytic techniques. Guilford thus states, "When the problem is approached from the standpoint of individual differences, the most natural scientific technique to apply is that of factor analysis" (Guilford, 1963b, p. 214). Elsewhere, he adds, ". . . our way of using factor analysis has one great advantage in that we do not have to worry about the criterion problem. Factor analysis provides its own criteria" (Guilford, 1964, p. 262).

Whether this latter viewpoint is shared by other psychologists is a moot question, since some workers have undoubtedly regarded the trend as "a narcissistic program of studying . . . tests as an end in themselves" (Cronbach, 1963, p. 9). Thus, Beittel (1964) states that "Guilford's 'Structure of the Intellect' idea has to be viewed as a self-sufficient system in which the logic of relations between the parts are important structurally and symbolically, without reference to the question of their external validity" (p. 273). To the foregoing can be added the comments of McNemar (1964, pp. 879–880) who argues strongly for evidence on empirical validity of creativity tests based upon independent criteria.

Whatever the merit of such reservations about Guilford's position, it is hard to deny the strength of his impact upon research on thinking and upon teaching practice. This appears to be particularly true of Guilford's idea that individual differences in problem-solving performance can be largely accounted for by differences in common-factor variance patterns in the structure of intellect (Guilford, 1963a, p. 107). Reification of Guilford's factors appears to be an unfortunate but possibly inevitable by-product of such a forceful formulation.

It is interesting in this context to observe that Guilford himself once recorded the following words in agreement with Cronbach (1963): "The unifying basis of theory comes from a wedding of the logic of experimental method and factor analysis. The latter, if it is to be used effectively in basic research, should never be separated from the former" (Guilford, 1959b, p. vii).

A possible way of resolving the experimenter versus correlator dilemma in the study of "the behavior or organism-in-situation" (Cronbach, 1963, p. 17) may be provided by computer simulation techniques (Newell, Shaw, & Simon, 1963; Tomkins & Messick, 1963). In such an approach, creative thinking seems to be defined in terms of behavior involving organization of information into novel combinations. If insight or "inspiration" is assumed to be an integral part of creative thinking (such a possibility is by no means ruled out by this group of workers), such processes admittedly cannot be programmed. On the other hand, the end product of creative thinking, namely, a novel arrangement of material or information, may certainly be accomplished (or approximated) by the use of a computer instead of a human brain. These combinations can be formulated on a computer either on the basis of a random model or by application of logical procedures. In this delimited sense creative work may be understood as a difficult but manageable case of general problem-solving behaviors.

It seems evident, as Newell, Shaw, and Simon (1963, p. 116) assert, that in the present stage of development the specific findings from such computer simulation are less significant than the methodology itself. A computer program which is intended to serve as a model must sooner or later be checked against independent observations (i.e., empirical findings) to establish its validity just as in the case of any other mathematical or verbal models. In addition, a considerable amount of knowledge of any behavioral phenomenon is probably required previous to its computer simulation. Nevertheless, modern computers offer the distinct advantages of speed and complexity and thus allow the experimenter to "change the parameters or values on several different variables at once, more than could easily be coped with conceptually or mathematically, . . ." (Messick, 1963, p. 310). With continuing efforts in the field of computer simulation, our understanding of the fundamental processes of the functioning of human mind, especially at its inventive best, may indeed be substantially facilitated.

EPILOGUE

I have suggested in this paper that the blind men of the present day have been experiencing some difficulties in mutual communication and understanding not so much because of their restricted exploratory abilities and spheres of scrutiny as because of their radically different philosophical positions or expectations with which they set out in their exploration. Thus, I have tried to point out the fact that the present "confused abundance" in the study of creativity is a result of (1) the different points of departure in the definition of creativity, (2) the differences in assumptions and presuppositions, and (3) the differences in research strategies among and within groups of workers of different orientations. There are some who believe that analytical studies of creativity are simply impossible without destroying the essence of the act of creation. There are others who, while believing that empirical investigation is possible, argue against reductionistic approaches and insist on the necessity to understand a man's creative behavior in its whole. Still others enthusiastically declare their faith in the universal creative potential of man and exhort others to follow certain procedures to foster creativity, basing their arguments on largely intuitive judgment and casual (i.e., uncontrolled) observations. And, finally, there are those who contend that reductionistic empiricism is the royal road to the understanding of creative behavior. Each group has its unique assumptions, adopts its particular definitions, and employs its preferred techniques of inquiry. Each group has its own language, its peculiar way of speaking about the problem which is not readily understood by other groups of workers. Obviously, these divergences in frame of reference and in form of communication add to the difficulty of integrating man's knowledge about his uniquely human behavior, namely, creativity.

A final word of caution is in order. I have intended this analytical exercise as an explication of the concept of creativity, as a means of placing the research problem in broader perspective, and as a possible stimulus to the reformulation of some of the relevant issues. Naturally, the paper should not be construed as an effort to classify (or "pigeonhole") various workers in creativity research. Attempts at rigid classification of concept formation and research strategy would work against the free and rich cross-fertilization of ideas which is essential for advancement of our knowledge in this complex field of inquiry.

REFERENCES

Allport, G. W., "European and American Theories of Personality," pp. 3–24 in H. P. David and H. von Bracken (eds.), *Perspectives in Personality Theory* (London: Tavistock Publications, 1957).

Anderson, H. H. (ed.) *Creativity and Its Cultivation* (New York: Harper, 1959).

Barker, R. G., "Explorations in Ecological Psychology," *American Psychologist,* 20 (1965), pp. 1–14.

Barron, F., *Creativity and Psychological Health* (Princeton, N.J.: Van Nostrand, 1963).

Beittel, K. R., "On the Relationships Between Art and General Creativity: A Biased History and Projection of a Partial Conquest," *School Review,* 72 (1964), pp. 272–288.

Blatt, S. J. and M. I. Stein, "Efficiency in Problem Solving," *Journal of Psychology,* 48 (1959), pp. 192–213.

Borko, H., "Do Computers Think?," pp. 12–21 in H. Borko (ed.), *Computer Applications in the Behavioral Sciences* (Englewood Cliffs, N.J.: Prentice-Hall, 1962).

Bram, J., "Book Review on *Creativity and Intelligence* by J. W. Getzels and P. W. Jackson," *Library Journal,* 87 (1962), p. 1798.

Brown, G. I., "Book Review on *Creativity and Psychological Health* by F. Barron," *Educational and Psychological Measurement,* 24 (1964), pp. 707–709. (a)

——, "Book Review on *Creativity and Psychological Health* by F. Barron," *Educational and Psychological Measurement,* 24 (1964), pp. 709–711. (b)

Burt, C., "The Psychology of Creative Ability," *British Journal of Educational Psychology,* 32 (1962), pp. 292–298.

Christensen, P. R., "Book Review on *Contemporary Approaches to Creative Thinking,* ed. by H. Gruber, G. Terrell, and M. Wertheimer," *Educational and Psychological Measurement,* 24 (1964), pp. 705–707.

Coffman, W. E., "Convergent and Divergent Excellence," *Contemporary Psychology,* 8 (1963), pp. 125–126.

Cronbach, L. J., "Book Review on *Creativity and Intelligence* by J. W. Getzels and P. W. Jackson," American Journal of Sociology, 68 (1962), pp. 278–279.

——, "The Two Disciplines of Scientific Psychology," pp. 3–22 in Martha Mednick and S. A. Mednick (eds.), *Research in Personality* (New York: Holt, Rinehart and Winston, 1963).

Cureton, Louise W., "Creativity Research and Test Theory," *American Psychologist,* 19 (1964), pp. 136–137.

DeMille, R. and P. R. Merrifield, "Book Review on *Creativity and Intelligence* by J. W. Getzels and P. W. Jackson," *Educational and Psychological Measurement,* 22 (1962), pp. 803–808.

Dollard, J. and N. E. Miller, *Personality and Psychotherapy* (New York: McGraw-Hill, 1950).

Faris, E. L., "Book Review on *Creativity and Intelligence* by J. W. Getzels and P. W. Jackson," *American Sociological Review,* 27 (1962), pp. 558–559.

Flanagan, J. C., "Progress Toward the Goals of Project Talent," *Bulletin of Project Talent,* (1965), No. 4.

Galagher, J. J., "Productive Thinking," pp. 349–381 in M. L. Hoffman and Lois W. Hoffman (eds.), *Review of Child Development Research*, vol. 1 (New York: Russell Sage, 1964).

Gardner, J. W., "Renewal in Societies and Men," *Annual Report of Carnegie Corporation*, 1962, pp. 3–13.

Getzels, J. W., "Creative Thinking, Problem-solving, and Instruction," pp. 240–267 in E. R. Hilgard (ed.), "Theories of Learning and Instruction," *Yearbook of the National Society for the Study of Education*, 63 (1964), Part I.

Getzels, J. W. and P. W. Jackson, *Creativity and Intelligence* (New York: Wiley, 1962).

Gowan, J. C., "Annotated Bibliography on Creativity and Giftedness," Final Report, U.S. Office of Education, Cooperative Research Project No. S–056. Northridge, Calif.: San Fernando Valley State College Foundation, 1965).

Gruber, H. E., G. Terrell, and M. Wertheimer (eds.), *Contemporary Approaches to Creative Thinking* (New York: Atherton, 1963).

Guilford, J. P., "Creativity," *American Psychologist*, 5 (1950), pp. 444–454.

——, "Three Faces of Intellect," *American Psychologist*, 14 (1959), pp. 469–479. (a)

——, *Personality* (New York: McGraw-Hill, 1959). (b)

——, "Intellectual Resources and Their Values as Seen by Scientists," pp. 101–118 in C. W. Taylor and F. Barron (eds.), *Scientific Creativity: Its Recognition and Development* (New York: Wiley, 1963). (a)

Hughes, Marie M., "Integrity in Classroom Relationships," pp. 77–106 in Alice Miel (ed.), *Creativity in Teaching* (Belmont, Calif.: Wadsworth, 1961).

Joncich, Geraldine, "A Culture-bound Concept of Creativity: A Social Historian's Critique, Centering on a Recent American Research Report," *Educational Theory*, 14 (1964), pp. 133–143.

Kneller, G. F., *The Art and Science of Creativity* (New York: Holt, Rinehart and Winston, 1965).

Kubie, L. S., *Neurotic Distortion of the Creative Process* (Lawrence, Kans.: University of Kansas Press, 1958).

Lowenfeld, V., *Creativity and Mental Growth*, 2nd ed. (New York: Macmillan, 1952).

MacKinnon, D. W., "The Nature and Nurture of Creative Talent," *American Psychologist*, 17 (1962), pp. 484–495).

MacKinnon, D. W., (ed.), *Report of Proceedings for Conference on "The Creative Person"* (Berkeley, Calif.: University Extension, University of California, 1961).

——, "Creativity and Images of the Self," pp. 251–278 in R. W. White (ed.), *The Study of Lives* (New York: Atherton, 1963).

——, "Personality and the Realization of Creative Potential," *American Psychologist*, 20 (1965), pp. 273–281.

Mackworth, N. H., "Originality," *American Psychologist*, 20 (1965), pp. 51–66.

MacLeod, R. B., "Retrospect and Prospect," pp. 175–212 in H. E. Gruber, G. Terrell, and M. Wertheimer (eds.), *Contemporary Approaches to Creative Thinking* (New York: Atherton, 1963).

McNemar, Q., "Lost: Our Intelligence? Why?" *American Psychologist*, 19 (1964), pp. 871–882.

Maltzman, I., "On the Training of Originality," *Psychological Review*, 67 (1960), pp. 229–242.

Maltzman, I., S. Simon, D. Raskin, and L. Licht, "Experimental Studies in the Training of Originality," *Psychological Monographs*, 74, No. 6 (whole no. 493) (1960).

Marksbury, Mary L., *Foundation of Creativity* (New York: Harper and Row, 1963).

Martindale, D., "Limits of and Alternatives to Functionalism in Sociology," pp. 144–162 in D. Martindale (ed.), *Functionalism in the Social Sciences* (Philadelphia: American Academy of Political and Social Science, 1965).

Marx, M. H. and W. A. Hillix (eds.), *Systems and Theories in Psychology* (New York: McGraw-Hill, 1963).

Maslow, A. H., "Existential Psychology—What's in It for Us?" pp. 52–60 in R. May (ed.), *Existential Psychology* (New York: Random House, 1961).

Mearns, H., *Creative Power* (New York: Dover, 1958).

Mednick, S. A., "The Associative Basis of the Creative Process," *Psychological Review,* 69 (1962), pp. 220–232.

Mednick, S. A. and Martha T. Mednick, "An Associative Interpretation of the Creative Process," pp. 54–68 in C. W. Taylor (ed.), *Widening Horizons of Creativity* (New York: Wiley, 1964).

Merrifield, R. R., "Book Review on *Guiding Creative Talent* by E. P. Torrance," *Educational and Psychological Measurement,* 24 (1964), pp. 711–715.

Messick, S., "Computer Models and Personality Theory," pp. 305–317 in S. S. Tomkins and S. Messick (eds.), *Computer Simulation of Personality* (New York: Wiley, 1963).

Michael, W. B., "Book Review on *Scientific Creativity: Its Recognition and Development* edited by C. W. Taylor and F. Barron," *Educational and Psychological Measurement,* 24 (1964), pp. 711–715.

Miel, Alice, "Teaching as a Creative Process," pp. 3–9 in Alice Miel (ed.), *Creativity in Teaching* (Belmont, Calif.: Wadsworth, 1961).

Mooney, R. L., "A Conceptual Model for Integrating Four Approaches to the Identification of Creative Talent," pp. 331–340 in C. W. Taylor and F. Barron (eds.), *Scientific Creativity: Its Recognition and Development* (New York: Wiley, 1963).

———, "Creation and Teaching," pp. 45–62 in W. P. Street (ed.), *Creativity and College Teaching* (Lexington, Ky.: Bureau of School Services, University of Kentucky, 1963).

Newell, A., J. C. Shaw, and H. A. Simon, "The Processes of Creative Thinking," pp. 63–119 in H. E. Gruber, G. Terrell, and M. Wertheimer (eds.), *Contemporary Approaches to Creative Thinking* (New York: Atherton, 1963).

Osborn, A. F., *Applied Imagination*, 2nd ed. (New York: Scribner's Sons, 1957).

Rhodes, M., "An Analysis of Creativity," *Phi Delta Kappan,* 42 (1961), pp. 305–310.

Rogers, C. R., "Toward a Theory of Creativity," pp. 347–359 in C. R. Rogers, *On Becoming a Person* (Boston: Houghton Mifflin, 1961). (a)

———, "Two Divergent Trends," pp. 85–93 in R. May (ed.), *Existential Psychology* (New York: Random House, 1961). (b)

Rugg, H., *Imagination* (New York: Harper and Row, 1963).

Sanford, N., "Will Psychologists Study Human Problems?" *American Psychologist,* 20 (1965), pp. 192–202.

Staats, A. W. and Carolyn K. Staats, *Complex Human Behavoir* (New York: Holt, Rinehart, and Winston, 1963).

Stein, M. I., "Survey of the Psychological Literature in the Area of Creativity with a View Toward Needed Research," Final Report, U.S. Office of Education, Cooperative Research Project No. E–3 (New York: Research Center for Human Relations, New York University, 1962).

———, "Explorations in Typology," pp. 281–303 in R. W. White (ed.), *The Study of Lives* (New York: Atherton, 1963).

Stein, M. I. and Shirley J. Heinze, *Creativity and the Individual* (Glencoe, Ill.: Free Press, 1960).

Street, W. P. (ed.), *Creativity and College Teaching* (Lexington, Ky.: Bureau of School Services, University of Kentucky, 1963).

—— (ed.), *Creativity in Its Classroom Context* (Lexington, Ky.: Bureau of School Services, University of Kentucky, 1964).

Taylor, C. W. (ed.), *Widening Horizons in Creativity* (New York: Wiley, 1964). (a)

—— (ed.), *Creativity: Progress and Potential* (New York: McGraw-Hill, 1964). (b)

Taylor, C. W. and F. Barron (eds.), *Scientific Creativity: Its Recognition and Development* (New York: Wiley, 1963).

Taylor, C. W. and J. L. Holland, "Development and Application of Tests of Creativity," *Review of Educational Research*, 32 (1962), pp. 91–102.

Thorndike, R. L., "The Measurement of Creativity," *Teachers College Record*, 64 (1963), pp. 422–424. (a)

——, "Some Methodological Issues in the Study of Creativity," pp. 40–54 in E. F. Gardner (ed.), *Proceedings of the 1962 Invitational Conference on Testing Problems* (Princeton, N.J.: Educational Testing Services, 1963). (b)

Tomkins, S. S. and S. Messick (ed.), *Computer Simulation of Personality* (New York: Wiley, 1963).

Torrance, E. P. (ed.), *Creativity: Proceedings of the Second Minnesota Conference on Gifted Children* (Minneapolis: Center for Continuation Study, University of Minnesota, 1959).

—— (ed.), *Talent and Education* (Minneapolis: University of Minnesota Press, 1960).

—— (ed.), *New Educational Ideas: Proceedings of the Third Minnesota Conference on Gifted Children* (Minneapolis: Center for Continuation Study, University of Minnesota, 1961).

——, *Guiding Creative Talent* (Englewood Cliffs, N.J.: Prentice-Hall, 1962).

——, *Education and the Creative Potential* (Minneapolis: University of Minnesota Press, 1963).

——, *Rewarding Creative Behavior* (Englewood Cliffs, N.J.: Prentice-Hall, 1965). (a)

——, *Gifted Children in the Classroom* (New York: Macmillan, 1965). (b)

Toynbee, A., "Is America Neglecting Her Creative Minority?" pp. 3–9 in C. W. Taylor (ed.), *Widening Horizons in Creativity* (New York: Wiley, 1964).

Vernon, P. E., "Creativity and Intelligence," *Educational Research*, 6 (1964), pp. 163–169.

Wertheimer, M., *Productive Thinking* (New York: Harper, 1945).

Wilson, R. C., "Creativity," pp. 108–126 in N. B. Henry (ed.), "Education for the Gifted," *Yearbook of the National Society for the Study of Education* 57 (1958), Part II.

Wilt, Miriam E., *Creativity in the Elementary School* (New York: Appleton-Century-Crofts, 1959).

Wodtke, K. H., "Book Review on *Creativity: Progress and Potential* edited by C. W. Taylor," *Educational and Psychological Measurement*, 24 (1964), pp. 715–720.

Yamamoto, K., "Creative Thinking: Some Thoughts on Research," *Exceptional Children*, 30 (1964), pp. 403–410.

Zirbes, Laura, *Spurs to Creative Teaching* (New York: Putnam's Sons, 1959).

** 4 **

Educational Acceleration:
Occasional Procedure or Major Issue?

SIDNEY L. PRESSEY

At long last, it is becoming generally admitted that some acceleration of some gifted youngsters is desirable.   Thus a conference of representatives of the American Psychological Association, American Educational Research Association, and Association for Supervision and Curriculum Development concluded that "The research testimony as to the advantages of acceleration is weighty, consistent, and continuous over several decades." However, acceleration was judged not "the best method for dealing with the able," and very limited in application; "It is probable that acceleration should *not* take place with youngsters whose IQ is below 130" [italics theirs] or below about the top five per cent of all school children in ability (*1, pp. 60–62*). This paper presents considerations arguing that acceleration is certainly the most advantage-yielding and, on the whole, most sound method of dealing with talented youngsters, that the top fifth or more of all pupils might well progress faster than the usual lock-step pace, that acceleration may occur desirably anywhere from kindergarten to professional school—and presents the most rewarding of all opportunities for wise student personnel policy.

THE NEGLECTED VALUES OF TIMESAVING

The chapter on evaluation and research of a recent book on education of the gifted presents elaborate schedules for appraising programs, but nowhere is there mention of the time they take. The careful design of a well-financed investigation provided excellent controls and broad appraisals but nowhere took account of timesaving, nor did the report mention that the accelerates, besides doing better than the controls, had also saved

* From *The Personnel and Guidance Journal* 1962, *41*, 12–17. Reprinted by permission of the author and the publisher. Copyright, 1962, American Personnel and Guidance Association.

a year! There is now a nationwide effort to get more able young people to go to college; those who do so increasingly go on into graduate or professional school; of these, the ones who (for example) obtain a doctorate in a science do so at a median age of around 30. A physician who specializes gets into his career even later. Reasonable programs of acceleration would lower these ages at least two years—thus adding two years to career! A medical discovery which added two years to life would receive worldwide acclaim. An educational procedure accomplishing somewhat the same result still tends to be looked at askance.

A variety of investigations indicate that able youngsters can complete secondary school at the age of 17 or 16 instead of the usual 18, that they are then more likely to go on to college (where they do better work and are more likely to graduate than controls of the same ability but the usual entering age), that those graduating young are more likely to go on to graduate or professional school and more likely to have successful careers. Thus Terman found that most of his famous gifted group were accelerated in age of graduating from high school, and comparison of those graduating at age 17, 16, and 15 showed progressive increases from oldest group to youngest in percentages graduating from college, taking one or more years of graduate work, and (for men) in the highest classification as to vocational success—though there was relatively little difference among these three groups in childhood IQ (13). The writer has obtained similar findings. A substantial number of other investigations are to the same effect (10).

Why should all this be so? Obviously early graduation from high school or college leaves more time in youth for further education, for which there may remain more family funds with less likelihood of death of a parent or other reverse; and leaving school for marriage or job is less likely. Earlier beginning of career leaves more time for it. These would seem obvious but neglected timesaving advantages of acceleration. But other factors seem likely.

EDUCABILITY, CREATIVITY, MATURITY

First an intriguing but seemingly completely neglected possibility. Forty years ago, Bagley showed that draftees in the First World War from the various states varied in tested "intelligence" according to the adequacy (largely the average length) of the schooling in those states. Draftees in the Second World War had had about two years more schooling than those in the first and tested as roughly that much higher in "general ability." Lorge found that boys given tests of "intelligence" in 1921 and again in 1941 showed increases in scores roughly proportional to the amount of their schooling since 1921. Several investigations have compared groups of bright pupils who completed the usual three-year junior high school program in two years with groups similar to them in initial school record and ability but taking the usual three years as to record in senior high, and found the accelerates there doing as well or better academically—and satisfactory in social adjustment. Similar results have been reported for groups doing the three years of senior high in two years as regards record in college. If at the end of its intensive two years an accelerate group and its control had been given tests of "general ability," might the accelerates have been found gaining over their controls in "intelligence"?

The writer knows of no such comparisons. But surely a junior high program includes vocabulary, concepts, and study skills of some general value which gained in two years should show on such tests as gains over the controls, if not in "intelligence" in part of what the usual "intelligence" tests measure. This might perhaps best be called "educability." At least the accelerates in the two years gained more education. There may be other gains. Thus over two-thirds of the students who, under subvention of the Ford Foundation, skipped the last year of high school (42 per cent had only 10 years of public school) reported as an advantage "a much greater academic challenge in college than in high school." Parents reported gains in maturity. As a result of these and other factors not only did the "Fordies" do better in college than cases paired with them as to aptitude but who had completed high school and were about two years older, but gained more from college sophomore to senior year on the Graduate Record Examination (2).

Lehman's findings that most outstanding creative work has tended to come early in the careers of famous scientists, inventors, authors, artists, musicians are widely known (5). However, it is not generally recognized that his curves for years of optimal creativity show mostly ages of patenting an invention or publishing a report of a scientific discovery or a book, and the brilliant ideas probably came a year or more earlier. Push these curves down a couple of years and they are close to his curves for ages of winning athletic championships, and in coordination with data on ages of maximal health, capability for learning difficult material, and strong outranging interests (12, 14). Not only greatest creative potential, but also greatest health and enthusiasm to support creative effort, appears usually to come in the twenties and earlier thirties; and if full-time education extends well into these years, maximal productivity might be reduced.

Not only are the increasing numbers of college and advanced students an increasing burden on the economy for both their keep and their schooling, increasingly they are married—32 per cent of a sampling of senior men in the undergraduate colleges of The Ohio State University in the autumn quarter of 1961 and 58 per cent of graduate school men, many with children. Housing for married students is a distinctive problem of the post-war campus, and scholarship or other support for them a substantial charge on funds available for such purposes. However, in the writer's opinion it is not primarily their costs that make student marriages a threat to the prolonging of advanced training, but more broadly the desire shown by young people that they be allowed the realization of adulthood without long delay, after maturity has been reached. Adulthood means not only marriage, but the beginning of career and an independent place in the community. So earlier completion of full-time education will, the writer believes, increasingly be sought by students. That the result may be healthy educationally is well expressed in a letter from a former president of the American Psychological Association and authority on child development, now an administrator in a famous university, in answer to an inquiry about his having obtained his doctorate at the age of 23:

> I cannot speak too strongly for the value of finishing up the educational process as early as possible. I am quite convinced that the greatest creativity and greatest enthusiasm for research comes before the age of 35. Certainly many of our students today are far better trained when they get a Ph.D. than I was. But in the next five years I learned probably as much factually as they do and I had the enormous advantage of already having a good leg up on my career, and the satisfaction of being an independent operator with a few small successes that unquestionably served to motivate me vitally toward a continuation of that career. I think it is almost criminal to let people stay in the social role of student any longer than is absolutely necessary. The only progress I see in people's development is that which comes from their own independent work. The longer they remain students, the longer they remain subordinate, passive, always looking up to others instead of out toward the horizon for themselves. What we need to do is get more people into their careers and let them begin to enjoy the rewards and excitements of independent endeavor.

The preceding paragraphs have argued that accelerated programs for the gifted should: (a) certainly give more education in a given time, but perhaps also result in more and more mature general competencies, (b) make more career use of the potentially most productive early adult years, (c) make feasible earlier realization of adult status as in beginning of career, socio-economic independence, and marriage. If all this is desirably so, then in general those finishing an educational program young should be more successful than those finishing later. As already mentioned, Terman found those graduating from high school early most successful in later education and career. The writer gathered data indicating that those graduating young from a New England arts college and from a midwestern teachers college were vocationally more successful than those graduating at the usual age. Recently he has compiled material as to the relations of age of obtaining the doctorate to professional success. Currently, median age of obtaining the doctorate in psychology is around 31 (with only one per cent getting the degree at 24 or younger); however, the last 25 presidents of the American Psychological Association earned the degree at a median age of 25.7! Analogous findings were obtained for chemists, sociologists, economists, and political scientists and the presidents of their national organizations. Indeed, of the presidents of these various learned societies, 32 per cent of the psychologists, 25 per cent of the chemists, and 15 per cent of the social scientists had obtained the doctorate at the age of 24 or younger. Further, median age of obtaining the doctorate was

26.1 for a sampling of members of the American Academy of Sciences
and 25.0 for Nobel Prize winners in physics and chemistry; 22 per cent of
the first group and 50 per cent of the second obtained the degree at the age
of 24 or younger (7, 8). In total, the evidence for acceleration, especially
as regards career outcomes, would seem varied and impressive.

APPLICATIONS, IMPLICATIONS

Such evidence (in contrast to the negligible good research supporting enrichment) would seem to warrant the conclusion that acceleration was the
best of generally recognized methods of dealing with the gifted. And
surely such benefits should not be limited to the top 5 per cent of pupils;
at least the top 20 per cent should be considered for some advancement
over the lock-step pace. The total of such likely desirable outcomes should
make acceleration the most rewarding of all personnel procedures, and
counseling looking thereto especially pleasant—and especially needed now.
For acceleration recognizes ability by advancement earlier to complete
more education for better vocational opportunities—sooner to meet the
nation's needs with more trained manpower. And if a fifth of all high
school graduates might well finish the usual 12 years of public school in
11 years or less (in the writer's judgment, a reasonable estimate on the
basis of a variety of data, some shortly to be mentioned) and a fifth of all
college graduates finish in three years, then the relief to crowded schools
and colleges would be considerable.

But why keep the age-grade lock-step as the basic procedure, deviation
from which becomes a special issue? Why not admit each child to the first
grade when he is "ready"; numerous experiments have shown bright
children admitted before six doing well—better than their controls when
followed even through the eighth grade (15). Why not non-graded schools,
in which each child may progress as he can? More might then "accelerate"
than before. At slowdown and overlap places in the present ill-coordinated
American educational system (perhaps around second grade, junior high,
senior year of high school and college freshman year) a large portion
of all the youngsters might edge ahead. And why not "classless" colleges? Now some students enter as sophomores because of anticipatory
examinations in such institutions as Harvard, and many universities permit
earning of graduate credit in the senior undergraduate year. The able
might, if permitted to move easily over grade-class boundaries, advance
yet more rapidly. An elaborate California investigation of gifted children
showed one-fourth of a group of first graders at the end of that school year
reading at fourth grade level; in arithmetic they were two years advanced.
The upper half of fourth and fifth grade gifted pupils were close to or
beyond ninth grade level on a battery of tests of achievement (6). About
a tenth of all high school seniors scored above the college senior mean on
an elaborate examination supposedly covering the essentials of a college

education (4). Over three-fourths of the "Fordies," who had skipped the last one or two years of high school, when college sophomores scored above the mean for first-year graduate students on the Graduate Record Examination (2).

Might social maladjustment result from any substantial acceleration, even in a non-graded school or college? Gifted youngsters have been found to prefer the companionship of older and other gifted associates (9). The California study noted the "striking and consistent early emotional maturity" of the gifted, who "at both the junior and senior high levels resembled college and adult populations more closely than they resembled their own age mates" on a personality inventory (6, p. 4). In fields now less subject to age-grade rigidities—music, the graphic arts, the performing arts, athletics—those excelling usually begin early and progress rapidly, and different ages associate easily in their common interest. But if age-grade rigidities be done away with *and* personnel policy is alert to the opportunities thereby presented, might the *average* student accelerate a little, making marked acceleration of the able less marked?

For it seems hardly too harsh to say that the total American educational system is an ill-coordinated conglomerate, irresponsible in its readiness to take over some of life's best years. Fifty years ago an American doctorate regularly took three years, but now four or more; and if it is argued that now much more need be learned, Oppenheimer's remark should be recalled that with the present rapid changes in knowledge, soon all one learned in schools is not so (incidentally, he obtained his doctorate at the age of 23). The Ph.D. program, imported less than a century ago from Germany where it followed the secondary school "gymnasium," was here put after the four-year college. So the doctorate is obtained about four years earlier in Germany than here—four years added to career which might be a factor in German scientific productivity. The American college was imported over three centuries ago from England where Cambridge had had four-year programs; that institution went to three, but not the American college, in spite of many efforts so to do, led by such people as Harvard's President Eliot. The American high school is largely home-grown, and may almost completely overlap the first year of college. Not many years ago, excellent school systems had seven elementary grades instead of eight—and research evidence indicates that they were doing about as much educationally in the shorter time. With guided progress aware of all this and of the brighter student's capacity to move ahead, might the median age for the doctorate drop to 25, for the A.B. to 20? And if the present "going steady" with one's own age group was broken up, might that be socially healthy, perhaps reducing the number of too early marriages?

Guidance might well first stress to students, parents, and teachers the considerations outlined in this paper. Faster progress than the lock-step may sometimes be by skipping: so by substantial advanced placement credit a student may enter college with sophomore standing (3), or like the "Fordies" skip the high school senior year; or a bright child may skip the last year of junior high into senior high or sixth grade into junior high, or begin primary school in the second grade if he enters already able to read. Better are smoother means: in college, accelerative honors programs, or independent study; in the public schools, rapid progress sections or non-graded structuring (perhaps aided by "teaching machines"). Wisely guided acceleration may add two or three years to the careers of able young people, not merely without educational loss but with gains in competence sometimes notable (*11*).

SUMMARY

Belatedly, it is being recognized that research evidence in favor of acceleration is overwhelming. But old doubts persist. And the larger significance of the evidence seems not seen.

1. Fifty years ago the effort was to keep young people in school longer; now much evidence indicates that many are being kept there too long. Yet "timesaving in education" has been little mentioned since the twenties, and both school programs for the gifted and the college honors programs often ignore the issue.

2. Acceleration may not only give a student more education in a given time, but increase his functioning abilities. That greatest physical vigor *and* intellectual creativity come in the earlier adult years is now well evidenced. That young people are increasingly insisting on less delay in adult status is evidenced by the increase in student marriages. A variety of evidence indicates that early beginning of career is associated with outstanding success therein.

3. Personnel policies fostering acceleration of able students should thus be richly rewarding. Now, years in their lives may be frittered away in ill-coordinated, slow-paced, over-extended educational programs. Guided acceleration may well not only prevent such waste, but be the cutting edge of efforts toward programs better coordinated and paced, for all in the schools.

REFERENCES

Anderson, K. E. (ed.), *Research on the Academically Talented Student* (Washington, D.C.: National Education Association, 1961).

Fund for the Advancement of Education, *They Went to College Early* (New York: The Fund, 1957).

Jones, E. S. and Gloria K. Ortner, "College Credit by Examination," *University of Buffalo Studies*, 21 (1954).

Learned, W. L. and B. D. Wood, *The Student and His Knowledge* (New York: Carnegie Foundation for the Advancement of Teaching, 1938).

Lehman, H. C., *Age and Achievement* (Princeton, N.J.: Princeton University Press, 1953).

Martison, Ruth A., *Educational Programs for Gifted Pupils* (Sacramento, Calif.: California State Department of Education, 1961).

McCallum, T. W. and A. S. Taylor, *Nobel Prize Winners* (Zurich: Central European Times Publishing, 1938).

National Academy of Sciences, *Biographical Memoirs*, 27–30 (New York: Columbia University Press, 1949), pp. 1952–1956.

O'Shea, Harriet E., "Friendship and the Intellectually Gifted Child," *Exceptional Children*, 26 (1960), pp. 327–335.

Pressey, S. L., *Educational Acceleration: Appraisals and Basic Problems* (Columbus, Ohio: State University Press, 1949).

———, "Concerning the Nature and Nurture of Genius," *Scientific Monthly*, 68 (1955), pp. 123–129.

Pressey, S. L. and R. G. Kuhlen, *Psychological Development Through the Life Span* (New York: Harper, 1957).

Terman, L. M. and Milita H. Oden, *The Gifted Child Grows Up* (Stanford, Calif.: Stanford University Press, 1947).

Welford, A. T., *Ageing and Human Skill* (London: Oxford University Press, 1958).

Worcester, D. A., *Education of Children of Above-Average Ability* (Lincoln, Nebr.: University of Nebraska Press, 1956).

** 5 **

Programs for the Superior:
Happenstansical or Conceptual?

T. ERNEST NEWLAND

Imagine with me a home with a lovely picture window installed in a wobbly wall capable of holding it only until a 40-mile wind blows. Or a home constructed by joining the studding with six penny nails and by applying the siding with four penny nails. Imagine trying to answer the question, "What is the best house in the United States?" Imagine trying

* From *Teachers College Record* 1961, 62, 513–523. By permission of the author and the publisher.

to justify economically a gas transmission line that has a 40 per cent leakage. Imagine efforts to treat orthopedic defects solely with thermo-therapy. Weird imaginings! But they suggest crude analogues to what we see reflected all too frequently in educational practices for and attitudes toward our mentally superior children.

On the basis of the special provisions that are reported for the "gifted" in our schools, one can, perhaps, be excused for being more depressed by the happenstansical nature of educational practices perpetrated in the name of these children than impressed by the extent to which provisions for them are shored up by sound undergirdings of philosophy and psychology. To a dangerous extent, many of our schools are trying to "meet the needs of the gifted" in a perceptual rather than a conceptual manner. To support this judgment, we shall first consider only a limited number of examples, out of the unfortunately large number available, of practices that have been introduced which fall far short of being programs for the mentally superior. Secondly, we shall attempt to identify only some of the factors which have contributed to the patching of educational cloth, sometimes itself of limited quality, with, at times, bright colored swatches. Lastly, some fundamental steps will be suggested which must be taken in order to avoid putting the education of the mentally superior in a worse condition than it was in before the impetus of Sputnik I.

SUPERIOR LEARNING

The term "mentally superior" is more appropriate to our consideration than is the more popular but ambiguous term "gifted." Even though it is not errorless to do so, the children in whose interest this is written will be regarded as those who earn or who can earn IQ's of 120 to 125 and above on the Revised or 1960 Stanford-Binet or on the verbal portion of the Wechsler individual test. To this admittedly oversimplified but still primary denotation of these children may be added other significant characteristics so long as they do not negate or detract from the primary criterion of superior conceptualization potential. The "talented" will be only alluded to, since what this term long has connoted is not central to our purpose. Further, we shall be concerned here with only the sub-college school age range.

Certain limitations must be borne in mind. No single criticism applies to all school systems attempting to improve the lot of the mentally superior. As we seek to obtain objective evidence regarding the children who are intellectually superior, we must recognize that, even as in the domain of the physical sciences, we have measurement error. But we need to learn how to operate in the presence of such error, rather than refuse to use devices that have reasonable error. We need constantly to recognize the fact that an IQ is not an IQ is not an IQ, particularly in the cases of group tests of learning aptitude. What we have yet to learn about the nature of the learning potential of school children is great; yet much educational good can be done if we will only use understandingly what we thus far know. We shall see an increased interest in the operation of creative thinking, based upon Guilford's recent work (2) on high level intelligence, but we hope that it doesn't lead into a fad of children being taught just to be different. We shall need to be sensitive to the fact of talent, curious about the extent to which it may exist in the absence of high level intelligence, and wary of any tendency to identify any highly skilled behavior as talent. We shall become increasingly aware of the roles played by the social dynamics of the various situations within which the mentally superior will have learned and in which they function, particularly with regard to their effects upon the value systems and personalities of these superior youngsters. Important as all these and other factors may be, they still must be perceived as only facilitative or inhibitive to the fundamental phenomenon of the operation of inherent superior learning aptitude in the schools.

PRACTICE OR PROGRAM

Unfortunately, we have no real evidence on which to base judgments concerning the extent to which provisions for the mentally superior in our schools fall into the category of practice rather than program. Our professional literature teems with inquiries about "programs" which school systems are asked to identify and describe. But the bulk of these describe only practices—some at a single grade level or even in a single school or classroom. Without objective evidence, there is still the strong impression that school systems have tended predominantly to institute practices devoid (at the time of their being instituted) of programmatic or major conceptual anchorage. Bear in mind that practices may have merit or potential value when employed in relation to other potentially good practices; but it is the *pattern* of practices which has the greater promise of yielding the more significant return. A brick may be a good brick, but it is not a house.

Let us consider only a few illustrative practices of varying potential merit or harm. One of the more stereotypic attempts to provide more adequately for the mentally superior has been the introduction of foreign languages at some point in the elementary school. Depending on the enthusiasm and strength of opinions held rather than on the findings of objective research, foreign language learning has been introduced into the school program at points ranging from the first to the seventh grade. Such a provision has a kind of face validity in that it is socially perceived as "intellectual" and has tended to be regarded as a form of learning and acculturation more appropriate to the classes than to the masses. Bright children enjoy learning foreign languages, just as they enjoy any diversion from the lockstep of regular school work. Foreign language textbooks and information on methods of teaching foreign languages have long been readily at hand.

This form of "doing something" is, then, much more convenient than, say, a school's going into the community to make it possible for its youngsters to have a fuller understanding of the operations of governmental and social agencies. It is possible that more teachers and parents know more about conjugating irregular verbs than about how the many taxing units in their cities, townships, and counties operate. The enthusiasm of the teachers so involved has by no means been any guarantee that the study of the foreign language has facilitated the fuller understanding of English, nor do we seem generally to expect that the regular class teachers of the youngsters studying foreign languages have been particularly effective in connecting foreign language learning with other learnings in regular class-rooms. Every bit as discouraging is the fact that after the children have, perhaps, learned some foreign language in the elementary grades, often no realistic provision has been made for them to continue their study as an integral part of the curriculum at the next higher level. Pupil frustration and an aura of educational hypocrisy subtly attend a practice which probably has lulled into a false sense of educational effectiveness many of those parents who wanted "something done for the gifted."

ENRICHMENT?

Of the same order, in terms of essential educational and psychological factors, is a large amount of school window dressing so often regarded as "enrichment." Witness the incident of the elementary school principal who, when it was suggested to him that he might "free" some of his brighter children who were interested in things scientific, allowed a small, select group of youngsters to meet once a week as a science club and then arranged for persons of considerable scientific competence to meet each week with the club to lecture about their particular areas of competence. The youngsters were passingly interested in the lectures, as would be expected, but it was, in effect, an elementary school Chautauqua which provided no opportunity for these youngsters to study intensively and integratively the scientific phenomena and concepts in which they were beginning to show more than superficial interest. Similarly, the numerous, and soon monotonous, things which bright children can do as teacher aids, the number puzzles which may be solved, the wide variety of charts (at least equally educationally valuable for the retarded) to be constructed and maintained, and the like are but intellectual atoms which too often are more a gesture of a shallow educational diversion than of true enrichment.

Such usually interesting but often intellectually barren practices tend too much to constitute the form but not the essence of intellectual enrichment. Take, for instance, the provisions made by a civic women's group which offered the school the opportunity of sending its more promising youngsters each Saturday morning to the local art museum, where the well intentioned ladies took turns telling the youngsters about different art forms and art eras. Yet the local school in no way capitalized upon this adjunctive facility by means of any potentially valuable feedback. Witness, too, the policy of certain schools which, while ardently advocating enrichment, limits it to the use of only those materials known or believed to be appropriate only to the grade level to which the bright pupil may, for some reason, be officially anchored at any given time. Too often, one encounters the administrative edict that fifth (or some other) graders must use only the textbooks prescribed for their grade in order that the work of the teacher of the next higher grade will not be interfered with. Omitted intentionally from these illustrations is the exploration of the fact that the educational experiences of some bright children are believed to be enriched by having these children do more of the same thing when they actually need fewer practice exercises or problems in order to comprehend the operation of a principle or process.

There comes a time when certain legitimate enrichment activities constitute, in fact, acceleration for the child. "Enrichment in depth" is a case in point, since it is at once apparent that the so-called depth actually involves the employment of concepts and thought processes which are generally expected of more advanced children. Accelerative practices which do not take place within the structure of total programming can have unfortunate side effects. In many of our schools, potentially sound accelerative practices may be employed at the elementary level only to have the children so accelerated move into a separately administered secondary school where a most primitive lockstep scheduling may be in operation. Even in a school district where all the grade levels may be under the same administrator, such accelerated youngsters may encounter similar frustration. Some children may be soundly advanced to a higher grade level where their chances of good learning are materially enhanced, only to move the year after that into the room of a teacher who is completely opposed to any acceleration. Others are uprooted in mid-semester from their well-established social groups because they happened to be going to a school in which the responsible administrator suddenly sees merit in advancing some children a bit more rapidly than others, especially if it will help ease crowded conditions in certain rooms.

In one school system, the recognition of the possible merits of a part-day, special group program for some of the more promising students led the administrator forthwith to cause such groups to be established. It all happened so suddenly that neither the home-room teachers of the youngsters involved nor the teachers of the special groups themselves were sensitive to the nature of the relationships which should characterize the learnings in such special groups and in regular classes. In fact, one person, writing a doctoral dissertation on the social relationships among all the children involved in this situation, had to admit that the lack of communication and understanding between the regular class teachers and the special group teachers may have affected the nature of her findings.

But this list of education gaucheries must not be extended here, even though it could be. Perhaps it is not even adequately representative of the fact that so often the form of doing something for the mentally superior may have been partially perceived without its essence being comprehended. Perhaps the kinds of things described here do not characterize the efforts of the majority of our schools. But the kind of educational shortsightedness illustrated by these incidents characterizes far more of our school programs than any of us would wish to be the case. Remember that the school people who inaugurated these and similar educational practices of limited perspective are well intentioned people, even though they may have responded more in terms of the pressures of the moment than of considered thought and available knowledge. Remember, too, that those who did these kinds of things are products of our professional educational training and selection program. And I remember, on the other hand, that many of the bright children involved in these educational practices may well have enjoyed many of their novel experiences either by virtue of the intellectual stimulation they experienced in such activities or by the less socially significant fact that they enjoyed temporary distraction from intellectually impoverishing school practices.

BASIC LACK

Let us turn, now to a consideration of "how we got that way." The general situation, epitomized by the different kinds of real life examples which have been cited, has developed for known or knowable reasons. Some we shall merely notice in passing; others we shall explore a bit more intensively.

The major foundation for what is shoddy in our educational structure is the lack on the part of teachers, their supervisors, and administrators, of a clear and firm philosophy of education that reflects sensitivity both to the needs of society and to the facts and principles of psychology. It is neither possible nor appropriate here to delineate all the points of impact which the necessary interaction of philosophy and the findings of psychology should have upon the school program. Illustrative, however, is the disturbing extent to which educational content and methodology fail to reflect the socially more promising educational philosophies so long propounded and the psychological facts so long a matter of record. Ward (6), for instance, has called our attention to three significant elements in this connection: (1) that the mentally superior child should be perceived more as a learner than as one who must be taught all he will ever know, recognizing the need for "the reservation of the class hour for engagement in the complex and elusive subtleties lying in the richest instance just beyond the individual's present unaided grasp"; (2) that not just knowledge, but "knowledge about knowledge" is the major domain of the mentally superior, and (3) that a studied diminution of emphasis upon the concrete and an attending greater recognition of generalization should be reflected in methods employed with the mentally superior.

Further illustrative of limitations in this general area is the lack of psychologically sound conceptualizations of the nature of the intelligence with which these children are so specially endowed. The uncritical uses made of most anything turned out by an author or publisher under the name "intelligence tests" and certain subsequent actions taken in terms of those test results are symptomatic of a frightening psychological naiveté. If we start from the fundamental position that the children with whom we are concerned are those who are able quickly to grasp concepts of greater difficulty, are able to acquire symbols and understand them, are able to deal effectively with abstractions, are quick with sound generalizations, and often come up with novel but sound approaches and ideas, then we shall be profitably approaching the complex notion of intelligence. That these children with high conceptualization potential differ among themselves and have varying degrees of competence within themselves in no way removes them from the category of those with high academic potential. However, some kinds of behavior samples reflected in some tests bear little significant relationship to the high potential with which we are concerned. Such is the case with various motor and mechanical performance tests. Hence, confusion sometimes is introduced by results from tests selected more for convenience than for their relationship to conceptual behavior.

CONFUSION IN COMMUNICATION

Communication about the mentally superior is becoming increasingly confused. We are having to contend with the reckless abandon with which newcomers to the field of the mentally superior either make idiosyncratic uses of terms which had reasonably well established communication value or introduce neologisms loaded with ambiguity. For some 25 years, our communication was reasonably precise. When we used the term "gifted," we denoted both those who were mentally superior and those who were talented. The term "talented" was then used with some restraint. To the psychologically trained, talented persons were, in very large part if not entirely so, mentally superior persons who had demonstrated or who were believed capable of demonstrating outstanding performance in one of the arts. Then came the "talent epidemic," which seems to have had one important characteristic: As more and more kinds of behavior are called talent, mental superiority tends less and less to be recognized as a primary or even essential component of talent. On the other hand, the term "mental superiority" is perceived as a social class tag, a rather undesirable phenomenon in a society where we overtly profess classlessness but covertly struggle constantly to improve social position.

But our confusion doesn't stop here. We designate those whom we regard as mentally superior in terms of different test performances that are known not to have the same meanings, even so far as intellectual level is concerned. Our communication is further clouded by the fact that the *degree* of mental superiority, in terms of IQ or other derived score on any given test, often is not stated. Even when these degrees are explicit, we carelessly seek for commonalities between the findings of one study made on children with Binet IQ's ranging from 120 to 185 and the findings of another made on children scoring only above 150 on that test. School District A "does something" for its children above 120 I.Q. on some group test. School District B "does something" for its children above Binet 140 or 150. If the outcomes are different, too often we forget to bear in mind how different the populations were on a crucial variable. In terms of intelligence quotients, admittedly an over-simplified frame of reference, the fact is often overlooked that there are differences among the extremes of the mentally superior that are as great as are the differences between the dull normal and the idiot.

Like love, our superior population is a many splendored thing, and we are obligated to state precisely just how the samples we draw from it are defined. We must communicate clearly rather than hide behind ambiguous terminology. Nor can we afford to sink to the level of irresponsibility at which Abraham solves his problem thus:

> Nor should we become involved in an argument over some kinds of words . . . like "superior," "gifted," or "exceptional." The last is now accepted as including all who deviate from the so-called normal, and what difference does it make what the exact term is anyway? It is the *idea* that counts, the idea that evolves from a child whose contribution to our society is far less than his wonderful capacity could provide. That's the problem, and that's the child—and we can no longer afford to get bogged down in definitions and confusion (*1*, p. 28).

The implications of the current terminological abandon are unmistakably clear. How can we expect anything other than a completely happenstansical approach to meeting the needs of the mentally superior when those recommending, introducing, or carrying out educational practices are so unclear and ambiguous in their own perceptions of the children in whose interests they presumably are working?

IGNORANCE

One factor which has contributed to spotty, makeshift educational provisions for the mentally superior is the almost studied unfamiliarity with the professional and scientific literature on this type of child and his educational needs. One hardly knows where to start or how to deal with this newness-of-it-all attitude professed by so many educators. A state director of special education says, "Tell us what to do for these children, and we'll do it." All too many superintendents and principals admit that, whereas they know they have such superior children in their schools, they just don't know what to do for them. An educator, nationally prominent in the field of special education, opposed the introduction of a course on the gifted into a college curriculum "because there wasn't enough research on them" to warrant the offering of such a course. The disturbingly large numbers of studies in several states of what is or what "can be" done for mentally superior school children are highly duplicative and add little to research knowledge.

Their main value lies in their demonstrating to the current crop of those concerned what long has been a matter of descriptive and research record. Stedman's 1924 book (4) described her special class program for bright children. The Cleveland special classes (3) have been in operation nearly 40 years. The ten-year report on the Hunter College Elementary School for gifted children was published in 1952. A follow-up study on children admitted early to school on the basis of their superior early promise has followed these children through the second year of post college life. Terman's famous study most recently resulted in a report on his gifted sample 35 years after the inception of his observations (5). Professions of ignorance as to what can be done do not speak well for people who presumably have had professional training. A large and helpful literature is available, but it must be read!

MARKING SYSTEMS

Time and again, frustration has been expressed about the marking systems employed in evaluating academic performance. Practices of considerable potential promise have been jeopardized by the difficulties or absurdities in attempts to characterize or evaluate the academic performances of mentally superior children. A typical illustrative problem involves the use of an implicit single standard of performance with a multiple-track practice. In such a grading situation, certain of the bright children consciously achieve in ways which cause their being placed in that "track" where their chances for receiving favorable marks are increased. One question fundamental to the whole marking issue is whether a child's achievement is to be evaluated in terms of how well he performs compared with others in his (real or imaginary) group or in terms of how well he performs relative to his assessed capacities. Those committed to an egalitarian philosophy of education subscribe to the giving to all the "same" opportunity to achieve and then noting the fact of differential achievement, whereas some of those subscribing to a democratic philosophy are sensitive to individual differences in basic learning capacity and try to relate differential achievement, at least in part, to such differences. Generally, educators have been caught up in unwarranted attempts to fuse into a single index of performance the two incompatible frames of reference of how the child learns in terms of his own potential and how the child performs in comparison with the Joneses.

Put briefly and bluntly, educators tend to function more at a perceptual than at a conceptual level. Teachers want methods courses much more than those dealing with the major social phenomena relevant to the mentally superior or with the philosophical and psychological principles basic to a number of specific methodologies. Illustrative of how they get that way was a recent incident in which a student (in a methods course) was overheard to ask his instructor if he could turn in a report on a book having a title something like "The Intellect of Man," only to have his instructor tell him to report on one of the recommended methods books. Perhaps to a distressing extent—at least to some—teachers have more often been taught what to do when than the principles which facilitate sustained thought and the development of programmatic solutions to problems. The perceptual-conceptual continuum is a significant dimension in terms of which we see the introduction of specific educational practices which simply fail to meet the on-going needs of the mentally superior. Educational tactics lie readily to hand; educational strategy requires knowledge, thought, and an imagination born of principles critically reflected upon.

VALUE SYSTEMS

Another factor contributing to concern about what is being attempted for the mentally superior is a rather nebulous but very potent one. It is the system of values of teachers and administrators which so largely determines the intellectual quality of the atmosphere in which our school children are expected to do their growing. The omission from this discussion of the matter of value systems in the family, the church, or society generally should not be construed as implying that it is unimportant. Such value systems are highly contributive to certain of the schools' problems. But this in no way relieves the schools of the responsibility of addressing themselves to the problem with which we are here concerned. Often overlooked is the fact that the adults who determine these extra-school milieus of children are themselves products of the schools. Further, a fundamental purpose of the schools is to compensate for the deficiencies of children's homes.

Some aspects of this problem can better be reflected in the raising of certain questions, recognizing that objective answers to them would be most difficult to obtain. To what extent and in what ways are the intellectual tone, the nature of intellectual aspiration levels, the prizing highly of the thrill of learning, and intellectual growth affected by the intellectual outlook and sensitivities of both school administrators and teachers? Without in any way implying that athletic coaches are mentally limited, one can't help wondering about the cultural nurturance provided by the superintendents, a majority in some states, who rose to their positions of educational leadership via the coaching route. With respect to the cultivation of broad reading interests in our children and a rich cultural background for their learnings, what are the implications of the fact that so many of our teachers read so little beyond the demands of their work? A discouraging preponderance of the teachers in a number of samples report the annual reading of no more than one book of even current fiction beyond whatever professional reading they may do. To what extent are mentally superior children caused, perhaps unwittingly, to perceive their learning activities in terms of specific, often atomistic, tasks which carry only highly specific and superficially tangible rewards in contrast to the discovery that learning can be thrillingly enjoyable, that it feels good to grow rather than just to put on weight? Put a bit differently, to what extent and in what ways do the value systems of the teachers contribute to intrinsically rather than extrinsically motivated learning in mentally superior children? In what ways are the value systems of children affected by the constricted perspectives of teachers engaged in teaching subjects for which they have only a modicum of content preparation? The implications of these and similar questions, varying of course in degree of generality, can create an anxiety not only about the quality of *programs* for the mentally superior but also about even the *practices* instituted for them.

FOUR POSITIVE SUGGESTIONS

The purpose of this admittedly incomplete identification of factors which bear upon the all-too-often ill-considered introduction of educational practices in the name of the mentally superior is not intended as an invitation for an ineffective meeting at the wailing wall. Implicit in the description of these contributing factors is the nature of positive steps which should be taken in order to give integrity to what should be done for mentally superior children in our schools. There appear to be four major directions in which our thinking and action should proceed in this problem area if educators are to exercise the leadership for which they presumably are being trained. Effective action in these four directions could do much to correct the current condition whereby society appears to be failing to capitalize on from 25 to 40 per cent of its natural resources in human capability.

First, we need to formulate a socially and psychologically sound philosophy of education for the mentally superior. It need differ only in details from a sound general philosophy of education. Its relevance to the mentally superior will be largely in the way it is implemented. Presumably, it will be democratic rather than egalitarian, reflecting a full sensitivity to the fact of individual differences and to the psychological characteristics of the mentally superior. Associated with this philosophy must be a firm and abiding commitment to it. Any such commitment is not to be confused with the tendency to "get on the bandwagon," with the desire only to compete with other school systems, or with a fear of the implications of Sputniks. Even though it may well be that a Sputnik-induced fear has caused some schools to attempt to do the type of things advocated by some of our educational experimentalists as long as half a century ago, we can not afford to erect educational structures on the sands of fear.

Secondly, the kinds of problems encountered in providing educationally effective programs for mentally superior children bring into sharp focus again the importance of the kinds of professional programs offered by the colleges and universities for the purpose of preparing teachers, supervisors, and administrators to assume their socially crucial roles. The mentally superior need, and are particularly endowed to benefit more from, the broadly cultured educator rather than the narrowly trained educationist. This in no sense need lead to the elimination of all instruction in classroom methodology. But it must lead to the perception of methodology as a means to an end and to a readiness and ability to help children attain appropriate goals by whatever approach fits the characteristics of the child, the particular kind of learning activity which is at the moment involved, and the psychosocial situation within which the learning is to take place. It is quite possible that the area of greater concern for the professional schools is that of providing an increased philosophical, psychological, and broadly cultural orientation and perspective for supervisors and administrators.

Thirdly, we must face up to the importance and need of defining much more clearly than seems presently to be the case just whom we mean by mentally superior children. Such great legitimate concern has been expressed regarding the fact that even good mental test results do not tell us all we need to know about children that the proper use of good intelligence tests has been accorded a lower status than it deserves. Many have thrown out the baby with the bath water. But we also define the population with which we are concerned in terms of social needs. We can, for instance, ascertain the percentage of our total population needed to carry on work of a high conceptual level in our society and then, on the basis of such findings, arrive at a much firmer picture of the percentage of our school population for which we need to do different things educationally in order to qualify them to meet these social demands. Available data suggest that we need to do these kinds of things for children with a derived IQ of 125 upward. This type of designation need not imply any social stasis. Among other things, it would seem to have more foundation in fact than do designations born more of blind guessing or guilt feelings. Identification procedures should be implemented accordingly, with particular emphasis on early identification. Such identification must be initiated four or five years earlier than the fourth grade level, which is characteristic of current practice in so many school systems.

Lastly, thinking about doing something for mentally superior children must proceed first in terms of total program planning. Any practices that are introduced must be perceived only as means of moving toward the realization of a total program. New practices or modifications which are undertaken without this total program anchorage have too great a chance to prove only disillusioning and frustrating. Whatever is planned or done must be effected in terms of a sound social philosophy, on the basis of the psychological facts of the case, in terms of the unique realities of the local situation, and on the basis of any research findings that may be relevant.

THE PLURAL APPROACH

Thinking predicated upon the assumption that there must be a single educational practice which will provide effectively for mentally superior children is illusory. Providing properly for these children involves the doing of many things: sound and early identification; a willingness to accelerate when the total psychological picture warrants, but neither an addiction to nor a blanket aversion from the practice; psychologically and educationally sound enrichment, involving good library facilities and effective use of other ancillary services; special within-class groups, special groups within schools or school systems, or complete special classes; advanced accreditation facilities; correspondence courses, particularly for the relatively isolated small school, the use of a school system consultant working only in the interests of these youngsters, and numerous other provisions. Just what is needed must depend upon the pattern of factors in the community, in the school staff, and in the pupils themselves. Further, the pattern of provisions which can be effective in one school system at one time quite likely may not be the one which will be effective five years hence.

In the eyes of many, one glaring deficiency in this statement will lie in the failure to point out specific needs for research. Rather than close with the dissertation benediction that much research still is needed in this area, suffice it to point out that we have had on the record for many years the results of much more research than we have seen reflected in educational practice. Much recent research is essentially duplicative of or supportive to what has been available for him who would read. Some new research fronts have been developed and what is being learned can be most helpful. But whatever they may be, they do not alter the basic problems identified here.

REFERENCES

Abraham, W., *Common Sense About the Gifted* (New York: Harper, 1958).

Guilford, J. P., "The Structure of Intellect," *Psychological Bulletin*, 53 (1956), pp. 267–293.

Hildreth, Gertrude H., *Educating Gifted Children* (New York: Harper, 1942).

Stedman, Lulu M., *Education of Gifted Children* (Yonkers-on-Hudson, N.Y.: World Book, 1924).

Terman, L. M. and Melita H. Oden, *The Gifted Group at Mid-Life* (Stanford, Calif.: Stanford University Press, 1959).

Ward, V. S., "The Role and Nature of Theory in the Education of the Gifted," paper delivered Oct. 1, 1959, at the University of Pittsburgh Institute on "Education of Gifted Children and Youth."

** 6 **

The Maze of the Research on Ability Grouping

A. HARRY PASSOW

I

In the concern for improving the educational provisions for the gifted as well as for upgrading the quality of education for all students, questions about the relative advantages and disadvantages of ability grouping have once again been raised. A great deal of sentiment, both pro and con, about the merits of ability grouping is recorded in the literature together with descriptive accounts of various practices and programs. In the search for research findings, the quantity is great (dating back forty years or more), the quality is irregular, and the results generally inconclusive for reasons which soon become apparent.

A steady flow of studies and discussions about grouping began in the early 1920's, reached a peak in the mid-1930's, and then dwindled sharply. Surveying the status of and trends in grouping in 1932, Billett observed: "Perhaps no plan, method, or device for reaching the individual through class instruction has evoked more words written or spoken during the past ten years than homogeneous or ability grouping. The possible exception is individualized instruction." [1] Always responsive to the key issues of the day, the National Society for the Study of Education focused a 1936 yearbook on *The Grouping of Pupils*.[2] By 1950, in an article in the *Encyclopedia of Educational Research*, Otto stated that "no research studies on ability grouping have been reported during the past fifteen years." [3] While there actually were some studies in that period, the article accurately reflected

* From *Educational Forum* 1962, *26*, 281–288. Reprinted by permission of the author and Kappa Delta Pi, an Honor Society in Education, owners of the copyright.

the decline in research on grouping. The past decade has been marked by a sharp upswing in grouping proposals and in studies of the effects and effectiveness of grouping. In the 1960 edition of the *Encyclopedia of Educational Research* article on grouping, Goodlad commented that, "Perhaps the most controversial issue of classroom organization in recent years is whether or not students of like ability should be grouped together for instructional purposes." [4]

Homogeneous grouping is defined in the *Dictionary of Education* as "the classifications of pupils for the purpose of forming instructional groups having a relatively high degree of similarity in regard to certain factors that affect learning." Many different schemes fit this definition and a wide variety of programs and practices has emerged, all of which involve some form of classification or selection of students, each aiming to increase either teaching or learning effectiveness. For instance, of the many provisions for individual differences found in the 1932 National Survey of Secondary Education, *homogeneous grouping* and *special classes* were found to be the most popular, and were judged by the school respondents as the "most successful." Homogenous grouping in that survey included all efforts to "improve the teaching and learning environment through refined classification of pupils," while special classes encompassed various attempts to provide for extreme deviance in abilities and/or needs by means of such provisions as special coaching for slow or gifted pupils or by opportunity, remedial and adjustment classes.[5] Harap reported in 1936 that ability grouping was the "most common method of adjusting learning to individual differences." [6]

A United States Office of Education survey of practices and policies of elementary school administration and organization published in 1960 noted that "the methods of grouping and assigning pupils for instructional purposes represent another area of timely interest and one on which there is a great deal of public and professional discussion." The survey indicated that of the 4,307 urban places with populations of 2,500 or more which participated, in elementary schools, only 16.9 percent had a basic policy of homogeneous groupings in Grade 1–6; 34.4 per cent grouped homogeneously in Grades 7–8. Interestingly, schools using a policy of heterogeneous grouping and those using homogeneous grouping were in agreement that there would be an increase in homogeneous grouping in the future. In terms of the predicted trend, "those presently grouping heterogeneously show more than a 40 percent prediction towards homogeneous grouping, whereas about 8 percent in both grade groups who now group homogeneously suggest a change towards heterogeneous grouping." [8]

II

Although the practice of grouping students reached its peak in the 1920's and 1930's, the origins of grouping go back into the last century. W. T.

Harris's plan, initiated in St. Louis in 1867, is often cited as the first attempt at homogeneous grouping. Selected groups of bright students, chosen on achievement as determined by the teachers, were promoted rapidly through the elementary grades. A few years later, Elizabeth, New Jersey, inaugurated a somewhat similar plan with classes of bright pupils formed from each of the elementary grades and moved through the program as rapidly as possible. The Cambridge, Massachusetts, plan came into operation in 1891 with the pupils divided into groups so that the brightest might complete grades 4–9 in four years, while the slowest took seven or eight. The Santa Barbara Concentric Plan was begun at the turn of the century, with each grade divided into A, B, and C sections, each mastering the same fundamentals for each subject, but the A's doing more extensive work than the B's, and the B's more than the C's. These and other plans—the Newton Plan; the "Double Tillage Plan" of Woburn, Massachusetts; the New Richmond, Wisconsin Plan—are just a few of the dozens of schemes for flexible progress and promotion which were in operation sufficiently long to merit mention in the literature.

However, it was not until 1916 that any serious attempt was made to study homogeneous grouping with something resembling controlled experimentation. Guy M. Whipple studied a gifted class consisting of 13 boys and 17 girls, chosen on teacher recommendation from the fifth and sixth grades of an Urbana, Illinois school. Numerous other studies followed soon after, with the number greatest in the late 1920's. By the early 1930's, several good summaries and critical reviews of the research appeared. One of the earliest was a critical analysis of research evidence on ability grouping, made by Rock in 1929. Considering only those studied which he viewed as "scientific," Rock concluded that:

> The experimental studies of grouping which have been considered, fail to show consistent, statistically or educationally significant differences between the achievement of pupils in homogeneous groups and pupils of equal ability in heterogeneous groups. This failure to realize one of the important advantages claimed for ability grouping is not, however, evidence that homogeneous grouping cannot result in increased academic achievement. Neither do the experiments show that other claims made for grouping cannot be attained under proper organization.[9]

Billett reviewed 140 articles, including 108 "experimental or practical studies" which appeared in the literature between 1917–1928. Of the 108 studies, Billett listed 102 as "uncontrolled," two "partly" controlled, and four as "thoroughly controlled." Of the 102 "uncontrolled studies," 88 were favorable to grouping, 10 were doubtful, and four unfavorable. One of the "partly controlled" studies was favorable to grouping, the other doubtful. Two of the four "thoroughly controlled" studies were favorable to grouping, one doubtful, and one unfavorable.[10]

Among the trends in the study of homogeneous grouping, Billett found, the general recognition that "so-called homogeneous grouping in practice produces not homogeneity, but reduced heterogeneity."[11]

From an analysis of research on grouping made in 1931, Turney concluded that most of the studies purporting to evaluate ability grouping have proved nothing regarding grouping but have only added evidence bearing on the nature and extent of individual differences.[12]

Twenty studies were summarized by Miller and Otto in 1930, who criticized the methodology used in the studies and the experimental design. Their conclusions were as follows:

1. While the evidence is contradictory, at least two of the studies suggest that ability grouping is quite ineffective unless accompanied by proper changes in method. Unless adaptation of methods and materials is a necessary correlate to ability grouping, one of the purposes of the project is defeated.
2. So far as achievement is concerned, there is no clear-cut evidence, that homogeneous grouping is either advantageous or disadvantageous. The studies seem to indicate that homogeneous classification may be effective if accompanied by proper adaptation in methods and materials.[13]

In preparation for a large-scale grouping experiment in Australia, Wyndham studied the research and literature dealing with ability grouping in the United States. He concluded that in terms of improvement in scholastic achievements, the evidence is slightly in favor of ability grouping; that no experimental evidence is available which supports the contention that ability grouping produces undesirable attitudes on the part of pupils; and that the question of comparative ease and effectiveness of teaching remains virtually unanswered.[14]

Wyndham noted that, "Upon examination, the issues in this field proved to be much further from any kind of settlement than some writers had indicated; from no source could an unequivocal answer be found to any of the problems involved." Even at that date, Wyndham was able to observe a reaction to the practice of ability grouping—"without waiting for experimental evidence as to the effectiveness or the undesirability."

The National Society for the Study of Education's Thirty-Fifth Yearbook (1936), consisted of a comprehensive discussion of the practical, theoretical, and experimental considerations in grouping of pupils as of that time. Cornell's conclusion was that:

The results of ability grouping seem to depend less upon the fact of grouping itself than upon the philosophy behind the grouping, the accuracy with which grouping is made for the purposes intended, the differentiations in content, method, and speed, and the technique of the teacher, as well as upon more general environmental influences. Experimental studies have in general been too piecemeal to afford a true evaluation of the results, but when attitudes, methods, and curricula are well-adapted to further adjustment of the school to the child, results, both objective and subjective, seem favorable to grouping.[15]

A review of the literature on experimental studies of homogeneous grouping by Ruth Ekstrom in 1959 resulted in finding 13 studies which found differences favoring homogeneous grouping; 15 which found no differences or which found grouping detrimental; and 5 studies which gave mixed results. Ekstrom found: no consistent pattern for the effectiveness of homogeneous grouping related to age, ability level, course contents, or method of instruction.[16]

III

Looking specifically at the research related to special grouping for the gifted, Miles declared that, "The experimental work with the gifted children in which segregated are compared with non-segregated groups seems to point to the more favorable progress of the former as compared with the latter. The studies are too few to be completely convincing." [17] Similarly, while noting the lack of unanimity of findings with respect to homogeneous vs. heterogeneous grouping, Passow observed that "comparative studies of gifted students in regular and special classes on all educational levels tends to be more uniform in denoting beneficial effects of the special classes on academic, personal, and social growth." [18]

In the most recent edition of the *Encyclopedia of Education Research* (1960), Goodlad observed that studies since the 1930's "have not added to precision of the conclusions or clarification of the problems analyzed by Cornell" in the 1936 N.S.S.E. yearbook.

Even as the number of grouping studies have accumulated over the past three decades, the inconclusiveness of the research findings becomes more apparent as each reviewer couches his summary in tentative or equivocal fashion. While it is true, as Ekstrom observed, "the studies differ widely in quality, purpose, and significance," [19] there are also many other differences which make synthesis of research difficult in this area. The conflicting findings caused Cornell to observe in 1936 that "a review of the objective results of ability grouping leaves one convinced that we have not yet attained any unequivocal experimental results that are capable of wide generalization." [20] Two years earlier, Wyndham had noted that "the first general impression one gains from these studies is that, granted their unequal experimental significance, they raise more issues than they settle." [21]

Some of the reasons which may account for the difficulties in generalizing from the research are readily apparent from an examination of the studies themselves. Specifically, the problems of equating and synthesizing research findings stem from the following:

1. *The studies vary considerably in scope of aim and purpose.* Some experiments were relatively circumscribed, dealing with a single grade level; others, the entire elementary or junior high school level. In some instances, the studies were concerned with achievement in a single subject —reading, algebra, Latin, college physics—while other experiments attempted to assess scholastic growth in all content areas at a particular grade level. Some studies simply assessed pupil and teacher opinion. Most experiments were concerned solely with attainments in scholastic subjects. Little or no attention was given in most experiments to assessing the effects of grouping on other aspects of pupil growth—attitudes, interests, or personal development. The arguments pro and con ability grouping generally involve the effects of such practices on personal and social development but the purposes of most experiments have excluded these behavioral areas and dealt primarily with academic achievement.

2. *The studies differ in the number of students, the number of groups, and the size of the classes involved.* The total number of subjects and groups was too often far too small to provide any basis for valid generalizations. In some experiments, as few as two or three groups with 25–30 students each were used. Of the 20 studies, Miller and Otto summarized, the total number of pupils, when indicated at all, ranged from 80 to 333. The size of the classes varies considerably even within a single study. For instance, in the Billett studies (1924–1927) – cited by Wyndham as "among the most satisfactory from the point of view of method and form of presentation"– the 116 incoming ninth graders were divided into five groups, ranging in size from 13 to 39.[22] Comparisons of achievement in groups which were quite disparate in size are highly questionable– differences may well reflect the effects of class size rather than of grouping practices. The size of the sample is not the only consideration, of course, since some of the studies with the largest gross numbers of pupils employed such poor techniques of selection and grouping that the value of the findings is diminished.

3. *The studies differ in their duration—ranging from a semester or less to a year or more.* The question of length of an experiment is important in assessing how lasting or cumulative the results are. Pointing to the complexity of problems caused by inadequate duration, Wyndham noted that many experiments are begun at the beginning of the year and last for such a short time that

> it becomes pertinent to ask whether a teacher is thoroughly *en rapport* with her class during the first term of the school year, whether the children are properly adjusted to the new conditions, and whether the measures of the products of schooling during that time afford an adequate sample of what will be achieved during the year as a whole.[23]

This problem of inadequate duration of study is underlined by Ekstrom who notes that "the probable error of the reported test scores is frequently greater than the normal differences in scores for the period of experiment."

4. *The studies differ in the adequacy of the selection bases and the means of matching experimental and control groups.* With few exceptions, general intelligence as measured by group tests is the usual criterion for the selection of groups. Particularly in the earlier studies, pupils were classified into gross categories of dull, average, and bright. Seldom were classes or groups organized on the basis of more than a single variable. As a consequence, groups were only "homogeneous" with respect to one factor and, therefore, subject to the limitations involved in its measurement. The matching of experimental and control groups in many studies has been inadequate since most of the factors which affect individual learning are ignored. Even the description of the composition of groups has been incomplete in some studies. Matching of individuals on the basis of single scores is a doubtful procedure used in some experiments. While

some studies speak of paired control groups or matched pairs, the nature of the selection frequently leaves much to be desired even in terms of adequately describing the procedures and the groups which results. Many different bases for selection other than group intelligence test scores have been suggested—teachers' judgements, physical and social age, educational quotient, interest, and even anatomical age—but few studies have employed multiple criteria in selection for grouping.

5. *The studies differ in the "treatment"—i.e., the differentiation of curricula and methods of teaching.* In some studies, teachers were asked to keep course content and teaching methods essentially the same for all groups; in others, enriched materials and increased tempo of instruction were provided the bright groups, while other program modifications were made for the slower pupils. Some of the studies suggest that unless accompanied by curriculum and methodological changes, grouping is ineffective and its prime purpose—to facilitate differentiated instruction is lost. The difficulties in this area lie in the fact that variations in content and method are not controlled and yet they are treated as if they were controlled factors when assessing the effects of grouping. Billett noted that skillful teachers in charge of homogeneous classes differentiated subject matter and class procedures even though they followed essentially the same course of study.

6. *The studies differ in the deployment of teachers in various groups.* Sometimes a single teacher worked with both heterogeneous and homogeneous groups; sometimes a teacher worked with only one kind of group and each class had a separate teacher. Usually the teacher factor was completely ignored in the experimental design. Wyndham was convinced that any attempt to equate teachers on the basis of teaching efficiency was doomed to failure and could lead only to the "erection of statistical structures on foundations of shifting sand. The better plan would seem to be to attempt to obtain the best possible teaching situation for each type of class organization." [24] Implicit in this proposal is the assumption that the "best possible teaching situation" was probably different for each type of grouping and that the teacher's enthusiasm for working with a particular kind of child or group of children is an important criterion to be considered.

7. *The studies differ in the instruments and techniques used in evaluating changes in students.* Standardized tests of achievement, either in single subjects or batteries, and teacher grades are the most widely used means of evaluating in grouping studies. Some of the earlier studies noted change in the rates of failure or promotion, but the majority relied on some kind of objective tests to determine whether one kind of grouping was more favorable than another. Although the arguments pro and con grouping frequently refer to such changes as work-study habits, social adjustment, attitudes toward learning, self concepts, and other personal-social behaviors, few efforts have been made to evaluate the effects of grouping on these areas of development. Cornell noted that "many of the alleged desirable or undesirable results are either not susceptible of meas-

urement or are so difficult to measure that an experiment attack has not been made upon them." [25] Psychometric advances in the past twenty-five years have extended the areas of assessment of these procedures, but experimentation in grouping has not as yet taken full advantage of these procedures.

8. *The studies have generally failed to assess the effects of grouping on teacher and administrators.* Facilitation of teaching classroom management has been claimed as an advantage for ability grouping but few studies have attempted to assess the effects on teachers. Whatever studies have been done, particularly in the early research, have usually relied on various types of questionnaires to canvass teachers as to their views on grouping. Attitude and opinion surveys have been made by several researchers but no real experimental attack has been made on the question of ease or effectiveness of teaching in various grouping plans.

There are a great many questions still unanswered about the effects of ability grouping. Some more recent grouping plans—ungraded primary units, Dual Progress Plan, University of Chicago's "teachable groups"—are now being studied. These represent approaches to grouping which depart from the more traditional procedures based on a single ability criteria. Little, if any, evidence is available on the effectiveness of any of the newer grouping approaches to date. Research designs which deal with some of these unanswered questions in more comprehensive fashion than has been done in the past may help fill some of the gaps.

REFERENCES

1. Roy O. Billett, *The Administration and Supervision of Homogeneous Grouping* (Columbus, Ohio: Ohio State University Press, 1932).

2. Guy M. Whipple (ed.), *The Grouping of Pupils.* Thirty-fifth Yearbook, Part I, National Society for the Study of Education. (Bloomington, Ill.: Public School Publishing Company, 1936).

3. Henry J. Otto, "Elementary education—III. Organization and Administration," pp. 876–388 in Walter S. Monroe (ed.), *Encyclopedia of Educational Research* (New York: Macmillan, 1950).

4. John I. Goodlad, "Classroom Organization," pp. 223–225 in Chester W. Harris (ed.), *Encyclopedia of Educational Research* (New York: Macmillan, 1960).

5. Roy O. Billett, *Provisions for Individual Differences, Marketing, and Promotion.* Bulletin 1932, No. 17, National Survey of Education Monograph No. 13. (Washington, D.C.: U.S. Government Printing Office, 1933), p. 11.

6. Henry Harap, "Differentiation of Curriculum Practices and Instruction in Elementary Schools," pp. 161–172 in Guy M. Whipple (ed.), *The Grouping of Pupils, op. cit.*

7. Stuart E. Dean, *Elementary School Organization and Administration.* Bulletin 1960, No. 11, U.S. Office of Education (Washington, D.C.: U.S. Government Printing Office, 1960), pp. 67–73.

8. *Ibid.*, pp. 68–72.

9. Robert T. Rock, Jr., "A Critical Study of Current Practices in Ability Grouping," *Educational Research Bulletin, Catholic University of America*, Nos. 5 and 6 (1929).

10. Roy O. Billett, *op. cit.*, p. 6.

11. *Ibid.*, pp. 116–120.

12. Austin H. Turney, "The Status of Ability Grouping," *Educational Administration and Supervision,* 17 (January and February 1931), pp. 21–42, 110–127.

13. W. S. Miller and Henry J. Otto, "Analysis of Experimental Studies in Homogeneous Grouping," *Journal of Educational Research,* 21 (January–May 1930), pp. 95–102.

14. Harold S. Wyndham, *Ability Grouping* (Melbourne, Australia: Melbourne University Press, 1932).

15. Ethel L. Cornell, "Effects of Ability Grouping Determinable from Published Studies," pp. 289–302 in Guy M. Whipple (ed.), *The Ability Grouping of Pupils, op. cit.*

16. Ruth B. Ekstrom, *Experimental Studies of Homogeneous Grouping* (Princeton, N.J.: Educational Testing Service, April 1959).

17. Catherine C. Miles, "Gifted Children," pp. 984–1114 in Leonard Carmichael (ed.), *Manual of Child Psychology* (New York: John Wiley and Sons, 1954).

18. A. Harry Passow, "Enrichment of Education for the Gifted," pp. 193–221 in Nelson Henry (ed.), *Education for the Gifted.* Fifty-seventh Yearbook, part II, National Society for the Study of Education (Chicago: University of Chicago Press, 1958).

19. Ruth B. Ekstrom, *op. cit.*, p. 18.

20. Ethel L. Cornell, *op. cit.*, p. 290.

21. Harold S. Wyndham, *op. cit.*, p. 156.

22. Roy S. Billett, "A Controlled Experiment to Determine the Advantages of Homogeneous Grouping," *Educational Research Bulletin,* 7 (April–May 1928), pp. 133–140, 165–172, 190–196.

23. Harold S. Wyndham, *op. cit.*, p. 19.

24. Harold S. Wyndham, *op. cit.*, p. 157.

25. Ethel S. Cornell, *op. cit.*, p. 290.

* PART TWO

Mentally Retarded

In its ideal form a diagnosis of mental retardation involves a team of specialists including physicians, psychologists, social workers, and — depending on the age and circumstances of the case — educators. The process is costly, but if it is carried out effectively, a plan of action is laid down that will lead to optimal adjustment of the retardate and his family.

Unfortunately the diagnostic process is wrought with "superstitious beliefs" as Wolfensberger points out in the first article of the section ("Diagnosis Diagnosed"), written for a British audience. The need to provide feedback to families, the too frequent dead-end nature of the procedures, and the overdevelopment of diagnostic services to the exclusion of other resources are several problem areas given careful attention and critical evaluation.

The validity of measures of intelligence as predictors of future behavior is yet another source of embarrassment in the diagnostic arena, which, while it is not of the same order as those problems of a more administrative nature treated by Wolfensberger, does give pause for thought. The problem is illustrated by Butterfield's case study in which a mongoloid adult achieved at a level considerably higher than his measured IQs of 28 (Stanford-Binet Intelligence Scale, Form L-M) and 54 (Peabody Picture Vocabulary Test) or Vineland Social Maturity Social Quotient of 44 would suggest. Cases of a similar nature have been reported elsewhere (Seagoe 1965; Sarason, 1958). Perhaps these are rare cases of a discrepancy between ability and performance. However, they serve to remind us that instruments for the assessment of intellectual functioning are not without their problems, and that the relationship between measured intelligence and intelligent behavior is less than perfect.

Although there are problems in the diagnosis of mental retardation and questions sometimes about the validity of instruments used for assessing intelligence or, indeed, about the concept of intelligence itself (Liverant, 1960), there is perhaps clear agreement among specialists that the term mental retardation is useful for describing a group of individuals characterized by subaverage intellectual functioning and impairment in the ability to adapt in society at a level commensurate with their chronological age. Explanations of the deficiency, however, are the subject of some controversy. Zigler, in a paper reprinted in the present volume ("Cultural Familial Retardation: A Continuing Dilemma") sets forth arguments existing between developmental and defect approaches to mental retardation. This exposition is not without controversy itself, as witnessed by the critical replies to the article, written by Weir and Jastak, and Zigler's rejoinder. Still further debate on the topic is to be found in the writings of Milgram (1969), Zigler (1969), and Ellis (1969).

Bijou (1966) represents still another perspective, with his rejection of "hypothetical, internal determining factors and assumed biological processes." Instead, one who is developmentally retarded is said to be "one who has a limited repertory of behavior shaped by events that constitute his history." The above writings and those reprinted in this volume call our attention to the fact that theorizing about the basic nature of mental retardation is a very live issue indeed.

How shall the educable retarded be educated? By special classes, integration in regular classes, institutions, special schools? These questions have concerned special educators for a long time. The basic question motivating the research is whether or not special classes for the educable retarded are as effective as regular classes in facilitating the achievement and adjustment of such pupils. Early results seemed reasonably clear: academic achievement was fostered by placement in regular classes, social adjustment by placement in special classes. Methodological considerations, however, led to an abandonment of these generalizations (Quay, 1963). One sophisticated new study (Goldstein et al., 1965) has also been soundly criticized (Guskin and Spicker, 1968; Blackman, 1967).

Dunn, in an article reprinted in this volume, "Special Education for the Mildly Retarded—Is Much of It Justifiable?,"[1] suggests that special classes for the retarded be abandoned. Goldstein, on the other hand ("Issues in the Education of the Mentally Retarded"), discusses two key issues in the education of the mentally retarded, and suggests that alternate patterns for the education of retarded children be explored. He stops short of suggesting that the classes be eliminated, however. Indeed, taking a position diametrically opposed to that of Dunn, Goldstein suggests that the problem of stigma associated with special class placement—of such great concern to Dunn—may need to be viewed from a different perspective:

> Instead of becoming preoccupied with labels and stigma, we might do well to look at the other side of the coin and ask what effects delayed placement has on the personality development of the child, the status he acquires among his regular class peers, and the pressures placed on the family.

And Dunn writes:

> The assessment of educational potential has been left to the school psychologist who generally administers—in an hour or so—a psychometric battery, at best

---

[1] The Dunn article, although focusing on problems of the mentally retarded treats several very large general issues. For this reason it is reprinted in Section VII, "General Problems and Issues." It would not seem inappropriate, however, if the article were read within the context of the present chapter.

consisting of individual tests of intelligence, achievement, and social and personal adjustment. Again the purpose is to find out what is wrong with the child in order to label him and thus make him eligible for special education services. In large measure this has resulted in digging the educational graves of many racially and/or economically disadvantaged children by using a WISC or Binet IQ score to justify the label mentally retarded. The term then becomes a destructive, self-fulfilling prophecy.

In a similar critical vein, Olshansky, Schonfield, and Sternfeld ("Mentally Retarded or Culturally Different?") raise questions about the validity of the term mental retardation, particularly for those in the lower socioeconomic classes. Abandonment of the term is urged for those who show no demonstrable brain damage. Certain evidence for viewing lower socioeconomic children as "culturally different" rather than mentally retarded is taken from the Onondaga study which found "the prevalence rate for retardation or suspected retardation was more than three times as high as that for whites, and residence in the economically depressed areas was accompanied by higher rates for all colors." The authors make a strong case for differential labelling. It must be noted, however, that the Onondaga study from which the inferences were drawn has been itself the subject of some controversy (Kirk and Weiner, 1959).

The final article deals with the problem of multiple handicap among mental retardates. Multiple handicap is an important but neglected topic in special education. Indeed, there is ample evidence to indicate that in a great many cases—some suggest most—the problems are those of more than a single disability. Henderson ("Teaching the Multihandicapped Mentally Retarded Child") reviews studies of the incidence of multiple handicaps in the mentally retarded, and takes up the significance of secondary handicaps in retarded children from educational and social perspectives. It is not surprising that problems of diagnosis and educational programming, seen in the general area of mental retardation and other handicapping conditions, exist also for the multiply handicapped mentally retarded.

REFERENCES

Bijou, S. W., "A Functional Analysis of Retardated Development," in N. R. Ellis (ed.), *International Review of Research in Mental Retardation* (New York: Academic Press, 1966).

Blackman, L. S., "The Dimensions of a Science of Special Education," *Mental Retardation*, 5 (1967), pp. 7–11.

Ellis, N. R., "A Behavioral Research Strategy in Mental Retardation: Defense and Critique," *American Journal of Mental Deficiency*, 73 (1969), pp. 557–566.

Goldstein, H., J. W. Moss, and L. J. Jordan, *The Efficacy of Special Class Training on the Development of Mentally Retarded Children*. Cooperative Research Project No. 619, 1965 (Washington, D.C.: U.S. Office of Education).

Guskin, S. L. and H. H. Spicker, "Educational Research in Mental Retardation," in N. R. Ellis, *International Review of Research in Mental Retardation*, vol. 3 (New York: Academic Press, 1968).

Kirk, S. A. and B. B. Weiner, "The Onondaga Census—Fact or Artifact," *Exceptional Children*, 25 (1959), pp. 226–231.

Leland, H., "The Relationship Between Mental Retardation and Intelligence," *American Journal of Mental Deficiency*, 73 (1969), pp. 533–535.

Liverant, S., "Intelligence: A Concept in Need of Re-examination," *Journal of Consulting Psychology*, 24 (1960), pp. 101–110.

Milgram, N. A., "The Rational and the Irrational in Zigler's Motivational Approach to Mental Retardation," *American Journal of Mental Deficiency*, 73 (1969), pp. 527–532.

Quay, L. C., "Academic Skills," in N. R. Ellis (ed.), *Handbook of Mental Deficiency* (New York: McGraw-Hill, 1963).

Sarason, S. B., *Psychological Problems in Mental Deficiency* (New York: Harper, 1958).

Seagoe, M. V., "Verbal Development in a Mongoloid," *Exceptional Children*, 31 (1965), pp. 269–275.

Zigler, E., "Developmental Versus Difference Theories of Mental Retardation and the Problem of Motivation," *American Journal of Mental Deficiency*, 73 (1969), pp. 536–556.

** 7 **

Diagnosis Diagnosed

WOLF WOLFENSBERGER

In the U.K. I noticed that few retardates had had the type of comprehensive diagnostic evaluation which is relatively easy to obtain in the U.S. Indeed, many U.K. retardates had apparently not even had a standardized intelligence test, and if they did, the examiner's report usually included little except the MA and IQ. While this, at first, shocked my sensibilities, I also noted that some of the most remarkable services to the retarded that I had ever seen, as, for instance, the adult training centre programme in Middlesex, rendered outstanding services in spite of lack of extensive diagnosis.

This observation was so discordant with everything I had been taught that I decided that it called for further scrutiny. Perhaps, I thought, the remarkable performance of the trainees was due to their having been misdiagnosed. Perhaps they were really just schizophrenics, delinquents, etc.? Thus I decided to examine the casefolder of every single trainee in one of the Middlesex centres. I found that 40% of the 85 trainees had apparently never been tested, but that these seemed to be the lower, not the higher, functioning ones. The mean IQ of the other 60% was 44, with a range of 18–67 and a standard deviation of 13.

I still felt a need to ascertain that the trainees without tests were, in fact, the lower functioning ones as they appeared to be. Dr. Bennett, the Principal Mental Health Officer, Dr. Tizard and I interviewed every single trainee at another Middlesex centre which was thought to cater to higher functioning trainees. Each trainee was interviewed by at least two of us, and we made independent judgments and measurements on a number of criteria. In brief, we found that 32% of the trainees did not know their age and only 33% could write their name. While 56% could count to 20, 16% could count only to 10, and only 31% could tell which number came before 12. Forty-five per cent could identify six basic coins, but a

* From *The Journal of Mental Subnormality* 1965, *XI*, pp. 62–70. Reprinted by permission of the author and the publisher.

The writing of this paper was supported by USPHS Grant No. HD 00370.

Parts of this paper are excerpts reprinted by permission from *Mental Retardation*, 1965, 3, 29–31, a publication of the American Association on Mental Deficiency.

mere 13% could combine at least 2 coins from a pile to make 4d, 9d, 1/-, 1/3, and 2/6. Only 22% could tell time to within 5 minutes. Seventy-nine per cent were completely illiterate on the Schonell Reading Test, while 9% could read mechanically at the 10 year level. Only 10 trainees (12%) were judged to look and act in a fashion as to pass for normal on the street. In sum, the group appeared to be very similar to a random sample of hospitalized ambulatory retardates, and their good performance could not be ascribed to a significant number of misplacements or misdiagnoses. It took some months before I could make sense out of all this, and reconcile myself to the fact that good services *can* be rendered even in the absence of sophisticated diagnostics. At this point, I began to look for the origins and basis of a number of beliefs about and practices in the diagnostic process in mental retardation.

The treatment of mental retardation is primarily a problem of human management, and many approaches to human management, for a variety of historical and social reasons, are based upon a medical model. The treatment of mental retardation is one of these, and the field has inherited or derived many attitudes, practices, and, yes—even myths and lores from the medical models it has emulated. One complex of attitudes, practices, myths and lores has to do with the role and significance of case evaluation, or, as it is called in the medical tradition, diagnosis.

Among some clinicians, particularly in the medical field, there exists what can almost be described as a diagnosis compulsion. Sometimes diagnosis seems to become more important than anything else, and once diagnosis has been achieved the clinician may behave as if the main task of case management were completed. Even among less diagnosis-oriented professionals, diagnosis is viewed as a sacred cow which has been enshrined in a mystique, and there are many superstitious beliefs associated with its worship. Let me enumerate only a few:

1. Diagnosis is better than no diagnosis.
2. Early diagnosis is better than late diagnosis.
3. Diagnosis is essential to successful treatment or case management.
4. Differential diagnosis is important for differential treatment.
5. Extensive evaluation is better than limited evaluation.
6. Team diagnosis is better than individual diagnosis.

These beliefs, we may almost call them dogmas, are widely subscribed to in medicine. You will readily note that all have been applied to retardation and are generally encountered and accepted there. Yet we can show that these beliefs are not only not always true in the human management of retardates, but are also sometimes invalid even in the best practice of medicine.

Let us take a critical look at the six dogmas, one by one.
1. Is diagnosis always better than no diagnosis? I submit to you that

many cases of mental retardation would have been better off had they never been formally and professionally diagnosed. Some individuals, both professional and lay, see diagnosis as a magic solution to a human puzzle. Others, particularly service agencies, use it as an escape from responsibility. For whatever reason, diagnosis can quite often be a dead end for the family. Instead of leading to a meaningful service assignment it frequently results only in a frustrating series of fruitless cross-referrals. A typical case in my experience is that of a mildly retarded, homosexually inclined, moderately disturbed teenager who was referred back and forth between the following agencies: regular and special school programs, a child guidance and residential treatment centre, a state hospital for the mentally ill, two state institutions for the retarded, and the state vocational rehabilitation service. He was judged to be too retarded for the regular grades, too disturbing in the special class, too retarded for the outpatient and too old for the inpatient service of the disturbed children's center, too homosexual for the children's ward of the state hospital and too young for its adult wards, too high functioning for the first state retardation institution, not quite enough of a number of things for the special treatment unit of the second, and too effeminate for the programs vocational rehabilitation offered.

This cross-referring took place within a relatively short time span and three or four agencies ran him through their standard diagnostic mill. In the end, the boy somehow did not quite fit in anywhere and lived at home without any service whatever. On paper, however, he was a great success as far as the agencies were concerned. Since he was referred in each instance to what was considered to be an appropriate service by the agency one step ahead in the referral chain, he constituted at least six successful close-outs and will thus enter our national mental health, mental retardation and education statistics. A similar case has been recorded in the literature (Krush, 1964) where a boy was handed on between 18 physicians, four teachers, one chiropractor, two clinics, two hospitals and seven schools. After this, the boy became "unco-operative, untidy, disturbed," and the mother stated that "not even the worst prognosis he had received in all our long years of searching for help had prepared us for this."

Many a parent has questioned bitterly what good the diagnostic evaluation did if it failed to lead to assignation to a service, or, even worse, if it actually resulted in the child's exclusion from a program previously enrolled in. A rather extreme example of this occurs in one of our states which I will not name. There, severely retarded children need not be included in public education programs, and only a very small number of local school districts have chosen to provide classes voluntarily. In addition, the definition of severe retardation was manipulated so as to include children up to IQ 60. Finally, even if a school district does decide to offer so-called trainable classes on a voluntary basis, children must be at least eight years old. My advice to parents of children who are probably near IQ 60 in that state is to avoid, by all means available, the testing or evaluation of their school-age child. They have nothing to gain and all to lose from a professional diagnosis.

Quite aside from the *question* of when diagnosis is better then no diagnosis is the *fact* that unlike in most areas of medicine, diagnosis in retardation is not always possible anyway. Even the most careful study of a case may leave many diagnostic questions unanswered. Especially etiological diagnosis is often only an educated guess and rarely has the weight of evidence behind it that usually supports medical diagnoses. ". . . . The diagnostic label which is applied to an individual frequently reveals more about the orientation and bias of the diagnostician than about the causal agents responsible for the retardation" (Robinson & Robinson, 1965). Even where there is considerable evidence, there exist embarrassments. For example, a pregnant mother and apparently also the fetus suffered an infection and she delivered prematurely in a difficult birth. Is the child's retardation to be coded as due to pre-natal infection, prematurity or birth trauma? Most currently popular etiological and coding classification schemes permit only one entry.

The behavioral area has other kinds of problems. Here, we have heavy reliance on tests and techniques which have not been validated as regards predictions about retardates. The lack of concern for validating data on the part of some personnel in the applied areas is sometimes little short of shocking to those who take an empirical approach to behavior.

2. Is early diagnosis always desirable? I submit that perhaps it is in an ideal society, but that in the reality of everyday practice, early diagnosis can be a disaster. Let me give you a typical example. When a child is born into a family it is usually accepted and loved with little reservation. Should the child later turn out to be retarded, the problem may be worked out within the family because of the strong bonds that have been formed. However, a child diagnosed as retarded at or near birth may never find the crucial initial acceptance and may be viewed with conflicted attitudes which prevent the formation of deep parental love. This can lead to early and quite unnecessary institutionalization or other consequences detrimental to the child.

I have encountered many instances, numbering in the hundreds, where early diagnosis such as in mongolism exposed the family to professional management which appeared contrary to the welfare of either child, family or society. The most common counsel seems to be the stereotyped "put the child in the institution right away," often accompanied by the sincere admonition to "forget you ever had him" and perhaps the consolation to "have another one instead." This sort of advice is, by no means, the most inappropriate or callous one readily encountered and repeatedly documented in the literature. The dictum that early diagnosis is always optimal may thus need to be qualified. Early diagnosis is desirable when it leads to prevention, early treatment or constructive counseling; it is irrelevant if it is purely academic and does not change the course of events; it is harmful if, in balance, child or family reap more disadvantages than benefits.

3. Is diagnosis essential to successful treatment or management? In medicine we have many instances which illustrate that successful treatment can take place even when the nature of a condition is unknown. One of the classical examples is that of John Snow who was a public health pioneer during the 1854 cholera epidemic in London. Plotting the incidence of cholera on a map, he noticed that it centered around a well, *viz.* the Broad Street Pump. The mode of propagation of cholera was then not understood, but Snow did not wait for experiments and causal explanation. He noted the correlation between drinking from the well, and death from cholera, and resolutely closed the well. The epidemic promptly faded away. A more contemporary example is prophylactic treatment with antibiotics when one really has no idea what it is one is trying to prevent, or is, in fact, already treating.

I submit that in many cases where the main object of diagnosis is the identification of service needs, a brief interview with the family can sometimes even be sufficient. While the case itself may be complex, the *need* may be very simple. Thus, the need for a mother's helper, day care, trainable classes, public health nurse visits, etc., is often so blatant that an intelligent layman could render a good judgement, especially when the existence of retardation can no longer be doubted, and/or when previously obtained diagnostic data are already available. Yet some agencies, at least in this country, will blindly administer a mammoth and stereotyped dose of diagnostics to all comers, even where the needs are as obvious as the total lack of means to satisfy them. An example here is that of a clinic I know which routinely includes a speech evaluation in its "interdisciplinary" approach. To my amazement the speech pathologist evaluated a two-months old mongoloid infant, and came up with a diagnosis of "delayed language development."

4. Does differential diagnosis really imply differential treatment? The belief in the importance of differential diagnosis seems primarily derived from the medical emphasis on etiological diagnosis. It is argued that you must know what caused a disorder before you can really treat it effectively. This argument, of course, is not even valid in medicine even though I have heard many physicians repeat it. It is even less valid in human management problems. Even in situations where it is believed that differential etiological diagnosis implies differential treatment, the evidence may be extremely tenuous or lacking, and the treatment may be chosen on the basis of current dogma only. A typical example is the virtually universally accepted belief encountered in untold texts and articles, *viz.* that a diagnosis of mental retardation in a child calls for an entirely different type of treatment than a diagnosis of emotional disturbance. If this is so—and I personally doubt it—it certainly has never been subjected to an adequate empirical test even though such a test would not be all that difficult. Another, similar claim which has been tested, and has found only very limited

support, is that cultural-familial retardates need a different educational curriculum than retardates with presumed brain-injury.

Generally, practically useful prediction of outcome in various areas of disposition and treatment of *individual* retardates has been a spectacular failure. Literally hundreds of studies have unsuccessfully concerned themselves with this problem.

5. Is extensive evaluation always better than a limited one? Often it is, but sometimes it is not. Only too often diagnostic clinics or centers run every client through a fairly standard, little varying mill of tests and procedures. They may do this regardless of what the presenting question or problem is. Sometimes a very extensive but standardized evaluation is entirely wasted because it did not address itself to the presenting question. When a client is fed into the diagnostic mill, the mill should be set to grind in a certain way and for a certain length. Not all grain needs or even should be ground the same way or else there will be waste.

Considering the costs involved, diagnosis should be rendered only in terms of the question: "Diagnosis for what?" Often detailed pre-diagnostic questionnaires and letters to previous contact agencies will reveal that the family only needs counseling, selective evaluation, or a referral instead of "the works." Yet, in my experience, pre-diagnostic screening is often very cursory and inadequate. Even when diagnosis could be rendered in a meaningful context it is only too often of low utility. Diagnostic teams in retardation are new and are still learning, and even skilled diagnosticians do not always render reports of practical utility to those who are often the only ones actually doing anything meaningful for the client, namely the family and the teaching and habilitative professions.

6. Is team diagnosis better than individual diagnosis? Ordinarily, the answer appears to be yes, but we must keep clearly in mind the shortcomings which tend to be characteristic of team evaluations, and that is lack of integration of the findings, and fragmentation of the client. The getting together of six people once a week in a staff meeting and reading six written reports does *not* constitute integration and team diagnosis. Team evaluation should add up to more than the sum of its parts, but often it does not even add up to as much as the sum, as when contradictory or puzzling findings are left unresolved and dangling in the air.

The above discussion has several implications to program development in the U.K. Many times during my travels, program directors would apologize because retardates in their programs had rarely had the broad multidisciplinary evaluation which is relatively easy to obtain in this country, or because some retardates had not even been given a standardized intelligence test prior to service assignment. The program directors would tell me that this was regrettable and that they hoped that in the future more comprehensive evaluation centers or services would be developed. In other words, they viewed the sparsity of diagnostics as something which called for remedy.

Somehow, the British program directors' cry for diagnostic services re-

minds me of the Israelites' demand for a king. The Lord warned them that
a king would lay a heavy hand on them, tax their property, possess their
women and even take their lives. But the Israelites wanted a king, and
kings they got who did exactly as the Lord had foretold. The British
can have their diagnostic services and clinics just like we do, but such
services can be, like kings, expensive, incompetent, tyrannical, unreason-
able, destructive, remote from reality and the people, and even useless.
I am not prepared to say that diagnostics in mental retardation is bad,
should be abolished, or should not be established where it is not yet available. But just as we had (and still have) much to learn from U.K. service
patterns, so I want to warn you not to fail to learn from our experiences,
or, in this case, failures. Specifically, I would recommend to you that you
invest your money (remember, we can waste ours, but you can't) in diagnostic services only if the conditions discussed below are fulfilled:

**1. Diagnostic service development should not precede other service devel-
opment but should follow it.**

The best moment to activate a diagnostic center for retardates is probably when other services have reached the point where they are satisfying
the bulk of that demand which can be met without sophisticated diagnostics. To operate a diagnostic center in a service vacuum is very frustrating
for parents and sometimes even for professionals. Parents will have to be
told what they need and then informed that, too bad, so sad, the needed
service will not be developed until their child is too old for it anyway.

The state of the science being what it is, diagnosis and evaluation in
retardation must quite often be based upon observation of the client's
response to services, rather than precede it. For example, the prediction
of vocational adjustment of moderately retarded adults is virtually impossible or meaningless unless vocational placement and habilitation training
and counseling are available.

In the U.S. we have a situation where in many localities diagnostic services are greatly overdeveloped in comparison to other available resources.
Indeed, of services in the field, diagnosis is often the most readily available, and is the first and for years the only resource to be developed.
Curiously, this can create a manpower problem and far from stimulating
other service development may inhibit it as many professionals much prefer
to render diagnosis than to offer families of the retarded the kind of help
they need. There are a number of plausible reasons for this. Diagnosis is
an intellectual exercise which calls upon the basic skills the professional has
learned in his training and which can be carried out in his office. It gives
him a deceptive feeling of accomplishment and can do so several times
a week. In diagnosis, the professional can find many rewards and a good
deal of security—just the opposite of what the parent typically finds in it.
However, when it comes to other services, the professional finds neither
security nor easy satisfaction. Particularly in mental retardation, traditional
approaches used in mental health (and of questionable success even
there) have not been very successful. Furthermore, the rewards of most

services in mental retardation come very, very slowly as treatment is a long, drawn-out difficult and laborious process. Reinforcement in the form of visible progress in an individual case may be apparent sporadically through the years rather than several times a week as in diagnosis. Finally, most effective services simply cannot be rendered in an office. All of this may keep professionals clinging to diagnosis and shying away from other services.

2. The diagnostic service should be tied firmly into the mental retardation service continuum.

This tie-in must be real, not just a verbal or paper one. Preferably, the same administrative body which controls part or all of a service continuum should control the diagnostic service. Agencies which have no major interest in the retardate and little if any service responsibility to him are particularly ill-suited for a diagnostic role, even if their personnel are highly skilled in their own area. The trouble with many U.S. diagnostic services is that they are provided by psychiatrically oriented agencies to whom mental retardation is a stepchild. Too often they regard the retardate as a disturbed psychiatric case, and may mumble something about his ego being impounded by the libidinal id. In such agencies, the parent of the retardate is almost always stereotyped as guilty, rejecting, unaccepting of reality, and in need of psychotherapy. The mother with three children (the oldest being the retardate) in nappies who desperately needs the help of the public health nurse to teach her toilet training techniques may, instead, be told she needs psychotherapy to help her with her feeling about feces.

One of the big bonuses of tieing diagnostic agencies into the service continuum is the exposure of diagnostic personnel to the refreshing wind of feedback, which can be both embarrassing and educational. This should, in time, result in more cautious and/or more accurate prediction.

3. Diagnostic services should be structured to offer substantial feedback and interpretation to the family.

Many diagnostic centers in the past have considered their duty done the moment the diagnostic process is completed *to their satisfaction.* Once the professional staff involved had reached a conclusion, the case was closed except for one, often hurried, impatient and perhaps patronizing, feedback session with the parents. They were given the facts as seen by the professional and told to "accept" them. More than one feedback session was felt to be beyond the scope of diagnosis, and a series of sessions was sometimes already considered psychotherapy which, being a "service," the parent was supposed to get elsewhere. Parents who were dissatisfied with this type of management were considered maladjusted, difficult, and "nonaccepting."

Professionals look askance at the parent who does not "accept" their diagnosis and who keeps looking elsewhere for confirmation or disconfirmation. It is undoubtedly true that many a child has been subjected to redundant diagnostics because of the parents' emotional maladjustments and feelings of guilt and hostility. At the same time I believe strongly that a good deal of diagnosis "shopping" has been due to inadequate feedback counseling.

As long as parents do not have diagnostic centers to go to, they cannot be dissatisfied with what they are not being told. Once such services are established, however, parents will expect feedback. If this feedback is inadequate, they will begin to go shopping from one diagnostic center to another. This is a very prevalent phenomenon in the U.S. where a large number of retardates undergo repeated and redundant evaluations which parents can obtain at relatively little cost if they are willing to expend time and effort. In my own experience, the record was held by a boy who, within five years, was subjected to eight evaluations, most of these by a full clinical team, and several at well-known clinics. Obtaining needed services, however, was another matter.

I am now deeply convinced, and more and more of my colleagues who work with parents seem to agree, that it takes a series of sessions, spread out over several months, before most parents come even somewhat to grips with the nature and, particularly, the implications of a diagnosis. Time and again one finds that not even parents with professional and mental health backgrounds, nor those who profess a verbal understanding during the first feedback session, have even made a good start in working through their conflicts. For this reason, spaced and repeated feedback counseling should be viewed not as a luxury but as an integral part of the function of a diagnostic service. Such counseling should be offered even if it necessitates case load reduction since, in the long run, it will probably conserve professional manpower.

It is penny-wise and pound-foolish to invest substantial and valuable resources into the diagnostic process only to begrudge a few additional hours of counseling. If the parents are not adequately counseled, they may not only go shopping, but perhaps even worse, their defenses may harden and may render them inaccessible to help. In the end this may cost ten, a hundred and even a thousandfold what a few hours of counseling would have cost.

4. A program of staff training and attitude shaping should be a clearly structured element of a diagnostic center.

A significant proportion of the staff of our mental retardation diagnostic clinics are without any experience or training in the field, and some are without any awareness of a need for such training, and no compulsion to obtain it. In addition, they may not even have a deep interest in retardation. In short, they are what one might call "utilizers" who have no involvement in mental retardation and who might just as readily drift off to a psychiatric, geriatric, alcoholic, or any other kind of agency, depending on where the edge of personal advantage is to be found. Their services to the retardate are not infrequently worse than worthless as they may do more harm to a case than if it had been left alone. I have seen centers without a single adequately trained member on their staff.

Training is even more important for diagnostic center personnel than personnel in other services. Center personnel receive little verification, validation, or feedback in general about their work and they may rarely see retardates in any capacity other than diagnosis. As a result, they are more apt to grow dogmatic and careless in their judgements and prognoses. Particular care must be taken in the training or selection of parent counselors. There exists, at present, no certificate of training or academic degree which assures that a person is fit to manage or counsel parents of retarded children. Unfortunately, space does not permit a discussion of counselor qualification.

When setting up a mental retardation diagnostic service, training in mental retardation should be made mandatory. While this can be done on an inservice basis, it must not be done informally but in a structured and demanding fashion. Not even experience in the field can be assumed to be adequate, for I have seen professionals who, even after years of work in retardation, were as naive at the end as at the beginning. Quite often one will hear the objection that case load demands make an intensive and sustained training program impossible. In my experience, diagnostic centers where this argument is successfully advanced render very inadequate services. They would be much more useful if they reduced service load and improved quality.

This has brought me to the end of my little contribution to your journal. It has been very healthy and cathartic for me, because it is difficult to get a paper like this published in the U.S. Already, I have had a similar paper rejected as "too controversial." Maybe it is fortunate (for me) that not too many of my American colleagues read the *Journal of Mental Subnormality,* or they might skin me alive. Parochialism does have its advantages!

REFERENCES

Krush, T. P., "The Search for the Golden Key," *Bulletin of the Menninger Clinic,* 28 (1964), pp. 77–82.

Robinson, H. B. and Nancy M. Robinson, *The Mentally Retarded Child: A Psychological Approach* (New York: McGraw-Hill, 1965).

Wolfensberger, W., "Reminiscences on a British Psychological Society Convention," *American Psychologist,* 19 (1964), pp. 774–775.

———, "Some Observations on European Programs for the Mentally Retarded," *Mental Retardation,* 2 (1964), pp. 280–285. (b).

———, "Teaching and Training of the Retarded in European Countries," *Mental Retardation,* 2 (1964), pp. 331–337. (c)

———, "General Observations on European Programs," *Mental Retardation,* 3 (1965), pp. 8–11. (a)

———, "Embarrassments in the Diagnostic Process," *Mental Retardation,* 3 (1965), pp. 29–31. (b)

** 8 **

A Provocative Case of Over-Achievement
by a Mongoloid

EARL C. BUTTERFIELD

In this day of analysis of variance and factor analysis, the case study of a single individual seems scant basis for sound conclusions. However, a single case may suggest hypotheses. Indeed, if a single case is unusual enough it can cause one to consider revising concepts which he has regarded as well established and upon which he has regularly based decisions which radically affect the lives of others. The following appears to be such a case.

E. is a 36 year old male mongoloid who recently was admitted to a state institution for the mentally retarded.[1] At the time of his admission, E.'s extensive social history suggested that he was not a 'typical mongol.' Accordingly, E. was immediately examined by a medical doctor, a speech and hearing specialist, psychologists and staff personnel from the cottage where he was placed when he arrived at the institution. It was hoped that, by acting soon after his admission, information about E., which was as little biased by institutional influences as possible, could be obtained.

HISTORY

E. was born on January 1, 1924. The birth was by Caesarian section because his mother suffered from a severe deformity of the pelvis. E. weighed 7 lbs., 12 oz., at birth and was regarded as being physically normal.

E. was first examined psychologically in 1936 when he was 12–1. At that

* From *American Journal of Mental Deficiency* 1961, 66, pp. 444–448. Reprinted by permission of the author and the publisher. Copyright © 1961, American Association on Mental Deficiency.
[1] The author is indebted and extends his sincere thanks to the administrative staff of Southbury Training School, Southbury, Conn. for generously granting permission to report information from the training school files.

73

time, the Connecticut State Board of Education reported that E. had a
1916 Standford-Binet M.A. of 4–4 and IQ of 36. It was the examiner's
impression that E. was a "typical mongolian idiot. . . . Vision very poor.
. . . Speech defective. . . . Very short span of attention. . . . Hyperactive. . . . Immature. . . . Extremely dependent upon mother." It was
also reported that E.'s mother was "very much attached to the patient;
would not consider committing him to an institution; spends a great deal
of time tutoring him and training him in good habits." On the basis of
this report, E. was excluded from the public schools and institution authorities were told of his status.

In July, 1948, when E. was 24, he was referred to the New Haven Vocational Service by his mother's physician "for the purpose of determining
whether he could be made employable and in what area." Testing there
revealed a mental age "definitely below six years on the Stanford-Binet
(L) supported by performance on selected sections of the Wechsler-
Bellvue Scale (Form I)."

From 1951 to his admission to the institution in 1960, E. was visited regularly at his mother's home by social workers from the state institution for
the mentally retarded. The remainder of his history is drawn from the
written reports of these social workers.

June, 1951: E. "is eager to help around the house and to do errands for
the neighbors. He can go to a self-service store by himself. He goes into the
center of New Haven (population 150,000) by himself and goes around on
various errands for his mother, such as paying the gas and electric bills.
Patient is immaculately clean and is able to care for all of his personal
needs."

May, 1952: E. and his mother "played a (piano) duet for the worker."
E.'s mother is teaching him "to play the piano and he does this very well."

January, 1956: E.'s mother has been in a hospital for six months recover-
ing from a heart attack. (For the remaining four years of her life E.'s
mother was unable to do any physical work about the house.) E. "now
does all of the housework. He does the washing and ironing, vacuums,
makes beds, washes the floors and windows, takes out the rubbish, runs
all of the errands and pays all of the bills. . . . All Mrs. E. does is a little
cooking and baking."

August, 1956: "For spare money, E. makes potholders which he sells to
friends; he is also selling Christmas cards and ball point pens."

April, 1957: When worker arrived E. "was sitting at the table writing
and he immediately got up and spoke with the worker and was very po-
lite. . . . He showed the worker some of his writings and he is able to
write quite legibly. . . . He also enjoys music."

October, 1958: E. "recently had his name in the paper for finding a
pocketbook with $600.00 in it on a bus and turning it in to the driver."

January, 1959: Worker found house disrupted and workmen sealing a
hole in the kitchen ceiling. Water had flooded the apartment from above.
While Mrs. E. supervised the workmen in the kitchen, E. "came into the

living room, sat down and talked with the worker. . . . When the repair men left, E. began to set the kitchen to rights. Later, as the worker was leaving, she noticed that E. was setting up a rollaway bed which had been taken apart to dry. At this time, the worker's opinion was that "without E.'s help mother would be unable to continue her mode of living."

July, 1960: E.'s mother died and since there were no relatives who were able to keep him E. was committed to Southbury Training School.

MEDICAL FINDING

The STS medical department confirmed E.'s diagnosis of mental retardation due to mongolism and found no other abnormal physical symptoms. E. has subsequently developed a skin rash of unknown cause.

SPEECH AND HEARING EVALUATION

The STS speech and hearing clinic found that E. "is a secondary stutterer, complete with all of the earmarks of hesitation, repetition, elongation, circumlocution, cluttering, etc. His physical symptoms are characteristic of the advanced stutterer, i.e., tight stomach, constricted throat and grotesque facial movements."

PSYCHOLOGICAL EXAMINATION

On the Stanford-Binet Intelligence Scale, Form L–M, E. earned an M.A. of 5–0 and an IQ of 28. He succeeded in passing all of the items at the IV level; the Aesthetic Comparison, Opposite Analogies and Three Commissions at the IV–6 level; Paper Folding, Definitions and Copying a Square at the V level; and Number Concepts at the VI level.

On the Peabody Picture Vocabulary Test (Dunn, 1959), E. earned an M.A. of 7–6 and an IQ of 54.

The Vineland Social Maturity Scale was scored from the case history data and from reports of cottage attendants at STS. He earned an S.A. of 11.0 and an S.Q. of 44. He was given credit for all of the items at the IX–X level; writes short letters and does small remunerative work at the X–XI level; is left to care for self and others at the XI–XII level; and performs responsible routine chores at the XII–XV level.

On the Wide Range Achievement Test E. earned a reading grade level of 5.6, spelling grade level of 5.0 and an arithmetic grade level of 2.2.

On the Gray Standardized Oral Reading Paragraphs E. read through the sixth grade level with only one error.

The results of all of the psychological tests are summarized in Table I.

■ TABLE 1   *Summary of Objective Psychological Test Scores Secured for E.
Shortly After Institutionalization*

Stanford-Binet, LM	M.A. 5–0	IQ 28
PPVT	M.A. 7–6	IQ 54
Vineland	S.A. 11–0	S.Q. 44
Wide Range	Reading Grade	5.6
	Spelling Grade	5.0
	Arithmetic Grade	2.2

DISCUSSION

The main impact of this case study lies in the striking discrepancy between E.'s actual social maturity and academic achievement and the social maturity and academic achievement which would be predicted for someone of his M.A. and IQ. The special tutoring and care which his mother gave to him apparently resulted in a much higher level of general life and academic achievement than generally would be expected of a mongoloid or any other person of E.'s M.A. and IQ. However, this striking "predictive failure" is not inconsistent with the findings of a number of research programs which have investigated intensively various aspects of mental retardation.

A long series of researches begun with the hypothesis that normal and retarded children should react differently to success and failure experiences has shown that differential prediction cannot be made for groups constituted solely on the basis of the intellectual level of the Ss involved (Bialer, 1960; Gardner, 1958; Heber, 1957; Moss, 1958; Ringelheim, 1958). Rather, accurate predictions are possible only when personality factors which are common to both average and retarded groups are taken into account.

A series of interrelated studies which grew out of Kounin's (1941) and Lewin's (1936) contention that feebleminded, i.e., low IQ persons, are inherently more rigid than persons of average IQ has shown that rigid behaviors observed in mentally retarded Ss are best understood in terms of a number of motivational and developmental factors which are not uniquely dependent upon IQ (Green, 1960; Shallenberger, 1959; Stevenson and Zigler, 1957; Zigler, 1958; Zigler and deLabry, 1960; Zigler, Hodgen and Stevenson, 1958).

A variety of learning and reaction time experiments have shown that IQ differences are not so predictive of these phenomena as one might expect. G. Butterfield (1960) found no differences in the rate of acquisition of learning sets between "oddity items" in different M.A. levels of retarded Ss. Shipe (1960) found either no differences or differences in the direction opposite of that expected in the rate of acquisition of a probability learning task between average and retarded Ss. Although Bialer (in press) did find that "relatively higher IQ groups responded significantly more on the basis of secondary stimulus generalization," he found no differences in the rate of acquisition of either a form or color discrimination between different IQ levels of retarded and adolescent Ss. Barnett (1959) found no differences in stimulus generalization of a reaction time response to a visual stimulus in retarded and average adolescents. Berkson (1960) found no evidence that IQ and "perceptual and choice" functions in a reaction time task were related.

If there is a lesson to be learned from E.'s case history and the literature reviewed in this discussion, it is, perhaps, that M.A. and IQ are simply not sufficient bases for predicting many of the ways in which average and retarded Ss will differ. Although M.A. and IQ do predict some very important differences between average and retarded Ss, they are apparently not at all helpful in other kinds of predictions. This fact does not, of course, imply that M.A. and IQ are useless and should be abandoned. It does suggest, however, that more effort might profitably be expended in searching for other variables which are able to predict differences between average and retarded Ss.

In terms of research strategy, the suggestion that we search for variables to supplement M.A. and IQ implies that the time may have come to move away from the M.A. and IQ leveling research design to a prediction-criterion design. Studies of the mentally retarded and other quite different studies (Liverant, 1960; Rotter, 1960) both suggest that prediction might first be increased by moving to rigorously defined motivational and situational variables as predictors and narrowly defined response measures as criteria.

REFERENCES

Barnett, W. I., "Stimulus Generalization in Normals and Retardates on a Visual-Spatial Task Requiring Voluntary Response," *Abstract of Peabody Studies in Mental Deficiency*, 2 (1960), p. 50.

Berkson, G., "A Study of Reaction Time and Duration Threshold in Familial Mentally Deficient and Normal Adolescent Boys," unpublished doctoral dissertation, George Peabody College for Teachers, 1960.

Bialer, I., "Conceptualization of Success and Failure in Mentally Retarded and Normal Children," unpublished doctoral dissertation, George Peabody College for Teachers, 1960.

———, "Primary and Secondary Stimulus Generalization as Related to Intelligence Level," *Journal of Experimental Psychology*, 1961.

Butterfield, Gail B., "The Dependence of Learning Set upon Inter-Problem Interval," unpublished manuscript, Southbury Training School, 1960.

Dunn, L. M., *Peabody Picture Vocabulary Test* (Nashville, Tenn.: American Guidance Services, 1959).

Gardner, W. I., "Reactions of Intellectually Normal and Retarded Boys After Experimentally Induced Failure," unpublished doctoral dissertation, George Peabody College for Teachers, 1958.

Green, C. G., "Social Interaction in Feebleminded Children," unpublished master's thesis, University of Missouri, 1960.

Heber, R. F., "Expectancy and Expectancy Changes in Normal and Mentally Retarded Boys," unpublished doctoral dissertation, George Peabody College for Teachers, 1957.

Kounin, J., "Experimental Studies of Rigidity, I. The Measurement of Rigidity in Normal and Feebleminded Persons," *Character and Personality*, 9 (1941), pp. 251–273.

———, "Experimental Studies of Rigidity, II. The Explanatory Power of the Concept of Rigidity as Applied to Feeblemindedness," *Character and Personality*, 9 (1941), pp. 273–282.

Lewin, K., *A Dynamic Theory of Personality* (New York: McGraw-Hill, 1936).

Liverant, S., "Intelligence: A Concept in Need of Re-examination," *Journal of Consulting Psychology*, 24 (1960), pp. 101–110.

Moss, J. W., "Failure-Avoiding and Success-Striving in Retarded and Normal Children," unpublished doctoral dissertation, George Peabody College for Teachers, 1958.

Rotter, J. B., "Some Implications of a Social Learning Theory for the Prediction of Goal Directed Behavior from Testing Procedures," *Psychological Review*, 67 (1960), pp. 301–316.

Shallenberger, P., "The Cosatiation Score as a Measure of Positive and Negative Reaction Tendencies in Children," unpublished master's thesis, University of Missouri, 1959.

Shipe, Dorothy, "A Comparison of Probability Learning in Mentally Retarded and Normal Children," *Abstract of Peabody Studies in Mental Deficiency*, 2 (1960), p. 36.

Stevenson, H. and E. Zigler, "Discrimination Learning and Rigidity in Normal and Feebleminded Individuals," *Journal of Personality*, 25 (1957), pp. 699–711.

Terman, L. M. and Maud Merrill, *Stanford-Binet Intelligence Scale, Form LM* (Cambridge, Mass.: Riverside Press, 1960).

Zigler, E., "The Effect of Pre-Institutional Social Deprivation on the Performance of Feebleminded Children," unpublished doctoral dissertation, University of Texas, 1958.

Zigler, E. and J. O. deLabry, "Concept Formation as a Function of Reinforcement in Feebleminded and Normal Children," unpublished manuscript, Yale University, 1960.

Zigler, E., L. Hodgen, and H. Stevenson, "The Effect of Support on the Performance of Normal and Feebleminded Children," *Journal of Personality*, 26 (1958), pp. 106–122.

** 9 **

Familial Mental Retardation:
A Continuing Dilemma

EDWARD ZIGLER

The past decade has witnessed renewed interest in the problem of mental retardation. The interest has resulted in vigorous research activity and the construction of a number of theories which attempt an explanation of attenuated intellectual functioning. However, much of the research and many of the theoretical efforts in the area appear to be hampered by a variety of conceptual ambiguities. Much of this ambiguity is due to the very heterogeneity of phenomena included within the rubric of intellectual retardation. A portion of this ambiguity also appears to be the product of many workers' general conceptual orientation to the area of mental retardation.

The typical textbook pictures the distribution of intelligence as normal or Gaussian in nature, with approximately the lowest 3 percent of the distribution encompassing the mentally retarded (see Fig. 1a). A homogeneous class of persons is thus constructed, a class defined by intelligence-test performance which results in a score between 0 and 70. This schema has misled many laymen and students, and has subtly influenced the approach of experienced workers in the area. For if one fails to appreciate the arbitrary nature of the 70–I.Q. cutoff point, it is but a short step to the formulation that all persons falling below this point compose a homogeneous class of "subnormals," qualitatively different from persons having a higher I.Q. The view that mental retardates comprise a homogeneous group is seen in numerous research studies in which comparisons are made between retardates and normal individuals with the two groups defined solely on the basis of an I.Q. classification.

This practice gives rise to a "difference," or "defect," orientation to mental retardation. Such an approach historically included the notion of moral defect and had many origins, ranging from the belief that retardates were

* From *Science* 1967, *157*(*3788*), pp. 292–298. Reprinted by permission of the author and the publisher. Copyright 1967 by the American Association for the Advancement of Science.

possessed by a variety of devils to the empirical evidence of the higher incidence among them of socially unacceptable behaviors, such as crime and illegitimacy. More recently, the notion of defect has referred to defects in either physical or cognitive structures. This defect approach has one unquestionably valid component. There is a sizable group of retardates who suffer from any of a variety of known physical defects. For example, mental retardation may be due to a dominant gene, as in epiloia; to a single recessive gene, as in gargoylism, phenylketonuria, and amaurotic idiocy; to infections, such as congenital syphilis, encephalitis, or rubella in the mother; to chromosomal defects, as in mongolism; to toxic agents, as in retardation caused by radiation in utero, lead poisoning, or Rh incompatibility; and to cerebral trauma.

The diverse etiologies noted above have one factor in common; in every instance, examination reveals an abnormal physiological process. Persons who are retarded as a result of an abnormal physiological process *are* abnormal in the orthodox sense, since they suffer from a known physiological defect. However, in addition to this group, which forms a minority of all retardates, there is the group labeled "familial"—or, more recently, "cultural-familial"—which compromises approximately 75 percent of all retardates. This group presents the greatest mystery and has been the object of the most heated disputes in the area of mental retardation. The diagnosis of familial retardation is made when an examination reveals none of the physiological manifestations noted above, and when retardation of this same type exists among parents, siblings, or other relatives. Several writers have extended the defect notion to this type of retardate as well, although they differ as to what they propose as the specific nature of the defect. On the basis of differences in performance between retardates and normals on some experimental task rather than on the basis of physiological evidence, they have advanced the view that all retardates suffer from some specifiable defect over and above their general intellectual retardation.

Some order can be brought to the area of mental retardation if a distinction is maintained between physiologically defective retardates, with retardation of known etiology, and familial retardates, with retardation of unknown etiology. For the most part, work with physiologically defective retardates involves investigation into the exact nature of the underlying physiological processes, with prevention or amelioration of the physical and intellectual symptoms as the goal. Jervis (1) has suggested that such "pathological" mental deficiency is primarily in the domain of the medical sciences, whereas familial retardation represents a problem to be solved by behavioral scientists, including educators and behavioral geneticists. Diagnostic and incidence studies of these two types of retardates have disclosed certain striking differences. The retardate having an extremely low I.Q. (below 40) is almost invariably of the physiologically defective type. Familial retardates, on the other hand, are almost invariably mildly retarded, usually with I.Q.'s above 50. This difference in the general intellectual level of the two groups of retardates is an important empirical phenomenon that supports the two-group approach to mental retardation, the approach supported in this article.

A TWO-GROUP APPROACH

Hirsch (2) has asserted that we will not make much headway in understanding individual differences in intelligence and in many other traits, unless we recognize that, to a large degree such differences reflect the inherent biological properties of man. We can all agree that no genotype spells itself out in a vacuum, and that the phenotypic expression is firmly the result of environment interacting with the genotype. However, an appreciation of the importance of genetic differences allows us to bring considerable order to the area of mental retardation.

We need simply to accept the generally recognized fact that the gene pool of any population is such that there will always be variations in the behavioral or phenotypic expression of virtually every measurable trait or characteristic of man. From the polygenic model advanced by geneticists, we deduce that the distribution of intelligence is characterized by a bisymmetrical bell-shaped curve, which is characteristic of such a large number of distributions that we have come to refer to it as the normal curve. With the qualification noted below, this theoretical distribution is a fairly good approximation of the observed distribution of intelligence. In the polygenic model of intelligence (see 2–4), the genetic foundation of intelligence is not viewed as dependent upon a single gene. Rather, intelligence is viewed as the result of a number of discrete genetic units. (This is not to assert, however, that single gene effects are never encountered in mental retardation. As noted above, certain relatively rare types of mental retardation are the product of such simple genetic effects.)

Various specific polygenic models have been advanced which generate theoretical distributions of intelligence that are in keeping with observed distributions (3, 5, 6). An aspect of polygenic models of special importance for the two-group approach is the fact that they generate I.Q. distributions of approximately 50 to 150. Since an I.Q. of approximately 50 appears to be the lower limit for familial retardates, it has been concluded (4, 5, 7) that the etiology of this form of retardation reflects the same factors that determine "normal" intelligence. With this approach, the familial retardate may be viewed as normal, where "normal" is defined as meaning an integral part of the distribution of intelligence that we would expect from the normal manifestations of the genetic pool in our population. Within such a framework it is possible to refer to the familial retardate as less intelligent than other normal manifestations of the genetic pool, but he is just as integral a part of the normal distribution as are the 3 percent of the population whom we view as superior, or the more numerous group of individuals whom we consider to be average (8).

The two-group approach to mental retardation calls attention to the fact that the second group of retardates, those who have known physiological defects, represents a distribution of intelligence with a mean which is considerably lower than that of the familial retardates. Such children, for the most part, fall outside the range of normal intelligence—that is, below I.Q. of 50—although there are certain exceptions. Considerable clarity could be brought to the area of mental retardation through doing away

■ FIGURE 1

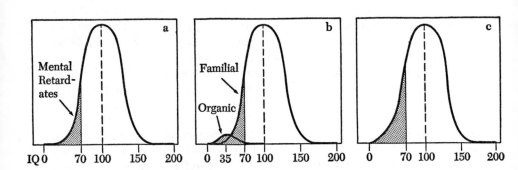

(a) *Conventional representation of the distribution of intelligence.*
(b) *Distribution of intelligence as represented in the two-group approach.*
(c) *Actual distribution of intelligence.*

with the practice of conceptualizing the intelligence distribution as a single, continuous, normal curve. Perhaps a more appropriate representation of the empirical distribution of intelligence would involve two curves, as Fig. 1b illustrates. The intelligence of the bulk of the population, including the familial retardate, would be depicted as a normal distribution having a mean of 100, with lower and upper limits of approximately 50 and 150, respectively. Superimposed on this curve would be a second, somewhat normal distribution having a mean of approximately 35 and a range from 0 to 70. (That the population encompassed by the second curve in Fig. 1b extends beyond the 70-I.Q. cutoff point is due to the fact that a very small number of individuals with known defects—for example, brain damage—may be found throughout the I.Q. continuum.) The first curve would represent the polygenic distribution of intelligence; the second would represent all those individuals whose intellectual functioning reflects factors other than the normal polygenic expression—that is, those retardates having an identifiable physiological defect. This two-group approach to the problem of mental retardation has been supported by Penrose (4), Roberts (9), and Lewis (10). The very nature of the observed distribution of I.Q.'s below the mean, especially in the range 0 to 50 (see Fig. 1c), seems to demand such an approach. This distribution, in which we find an overabundance of individuals at the very low I.Q. levels, is exactly what we would expect if we combined the two distributions discussed above, as is the general practice.

Limitations of space prevent consideration here of the controversy concerning the role of environmental factors in the etiology of familial retardation. Although such factors cannot be ignored by the serious student of mental retardation, the general dispute, discussed below, between adherents of the defect theory and of the general developmental theory can be examined somewhat independently of the environmental issue. That there will always be a distribution of a particular shape is a conclusion inherent in the polygenic argument, but the absolute amounts of intelligence represented by the various points on the distribution would still depend in large part on environmental factors.

DEVELOPMENTAL VERSUS DEFECT ORIENTATION

Once one adopts the position that the familial mental retardate is not defective or pathological but is essentially a normal individual of low intelligence, then the familial retardate no longer represents a mystery but, rather, is viewed as a particular manifestation of the general developmental process. According to this approach, the familial retardate's cognitive development differs from that of the normal individual only in respect to its rate and the upper limit achieved. Such a view generates the expectation that, when rate of development is controlled, as is grossly the case when groups of retardates and normals are matched with respect to mental age, there should be no difference in formal cognitive processes related to I.Q. Stated somewhat differently, this means that the familial retardate with a chronological age of 10, an I.Q. of 70, and thus a mental age of 7, would be viewed as being at the same developmental level intellectually as a child with a chronological age of 7 and an I.Q. of 100.

In contrast, according to the defect orientation, all retardates suffer from a specific physiological or cognitive defect over and above their slower general rate of cognitive development. This view generates the expectation that, even when the rate of cognitive development is controlled, as in the situation where mental ages are matched, differences in intellectual functioning which are related to I.Q. will be found. On their face, the repeated findings of differences in performance between groups of normals and retardates matched as to mental age have lent credence to the defect theory and have cast doubt on the validity of the developmental theory.

The developmental theorist's response to these frequently reported differences has been to point out that performance on any experimental task is not inexorably the product of the subject's cognitive structure alone but reflects a variety of emotional and motivational factors as well. To the developmentalist, then, it seems more reasonable to attribute differences in performance between normals and retardates of the same mental age to motivational differences which do not inhere in mental retardation but are, rather, the result of the particular histories of the retarded subjects.

It should be noted that most theories in the area of mental retardation are basically defect theories. These differ among themselves, however. A major difference involves the theoretician's effort to relate the postulated defect to some specific physiological structure. The theoretical language of some defect theoreticians is explicitly physiological, that of others is non-physiological, while that of others remains vague. Particular defects that have been attributed to the retarded include the following: relative impermeability of the boundaries between regions in the cognitive structure (11, 12); primary and secondary rigidity caused by subcortical and cortical malformations, respectively (13); inadequate neural satiation related to brain modifiability or cortical conductivity (14); malfunctioning disinhibitory mechanisms (15); improper development of the verbal system, resulting in a dissociation between verbal and motor systems (16, 17); relative brevity in the persistence of the stimulus trace (18); and impaired attention-directing mechanisms (19).

Where the hypothesized defect is an explicitly physiological one, it would appear to be a simple matter to obtain direct evidence that the defect does or does not exist. Such evidence would come from biochemical and physiological analyses as well as from pathological studies of familial retardates. A number of such studies have, of course, been carried out. Although there is an occasional report of some physical anomaly, the bulk of the evidence has indicated that the familial retardate does not suffer from any gross physiological defects. Indeed, if such evidence were readily available the defect theorist would cease relying on the more ambiguous data provided by studies of molar behavior. Failure to find direct evidence of a physiological defect in familial retardates has not deterred, and should not deter theorists from postulating such defects.

In spite of the negative physiological evidence, workers such as Spitz (14) maintain that all retardates, including familial retardates, are physically defective, and that our failure to discover defects in familial retardates is due to the relatively primitive nature of our diagnostic techniques. This view is bolstered by Masland (20), who has also noted the inadequacies of such techniques. It is perfectly legitimate for the defect theorist to assert that, although not at present observable, the physical defect that causes familial retardates to behave differently from normals of the same mental age will someday be seen. These theorists operate very much as the physicists of a not-too-distant era did when they asserted that the electron existed even though it was not directly observable. Analogously, defect theorists in the area of mental retardation undertake to validate the existence of a defect by first asserting that it should manifest itself in particular phenomena—that is, in particular behaviors of the retarded—and then devising experiments in which, if the predicted behavior is observed, the existence of the hypothesized defect is confirmed. Not only is this approach legitimate but, as noted above, it has become increasingly popular as well. A relatively comprehensive review of the literature emanating from the general defect position is now available (21). In the following paragraphs I briefly summarize the major defect positions.

An influential defect position is that of the Russian investigator A. R. Luria (16), whose work has now also influenced investigators in England and the United States. In the Soviet Union no distinction is made between retardates having known organic impairment and that larger group whose retardation is of unknown etiology, nor are genetic or cultural factors considered to be determinants of mental retardation. All grades of mental retardation are attributed to central-nervous-system damage believed to have occurred initially during the intrauterine period or during early childhood. Thus the diagnosis of mental retardation necessarily involves specification of a defect in some neurophysiological system; in fact, in the Soviet Union, professionals who work with the mentally retarded are called "defectologists."

Luria's interest in defective functioning appears to be an outgrowth of his more basic concern with the development of the higher cognitive processes in man. The influence of both Vygotsky and Pavlov may be seen in his work, which has been primarily concerned with the highly intricate development of the role of speech and language in regulating the child's behavior. In his comparisons between normal and retarded children, Luria has demonstrated that the behavior of retardates resembles that of chronologically younger normal children in that verbal instructions do not result in smooth regulation of motor behavior. Luria has found that retarded subjects have considerable difficulty with tasks requiring verbal mediation. Thus, Luria has inferred that the major defect in the retarded child involves an underdevelopment or a general "inertness" of the verbal system, and a dissociation of this system from the motor or action system. This dissociation is vaguely conceptualized as resulting from a disturbance in normal cortical activity.

The view that the behavior of a retardate resembles that of a chronologically younger child is, of course, consistent with the general developmental position. However, several English and American investigators (see, for example, 17 and 22) have demonstrated that, even with mental age level controlled, retardates have more difficulty on tasks requiring verbal mediation than normal subjects have. On the other hand, other such investigations have failed to provide support for Luria's position (23). To date, findings related to this position can best be described as equivocal.

Another major defect position is that of Herman Spitz (14), who has extended the Köhler-Wallach (24) cortical satiation theory to the area of mental retardation. According to Spitz, all retardates suffer from inadequate neural or cortical functioning; the inadequacy is best characterized by a certain sluggishness, or less-than-normal modifiability, in the functioning of cortical cells. Thus, Spitz believes that in retardates it takes longer to induce temporary, as well as permanent, electrical, chemical, and physical changes in stimulated cortical cells, and furthermore, that once such a change is produced, it is less readily modified than in the case of normal persons.

Spitz's evidence in support of his theory has come primarily from comparisons of the performance of retardates and normals of the same chronological age on a variety of perceptual tasks—for example, figural aftereffects and Necker-cube reversals. The heuristic value of Spitz's position may be seen in his recent efforts to extend his postulates beyond the visual perception area and employ them to generate specific predictions concerning the phenomena of learning, transposition, generalization, and problem solving. The evidence in favor of Spitz's position is far from clear-cut, however. Spivack (25) has pointed out that Spitz's findings are in marked contrast to those of other investigators. The very nature of many of Spitz's measures—for example, a verbal report—raises the troublesome issue of how well they reflect the perceptual responses being investigated. It should be noted that, in respect to this point as well as to other criticisms, Spitz himself has become one of the most cogent critics of his own efforts.

Many of Spitz's findings could be encompassed by the general developmental position. The developmental theorist would argue that it is not surprising that one gets different results for normals and for retardates matched with respect to chronological age, since such groups are at different developmental levels (as defined by mental age). One would be tempted to say that Spitz's work has little relevance to the issue of whether familial retardates suffer from a defect over and above their slower and more limited rate of cognitive development. However, Spitz has been quite explicit in his views that the differences he obtains are not developmental phenomena but reflect a physical deficit that should manifest itself even in comparisons with normal subjects matched in mental age to the retardates.

Ellis (18) has also advanced the view that the retardate is basically different from the normal individual and that this difference is a result of central-nervous-system pathology from which all retardates suffer. Ellis views this central-nervous-system pathology as producing a short-term memory deficit which, in turn, underlies the inadequacy of much of the retardate's behavior. The theoretical model presented by Ellis includes two major constructs, stimulus trace and neural integrity.

The stimulus trace, the mechanism underlying short-term memory functions, is conceptualized as a neural event or response which varies with the intensity, duration, and meaning of the stimulus situation confronting the subject. The stimulus-trace construct is thus anchored to stimulus characteristics on the one hand and to the subject's responses to these characteristics on the other. The neural-integrity construct is conceptualized as the determinant of the nature of stimulus-trace activity, and is defined by "measures of behavioral adequacy." The typical measure of neural integrity employed by Ellis is the I.Q. Thus, a person of low I.Q. is said to suffer from a lack of neural integrity. This lack, in turn, delimits or restricts stimulus-trace activity, and such restriction results in a variety of inadequate behaviors.

In support of his theory, Ellis has noted findings from numerous experiments involving short-term retention phenomena. These include studies on serial learning, delayed-reaction tasks, fixed-interval operant behavior, electroencephalographic investigations, reaction time, and factor analyses of the WISC test (the Wechsler Intelligence Scale for Children), as well as several studies of discrimination learning in brain-damaged animals (see 18). In respect to his own experimental tests, Ellis's reliance on the I.Q. as the measure of neural integrity has produced two types of comparisons: comparison of retardates and normals of the same chronological age and comparison of retardates and normals of the same mental age. In either comparison Ellis's model would predict that the retardates would be inferior on tasks involving short-term retention, due to their lower I.Q. In general, the findings obtained with groups matched as to chronological age have supported Ellis's position, while those obtained with groups matched as to mental age have not.

It should be noted that the demonstration that retardates do less well than normals of the same chronological age on tasks requiring short-term memory is a somewhat circular undertaking. It is circular to the extent that a deficit in short-term memory would influence the I.Q. score itself through its effect on certain of the intelligence subtests—for example, the digit-span test. Again, it should be emphasized that the discovery of a difference between normals and retardates of the same chronological age is just as amenable to a general developmental interpretation as to the view that all retardates suffer from central-nervous-system pathology, since the mental age of such retardates is necessarily lower than that of normal subjects in the control group.

Perhaps the oldest of the more influential defect positions is the Lewin-Kounin (11, 12) formulation that familial retardates are inherently more "rigid" than normal individuals of the same mental age. This position differs from the others discussed above in that the defect is conceptualized as inhering in a hypothesized cognitive structure without reference or reduction to any specific physiological entities. By the term *rigidity*, Lewin and Kounin were referring not to behaviors, as such, but rather to characteristics of the cognitive structure. These theorists felt that the essential defect, in retardation, was the lowered capacity for dynamic rearrangement in the "psychical system." This "stiffness" in cognitive functioning was conceptualized as being due to the relative impermeability of the boundaries between cells or regions of the cognitive structure. *Rigidity*, then, referred primarily to the nature of these boundaries, and to the resulting degree of communication or fluidity between regions.

Principal support for this position was contained in a series of experiments conducted by Kounin (11), in which he found differences between familial retardates and normals of the same mental age on a variety of tasks involving transfer phenomena, sorting, and concept-switching. Although the Lewin-Kounin position continues to receive some support (26), a fairly sizable amount of work (27, 28) now indicates that the differences discovered by Kounin between retardates and normals of the same mental age were due to differences in motivational variables rather than to an inherent cognitive rigidity of the retardate.

Lewin and Kounin appear to be the only defect theorists who have dealt adequately with the problem of etiology, which becomes a crucial issue in the controversy over the two theories. Their formulation was limited to familial retardates, and only such retardates were employed in Kounin's experiments. The other defect theorists have tended to argue that the distinction between familial and organic retardates is misleading, and, as a result, they have used groups of retardates of both types in their experiments. This presents an almost insurmountable problem when one attempts to evaluate the degree to which any uncovered differences in behavior support the major theoretical premise which underlies most defect approaches. This premise, clearly seen in the work of Luria, Spitz, and Ellis, is that all retardates, familials and organics alike, suffer from some specifiable defect. However, until the etiological issue is attended to in the research design, there is no way of assessing how much of the revealed difference between normals and retardates of the same mental age is a product of the gross organic pathology known to exist in the organic retardates included in the retarded group and how much is a product of the defect thought by the defect theorists to exist in all retardates.

The general developmental approach is applicable only to the familial retardate, and this approach does not speak to the issue of differences discovered between normal children and organic retardates. The developmental theorist also believes that, even when a difference in behavior is found between normals and familial retardates of the same mental age, it need not be attributed to any defect which inheres in familial mental retardation. Such differences are viewed as the possible outcome of differences in a variety of motivational factors which exist between the two groups. A sampling of the literature which lends credence to this view follows.

MOTIVATIONAL AND EMOTIONAL FACTORS

The view of those of us who believe that many of the reported differences between retardates and normals of the same mental age are a result of motivational and emotional differences which reflect differences in environmental histories does not imply that we ignore the importance of the lower intelligence per se. In some instances the personality characteristics of the retarded individual will reflect environmental factors that have little or nothing to do with intellectual endowment. For example, many of the effects of institutionalization may be constant, regardless of the person's intelligence level. In other instances we must think in terms of an inter-action; that is, a person with low intellectual ability will have certain experiences and develop certain behavior patterns differing from those of a person with greater intellectual endowment. An obvious example of this is the greater amount of failure which the retardate typically experiences. What must be emphasized is the fact that the behavior pattern developed by the retardate as a result of such a history of failure may not differ in kind or ontogenesis from patterns developed by an individual of normal intellect who, because of some environmental circumstance, also experi-ences an inordinate amount of failure. By the same token, if the retardate can somehow be guaranteed a history of greater success, we would expect his behavior to be more normal, regardless of his intellectual level. Within this framework, I now discuss several of the personality factors which have been known to influence the performance of the retarded.

It has become increasingly clear that our understanding of the per-formance of the institutionalized familial retardate will be enhanced if we consider the inordinate amount of social deprivation these individuals have experienced before being placed in institutions (29, 30). A series of recent studies (30–34) has indicated that one result of such early deprivation is a heightened motivation to interact with a supportive adult. These studies suggest that, given this heightened motivation, retardates exhibit con-siderable compliance with instructions when the effect of such compliance is to increase or maintain the social interaction with the adult. These findings would appear to be consistent with the often-made observation that the retarded seek attention and desire affection (35, 36).

Recent findings suggest that the perseveration so frequently noted in the behavior of the retarded is primarily a function of these motivational factors rather than a result of inherent cognitive rigidity, as suggested by Lewin (12) and Kounin (11). Evidence is now available indicating (i) that the degree of perseveration is directly related to the degree of depri-vation the individual experienced before being institutionalized (30), and (ii) that institutionalized children of normal intellect are just as persevera-tive as institutionalized retardates, while noninstitutionalized retardates are no more perseverative than noninstitutionalized children of normal intellect (31, 32).

Although there is considerable evidence that social deprivation results in a heightened motivation to interact with a supportive adult, it appears to have other effects as well. The nature of these effects is suggested in observations of fearfulness, wariness, or avoidance of strangers on the part of retardates, or of suspicion and mistrust (36, 37). The experimental work done by Zigler and his associates on the behavior of institutionalized re-tarded individuals has indicated that social deprivation results in both a heightened motivation to interact with supportive adults (a positive-reaction tendency) and a wariness of doing so (a negative-reaction tendency). The construct of a negative-reaction tendency has been em-ployed to explain certain differences between retardates and normals reported by Kounin, differences that have heretofore been attributed to the greater cognitive rigidity of retarded individuals. For instance, it has been demonstrated (38) that, once the institutionalized familial retardate's wariness has been allayed, he becomes much more responsive than the normal individual to social reinforcement. Thus, a motivational rather than a cognitive factor would seem to underlie certain rather mysterious behavioral phenomena frequently observed in familial retardates—for example, a tendency to persist longer on the second of two highly similar tasks than on the first.

Both positive- and negative-reaction tendencies have been recently investigated in a series of studies, with children of normal intellect (39), directed at further validation of the "valence position." Stated most simply, this position asserts that the effectiveness of an adult as a reinforcing agent depends upon the valence he has for the particular child whose behavior is being reinforced. (An adult's valence for a child refers to the degree to which that adult is sought or avoided by the child.) This valence is determined by the child's history of positive and negative experiences with adults. The studies noted above have produced considerable evidence that prior positive contacts between the child and the adult increase the adult's effectiveness as a reinforcer, while negative contacts decrease it. If the experimentally manipulated negative encounters in these experiments are viewed as experimental analogs of encounters institutionalized retardates actually have experienced, then the often-reported reluctance of such children to interact with adults and their wariness of such encounters become understandable. Thus it would appear that their relatively high negative-reactive tendency motivates them toward behaviors, such as withdrawal, that reduce the quality of their performance to a level lower than that which one would expect on the basis of their intellectual capacity alone.

Another factor frequently mentioned as a determinant in the performance of the retarded is their high expectancy of failure. This failure expectancy has been viewed as an outgrowth of a lifetime characterized by confrontations with tasks with which they are intellectually ill-equipped to deal. The work of Cromwell and his colleagues (40) has lent support to the general proposition that retardates have a higher expectancy of failure than normals have, and that this results in a style of problem-solving in which the retardate is much more highly motivated to avoid failure than to achieve success. However, the results of experimental work with retardates to investigate the success-failure dimension are still somewhat inconsistent, suggesting that even such a relatively simple proposition as this one is in need of further refinement.

Recent studies (31, 33, 41) have indicated that the many failures experienced by retardates generate a cognitive style of problem-solving characterized by outer-directedness. That is, the retarded child comes to distrust his own solutions to problems and therefore seeks guides to action in the immediate environment. This outer-directedness may explain the great suggestibility so frequently observed in the retarded child. Evidence has now been presented indicating that, relative to normals of the same mental age, the retarded child is more sensitive to verbal cues from an adult, is more imitative of the behavior of adults and of his peers, and does more visual scanning. Furthermore, certain findings (31) suggest that the noninstitutionalized retardate is more outer-directed in his problem solving than the institutionalized retardate is. This makes considerable sense if one remembers that the noninstitutionalized retardate lives in an environment that is not adjusted to his intellectual shortcomings and, therefore, probably experiences more failure than the institutionalized retardate.

Another nonintellective factor important in understanding the behavior of the retarded is the retardate's motivation to obtain various types of reinforcement. The social-deprivation work discussed indicates that retardates have an extremely strong desire for attention, praise, and encouragement. Several investigators (40, 42) have suggested that, in normal development, the effectiveness of attention and praise as reinforcers diminishes with maturity and is replaced by the reinforcement inherent in the awareness that one is correct. This latter type of reinforcer appears to serve primarily as a cue for self-reinforcement.

Zigler and his associates (27, 43, 44) have argued that various experiences in the lives of the retarded cause them to care less about being correct simply for the sake of correctness than normals of the same mental age. In other words, these investigators have argued that the position of various reinforcers in the reinforcer hierarchies of normal and of retarded children of the same mental age differ.

Clearest support for the view that the retardate cares much less about being correct than the middle-class child of normal intellect does is contained in a study by Zigler and deLabry (43). These investigators found, as Kounin (11) did, that when the only reinforcement was the information that the child was correct, retardates were poorer on a concept-switching task than middle-class normal children of the same mental age. However, when Zigler and deLabry added another condition, reward with a toy of the child's choice for concept-switching, they found that the retardates performed as well as the middle-class normal children. Since the satisfaction of giving the correct response is the incentive typically used in experimental studies, one wonders how many of the differences in performance found between retardates and normals are actually attributable to differences in capacity rather than to differences in the values such incentives may have for the two types of subjects.

Much of this work on motivational and emotional factors in the performance of the retarded is very recent. The research on several of the factors discussed is more suggestive than definitive. It is clear, however, that these factors are extremely important in determining the retardate's level of functioning. This is not to assert that these motivational factors cause familial mental retardation but to say, rather, that they lead to the retardate's behaving in a manner less effective than that dictated by his intellectual capacity. An increase in knowledge concerning motivational and emotional factors and their ontogenesis and manipulation would hold considerable promise for alleviating much of the social ineffectiveness displayed by that rather sizable group of persons who must function at a relatively low intellectual level.

SUMMARY

The heterogeneous nature of mental retardation, as well as certain common practices of workers in the area, has resulted in a variety of conceptual ambiguities. Considerable order could be brought to the area if, instead of viewing all retardates as a homogeneous group arbitrarily defined by some I.Q. score, workers would clearly distinguish between the group of retardates known to suffer from some organic defect and the larger group of retardates referred to as familial retardates. It is the etiology of familial retardation that currently constitutes the greatest mystery.

A number of authorities have emphasized the need for employing recent polygenic models of inheritance in an effort to understand the familial retardate. While appreciating the importance of environment in affecting the distribution determined by genetic inheritance, these workers have argued that familial retardates are not essentially different from individuals of greater intellect, but represent, rather, the lower portion of the intellectual curve which reflects normal intellectual variability. As emphasized by the two-group approach, retardates with known physiological or organic defect are viewed as presenting a quite different etiological problem. The familial retardate, on the other hand, is seen as a perfectly normal expression of the population gene pool, of slower and more limited intellectual development than the individual of average intellect.

This view generates the proposition that retardates and normals at the same general cognitive level—that is, of the same mental age—are similar in respect to their cognitive functioning. However, such a proposition runs headlong into findings that retardates and normals of the same mental age often differ in performance. Such findings have bolstered what is currently the most popular theoretical approach to retarded functioning—namely, the view that all retardates suffer from some specific defect which inheres in mental retardation and thus makes the retardate immutably "different" from normals, even when the general level of intellectual development is controlled. While these defect or difference approaches, as exemplified in the work of Luria, Spitz, Ellis, and Lewin and Kounin, dominate the area of mental retardation, the indirect, and therefore equivocal, nature of the evidence of these workers has generated considerable controversy.

In contrast to this approach, the general developmental position has emphasized systematic evaluation of the role of experiential, motivational, and personality factors. As a central thesis, this position asserts that performance on experimental and real-life tasks is never the single inexorable product of the retardate's cognitive structure but, rather, reflects a wide variety of relatively nonintellective factors which greatly influence the general adequacy of performance. Thus, many of the reported behavioral differences between normals and retardates of the same mental age are seen as products of motivational and experiential differences between these groups, rather than as the result of any inherent cognitive deficiency in the retardates. Factors thought to be of particular importance in the behavior of the retardate are social deprivation and the positive- and negative-reaction tendencies to which such deprivation gives rise; the high number of failure experiences and the particular approach to problem-solving which they generate; and atypical reinforcer hierarchies.

There is little question that we are witnessing a productive, exciting, and perhaps inevitably chaotic period in the history of man's concern with the problem of mental retardation. Even the disagreements that presently exist must be considered rather healthy phenomena. These disagreements will unquestionably generate new knowledge which, in the hands of practitioners, may become the vehicle through which the performance of children, regardless of intellectual level, may be improved.

REFERENCES

1. G. A. Jervis, pp. 1289–1313 in S. Arieti (ed.), *American Handbook of Psychiatry*, vol. 2 (New York: Basic Books, 1959).

2. J. Hirsch, *Science*, 142 (1963), p. 1436.

3. I. L. Gottesman, pp. 253–296 in N. R. Ellis (ed.), *Handbook of Mental Deficiency* (New York: McGraw-Hill, 1963).

4. L. S. Penrose, *The Biology of Mental Defect* (London: Sidgwick and Jackson, 1963).

5. C. Burt and M. Howard, *British Journal of Statistical Psychology*, 9 (1956), p. 95.

6. ———, *British Journal of Statistical Psychology*, 10, 33 (1957); C. C. Hurst, in *Proceedings of the Royal Society of London Services Bulletin*, 112, 80 (1932); R. W. Pickford, *Journal of Psychology*, 28, 129 (1949).

7. G. Allen, *American Journal of Mental Deficiency*, 62, 840 (1958); C. Burt, *American Psychologist*, 13, 1 (1958).

8. G. E. McClearn, pp. 144–252 in L. Postman (ed.), *Psychology in the Making* (New York: Knopf, 1962).

9. J. A. F. Roberts, *Eugenics Review*, 44, 71 (1952).

10. E. O. Lewis, *Journal of Mental Science*, 79, 298 (1933).

11. J. Kounin, *Character and Personality*, 9, 251 (1941); *ibid.*, p. 273.

12. K. Lewin, *A Dynamic Theory of Personality* (New York: McGraw-Hill, 1936).

13. K. Goldstein, *Character and Personality*, 11, 209 (1942–43).

14. H. H. Spitz, pp. 11–40 in N. R. Ellis (ed.), *Handbook of Mental Deficiency* (New York: McGraw-Hill, 1963).

15. P. S. Siegel and J. G. Foshee, *Journal of Abnormal and Social Psychology*, 61, 141 (1960).

16. A. R. Luria, pp. 353–387 in N. R. Ellis (ed.), *Handbook of Mental Deficiency* (New York: McGraw-Hill, 1963).

17. N. O'Connor and B. Hermelin, *Journal of Abnormal and Social Psychology*, 59, 409 (1959).

18. N. R. Ellis, pp. 134–158 in N. R. Ellis (ed.), *Handbook of Mental Deficiency* (New York: McGraw-Hill, 1963).

19. D. Zeaman and B. J. House, *ibid.*, p. 159.

20. R. L. Masland, *American Journal of Mental Deficiency*, 64, 305 (1959).

21. E. Zigler, in M. L. Hoffman and L. W. Hoffman (eds.), *Review of Child Development Research*, vol. 2 (New York: Russell Sage, 1967).

22. N. A. Milgram and H. G. Furth, *American Journal of Mental Deficiency*, 67, 733 (1963); *ibid.*, 70, 849 (1966).

23. D. Balla and E. Zigler, *Journal of Abnormal and Social Psychology*, 69, 664 (1964); M. Rieber, *American Journal of Mental Deficiency*, 68, 634 (1964).

24. W. Kohler and H. Wallach, *Proceedings of the American Philosophical Society*, 88, 269 (1964).

25. G. Spivack, pp. 280–511 in N. R. Ellis (ed.), *Handbook of Mental Deficiency* (New York: McGraw-Hill, 1963).

26. M. Budoff and W. Pagel, "Learning Potential and Rigidity in the Adolescent Mentally Retarded," paper presented before the Society for Research in Child Development (Minneapolis, March 1965).

27. E. Zigler, pp. 141–162 in E. P. Trapp and P. Himelstein (eds.), *Readings on the Exceptional Child* (New York: Appleton-Century-Crofts, 1962).

28. ————, pp. 77–105 in N. R. Ellis (ed.), *International Review of Research in Mental Retardation* (New York: Academic Press, 1966).

29. A. C. B. Clarke and A. M. Clarke, *British Journal of Psychology*, 45, 197 (1954); D. Kaplun, *Proceedings of the American Association of Mental Deficiency*, 40, 68 (1935).

30. E. Zigler, *Journal of Abnormal and Social Psychology*, 62, 413 (1961).

31. C. Green and E. Zigler, *Child Development*, 33, 499 (1962).

32. E. Zigler, *Journal of Personality*, 31, 258 (1963).

33. ————, L. Hodgden, H. Stevenson, *ibid.*, 26, 106 (1958).

34. R. Shepps and E. Zigler, *American Journal of Mental Deficiency*, 67, 262 (1962); H. Stevenson and L. Fahel, *Journal of Personality*, 29, 136 (1961); E. Zigler and J. Williams, *Journal of Abnormal and Social Psychology*, 66, 197 (1963).

35. W. M. Cruickshank, *Journal of Clinical Psychology*, 3, 381 (1947); E. E. Doll, pp. 21–68 in E. P. Trapp and P. Himelstein (eds.), *Readings on the Exceptional Child* (New York: Appleton-Century-Crofts, 1962).

36. E. A. Hirsh, *American Journal of Mental Deficiency*, 63, 639 (1959); B. L. Wellman, *Childhood Education*, 15, 108 (1938).

37. M. Woodward, *British Journal of Medicine and Psychology*, 33, 123 (1960).

38. P. Shallenberger and E. Zigler, *Journal of Abnormal and Social Psychology*, 63, 20 (1961); E. Zigler, thesis (Austin, Texas: University of Texas, 1958).

39. H. Berkowitz, E. C. Butterfield, E. Zigler, *Journal of Personality and Social Psychology*, 2, 706 (1965); H. Berkowitz and E. Zigler, *ibid.*, p. 500; N. McCoy and E. Zigler, *ibid.*, 1, 604 (1965).

40. R. L. Cromwell, pp. 41–91 in N. R. Ellis (ed.), *Handbook of Mental Deficiency* (New York: McGraw-Hill, 1963).

41. J. Turnure and E. Zigler, *Journal of Abnormal and Social Psychology*, 69, 427 (1964).

42. E. Beller, *Journal of Genetic Psychology*, 87, 25 (1955); J. Gewirtz, *Monographs of Social Research in Child Development*, No. 59 (1954), p. 19; G. Heathers, *Journal of Genetic Psychology*, 87, 37 (1955); E. Zigler, *American Journal of Orthopsychiatry*, 33, 614 (1963).

43. E. Zigler and J. deLabry, *Journal of Abnormal and Social Psychology*, 65, 267 (1962).

44. E. Zigler and E. Unell, *American Journal of Mental Deficiency*, 66, 651 (1962).

45. I am deeply indebted to Susan Harter for her help in organizing this article and for her assistance in clarifying many of the ideas presented. Preparation of the paper was facilitated by research grant MH–06809 from the National Institutes of Mental Health and by the Gunnar Dybwad award of the National Association for Retarded Children.

Mental Retardation

MORTON W. WEIR

Although I agree with many aspects of Zigler's "developmental" theory of retardation (*1*), several points appear to merit further discussion and clarification. A key portion of his developmental theory is given in the following: ". . . the familial retardate's cognitive development differs from that of the normal individual only in respect to its rate and the upper limit achieved. Such a view generates the expectation that, when rate of development is controlled, as is grossly the case when groups of retardates and normals are matched with respect to mental age, there should be no difference in formal cognitive processes related to I.Q." (*1*, p. 294).

In this statement, Zigler defines mental age (MA) as the rate of intellective development. In the same paragraph, however, he refers to MA as the "level" of intellective functioning. Zigler's apparent failure to distinguish rate of development from level of development leads to a questionable prediction from his theory—namely that retardates and normals of the same MA will be similar with respect to their cognitive functioning.

Mental age is a transformation of the score made in an intelligence test and is a measure of the current level of intellective functioning, not of the rate of accumulation of knowledge. If an individual's chronological age (CA) is also known, then the intelligence quotient (I.Q.) may be calculated: I.Q. = (MA/CA) × 100. The I.Q. score is a rough index of the amount of information accumulated in a given number of years of life; thus it is a measure of rate.

According to Zigler, if groups of retardates and normals are matched for MA there should be no difference in formal cognitive processes related to

* From *Science* 1967, *155*, pp. 576–577. Reprinted by permission of the author and the publisher. Copyright 1967 by the American Association for the Advancement of Science.

I.Q. Figure 1 reresents the growth in mental age of a hypothetical normal child, born in 1955, and progressing at the rate of one MA unit per year (I.Q. = 100), and of a retarded child born in 1950, who is progressing at the rate of one-half MA unit per year (I.Q. = 50).

Assume that the two children were chosen for a learning experiment in 1960 because they both had MA's of 5 years. According to Zigler, if non-intellective factors are held constant, the performance of the retarded child should equal that of the normal child. But note that the two children have different rates of intellectual growth. These differential rates should not

■ **Figure 1.** Growth of Mental Age of Two Hypothetical Children, one of IQ 100 and the Other of IQ 50.

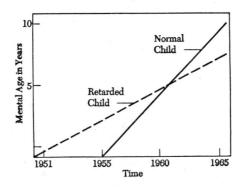

only appear as long-term phenomena but should also be evident in short-term laboratory tasks. It therefore appears imperative that Zigler's developmental theory should predict that the two children will perform differently, providing the task they are given is sufficiently complex to be sensitive to the abilities responsible for the differential growth shown in Fig. 1. The fact that these two children made identical MA scores on the intelligence test may be accounted for if one assumes that the intelligence test is more a test of recall of past learning, particularly vocabulary, than it is a test of the child's ability to deal with new and unfamiliar materials. Thus the MA score is basically a measure of achievement and may not be greatly affected by factors which determine the rate of accumulation of knowledge.

As evidence for his hypothesis of "equal-MA, equal cognitive functioning," Zigler cites research that demonstrates that the performances of normals and retardates, matched for MA, do not differ when motivational factors are controlled. However, it appears doubtful that the tasks used in the research cited are sensitive to the abilities which determine the rate of intellective growth. The tasks appear to involve a minimum of learning and information processing, and even one which is said to be relevant to "problem solving" is, according to the authors (2, pp. 501–502), "an extremely simple task with successful performance depending primarily upon compliance with E's instructions."

To summarize, I maintain that Zigler's developmental theory should predict differential performance of retardates and normals of equal MA on complex cognitive tasks, because such individuals differ drastically in the rate at which they are developing intellectually. The fact that Zigler and his associates have not found such differences is probably a function of the type of task which they have employed—one which is typically very simple and which would not be expected to be sensitive to those factors that produce differential intellective growth rates.

One final aspect of Zigler's article also deserves comment. The basic difference between his "developmental" theory of retardation and the so-called "defect" theories may be more apparent than real. There may have been theorists who separated individuals into two populations, one "retarded" and the other "normal," and claimed that the normals "had" something that the retardates did not. However, I do not think such a belief is prevalent in modern American psychology. I suggest that the term "deficit" is used in a relative sense by most modern retardation theorists; it is not that these theorists believe that normals "have" something that retardates do not, but instead that retardates may have less of something than normals do.

REFERENCES

1. E. F. Zigler, *Science*, 155, 292 (1967).
2. C. Green and E. Zigler, *Child Development*, 33, 499 (1962).

Mental Retardation

JOSEPH F. JASTAK

In Zigler's paper on the dilemma of mental retardation, an attempt is made to differentiate between two types of retardation—borderline familial and severe organic (1). At this stage it is difficult to establish with certainty the difference between intellectual superiority and inferiority, let alone

* From *Science* 1967, 157, pp. 577–578. Reprinted by permission of the author and the publisher. Copyright © 1967 by the American Association for the Advancement of Science.

discriminate between types and degrees of retardation. Zigler cites a number of theories and experiments on mental retardation, implying that the proponents of the theories and the experimenters really dealt with problems of mental retardation. As a matter of fact, the difficulty common to all such reports is the assumption that the individuals being investigated are mentally retarded individuals, when in reality they may not be. When multiple criteria are used in the determination of mental retardation, the I.Q. misclassifies four out of every five alleged retardates (2).

While Ellis's idea that the I.Q. represents neural integration is to some extent acceptable, it is also true that the greater part of the variance of the I.Q. does not represent neural integration. Until the multivariate nature of a test score (I.Q. or any other) is fully explained and its intellectual variance is determined, no one will know for sure who is retarded and who is not. That is why many a potential genius languishes in special classes and schools for the retarded and many a retarded individual supports himself in the community without ever having had his "cognitive rigidity" tested.

Luria's idea that defects in the medium of language are related to mental retardation is either circular or based on studies of highly constricted population samplings. When the Russians extend their sphere of interest, some surprises will await them, since severe speech handicaps are present in people of all degrees of intelligence. Neither language defects nor "cognitive rigidity" are typical of the retarded; they occur in all people at random.

Zigler's somewhat dogmatic references to cognitive processes as if they should be considered intellectual are but unconfirmed assumptions. Many behavioral scientists believe that the thinking functions, such as concept formation, judgment, and reasoning, have a larger emotional than cognitive variance. Zigler is apparently coming around to a point of view which he rejected even a few years ago. Vague speculations about motivational, cultural, genetic, and emotional influences only increase the ambiguities about which he is complaining. Speculations will not be necessary when we devote our full attention to the fundamental issue of the multivariate nature of behavioral measures and to the development of an acceptable theory of intelligence. Then the above factors may be measurable, and the two types of retardates discussed by Zigler will probably be found to have no existence in reality.

In the meantime we will make a real contribution to the study of mental retardation when we frankly admit that neither physicians nor psychologists know much about it, even in such so-called clear-cut cases as those accompanying phenylketonuria, mongolism, cretinism, microcephaly, cerebral palsy, and so forth. Above all, no one should take it for granted that an article or a reported experiment on mental retardation does really deal with mental retardation. A close look at the experimental population of any study would expose the astonishing fact that it comprises a mishmash of individuals with a wide variety of adjustment problems that have little to do with mental retardation. The true mental competency of these individuals is rarely established except by the most superficial of methods. We simply do not have the tools to do the job right. And the best tools we have are often misapplied and misinterpreted as measuring what they don't, for there are as many capricious theories and elegant nonmeasures of mental retardation as there are experimenters. Narrowly conceived experiments carried out on narrowly selected but heterogeneous groups only compound the unbelievable confusion in this important area of study.

REFERENCES

1. E. Zigler, *Science*, 155, 292 (1967).
2. J. F. Jastak, H. M. MacPhee, M. Whiteman, *Mental Retardation, Its Nature and Incidence* (Newark, Del.: University of Delaware Press, 1963).

Mental Retardation

EDWARD ZIGLER

Jastak's argument centers about the fact that I have used one classification system to categorize the mentally retarded, whereas he prefers another. As I have pointed out, provided two classificatory systems have satisfactory reliabilities, one cannot be considered "truer" than the other. The question is not one of truth or falsity but rather one of the usefulness of the particular system, usually defined by the number and magnitude of the behavioral correlates associated with class membership within the system. If one is employing the conventional classificatory principle used in my article, then it is Jastak's system that results in the misclassification of the vast majority of mental retardates. How useful any classification system will be in the development of an adequate theory of intelligence is an empirical question. Such a theory is, I agree, badly needed. One does not always have to decide between competing classificatory systems. Within an area several classificatory systems may exist side by side, provided those using

* From *Science* 1967, *157*, pp. 578–579. Reprinted by permission of the author and the publisher. Copyright 1967 by the American Association for the Advancement of Science.

the different systems have different goals in mind (for example, prediction of different behavioral correlates of class membership).

Jastak is wrong in suggesting that we cannot differentiate organic from familial retardates. Although we are not completely errorless, we can and do make this discrimination. A major point in my article was not that this two-category system of classification would illuminate all intellectual variables of interest, but that this simple differentiation must be made before any legitimate test can be conducted of issues separating developmental from defect theorists. I believe that these two broad types of retardation reflect two different types of etiology. Such a separation of the two, therefore, represents a reasonable first step preceding the construction in which much finer distinctions are made, systems which I think both Jastak and I would prefer. Nevertheless I take exception to Jastak's view that such a system would demonstrate that the two types of retardates I spoke of had "no existence in reality." To the extent that a classificatory system represents a conceptual construction of reality, then any system is just as "real" as any other system. To the extent that reality refers to the palpability or the physical evidence of the existence of an entity, Jastak is certainly wrong in regard to the organic types of mental retardation, where such evidence is readily available. It would appear premature to assert that, with advances in genetics, such evidence will not be forthcoming for the second broad class of retarded individuals now referred to as familial.

I wholly agree with Jastak's point that performance on so-called intellectual tasks invariably has an important emotional and motivational component. In fact, much of my article was directed toward supporting such a position. With respect to my changing my point of view, I see no great merit in an investigator never changing his mind. However, I do not believe I have changed my point of view over the past decade concerning the behavior of the retarded.

Weir makes a number of points meriting reply. His first criticism is based more on how I used the particular word "control" than on any substantive disagreement between us concerning the meaning of MA and I.Q. As should be clear from the total context of the paragraph cited by Weir, I asserted that in the MA-matched paradigm one takes into consideration the different rates of cognitive development (I.Q.'s) of normals and retardates. This procedure controls for known past differences in rate, and thus guarantees that, at the point in time at which the comparison is made, the two types of subjects are at the same cognitive level. The semantic confusion possible when one attempts to distinguish between rate and level of cognitive development is demonstrated in Weir's view that the I.Q. score, which is a measure of rate, is "a rough index of the amount of information accumulated in a given number of years of life." This is erroneous since the amount of information at any point is a level phenomenon. How long it took to acquire that amount of information is a rate phenomenon.

In whatever way I used the word "control" and Weir the phrase "amount of information," we are in total agreement that the I.Q. is a rate measure and MA is a level measure. However, I cannot agree that it is my failure to distinguish rate of development from level of development that leads to questionable predictions from my theory. As should become apparent in the remainder of my reply, developmental theorists such as myself may be wrong, but we are certainly not confused. Weir's major point hinges on one's conception of the cognitive characteristics of two individuals who at the same point in time are at the same cognitive level, but who have manifested different rates in achieving that level. The crucial question is: What does this different rate imply? Weir assumes that the rate phenomenon with its I.Q. measurement reflects speed of learning or information processing. Given this assumption, Weir predicts that at every cognitive level the child with a low I.Q. will do worse than that with a high I.Q. on tasks demanding such learning or information processing. But is the I.Q. indisputably a reflection of these cognitive abilities? Of course not. The I.Q. is only a rate measure in the sense that it relates a nonpsychological measure (passage of time) to a psychological one (level of cognition achieved). Approached in this way it is the MA (level) and not the I.Q. (the relationship of MA to chronological age) that determines the exact nature including the rate, of learning any task. If one really thinks that the rate of learning or information processing is related to I.Q. rather than to MA, I suggest that he compare the learning processes of a 3-year-old with an I.Q. of 150 and an 8-year-old with an I.Q. of 100.

Weir makes much of the different slopes of the MA curves presented in his figure, and argues that they tell us much about the cognitive functioning of normal and retarded children at particular points in time. Alas, understanding cognitive functioning is not so simple. If one took the trouble to extend Weir's curves for the two individuals through their adulthood, he would discover that eventually the slopes would be the same. The individual with an I.Q. of 50 would level off at MA 8 at the age of approximately 16, and therefore his MA would best be represented by a straight line. This is also true of the other individual, except that his MA curve would level off at MA 16. If it is the slope that allows us to make predictions concerning the quality of cognitive functioning, can we then argue that in adulthood the cognitive performances of normal and retarded individuals will be the same?

The major point is that one makes a number of theoretical assumptions when he asserts that, since the I.Q. is a measure of one kind of rate, then it must also be a measure of another kind of rate, namely a measure of the rate of learning or information processing on individual tasks. One can, of course, assert that both MA (level) and I.Q. (an hypothesized determinant of rate of cognitive functioning) influence cognitive tasks. But this is exactly the argument examined in my article. The person who holds that the I.Q., independent of level or MA, determines rate of cognitive functioning on short-term learning tasks is a difference or defect theorist. Which general position is correct is open to investigation, but there is no doubt that the two major approaches examined in my article generate quite different predictions.

I am in sympathy with Weir's argument that the MA obtained on standard intelligence tests is a far from perfect indicator of the nature of cognitive functioning (2). Indeed, if there were a consensus that the MA was a perfectly adequate measure of the formal features of cognition (for example, rate of information processing), there would be no argument between developmental and defect theorists, since by definition individuals of the same MA level would have identical cognitive structures. However, in his efforts to champion the predictive efficacy on cognitive tasks of the I.Q. over the MA, Weir appears to go too far. To argue that the MA is not an important determinant in the quality (including rate) of the child's learning of new and unfamiliar cognitive tasks is an error. Evidence on this point is clear, and I doubt whether anyone working in the area of cognition would take exception to it. In spite of its shortcomings, the single MA measure and its factorial components have more cognitive correlates, including performance on purer Piaget-like cognitive tasks, than any other measure in psychology.

With respect to Weir's task argument, he and I probably could agree that an investigator should use a task sensitive to the particular factor that the investigator would like to demonstrate as being operative. Thus one interested in demonstrating the effect of motivational factors employs experimental tasks sensitive to these factors. There is no argument, therefore, that if one wishes to test the hypothesis that I.Q. is a measure of rate of information processing he should use a task that makes this type of cognitive demand on his subjects. My criticism of the various difference or defect positions was not based solely on findings obtained with motivational tasks, but rested also on the fact that the findings obtained by the supporters of these positions on tasks of their own choosing frequently have been equivocal. Furthermore, to imply that the holders of the developmental position have been reluctant to adequately test their views by using cognitively demanding tasks is to do them an injustice. They have frequently employed the same tasks used by the expounders of the various defect positions. These tasks include not only the concept-switching tasks referred to by Weir but a variety of discrimination learning, reversal learning, transposition, and learning of set tasks. Indeed, workers sympathetic to the developmental position have employed the probability-learning task used by Weir in his laboratory. Although Weir does not state the criteria by which we might know if a task were truly cognitive in nature, I find it difficult to believe that none of these tasks involves information processing and that they are therefore inadequate tests of the hypothesis of "equal MA-equal cognitive" functioning.

Weir attempts to close the gap between the developmental theory of familial mental retardation and the various "defect" positions by noting that certain "defect" theorists argue that retardates have less of something that normals of the same MA have, rather than having something that the normals do not have. This is true; however, other defect theorists have argued that retardates are qualitatively different from normals. It is for this reason that throughout my article I referred to the general approach as a defect or difference orientation. It is the difference between familial retardates and normals of the same MA that is the point of contention between the developmental theorist and the difference theorist, whatever the hypothesized deficit underlying this difference may be. The gap between the developmental theorist and all the defect or difference theorists remains a wide one since the developmental position generates the hypothesis that there are no differences in formal cognitive functioning between familial retardates and normals matched on general level of cognition (typically measured by MA). What should be emphasized is that the developmental position at this point in time represents a tenable hypothesis. As long as the hypothesis clearly generates behavioral predictions, I would certainly entertain the possibility that it is wrong. Clearly, as my article pointed out, most theoretical workers in the area are entertaining this possibility. The argument presented in Weir's letter indicates that he shares their views. Fortunately, resolution of this can be achieved through thoughtful experimentation.

REFERENCES

1. E. Zigler and L. Phillips, *Social Psychology*, 63, 607 (1961).
2. E. Zigler, pp. 107–68 in *Review of Child Development Research*, M. L. Hoffman and L. W. Hoffman, (eds.), vol. 2 , (Russell Sage Foundation, New York, 1967).

** 10 **

Issues in the Education of the
Mentally Retarded

.

HERBERT GOLDSTEIN

Until comparatively recently, the responsibility for preparing the retarded youth to assume the obligations of a mature citizen was almost exclusively that of the school. There then came on the scene certain social and vocational services external to the school which had as their purpose the rendering of training and placement services to handicapped persons of post-school age. These agencies developed separately from the school and remained at some distance until recently when they and the schools recognized a mutuality of interests and purposes.

Today, the nature of the interaction between schools and other community agencies is of such a nature that there has come to be a dependency of one on the other to so accomplish its mission that a continuity and harmony between them be effected. It is now quite clear that failure or inefficiency in one can have serious and limiting effects on the contribution of the other. Specifically, there is always the hazard that one, the school, will lose contact with the realities of a rapidly changing society while the other, community agencies, will lose sight of or misinterpret the functions of the school. Either or both conditions tend to vitiate the contribution of each. We will examine this issue as it applies to the school.

Two issues stand out among the problem areas of the school. First, there is the issue of maintaining a harmony between a program of education and the nature of the society for which education is to provide orientation. Second, there is the issue found in the relationship between a program of education and the rules and rituals designed to facilitate the implementation of the program.

* Reprinted by permission of the author and the publisher from *Mental Retardation* 1963, 1, pp. 10–12, 52–53, a publication of the American Association on Mental Deficiency.

THE ISSUE OF TIMELINESS

It might be said that the ideal program of education for retarded children anticipates the shifts and changes in society and makes curriculum adjustments accordingly. A lesser but still acceptable condition would be where the school is not able to anticipate social change but is able to recognize change as it begins to occur and is able to stay abreast of it. The least desirable but always imminent condition is where the school, for some reason, loses sight of the nature of social change and proceeds on its own way unaware that its program is preparing people for a world that used to be. One of the principle reasons for losing sight of the nature and extent of social change is in the tendency for some to operate on the basis of home-made policy rather than from facts that are, in themselves, indicators of the nature and direction of change.

Most educators would agree that it takes more concerted effort today to find and maintain occupational placement for the graduating retardate than it did not too long ago. Most would also agree that the difficulty stems from two related sources. First, there is the growing complexity of an already intricate society whose mores and customs are proliferating at a great pace. Second, there are the lightning changes in the labor scene due to technological trends away from men and toward machines as the source of production and service.

We would have to be remarkably insensitive to the world around us not to identify and realize the extent of the trend toward complexity. Getting to places, management of financial affairs, communication, and parcelling out non-occupational time require planning and decisions rarely required before. Unfortunately, we cannot quantify the nature and extent of change to illustrate a rate or proportion.

The picture is a bit more clear in the case of technological change. Here we have agencies and services whose business it is to count noses and places for noses and then, based on an accumulation of quantified experiences, to make predictions.

Such agencies as the U.S. Dept. of Labor, the Fed. Sec. Agency, and the Bureau of Labor Statistics, among others, tell us that:

1. There has risen a new class among the unemployed known as the "unemployables." These are persons of working age who lack marketable skills either because of lack of training or because their skills are obsolete;

2. The proportion of high school drop-outs continues to be about one-third of the high school population. These generally tend to enter the category of unemployables or the ranks of the unskilled;

3. The proportion of occupations in the unskilled categories is on the wane. Whereas six of every 10 members of the labor force in 1900 were in unskilled jobs, less than three in 10 were so occupied by 1950;

4. Teen-agers constitute by far the largest group of unemployed;

5. The Bureau of Labor Statistics predicts a further decrease of unskilled positions, i.e., they predict that one in four members of the labor force will be in an unskilled job in 1965 and about one in five by 1975, and

6. The Dept. of Labor predicts a 30% increase in teenagers by 1965.

The foregoing facts are just a sketch of a very complicated picture. Despite their sparseness, they point out quite clearly that we are faced with the challenge of preparing educable mentally retarded youth to be more effective competitors in a highly competitive world and, at the same time, educating the community so that it will be more aware of the contribution of the retarded in the world of work.

It would be too easy to retreat behind the complaint that there are too many workers and too few jobs. It is also easy, and some have already succumbed to this procedure, to say that we will only admit to our programs those who possess the inherent ability to enter into competition with some chance of success. This issue is greater than internal accommodation of external conditions. Conditions face us with the need to reassess our present programs to ascertain their relevance. We need to ask ourselves: is habituation consonant with conceptualization? To put it another way —should we be teaching for concrete behaviors in an abstract world? The answer to this question requires an examination of the total program from primary through secondary levels. Then we must ask if our traditional practices are appropriate in a changing world? Probably we need more than one kind of program to accomodate more than one kind of retardate. Finally, this issue demands that we in education examine our relationships with community agencies. There is a good possibility that changes in both areas of operation are indicated.

KEEPING APACE OF SOCIAL CHANGE

This brings us to the second issue—the question as to whether our present rules and rituals for doing things in the education of the retarded help or hinder efforts to keep apace of social change.

No one can deny the positive role of rules and rituals in the facilitation of functions and services. As long as these administrative provisions are looked upon and applied as means toward an end, the end being effective and contributing programming, we stand a good chance of making progress. When, however, we ascribe to rules and rituals a kind of sacredness and begin to modify our functions so that administrative procedures will remain unchanged, we stop moving ahead and, at best, maintain the status quo.

With the rapid and dramatic changes taking place in diagnostic techniques and in the number of children entering school, some school systems are only able to maintain the status quo by altering the rules to minimize numbers. For example, some have decreed a decrease of five IQ points in upper limits of eligibility for special class placement and thereby have changed the classification of a sizeable proportion of children from educable mentally retarded to something else.

In the face of the changing occupational scene and in increasing competition by high school drop-outs and displaced workers, it might be well to look at our so-called facilitating devices to ascertain whether they are helping or hindering services. The order is of no particular significance.

First, there is the ritual of letting the educable mentally retarded child prove to all concerned that he is retarded before considering him for special class placement. Many of these children go undiscovered, officially that is, until the third grade before they are legalized into the special class. This might have been a necessary precaution some 25 or 30 years ago when the reliability of diagnostic procedures was much less than today. Today, when every instructional and experimental moment is important to the child's development, this seems an expensive ritual to sustain.

There are those who wish to avoid the false positives inherent in early placement. They express the very reasonable fear that some children will be tainted unjustifiably with the label "retarded" if they are admitted to a special class at age six and later gain intellectually beyond the upper limits for such classes. However, we must not overlook the fact that such a child, through his adequate achievement in an appropriate regular class placement, stands an excellent chance of erasing the label.

Instead of becoming preoccupied solely with labels and stigma, we might do well to look at the other side of the coin and ask what effects delayed placement has on the personality development of the child, the status he acquires among his regular class peers, and the pressures, placed on the family. In all justice, we cannot close our eyes to the fact that the retarded child in the regular class can be and frequently is labelled by his peers in much the same way as children in special classes.

Second, there is the old and sacred 50–75 rule. On the one hand, we decry the use of the IQ as a sole criterion for anything. On the other, we duck behind this numerical fence to keep special class programs respectable statistically. It is not often stated openly, but most every administrator and teacher knows that raising the lower and upper limits of eligibility by 10 IQ points quadruples and, in some types of communities, quintuples the number of eligibles for special class placement.

Agreed that boards of education do not provide us with the personnel and facilities to fulfill our mission as adequately and effectively as we would like and that the colleges and universities are barely meeting attrition in teacher ranks due to retirement, marriage, and other less felicitous reasons for leaving the special class. What plans and procedures are afoot to face up to the anticipated needs of the increasing number of children with IQ's above 75 who need the special class program?

If we look at our history of the past half century, we can see that the

IQ 50–75 fence has grown higher and more opaque. Once it was intended as but one of a number of pieces of information that might contribute to understanding of a certain category of children. In recent years, it has become a corral to keep some in and others out. For one, the lower wall became so opaque that we couldn't see below IQ 50 with any degree of constructiveness. The philosophy was simply "keep those with IQ's below 50 out." The same philosophy continues to prevail for the above 75's and 80's. It was clear that special education for the retarded began at IQ 50 and terminated at IQ 75. Now we have classes for those with IQ's below 50 but not because we changed our philosophy in some burst of enlightenment. No, the parents of these children changed it for us and, from the looks of things, they will have to continue to goad us on if commensurate changes in programs and procedures are to be effected.

At the other extreme, we have kept out of our area of responsibility those children who score above the upper limit of eligibility to special classes. In fact, it is not an unusual practice to see special education programs literally eject children who, after a number of years in a special class, score above the upper limit. We act as though the new and higher score absolves us from any responsibility other than a solemn prayer that someone in the school system will find accommodation for the child and that he will survive.

We cannot resolve the issue of the role of criteria for special class scope, placement, and retention until we begin to ask the question "Where does mental retardation begin?" Until we look at mental retardation as a complex set of phenomena and not as an IQ span we will probably continue to go through life with our eyes in blinders.

Finally, there is the issue of efficacy in the preparation of the retarded for socio-occupational adjustment but this time from a quantitative point of view. We must face up to the fact that, even if we were qualitatively superior, we are preparing no better than 25% of all of the educable mentally retarded in our public schools. Admittedly, we are faced with such shortages of space, personnel, and equipment that we can do little to admit the "other 75%" to special classes. But special education is not confined to the physical limits of the special class. If we can't act outside of the walls of the special class because of administrative and physical reasons, we can think within the school as a whole. The community would be justified in assuming that we, as specialists, take responsibility for all retardates in our school systems and expect us to develop not one but as many programs as circumstances require.

SUMMARY

Two major issues in the socio-occupational preparation of the retarded are discussed. One issue has to do with the qualitative aspects of the school program and focuses upon the relationship between educational procedures and timeliness. In this area, there are a number of subissues related to the extent to which leadership personnel are guided by facts or by hunches.

The second issue involves the extent to which we perceive the limits of special education for the retarded and the implication of these perceptions on the number and kinds of retardates for whom we take responsibility.

CONCLUSION

From a positive point of view, we need a systematic approach to the constructive exploitation of data pertinent to the education of the retarded. The gathering and implementation of facts arising out of the relevant data is the responsibility of all echelons in the education of these children from the university teacher preparation and/or research program up to the public school class. Appropriate agencies in federal and state governments could contribute a great deal by collecting these facts from the sources and collating them into related bodies of information. In some cases, they could make general interpretations to guide local districts.

In terms of public school functions, we need to reassess our own concepts of what constitutes mental retardation and its relationship to the function of public education. In this sense, we need a broader definition of both "education" and "socio-occupation" adjustment. Our first positive move might be to restate trainability and educability to see whether or not we are talking about such different phenomena within the framework of a broad interpretation of socio-occupational adjustment.

Finally, we need to look again at the limits and character of what we call special education. The concept that special education takes place under a limited set of conditions is far too narrow. We need to look wider and see what accomodations other than the traditional will gain for more retardates better and more extensive provisions.

11

Mentally Retarded or Culturally Different?

SIMON OLSHANSKY, JACOB SCHONFIELD, LEON STERNFELD

The authors in this article urge the abandonment of the term "mental retardation" for two reasons: First, it is inaccurate. It suggests the existence of central nervous system pathology where there is no *present* evidence of such defect. In fact, the term *mental retardation* is used currently by professionals to categorize children without brain damage in contrast to the term *mental deficiency*, which applies to children with known brain damage. Even with some of these latter children it may be extremely difficult to separate consequences of brain damage from the consequences of poor parental management and miseducation. It is often assumed that a direct causal connection exists between brain damage and certain kinds of behavior. What is overlooked is the idiosyncratic nature of individual experience, and the transactional, as opposed to interactional, relation between an individual and his environment. Though in theory we may acknowledge the idiosyncratic and transactional nature of individual experience, clinically we tend to disregard it. Second, the label of mental retardation produces unhappy consequences for many of the children so described, reducing their self-confidence in their learning abilities and discouraging efforts in behalf of these children as well as research into their learning problems.

The authors believe that these children without brain damage are more aptly described at this time as "culturally different" rather than mentally retarded. Though improved neurological and psychological techniques may lead to the discovery of brain defect in these children presently found free of such defect, the question of cause and effect would still be unanswered: is the brain defect sufficient to account for their poor school performance? And the fact remains that the majority of these so-called mentally retarded children are able to meet most of life's changing expectations, except those of the schools *as currently structured.*

What is the evidence for viewing these children as culturally different rather than mentally retarded? In the Onondaga study (N.Y. Dept. Men-

* From *Training School Bulletin* 1963, 59, pp. 18–21. Reprinted by permission of the senior author and the publisher.

tal Hygiene, 1955) the prevalence rate for retardation or suspected retardation among non-whites was more than three times as high as that for whites, and residence in the economically depressed areas was accompanied by higher rates for all colors. That poverty and minority group status (associated with different kinds of experiences, values, and opportunities) are involved in the prospect of one's being defined as mentally retarded is borne out by the fact that in World War II the rejection rate for mental deficiency (what is currently called mental retardation) ranged between 9 per 1000 for whites in the far West and 202 per 1000 for Negroes in the Southeast (Ginsberg-Bray, 1953). Unless there is evidence for gross constitutional differences in mental capacity among various social, racial and ethnic groups, we are compelled to accept these differences as stemming from differences in experiences and opportunities.

Knobloch and Passamanick (1960) recently observed that "the findings of recent studies, our own as well as others, indicate that, in the absence of organic brain damage, it is life experiences and socio-cultural milieu modifying biologic and psychologic functioning which make the behavior of one individual *significantly** different from that of another."

In consideration of the above, is it accurate to label children with different experiences and values and *without central nervous system pathology* as mentally retarded? In the Onondaga study 60 per cent of the children with known I.Q.'s who were classified as retarded or suspected of retardation had I.Q.'s of 75 or better, and almost half of this latter group had I.Q.'s of 90 or better. Thus, even on the basis of culturally biased tests these children can not be called mentally retarded.

In passing, it is acknowledged that the investigators in the Onondaga study had used questionable criteria in classifying children as mentally retarded or suspected of mental retardation. But the criteria used are those generally used by schools and other social agencies.

It should be noted that the bulk of children labelled mentally retarded are so labelled generally by the schools on the basis of poor school performance and low I.Q. Comprehensive diagnostic work-ups are rarely available for most of these children.

Our point is that as long as a category of mental retardation exists it will be used as a convenient "dumping ground," especially for children disadvantaged by poverty and minority group status. The more important point is that many of these children in Onondaga County who were not mentally retarded were perceived and treated by schools and social agencies as if they were.

Some of the consequences of locating the school learning difficulties within the minds of these children are to limit efforts in their behalf as well as to persuade the children and some of their parents and peers that they are "dumb"[1] rather than different. In addition such a classification

---

* Italics in original

[1] Many children placed in so-called "special classes" for the mentally retarded describe them as "dumb" classes.

tends to relieve educators and others of some feelings of responsibility for intervention in behalf of these children since their problems are viewed as "mental" and "genetic" and therefore as essentially irreversible. In effect, besides adding the insult of stigmatization to the injury resulting from poverty and minority group status, we limit our confidence in our ability to affect change as well as diminish our interests in attempting change. Thus, within these terms many of these children are viewed patronizingly as "educable'" meaning that they have little capacity to learn as middle class children may be expected to learn, given their experiences and values.

Significantly, the majority of these "special class" children without brain damage, despite the stigmatization of special class placement, are able, upon leaving school, to find employment and become self-supporting citizens. (Masland, Sarason, Gladwin, 1958). We can only speculate about the quality of their post school adjustment had they been offered school training which stimulated their growth, capitalized on their abilities, and encouraged a more optimistic view of themselves as capable youngsters. Needless to say, these outcomes would entail the development of new kinds of curricula, (Eells, 1953), new educational objectives, new teaching methods.[2] Concurrent with, and in addition to, these educational changes it would be necessary to attempt to deal in a more concerted and concerned way with the poverty which chronically surrounds these children. At a minimum, this would entail improved health services, improved housing, and increased opportunity to share in some of the fruits of our affluent and democratic society. Motivation for exertion and achievement among children may depend as much on factors outside the schools as within them.

Abandonment of the term mental retardation with its clear implication of organic defect limiting growth and development might stimulate increased research into the socio-cultural factors which influence and determine the early learning patterns of these children. At present research interest in the field of mental retardation is overwhelmingly in the direction of bio-chemical investigations. We do not suggest a diminution of research in this area, but rather increased attention to the socio-cultural area which, we feel, may produce equally important results. But such an upsurge of research interest is not likely as long as we view school learning problems with the kind of finality implied by the frozen category, mental retardation.

In summary, we would urge the abandonment of the term mental retardation. One gain would be a re-definition [3] of each child, helping him view

[2] We recognize the extreme difficulty involved in the development of an educational program appropriate for lower class children, especially at a time of shortages in staff, money, and school buildings.

[3] It is relevant to compare the consequences which attended the recent re-definition of mental patients. As long as they were viewed and treated as violent and irreversibly crazy they conformed to those expectations. When those expectations were altered the mental patients altered their behavior.

himself, and be viewed by others, as essentially normal. By admitting that the school learning problems of some lower class children may stem in a large measure from their familial and cultural setting, which differentiates them from middle class children, rather than insisting that these learning problems inhere in their minds, we open up many possibilities for effective educational changes. In addition we bring a sense of hopefulness and optimism regarding future growth and development to both the children and their families, and to the professionals trying to help them. Lastly, professional attention may begin to shift from overwhelming concern with the problems of measuring a child's capacity to the problems of constructing environments which will facilitate and maximize the child's capacity for self-fulfillment.

Binet, whose spirit and intentions have been violated, expressed the matter well when he wrote: (Skeels, Dye, 1939) "Some recent philosophers appear to have given their moral support to the deplorable verdict that the intelligence of an individual is a fixed quantity, a quantity which cannot be augmented. We must protest and act against this brutal pessimism. We shall endeavour to show that it has no foundation whatsoever . . . A child's mind is like a field for which an expert farmer has advised a change in the method of cultivating, with the result that in place of desert land we now have a harvest. It is in the particular sense, the only one that is significant, that we say that the intelligence of children may be increased. One increases that which constitutes the intelligence of a school child; namely the capacity to learn, to improve with instruction."

REFERENCES

Eells, K., 1953. Some implications for school practice of the Chicago Studies of Cultural Bias in Intelligence Tests. *Harvard Education Review*, 23 (4).

Ginzberg, E., and Bray, D. W., 1953. *The Uneducated.* Columbia University Press.

Knoblock, N, and Passamanick, B., 1960. Environmental factors affecting human development, before and after birth. *Pediatrics*, 26 (2).

Masland, R. L., Sarason, S. B., and Gladwin, T., 1958. *Mental Subnormality.* Basic Books.

New York State Department of Mental Hygiene, Mental Health Research Unit, 1955. Technical Report.

Quoted from Skeels, H. M., and Dye, M. B., 1939. A study of the effects of differential stimulation on mentally retarded children. *Proceedings American Association of Mental Deficiency.* 44.

** 12 **

Teaching
the Multiply Handicapped
Mentally Retarded Child

ROBERT A. HENDERSON

Although there has been, for many years, a recognition of the higher incidence of multiple handicapping conditions among mentally retarded school children as compared with "normal" or above average pupils, neither the accurate census of the number and kinds of additional handicaps nor the methodology for teaching such multiply handicapped children in public school or residential school facilities is available.

REVIEW OF INCIDENCE STUDIES

Ayres (2) found in 1909 that while the "normal" child averaged 1.30 physical defects, the bright had only 1.07, while the "dull pupil" averaged 1.65 defects.

Sandwick (25) found a positive correlation between health and intelligence in his 1920 study, and Dayton (8) substantiated this in 1928 by reporting a negative correlation between physical defects and intelligence.

A recent controlled study (12) of motor characteristics of mentally retarded children found that the retarded were significantly poorer in the performance of all motor tasks. The authors recommended a structured physical education program in the curriculum of the mentally retarded pupil to provide specific training to overcome these deficiencies. Using a larger population, the same authors (13) found the mentally retarded public school pupil was lower than children of the same chronological age in all of the 11 gross motor tests administered, averaging two to four years behind normal pupils.

Blatt (4) compared mentally retarded children in a special class with

* From *Exceptional Children* 1960, 27, pp. 90–93. Reprinted by permission of the author and the publisher.

mentally retarded children in the same city who were enrolled in regular classes, and found that the number of physical defects in the special class children averaled 1.55, while those still in regular classes averaged only 1.08.

Beck (3) studying the incidence of brain injury in public school special classes for the educable mentally retarded in Southern Illinois, found 60 to 70% of the pupils had some neurological damage and that approximately 25% were on anticonvulsive medication. Although there is a wide discrepancy between authors, a 1955 book edited by Cruickshank and Raus (7) estimates that between 50 and 75% of cerebral palsied children are also mentally retarded.

DiMichael (10) indicates that 10 to 14% of blind children in the chronological age range 5–17 are retarded.

Myklebust (22) reports a study by Frisina showing 12% of the pupils at a residential school for the deaf to be between 60 and 75% IQ. In two audiometric studies (24) and (26) of school aged children in institutions for the mentally retarded, 19.8% and 17% respectively, were found to have a "significant hearing loss"—where that term is defined at 15 db loss or greater in two or more frequencies. Johnson and Farrell (18) report on a study of mentally retarded children at the Fernald State School in Massachusetts confirming the percentages above, and indicating that hearing loss is five times the incidence we would expect from a similar survey among public school children. Rittmanic (24) also reports on five other audiometric studies of mentally retarded children.

Many studies of speech handicaps among retarded children are available. Goertzen (14) reports two studies of institutionalized mentally retarded children which offered the following percentages of patients with speech defects (or no speech at all) in the three common subdivisions of the retarded level:

Intellectual Level	(Kennedy) % Speech Def.	(Sirkin, Jacob & Lyons) % Speech Def.
Educable M. R.	42.6	43
Severely M. R.	96.9	74
Total-Care M. R.	100.0	100

Lubman (20), reporting on a speech program for severely retarded children enrolled in parent-operated classes in Cleveland, Ohio, found only 7 of 150 children did not need speech therapy. Wallin (14) comparing mentally retarded and normal pupils in the public schools, found that 2.8% of the average school population had speech defects, while 26.3% of the mentally retarded special class children were afflicted. Kastein (19) discovered that of the 467 children accepted as patients at the Speech and Hearing Clinic of the Columbia Presbyterian Medical Center, New York, 267, or about 60% seemed retarded.

This review makes no pretense at being comprehensive or even representative of the available studies. It should serve, however, to indicate that no matter from what direction the problem is studied, the mentally retarded as a group have a rather high incidence of physical defects of all kinds including sensory and speech handicaps. Another insight to be gained from the assortment of studies reported is that for the child with multiply handicapping conditions, a differential diagnosis of the major handicapping condition and the extent of the mental handicap is often a difficult and demanding task. As Norris, Spaulding and Brodie (23, p. 41) point out, "The use of numerical scores and concepts, such as mental age and intelligence quotient, or social age and social quotient, has been found of limited value in understanding the capacity of a blind child." How much more limited they must be if the child also appears to be mentally retarded, with an undetermined hearing loss and perhaps mild cerebral palsy, accompanied by distorted speech!

SIGNIFICANCE OF SECONDARY HANDICAPS
ON A MENTALLY RETARDED CHILD

Let us consider for a moment what are the significant differences between multiply handicapped and otherwise unafflicted mentally retarded children.

First, I think, is the very pertinent question, is he really retarded? In the public school situation especially, the psychologist is under tremendous pressures to "test and certify" for special classes—usually on the basis of a single psychometric examination. Parents of multiply handicapped children are too often told their child is hopelessly retarded and should be committed to an institution forthwith, with even less evidence than that required for special class placement. Clinical diagnostic evidence seems to indicate that there is a wide variability in the functioning of individual children with multiple handicaps at different times, whether measured by intelligence or social maturity scales. This lack of reliability raises serious questions regarding the application of any single observation as an adequate basis for social or educational recommendations. Furthermore, I can find no instrument available which is designed for, and which has been standardized for the measurement of intelligence of children with multiple handicaps such as blind-retarded or deaf-retarded. Therefore we can and should expect that more extensive differential diagnostic studies be made in the case of mentally retarded children found to have additional handicapping conditions.

Secondly, I think we must consider the effect of multiple handicapping conditions upon the parents of the retarded child. Even with most retarded children, a bit of Emerson's Law of Compensation is possible: "He may not be able to go on to college, but he will be able to hold a job, pay his own way, and participate as an independent, tax-paying citizen of his community." The larger the number, and the greater the degree of multiple handicaps, the less likely that these goals of independent self-sufficiency will be reached. Thus assisting the parents in attaining realistic educational, social and vocational aspirations for their child becomes of increasing importance as additional handicaps are added to the diagnosis of mental retardation.

Thirdly, we must consider the question of the type of educational services needed by multiply handicapped mentally retarded children. Can we even talk of educating the "multiply handicapped mentally retarded," or must we break it down into the categories, blind-retarded, deaf-retarded, cerebral palsied-retarded, etc.? Can we expect the teacher of the mentally retarded to be adequately equipped to educate any and all retarded children regardless of additional handicaps, such as blindness, deafness, or cerebral palsy? Are there sufficient numbers to justify, and would it be desirable to encourage in our larger metropolitan areas the establishment of special centers for the multiply handicapped which would contain specialists in the various categories of handicapped children, working together as a team to provide educational services?

IMPLICATIONS

1. The lack of reliability and validity of current diagnostic instruments when used with multiply handicapped children requires more frequent re-evaluations and case conferences to assess the child's educational progress. These diagnostic shortcomings should not be viewed by psychologists or teachers as overpowering handicaps, but rather as more challenging areas with uneven and unique developmental patterns.

2. Coupled with the diagnostic problems is the lack of specific clinical teaching methods and materials for use with retarded children suffering with one or more physically handicapping conditions. Even now there are a few bright spots in this picture, and the future promises more. For instance, Ashcroft (1, p. 526) reports that, "The passing of the wave of retrolental fibroplasia, use of improved optical and technical aids, and expanded day school programs offer needed services. More attention can now be given to the visually handicapped child who has additional problems or handicapping conditions. Facilities once crowded by RLF children and others can be made available to children previously not considered for services." Most of the latter are blind-retarded children, I am sure.

3. There is the more general problem of who should educate each category of the multiply handicapped retarded, and in what setting: special classes for the mentally retarded, special regional day centers for multiply handicapped, or residential school special facilities?

All of these problems indicate how lightly the surface has been scratched, and how richly endowed this area is for research workers. We can be confident that increasing attention, stimulated by federal and private research monies, will provide answers soon to some of our problems of teaching multiply handicapped mentally retarded children.

REFERENCES

Ashcroft, S. C., "The Blind and Partially Seeing," *Review of Educational Research,* 24 (December 1959), pp. 519–28.

Ayres, L. P., "The Effect of Physical Defect on School Progress," *Psychological Clinic,* 3 (1909), pp. 71–77.

Beck, Harry S., "The Incidence of Brain Injury in Public School Special Classes for the Educable Mentally Handicapped," *American Journal of Mental Deficiency,* 60 (April 1956), pp. 818–822.

Blatt, Barton, "The Physical Personality and Academic Status of Children Who Are Mentally Retarded Attending Special Class as Compared with Retarded Children Attending Regular Class," *American Journal of Mental Deficiency,* 62 (March 1958), pp. 810–818.

Blodgett, Harriet, "A Keystone in Rehabilitation," *The Crippled Child,* 35 (6) and 36 (1) (April 1956).

Boly, L. F. and C. M. DeLeo, "A Survey of Educational Provisions for the Institutionalized Mentally Subnormal Blind," American Journal of Mental Deficiency, 60 (April 1956), pp. 774–749.

Cruickshank and Raus (eds.), *Cerebral Palsy* (Syracuse, N.Y.: Syracuse University Press, 1955.

Dayton, N. A., "The Relationship Between Physical Defects and Intelligence," *Journal of Psycho-Astenics,* 34 (1928–1929), pp. 112–139.

DeLeo, C. M. and L. F. Boly, "Some Considerations in Establishing an Educational Program for the Institutionally Blind and Partially Sighted Mentally Subnormal," *American Journal of Mental Deficiency,* 61 (July 1956), pp. 134–140.

DeMichael, Salvatore C., "Meeting the Needs of Retarded Blind Children," report at the American Association of Instructors of the Blind (June 1956).

Dunn, L. M. and R. J. Capobianco, "Mental Retardation," *Review of Educational Research,* 24 (December 1959), pp. 451–470.

Francis, R. J. and G. L. Rarick, "Motor Characteristics of the Mentally Retarded Children," (mimeo) (Madison, Wisc.: University of Wisconsin, Department of Physical Education for Men, 1957).

———, "Motor Characteristics of the Mentally Retarded," *American Journal of Mental Deficiency,* 63 (March 1959), pp. 792–811.

Goertzen, Stanley M., "Speech and the Mentally Retarded Child," *American Journal of Mental Deficiency,* 62 (September 1957), pp. 244–253.

Hardy, William G., "The Relation Between Impaired Hearing and Feeblemindedness," *The Nervous Child,* 7 (October 1948), pp. 432–445.

Hill, Arthur S., "The Status of Mental Retardation Today with Emphasis on Services," *Exceptional Children,* 25 (March 1959), pp. 298–299.

Huffman, Mildred B., *Fun Comes First for the Blind Slow-Learner* (Springfield, Ill.: C. C. Thomas, 1957).

Johnson and Farrell, "An Experiment in Improving Medical and Educational Services for Hard of Hearing Children at the Walter E. Fernald State School," *American Journal of Mental Deficiency*, 62 (September 1957), pp. 230–237.

Kastein, Shulamith, "The Responsibility of the Speech Pathologist to the Retarded Child," *American Journal of Mental Deficiency*, 60 (April 1956), pp. 750–754.

Lubman, C. G., "Speech Program for Severely Retarded Children," *American Journal of Mental Deficiency*, 60 (October 1955), pp. 297–300.

Minski, Louis, *Deafness, Mutism and Mental Deficiency in Children* (New York: Philosophical Library, 1957).

Myklebust, H. R., "The Deaf Child with Other Handicaps," *American Annals of the Deaf*, 103 (September 1958), pp. 496–509.

Norris, M., P. J. Spaulding and F. H. Brodie, *Blindness in Children* (Chicago: University of Chicago Press, 1957).

Rittmanic, Paul A., "Hearing Rehabilitation for the Institutionalized Mentally Retarded," *American Journal of Mental Deficiency*, 63 (March 1959), pp. 778–783.

Sanzwick, R. L., "Correlation of Physical Health and Mental Efficiency," *Journal of Educational Research*, 1 (1920), pp. 199–203.

Schlanger, B. B., and R. H. Gottsleben, "Clinical Speech Program at the Training School at Vineland," American Journal of Mental Deficiency, 61 (January 1957), pp. 516–55.

Tretakoff, M. I. and M. J. Farrell, "Developing a Curriculum for the Blind Retarded," *American Journal of Mental Deficiency*, 62 (January 1958), pp. 610–615.

PART THREE

Visually Handicapped

Problems of definition, of assessment, and of educational programming are as acute and as current in the area of visual handicap as in areas of other handicapping conditions. A most critical problem is that current definitions of visual handicap—based as they are upon measures of visual acuity—have little educational relevance. In the first article in this section, Jones ("Problems in Identifying and Classifying Blindness") points up limitations resulting from an over-reliance upon measures of visual acuity in defining or arranging educational placement for visually handicapped pupils. The observation that educational procedures for visually limited pupils are in many instances unrelated to the degree of visual acuity is indicative of the value of current definitions of visual handicap for educational placement. As Jones notes, problems of definition await resolution.

The psycho-educational assessment of blind children presents as many problems as are found in defining blindness for educational purposes. According to the canons of acceptable psychological testing procedures, meaningful interpretation of test scores can be made only if the instruments have been standardized on populations comparable to those with whom they will be used. In most instances (with the possible exception of the mentally retarded and the gifted), exceptional children are excluded from standardization populations. How then is the psycho-educational diagnostician to assess meaningfully the behavior of blind or other exceptional children? How much reliance can be (or should be) placed on the diagnostician's clinical judgment, accumulated hopefully as a result of the study and assessment of many exceptional children? And upon what can the diagnostician rely until he has accumulated such experience? These problems and related ones are taken up by Bateman in the second article of this section ("Psychological Evaluation of Blind Children"). Although the article deals with the assessment of blind children, it is apparent that the concerns expressed in this article apply to other groups of exceptional children as well.

Avery takes up the controversy of public school versus residential school placement for blind children. As the author notes, this issue has been debated for many years. In this article major arguments supporting the two types of arrangements are discussed and directions for a rapprochement suggested. As with arrangements for other exceptionalities, Avery suggests, appropriately, that the question of the most satisfactory educational arrangement for blind children is not an either/or proposition. Rather, the problem is one of fitting the child to the educational environment most appropriate for meeting educational, psychological, and social needs at that point in time; movement from the residential school to public school (or vice versa) may occur in some instances, and the possibilities should always be left open.

Avery has highlighted well the issues and problems associated with day school and residential school placement of blind children. However, questions about the value of these and other educational arrangements for blind and other categories of exceptional children will remain essentially unanswered unless the well-reasoned armchair arguments are accompanied by programs of research.

A number of additional psychological and educational problems in the area of blindness have yet to be addressed in systematic fashion. Nolan has discussed these topics in a recent paper, the major aspects of which are summarized below. In accounting for the relative paucity of psychological and educational research on the blind, Nolan points to the small number of doctoral-level persons who have full-time concern with research on education of the blind ("probably no more than five . . ."), and to the small number of institutions actually preparing teachers to work in this field.

Among the critical problems described by Nolan are the following: (1) *tactual perception*—(a) the dimensions of texture ("We still have no clear idea of the dimensions by which textures are tactually discriminated. Such information is critical, of course, for the development of maps and other tactual graphics.") and (b) form perception ("No information exists concerning what factors determine figure-ground relationships in tactual stimulus fields."); (2) *perception of space* ("How do the blind develop their concepts of space? How accurately is space perceived? What are the roles and limitations of the various sensory channels in space perception? Answers to these questions have implications for mobility instruction as well as instruction in mathematics and science."); (3) *visual perception* ("Most individuals who qualify as legally blind have some residual vision. However, very little information describing the effects of types and degrees of visual handicaps on visual perceptual processes is available. . . . Study is needed of ways in which the visually handicapped can make use of residual vision."); (4) *concept development* ("Visual deprivation results in a great reduction in the possible amounts of direct and vicarious contact with the environment. As a consequence, the proportion of experiences that must be classified as abstract is greatly increased for the blind. . . . Implications for education have never been explored."); and (5) *communications in education* ("Educational communications is an area that is affected greatly by the perceptual differences between visually handicapped and normal children. Rates of communication are much slower when either braille or large type media are used. Greater emphasis is placed on aural communication in the education of the blind. Many problems for research exist in this area.") Differences between visual and tactual reading, developing readiness for braille reading, developing readiness for large type reading, and making the most effective use of listening as a substitute for reading—all are problems in need of additional investigation.

Among the visually handicapped, most research and writing has focused upon the blind. For educational purposes, however, as Jones has pointed out in his article on problems of identifying blindness, distinctions between the blind and the partially seeing frequently are inappropriate; some individuals classified as blind use print, while those classified as partially seeing may use braille as their primary reading medium. Nevertheless, questions remain about the most appropriate arrangement for educating the partially seeing as well as the blind. For the partially seeing as for the blind, a number of administrative arrangements present themselves for consideration. These plans along with their pros and cons are summarized in the Stephens and Birch article, "Merits of Special Class, Resource, and Itinerant Plans for Teaching Partially Seeing Children."

The visually handicapped can—and frequently do—have concomitant handicaps. As with other exceptionalities, multiple disabilities in the area of blindness have been relatively neglected. Problems of multiple disability in visual handicap (particularly the mentally retarded blind) and in other areas are summarized by Wolf ("Multiple Disabilities—An Old Problem with a New Challenge") in a final article in this section.

REFERENCES

Nolan, C. Y., "Research in Education of the Blind," in *Blindness Research: The Expanding Frontier* (University Park and London: The Pennsylvania State University Press, 1969).

** 13 **

Problems in Defining
and Classifying Blindness

JOHN WALKER JONES

Much confusion stems from terminology presently used to describe visually handicapped children. This confusion tends to make it difficult for teachers and administrators to plan, evaluate and justify special programs. It also complicates the collection of basic statistics and estimations of incidence and prevalence in this area of special education. The growing concern of educators about problems related to defining and classifying blind and partially seeing children is summarized in this article. A brief review also is made of some program adjustments and of attempts by educators to refine the process of pupil selection and dismissal.

Little more than a decade ago, it was commonly believed that children with limited vision would damage their eyes if they used them to full extent for school work. Special educators encountered relatively minor problems in selecting pupils believed to be in need of placement in special programs. These educators found that their practices tended to support the application to school programs of the accepted definition of 20/200. Many applied this definition to education even though it had been developed primarily for use with adults in determining their eligibility for public assistance or for vocational rehabilitation. Similar experience was found with the visual acuity of 20/70 to 20/200 for children placed in special education programs for the partially seeing. As long as use of residual vision was believed to be associated with ocular damage, few educators or parents were concerned about the fact that many children selected *primarily* on the basis of their *visual acuity* and taught to read by means of braille, had enough vision to read print. Very few were concerned that many children placed in special programs for partially seeing students demonstrated the ability to read ordinary print with reasonable efficiency and appeared able to progress well in regular school programs.

* From *The New Outlook for the Blind* 1962, 56, pp. 115–121. Reprinted by permission of the author and the publisher.

SEEKING NEW GUIDELINES

Education of visually impaired children entered a new era when it was recognized that use of vision seldom if ever results in damage, even where serious impairments are present. With this new era came a renewed interest in exact retractions and in the use of low vision optical aids. With this new era also came a questioning of educational practices by educators, eye specialists, and parents of children with visual limitations. Empirical evidence began to indicate that under proper conditions many of these children learn to make good use of even slight amounts of residual vision. The realization began to grow that some children with limited vision not only could be, but should be, put back into regular classrooms for all or part of their education. New teaching techniques and types of special education programs began to evolve. Educators became dissatisfied with the visual acuity cut-off points on which many had relied so extensively in the past. They began to seek new criteria for defining, classifying and placing children.

The search for new guidelines to aid in classifying and defining visually handicapped children has gathered momentum in recent years. This is reflected in the following excerpts taken from the literature. Participants in a national conference on the education of blind persons in 1953 stated:

> The generally accepted definition of blindness places 20/200 as the dividing line between individuals considered legally blind and individuals considered sighted. However, this arbitrary definition does not seem realistic as applied to the educational needs of all children whose visual acuity falls below 20/200. Some . . . below this dividing line have unusual visual efficiency and, on the basis of recommendations of their ophthalmologists and the observations of their teachers, may be better off—physically, psychologically and socially—through using their vision in their education.[7]

Educators of partially seeing children reinforced this statement in one of their publications in 1959 as follows:

> Experience has shown that many children with visual acuity of less than 20/200 can see well enough to make use of the equipment and special education media provided for the partially seeing and should, therefore, be identified as partially seeing rather than blind.[5]

The overlap between the definitions of blind and partially seeing children has had many ramifications. Participants in a conference on teacher preparation programs suggested:

> The large number of children who seem to fall within *both* categories can be separated and constructively served only if we are able to view these children according to a *functional* definition which describes the child, with all of his potentialities and needs after medical, psychological, and sociological information has been considered, in terms of the best possible educational placement. This makes it necessary and very important for teachers of blind children to

have the related knowledge concerning the education of children with *varying degrees of visual problems.*[8]

An eminent ophthalmologist stated recently:

Classification of blindness is necessary because definition of blindness includes vision ranging from no light perception to 20/120. Only the totally blind need no definition. For all practical purposes, therefore, classification of residual vision is necessary to aid in the placement of partially seeing persons.[4]

He recommends that persons with vision of 1/200 or less be taught to read by means of braille but that those whose residual vision exceeds 2/200 be encouraged to the highest degree possible to read by means of print.

A small study of conference specialists in the education of visually handicapped children was called by the Section on Exceptional Children and Youth of the U.S. Office of Education during the summer of 1960 to study the definition and placement of these children.[1] Several tentative recommendations were made including:

A) Educators shoud seek to develop *functional educational* definitions of blind and partially seeing children rather than rely on definitions used by medicine, rehabilitation, and welfare.[*]

B) The current definition of legal blindness is of little use to educators either as a definition or as a criterion for placement. Immediate proposals to change existing state and federal laws, however, probably would be premature until further study has been given this important problem.

The following were among suggestions submitted by this group for further study and research exploration:

1) The educational classification of blindness should be reserved for children who have no measurable vision or vision which is so limited as to be of little if any practical use as a channel of learning. Such children use braille as their primary mode of reading and as an important source of learning.

2) Partially seeing children would be those whose visual limitation interferes with their learning efficiency to such an extent that they require special teaching services and aids if they are to attain performance standards appropriate for normally sighted students of comparable ability but who rely on vision as a chief channel of learning and use of print as the primary mode of reading.

3) Recognizing that some children with limited vision cannot be classified readily as either blind or partially seeing, a third or borderline group was suggested to include those partially seeing children able to use vision as an important channel of learning, some of whom may read by means of both print and braille.

Further evidence of need to resolve some of the issues pertaining to defining and classifying blind and partially seeing children and of the possible

---

* Definition and classification problems in the field of vocational rehabilitation, as they apply to visually handicapped persons, currently are under study by the Subcommittee on Impairments of Visual Function of the Rehabilitation Codes being conducted by the Association for the Aid of Crippled Children under the direction of Dr. Maya Riviere. The National Institute of Neurological Diseases and Blindness is studying broad aspects of the problem and the Biometrics Branch of this institute is giving special attention to epidemiological studies of incidence, prevalence, and etiology of blindness and other severe visual defects as is the National Society for the Prevention of Blindness.

magnitude of the problem were revealed by a study conducted in the Office of Education. This study was based on information provided with the registration of children with the American Printing House for the Blind in January of 1960. Analysis and comparison of data on more than 14,000 "legally" blind children enrolled in school at that time showed: 24 per cent were reported as totally blind; 16 per cent as perceiving light only, and approximately 60 per cent as able to perceive more than light.[6]

Projection of these percentages to current enrollments reveals the probability that there are now more than 10,000 "blind" children in school who have sufficient vision (more than light perception) to be considered as potential readers of either print or of both print and braille. Selecting the most appropriate reading medium and educational placement for these students is difficult but of great importance to each child. In communities where separate facilities are maintained for blind and for partially seeing children this decision may determine whether the child will be educated essentially as a blind or as a seeing person. Some of the 10,000 or more children currently classified as legally blind who have more than light perception are able to function satisfactorily in the regular school program without special instruction. Many in this group, however, require educational aids and instruction by specially prepared teachers if they are to progress at a rate in accord with their ability. Some within this latter group will need to be educated primarily as blind children and others primarily as partially seeing children if placements are made in keeping with their most essential needs.

MODE OF READING

Educators have recognized for some time the necessity of using functional characteristics of visually handicapped children as criteria for classification and placement. Basic among important characteristics distinguishing blind from partially seeing children is the mode of reading best suited to each child. Increasingly, educational reference to a child as blind has come to mean that he reads and writes primarily by means of braille. Those "legally" blind children who, in the opinion of education specialists, demonstrate an ability to use print as their basic reading medium are generally classified as partially seeing.

But there is evidence to suggest that, among programs for visually handicapped children, widely diverse practices may exist in regard to the mode of reading children with limited vision are encouraged to adopt. Comparisons of the modes of reading of legally blind children whose residual vision exceeds light perception as reported by local and residential schools to the American Printing House for the Blind in 1960 disclose some revealing differences.[6]

Among the approximately 5,250 *local* school registrants with this much vision, about 82 per cent were listed as reading primarily by means of print;

14 per cent by means of braille; and 4 per cent by means of both print and braille.

Among the more than 3,000 *residential school* registrants within this same range of vision, 29 per cent were listed as reading primarily by means of print; 61 per cent by means of braille; and 10 per cent by means of both print and braille.

While several factors may contribute to the extensive differences found between local and residential school students in this respect, these differences are of such magnitude as to suggest the likelihood that conflicting opinions and practices are involved. Differences exist not only between local and residential school pupils within this range of vision, but also among different schools or programs within each of these groups. It is evident, for instance, that a few residential schools teach braille to all students, even though many are registered as having 20/200 visual acuity. Data from most residential schools, however, suggest that practices are more selective. Somewhat similar differences are found among local school systems, even at times within the same state or region.

Because of this diversity of opinion and the wide differences in practice, it would appear that reliance cannot be placed upon the mode of reading as a criterion for educational definition and program placement. The visual characteristics and educational needs of children with limited vision who read by means of either braille or print vary greatly. Therefore, use of the mode of reading to define and classify these children seems merely to move the problem from the visual acuity horn of the dilemma to another equally impractical one. It would seem that many children reading by means of braille have as much visual acuity as many others who use print as their primary mode of reading.

VISUAL ACUITY

It is widely recognized that visual acuity alone is *not* a reliable criterion for defining or placing visually handicapped children. Reliance upon it as the most important single factor also is being challenged. In addition, many questions raised in connection with the use of present visual acuity designations center upon the fact that they do not correspond to the way children function in school. Yet, in many instances, administrators have used the visual acuity limits as the determining factor for placement rather than as a guideline. It frequently has been contended that wide variations are found in the needs of these children, particularly among those in the upper ranges of vision. Some educators maintain that continued use of these upper acuity designations is not in the best interest of children and is confusing to the public and to educators as well. Children falling within given visual acuity designations can be identified. But, if these visual acuity designations actually identify only children with visual limitations and not those for whom the limitations constitute educational handicaps, they are of very limited value in determining or predicting special program needs.

An example is the upper visual acuity limit of 20/70 which has been suggested as a guide for definition and placement of partially seeing children. It is now being contended that relatively few children with this much visual acuity require special consideration in their school program beyond that which can be easily arranged within the regular classroom. Repeated estimates have been made over the years that about one child in every 500 of the general school population may be expected to have corrected visual acuity in the better eye of 20/70 or less. However, a considerable number of specially prepared supervisors and consultants of visually handicapped children in charge of large state or local programs report that according to their experience as many as two-thirds or more of these children with 20/70 and less visual acuity are progressing well in regular classrooms without special instruction. They urge the retention of those visually limited children who make good progress in the general school program, but stress that routine checks should be made on their progress. On the other hand, evidence is beginning to accumulate that a few children with certain types of eye conditions whose visual acuity is better than 20/70 in the better eye after correction, tend to develop problems in school which may be related to difficulty in using their eyes effectively.[3] In general, however, it would appear that at this visual acuity level the exceptions may exceed the rule, resulting in some perplexing administrative problems. A thorough study of how approximate the 20/70 visual acuity designation is and the development of additional criteria would seem essential to progress in this field.

Recent experience in teaching children with impaired vision is beginning to indicate that many, perhaps most, of those whose corrected acuity is found to approximate 20/200 (the upper limit of legal blindness) are able to become reasonably effective readers of print. Comparisons of data on degree of vision and modes of reading provided with the 1960 registration of children with the American Printing House for the Blind appear to raise further questions about the 20/200 visual acuity cut-off point.[6] The analysis conducted in the Office of Education included 4,400 children who were reported to have approximately 20/200 visual acuity. Almost 82 per cent of these were registered as reading print, about 12 per cent braille, and 6 per cent both print and braille.

Included in this same analysis were data on 600 students reported to the American Printing House for the Blind as having approximately 15/200 visual acuity. Among this group it was found that about 67 per cent were listed as readers of print, 27 per cent braille, and 6 per cent both. Study of data on 1,250 students whose visual acuity approximated 10/200 showed that 59 per cent were registered as readers of print, 32 per cent braille, and 9 per cent both. The validity of these findings may be subject to question since there was no way to verify how precisely the eye information about the children was reported to the American Printing House for the Blind or how recently the eye examinations on which these reports were based had been conducted. However, since fairly large numbers of children were involved, it may be assumed that they are somewhat indicative of the true situation. They are grossly comparable to the findings on the visual nature and mode of reading of children in the study, *Services to Blind Children in New York State.*[2]

REFINING SELECTION AND DISMISSAL PROCESSES

Educators are attempting to cope with problems associated with defining and classifying visually handicapped children in a variety of ways.

Local and regional advisory committees or councils of educators are being formed to guide special teachers and local directors in the selection, placement, re-appraisal, and dismissal of visually handicapped children. The needs of individual children are reviewed in the light of local, regional, and state facilities available to meet these needs. Group recommendations are made, thus relieving any one person of taking full responsibility for placement of a child in a special program or for withdrawing a child from such a program.

Eye report forms used by the schools are being revised to contain requests for specific and detailed information from eye specialists who examine children who are considered for placement in special programs. Forms which indicate the exact type of information needed usually save considerable time for both the school and the eye specialists. Information on diagnosis, prognosis, and measurements of near as well as far vision is usually included in these requests. Interest is growing, also, in requesting measurements of visual fields. Annual eye examinations are being required for children enrolled in some special programs to assure the availability of current information and to help prevent unnecessary loss of vision among those whose vision is already limited.

The functional characteristics of children with limited vision are being studied in an effort to select those whose visual limitations actually constitute educational handicaps. Information about intellectual ability is being reviewed and compared with that on scholastic progress. Children with visual limitations who are making appropriate school progress without the aid of special teachers are encouraged to remain in regular classrooms. Their progress is reviewed periodically by regular and special teachers or supervisors. When a discrepancy is found between the ability and the progress of a child with limited vision, a more thorough analysis is made of the nature of his problem. Special consideration is given those children with visual limitations whose eye conditions appear to be making it difficult or impossible for them to complete long reading assignments or other school tasks involving close eye work; to copy accurately material from texts, workbooks, or chalkboards; to those whose listening comprehension substantially exceeds that of their own silent reading; to those who tend to skip letters and words which look somewhat alike when blurred or distorted; and to those who may understand the basic principles involved in certain concepts such as those used in arithmetic but who make errors in the more routine computations, particularly when working with long columns of numbers. Thus, the child's visual acuity, which formerly constituted a major criterion for special placement, is coming to be considered as one among many factors.

General recognition is being given the fact that proper selection of the most useful reading medium (braille, print, or both) is very important to the child, requires special knowledge and skills on the part of the teacher, and is a choice confronting a sizeable number of children with limited vision. Teachers entering this field are being encouraged and even required in a growing number of places to study the needs and methods applicable to both blind and partially seeing children. The practicality of employing teachers properly prepared to serve both groups is being realized. This practice is helpful in many rural areas and in small and medium sized school districts where the number of visually handicapped children tends to be too small to justify special programs for each child. In such programs the needs of children with borderline vision can be studied intensively, over rather long periods of time, if necessary, by teachers prepared to teach reading by means of either braille or print. It is suggested that these teachers are less inclined to favor one or the other mode of reading. The need for making an early placement of children in either a special program for blind or for partially seeing children is removed.

NEW KNOWLEDGE

Educators in this field as in other areas of special education are faced with the necessity of developing a new body of scientific knowledge if realistic definitions and guidelines to educational classification are to evolve. Teachers and supervisors in this special area have proved to be receptive to new ideas and the application of these to educational practices has enabled them to set patterns for others to follow. Their present concern for developing and refining definitions and placement practices once again reflects the thinking of forward looking people.

Search for agreement among experts in this field should continue. Local and regional surveys based on precise information of known validity about the primary diagnosis and the effect of the visual disabilities on both near and far point visual acuity of children in special programs are needed. Such surveys, replicated in various places by state and local educators, would be particularly helpful if visual acuity designations were to be sharpened and their use for purposes of educational definitions retained. The seemingly wide differences in modes of reading among students with similar degrees of vision appear to be so pronounced that reasons for them should be explored. Controlled studies seeking answers to many related questions should be undertaken. What factors other than visual acuity tested beyond the reading distance are important in determining the mode of reading performance of children with very low vision? Does the average child whose visual loss is associated with a particular condition such as nystagmus tend to be a more likely candidate for special education than one with a different condition but a similar degree of visual acuity? Is he more likely to succeed in reading by means of braille or by means of print? How extensively is large print material used by children with visual limitations? Which among them must rely upon it for their independent reading? Does the introduction of braille as the first trial reading medium result in a loss of the opportunity for young children to develop print reading skills and use of residual vision at an age when the chance for this development is optimum? Or does the introduction of print as the first trial reading medium to children with inadequate vision result in a loss of the opportunity for them to develop adequate skill in reading by means of braille? What constitutes a good trial climate and an adequate trial period for most of these children?

More children with impaired vision are enrolled in the nation's schools than ever before. Predictions of future enrollments are being adjusted upward as it now appears that larger numbers of visually handicapped children resulting from the general population increase may be following the "wave" of those whose limited vision or blindness was caused by retrolental fibroplasia. The opportunity and need to study and improve methods and practices pertaining to the educational definition and classification of these children is at hand.

REFERENCES

1. "Conference on Educational Definition and Classification of Visually Handicapped Children and Youth." Section on Exceptional Children and Youth, U.S. Office of Education, Summary Report (unpublished report).
2. Cruckshank, William M., Trippe, Matthew J., *Services to Blind Children in New York State.* Syracuse University Press, 1959.
3. Eames, Thomas H., "Visual Handicaps to Reading," *Journal of Education,* Vol. 141, No. 3, February 1959.
4. Fonda, Gerald, "Definition and Classification of Blindness with Respect to Ability to Use Residual Vision," *New Outlook for the Blind,* Vol. 55, No. 5, May 1961.
5. Foote, Franklin M., Bryan, Dorothy, Gibbons, Helen, *Education and Health of the Partially Seeing Child.* Fourth edition. Columbia University Press, 1959. p. 17.
6. Jones, John Walker, *Blind Children, Degree of Vision, Mode of Reading.* U.S. Department of Health, Education, and Welfare, Office of Education, Section on Exceptional Children and Youth. Bulletin #24, 1961.
7. *The Pine Brook Report.* New York: American Foundation for the Blind, 1954, p. 26.
8. *A Teacher Education Program for Those Who Serve Blind Children and Youth.* New York: American Foundation for the Blind, 1961. p. 9.

** 14 **

Psychological Evaluation
of Blind Children

BARBARA BATEMAN

Many of the major issues confronting the psychologist in the evaluation of blind children are essentially the same as those he faces in diagnostic work with any and all exceptional children. One of the first issues he must deal with concerns the use he wishes to make of normative data; or, in other words, from what frame of reference or vantage point is he assessing the blind child? Is he concerned with how well the blind child functions compared to sighted children? If so, in what areas of behavior is this question meaningful? Is he concerned with how the child compares with other blind children? If so, how does he weigh age at onset of blindness, degree of remaining vision, previous educational experiences, home environment, etc.? Is he interested in estimating how well the child might be functioning if he weren't blind? Is he concerned with some assessment of manifest intelligence in contrast to potential intelligence?

There are no easy answers, no global answers, to these questions. But the examining psychologist must be aware of these and other possible approaches to his diagnostic procedures. The meaningfulness of the data he obtains will depend on the extent to which he makes clear the frame of reference he is using. He may, of course, use several simultaneously. This problem in psychological diagnosis is one which always confronts us with children who are, as a given, substantially different from the sample on which our normative data are obtained. But the obvious answer of obtaining norms for each group of exceptional children falls short of adequacy for several reasons. A primary consideration is that many times the psychologist's purpose in diagnosis is to examine the possibility of the exceptional child being able to operate among nonhandicapped children. A further problem in using separate norms, especially for blind children, is that it implies a homogeneity of handicapped groups which doesn't in fact exist.

* From *The New Outlook for the Blind* 1965, 59, pp. 193–196. Reprinted by permission of the author and the publisher.

Once the frame of reference, or the purpose of testing, has been clearly established, the examiner is then bound to be confronted with problems in test administration. He must address himself to two more somewhat difficult questions. He must ask "How meaningful is it to administer, in unmodified form, an item which isn't entirely suitable or relevant for a blind child?" On the other hand, "How appropriate is it to modify an item without such modification being explicitly in line with standardized procedure?"

The problems posed so far suggest that total reliance on standardized procedures is perhaps impossible and/or foolhardy. But the alternative of clinical interpretation and informal testing and observational techniques should be based on "built-in" standards for blind children's behavior.

And, if we are to be quite frank and realistic, how many school psychologists have had the extensive experience with blind children necessary for the development of such an internalized comparator? Worse yet, such a comparator must be continually revised and sharpened by feedback on the accuracy of our hunches and predictions. Seldom do we get adequate feedback on our reports of routine diagnoses and prognoses, let alone on a large sample of blind children.

In short, heavy reliance on clinical judgment alone does not seem much more feasible than does mechanical applications of standardized measures. Regardless of what diagnostic approaches and procedures we adopt and the success with which we answer the questions posed so far, we are still faced with one more difficulty.

The assessment of cognitive processes and products is a challenging task under the best of conditions. Many of our instruments and judgments are simultaneously relatively insensitive to variables we wish to tap and too sensitive to extraneous variables. Now, when we add not just one, but two or three confounding variables—sensory deprivation, inadequate or unusual opportunities for learning, and emotional smothering or deprivation—our job seems almost overwhelming.

In short, the problems in psychological evaluation of blind children are many and complex. Final answers have we none. However, the following tentative guidelines are suggested as possible means of approaching and minimizing, if not solving, some of the problems raised.

Standardized tests which have been designed or modified for use with the blind are much more abundant than is often realized. Lende's *Books About the Blind* [1] lists over 120 articles dealing with such standardized tests. If the compilation were brought up to date it would perhaps double. The tests which have been used with the blind include projective techniques, achievement tests and interest inventories in addition to intelligence and aptitude tests. Most of the literature, however, deals with the use of these tests with groups of blind subjects rather than in individual diagnosis. The criticism of this group research is also voluminous and points out the problems of norms, item appropriateness, etc.

But the fact remains that there are many standardized tests which can be used with blind persons, especially beyond the early school ages. Among the tests currently widely used and recommended for blind children are the Interim Hayes-Binet Intelligence Test, WISC Verbal Scale, Merrill Palmer Scale of Mental Tests, the Maxfield-Buchholz Scale of Social Competence (pre-school blind), the Guess Who Game, Vineland Social Maturity Scale, and the Emotional Factors Inventory (age thirteen and up).

A possible addition to this list in future years will be the auditory-vocal channel subtests of the Illinois Test of Psycholinguistic Abilities (ITPA). The norms extend from age 2–6 through 9–0 years. Language development of blind children is frequently an area which the psychologist must examine. The ITPA appears to be a promising instrument in determining both level of language behavior and patterns of strengths and weaknesses.

However useful some standardized tests may be for certain purposes with some children, it would seem desirable to view such tests only as launching pads from which the diagnostic flight may begin. One guideline in the use of standardized uses is derived from the concept of diagnosis *for* the purposes of decision-making, recommending remedial or educational procedures, or answering specific questions. This concept of diagnosis is actually very different from the notion of diagnosis as classification or naming. It is easy enough to conclude a report of formal or informal testing with a label such as "educationally blind," or "low average intelligence" or "eligible for placement as multiply handicapped." More sophisticated clinical powers are required to make such recommendations and prognoses as "readiness training for braille should include work on tactile spatial orientation, for which a raised version of Frostig's spatial relations materials is suggested," or "performance on the Hayes Binet and the ITPA auditory-vocal association indicate that auditory closure is inadequate and exercises in riddles, rhyming, and categorization are recommended," or "while subject is technically eligible for multiply handicapped, the problems in auditory comprehension (resembling receptive aphasia) are probably remediable and therefore intensive work in noise recognition, sound localization, noise comparisons, following simple two-word commands, etc., is recommended. After such work is successfully completed, placement in a program for visually handicapped will probably be appropriate."

If the psychologist, in cooperation with parents, school personnel, or other professionals can obtain clear questions to be answered, rather than the typically general and broad referrals, his job will be clarified and the selection of evaluative procedures simplified. For example, instead of seeing a six-year-old blind child to make an "educational prognosis," a series of specific diagnostic questions are posed, e.g., "Are his attention span, his auditory comprehension, etc., adequate to enable him to function in a first grade classroom?" "Is his tactual discrimination adequate for beginning braille?" "Does he use his hands adequately in exploring new objects?" "Does he localize and remember sounds and objects?" "Are his self-help skills in toileting, dressing and eating sufficient to handle first grade demands?" "Is his neighborhood school or local district able to provide the necessary special education services?"

Responsiveness to teaching is often more important than a blind child's present level of functioning. This is especially true in the area of mobility, where the youngster may have been grossly restricted and over-protected. Some children will not walk without tangible support or hand-holding. Occasionally, in a few minutes, the psychologist can shape this behavior substantially by using a taut rope (for support) which is gradually slackened.

Auditory receptive language can sometimes be assessed, even in the absence of expressive vocal language, by asking the child simple questions of high interest to him. Candy bars or soda pop, while not found in Hoyle's rules of testing, may be useful not only in checking auditory comprehension but also sound localization.

To sum up so far, standardized as well as informal assessment techniques form the launching pad from which the diagnostic-treatment flight begins. If we keep in mind that evaluation must go beyond a mere classifying or labelling and answer questions with specific recommendations, then the formulation of these specific questions will lead almost automatically to a proper selection of testing procedures. The information obtained from these measures can then be translated into educational procedures recommended for maximum development.

This concept of evaluation for the purpose of recommending procedures to maximize development is based on the underlying notion of the educability of the exceptional child. More and more evidence is accumulating which underscores the importance of recognizing that cognitive development is inextricably dependent upon and related to experience. If we err, and err we must occasionally, we must do so on the side of being willing to explore the possible beneficial effects of a stimulating environment in overcoming earlier deprivation.

In the context of environmental and sensory deprivation it is well to briefly examine the continuum of the sighted world's perceptions of the limitations inherent in blindness. The extremes are perhaps exemplified by blindness seen as a minor annoyance and hindrance to unencumbered mobility versus blindness seen as the greatest deprivation, sensory and emotional, that can befall man. While psychiatric and psychoanalytic literature has had a heyday with speculations about blindness perceived as punishment for sin or as castration, etc., most educators prefer to emphasize that we are dealing with a *child* who doesn't see. It is very possible to impose limitations beyond those of loss of vision. The story is told of the young boy who wanted his blind father to go horseback riding. When the father protested that he couldn't because he was blind, the child countered "But, Daddy, the *horse* isn't!" All psychologists who evaluate blind children should examine their own attitudes toward expectations for the blind. Extreme positions of either denying the real limitations or of imposing unreal and unnecessary restrictions can bias the interpretation of a child's behavior.

One of the particular problems with which psychologists might be asked to deal it that of whether a visually handicapped child should be educationally classed as blind or partially seeing. In an ideal situation, the opthalmologist and optometrist can help translate the child's visual functioning into an educational recommendation. But occasionally the data given to the school is limited to a Snellen notation of 20/200 in each eye, or "counts fingers as five feet," etc. One eye specialist's report was seen recently which indicated that the child's visual acuity could not be determined and therefore he should "be put in the front row or in the blind school." This kind of information is not too helpful in deciding whether a child should be taught braille or print reading. How should the psychologist proceed? Every effort, of course, should be made to obtain all pertinent medical information.

But the correlation between functional vision and visual acuity is far from perfect and these are cases where the child must be given an opportunity to answer the question for us by a trial period with print. He can also be a valuable guide in selecting type size, lighting conditions, and reading posture. Barraga (1963)[2] provides convincing evidence that specific training significantly increased the level of visual functioning of blind children, although acuity was unchanged. This study should perhaps become required reading for those professionally concerned with the legally blind child who is "borderline" educationally blind.

Whatever else blindness may or may not limit, it does hinder mobility. Thus willingness and ability to explore the environment often become of special interest. A few years ago a psychologist who specializes in the diagnosis of language disorders was observed evaluating a non-speaking four-year-old blind child. The child wasn't the least interested in the red plastic cars offered to him but was highly intrigued by the radiator gurglings which he located immediately. Several times he left the too-large chair in which he had been placed in front of the pegboard and went swiftly and surely to his mother who was on the far side of the unfamiliar room. He thoroughly and systematically explored (orally, manually, and auditorily) several objects which he encountered in his unauthorized roamings around the room. However, the combination of his lack of language and his refusal to play the planned games (actually he appeared very undisciplined) totally outweighed his mobility and explorative skills in the psychologists' judgment and he was classified as severely mentally retarded.

Language problems are not infrequent in young blind children. Sometimes speech has not developed by the age or three or four. Occasionally excessive echolalia or other deviant verbal patterns (e.g., improper pronoun usage) associated with autistic behavior are reported. The fact that these language disorders perhaps occur more frequently in blind than in seeing youngsters suggests interesting etiological speculations. The implications of this greater incidence of language disorders (if thoroughly substantiated) could conceivably point either toward parental attitudes or toward physical factors as the etiological culprits. But neither line would be of immediate use to the psychologist who is attempting, hopefully, to recommend procedures for developing language, rather than settling for a diag-

Evaluation of Blind Child

Test and Observation Data	Psychological Evaluation	Decision-Making or Recommendations
Language	1. Determination of area concern (Column 3). Exactly *what* is to be evaluated and for what purpose?	Type of nursery school
Speech present		School readiness
Speech echolalic		
Auditory comprehension		Speech correction
Auditory memory		Braille vs. print
Grammar & syntax	2. Choosing best instruments and techniques available (Column 1) in order to check the *relevant* areas of function.	Continuance in public school
Etc.		
Mobility		Placement as multiply handicapped
Motor coordination		
Strength	3. Properly interpreting the data obtained in step 2, in order to make appropriate recommendations.	Removal from home
Attitude toward mobility		Parent counseling
Sound localization		Need for travel training
Etc.		Etc.
Tactile Sensitivity		
Discrimination		(These are illustrative only)
Recognition		
Memory		
Attitude toward exploration		

nosis of "delayed language development" or "inadequate language with some autistic-like characteristics." Some evidence (Eisenberg, 1956) [3] suggests that presence of speech by the age of five is a fairly good prognostication of future language development. Comprehension of the spoken word and the presence of any consistent, meaningful use of vocalization should certainly suggest that a trial period of specific language training is in order before a definite prognosis is attempted. The blind child's need and opportunity for expressive language in the home must be considered relevant.

Questions of where a blind child should be educated are often heard, perhaps ever more frequently now that public schools are providing local programs for half the blind children of school age in this country. Years ago, in its *Pinebrook Report*, the American Foundation for the Blind outlined its position: namely, that residential schools, resource rooms, and intinerant teacher services all have necessary roles to play and that none will completely replace another. This position is as valid as ever and suggests to the psychologist that the problem is not one of residential school versus public school, but rather one of which facility can best serve the individual blind child. Often the desirability of living at home or of being away from home will be a major consideration. In cases of borderline vision, the tendency found by Jones (1961) [4] for such children in residential schools to be braille readers and those in public schools to be print readers should be weighed.

Perhaps the process of evaluating a blind child can be schematically presented as shown above [*p. 139*]:

The reader will notice an absence of emphasis on global measures such as IQ and, instead, a concentration on specific abilities. This represents a bias, but one which is advocated on the grounds that it is practical. The bias is seen to extend to the concept that, above all, psychological evaluation of blind children "ought" to be practical, i.e., ought to lead to more definite action and procedures than mere classification or determination of eligibility for program *x* or *y*. The teacher, parent, speech correctionist, or whoever else might be concerned should know more about *what to do* with or for the child after the psychological evaluation than they knew before.

REFERENCES

1. Lende, Helga. *Books About the Blind*, New York: American Foundation for the Blind, 1953.
2. Barraga, Natalie. "Effects of Experimental Teaching on the Visual Behavior of Children Educated as Though They Had No Vision." *New Outlook for the Blind*, December 1964. (Published under the title "Teaching Children with Low Vision.")
3. Eisenberg, Leon. "The Autistic Child in Adolescence." *American Journal of Psychiatry*, 1956, 112: 607.
4. Jones, J. W. *Blind Children, Degree of Vision, Mode of Reading*. Bulletin No. 24. Washington: Section on Exceptional Children and Youth, U.S. Office of Education, 1961.

15

A Psychologist Looks at the Issue of Public vs. Residential School Placement for the Blind

CONSTANCE D. AVERY

The issue of whether to place youngsters in a public school or a residential school program has been a controversial and greatly debated one for many years. There are those who have taken a very active stand in favor of public school attendance for all blind children while there are those who feel that the residential school is better qualified to handle their academic training, social development, recreational activities, and physical and manual activities. There are several issues to be considered and it is quite difficult to take a categorical stand in favor of one or the other. The factors involved in the decision of public versus residential school revolve around the individual child's intellectual level, emotional maturity, social adaptability, and the presence of additional handicaps. There are times when a child would be equally well-placed in either a public or a residential school and there are circumstances that are more appropriate for placement in one in preference to the other.

HOW THE PUBLIC SCHOOL EDUCATES THE BLIND CHILD

In some public schools the blind child is absorbed into the regular classroom. He is provided with braille materials for the blind with no useful vision or large print materials for the legally blind with limited vision. In some public schools, he remains in the same classroom and grade year after year because he does not advance at the same rate of speed as the sighted children in the same grade. The sighted children are promoted while he remains. It has not been unusual for a blind child to repeat

* From *The New Outlook for the Blind* 1968, 62, pp. 221–226. Reprinted by permission of the author and the publisher. Mrs. Avery is a school psychologist for the Mount Vernon, New York, school system.

first grade, two, three, or even four times, because his progress was measured against that of a sighted child of comparable grade.

Time Spent with Itinerant Teachers Varies

In elementary school, he may be visited by an itinerant (traveling) teacher, trained in the special techniques of teaching the blind, on a regular daily basis for a half hour to an hour. Sometimes he is seen only once a week because of the large area the itinerant teacher has to cover, and in some instances only once or twice a month because of the scarcity of itinerant teachers. The itinerant teacher uses braille textbooks and supplies the student with raised maps, diagrams, records, and tapes as teaching aids. After his session with the itinerant teacher he is again absorbed into the regular classroom with a teacher who is not usually trained in the special teaching methodology for the blind.

There are also difficulties in obtaining large print materials for all academic subjects in public schools. Sometimes it is the teacher who must have the foresight to prepare separate materials for the visually limited student ahead of time, so that he will have his own materials to use when the other students are using regular print books, the blackboard, or mimeographed materials.

Certain unusual communities have their own teacher for the blind with a resource room especially equipped with materials for teaching the blind within the school. The blind child meets with this resource teacher for regular periods during the day. The remainder of the day he attends the regular classroom, using braille or large print materials.

SOME "ADVANTAGES" OF PUBLIC SCHOOLS MIXED BLESSINGS

In public school the blind child tends to get some disconcerting "advantages." Different requirements and expectations and in general lesser degrees of performance are expected from the blind child integrated into a sighted classroom. Many teachers, used to teaching the sighted, do not appreciate the differences in the level of academic and physical performance that can be expected of the blind. As a result, they have a lower level of expectation for them and are satisfied with minimal performance and small accomplishments.

Besides the greater tendency for permissiveness towards the blind student in the public school, there exists an attitude of sympathy that is psychologically detrimental to them. There are also many people not familiar with the capacities of the blind who have unrealistically high expectations for them and are over-critical of their slowness in such things as reading, mobility, and motor coordination.

HOW THE RESIDENTIAL SCHOOL EDUCATES THE BLIND CHILD

At a residential school, the blind child is placed at the grade or group level at which he is currently functioning. Residential schools usually have fewer pupils in each classroom than public schools. They have an academic curriculum geared to the needs of blind children and are equipped with braille materials, large print texts, and special equipment, such as slate and stylus, cube slates, raised maps, and charts as aids for teaching the blind. The blind student's other qualities—intellectual level, emotional maturity, and social adaptability—are also considered in his grade placement. His academic standing changes according to his progress. There is no automatic promotion from one year to the next. In a residential school, the academic environment is just one part of the day's activities. The children have an all encompassing program geared to their needs. There are extra-curricular activities after school, sports, recreational programs, individual religious instruction, scout programs. Dormitory living, which provides opportunity for social interaction with other blind children of the same age and social maturity, is an important part of residential school life. It is a live-in social experience as well as an academic one.

It is the rare public school system that has special library facilities for the blind, whereas this is an essential part of a residential school program. The blind child in a public school is denied the advantage of large collections of braille and large print materials, as well as a source of auditory and tactile academic aids.

Paucity of Electives in Residential Schools

Because of the greater number of pupils there is a wider scope of academic electives in high school than can be provided in a residential school. There is also a greater choice of language than the single foreign language offered in many schools for the blind. There are other electives available to the high school student, but the blind student usually cannot take advantage of many of them such as bookkeeping and shorthand.

One argument states that the blind should be educated with sighted students so that they may be treated as normally as possible. However, in the process of being treated "normally" in a public school setting the particular limitations of the blind are more likely denied than recognized, accepted, and respected in drawing up an academic curriculum. If blind persons must compete with sighted people after graduation, as residential and public school personnel both recognize, they should be educated and prepared in the best manner available. This means taking into consideration their limitations, while still preparing them to compete vocationally in a sighted world. It must be remembered, when exposing the blind to the sighted world of a public school setting, it is the needs of the majority, the sighted, who are considered. The best preparation for a recognizedly different population is a special approach and individualized facilities that will still achieve the end result of a thorough education.

Few Services for Multi-handicapped Blind in Public Schools

There are practically no services available for the multi-handicapped blind child in the present public school curriculum. Thus, the mentally retarded blind, the deaf-blind, the organically brain-damaged blind, and the psychologically disturbed blind are relatively neglected in the public schools, if they are allowed to attend at all.

Due to the limited number of blind children, there are limited facilities for manual and physical activities in a public school setting. Blind children in public schools most often do without physical education, sports, industrial arts, metal, electrical, and woodworking shop, and art instruction because there are not enough of them to warrant the facilities and special teaching methods required. The blind child may go to public school for his academic work, but he is provided with little or no exposure to the supplementary activities that are considered a requisite part of a well-rounded school program for the sighted. The blind child is supposedly "absorbed" within a regular sighted gymnastic program. On investigation, however, he remains on the sidelines and is not involved in the entire gymnastic program. The blind child has to adapt himself as best he can to the existing facilities geared to the sighted or be eliminated from playground, physical, and recreational activities altogether.

Within the school curriculum there are rarely special braille music programs. Public school teachers are not familiar with braille music so the blind cannot be taught a musical instrument within the school setting. Art is not adapted for a blind child and so he is excluded from an arts and crafts program. Dramatic activities and scientific field trips are additional activities from which he is excluded. Nor are courses in mobility training customarily available within public schools.

Special Programs in Residential Schools

Residential schools have playground activities geared to the blind student, and gymnasium facilities and music, art, and crafts programs that are adapted and taught with special attention to the limitations of the students. There are shop programs, that may include cabinetmaking, chair caning, metal work, and electrical maintenance and repair, available under the supervision of manual arts instructors trained in teaching the blind. Many residential schools have programs in ceramics and piano tuning, that are not available in public school. The public school depends on outside agencies for services that are usually considered an integral part of residential school services, such as medical services, readers, and mobility instruction.

Social Integration Limited in Residential Schools

Most residential schools afford only limited interaction between the blind students at school and sighted population in public school. Some residential schools make the attempt to bring blind and sighted groups together. Sighted scout troops and 4-H groups are invited to have joint sessions with the blind.

It is very difficult to arrange integrated dances for blind and sighted groups, however, because sighted teenagers are not anxious to attend. Thus the blind are denied extensive socializing with sighted peers. Both blind and sighted educators working with the blind recognize that no matter how the blind try to rationalize it and how charitable the sighted try to be, the blind child is different from the sighted. Some blind persons make use of mannerisms, such as poking fingers in their eyes and rocking back and forth, making them appear even more different and strange to the sighted.

Is the Blind Child Accepted in a Public School?

The blind child has great expectations when he goes to public school that he will be accepted on an equal basis with the sighted. He imagines that he will be welcomed as "one of the group" and absorbed into the social milieu like a sighted person. Unfortunately the sighted in public school do not mingle with a blind person readily or comfortably. The blind student's differences are easily recognized. The sighted child, who in the beginning might enjoy the novelty of guiding the blind person to class, eventually rebels against this imposition on his time and freedom. The blind student, no matter how pleasing and mobile, is still recognized as blind. He is accepted and integrated in a limited fashion within the sighted regime of a public school. Unfortunately, after a blind child begins public school, he and his family cannot easily admit that he is not faring as well as expected. The family becomes defensive because the child has been put in public school with great expectations. The parents defend their decision and are committed to saying that the child is doing well socially.

The blind child in both public and residential school is usually not afforded sufficient training in the skills of grooming, dressing, and eating, that are taken for granted as social amenities learned by the sighted before entering school. The physical appearance of a blind person who is not given special training in good grooming, dressing, and eating, is labeled as strange. Public schools do not attempt to train the blind in daily living skills. Residential schools make an effort to give this training, although many are admittedly weak in teaching these basic skills.

A great concern of residential school students is that they have no one with whom to socialize on weekends and during the summer, when school is out. Their blind companions at school come from different parts of the state and are difficult to contact or visit with when school is over. The blind are lonely on weekends and during the summer recess at home. Not being absorbed into their sighted neighborhood through attending a school in the community, they lack contact with their sighted peers, and there are few or no blind friends nearby with whom to socialize. Public school attendance enables the blind to make contact with children in their own communities with whom they can become better acquainted after school hours.

BLIND STUDENTS PROFIT SOCIALLY FROM PUBLIC HIGH SCHOOLS

Blind students appear to do better at public high school than they do at public elementary school. They profit more socially from the mixed milieu of sighted and blind since the sighted population is older and more sophisticated. At the elementary and junior high level, youngsters tend to discriminate on the basis of superficialities, such as a person's comeliness, the intactness of his physical faculties, whether his dress is fashionable, and whether he is "like everybody else." At the high school and, particularly, at the college level the blind student's sighted peers are better able to accept him on the basis of his character and personality assets, his academic achievement, and his vocational direction rather than on the basis of his physical appearance and physical limitations. The real social integration of the blind and sighted probably comes after they have finished their academic training and work together vocationally and professionally. The great equalizer of acceptance is more apt to be work performance than physical appearance or physical limitations. Vocational efficiency and productivity become the measure of a person's value.

There are many issues to be considered and several problems to be resolved to effect better solutions for the training of the blind in both residential and public schools. Both have advantages and special disadvantages for the academic training, social interaction, recreational, physical, and manual arts activities that are part of a total educational background. Part of the solution for bettering the education and training of the blind child is for public and residential schools to work closer together to incorporate the advantages of each within the regime of the other, while still recognizing the special attributes and advantages of each.

RESIDENTIAL SCHOOL SHOULD OFFER MORE ELECTIVES

The residential schools could profit from incorporating a wider scope of academic electives for their students including a wider choice of languages. They could allow their students greater social opportunities, by offering more activities whereby sighted groups attend functions at the residential school or residential students attend integrated school dances and community activities. The child in a residential school should be afforded more social activities in his own community. He should be encouraged to join local social and recreational organizations and not to confine his socializing to the residential school setting alone. Community organizations such as the YMCA, community centers, and church groups should afford recreational facilities for the blind so that the blind in both residential and public schools may have programs geared to their limitations as well as integrated social, physical, and recreational activities with the sighted, where this is feasible.

Public Schools Should be More Flexible with Blind Students

The public school needs to take into consideration not only the chronological age of the blind student in grade or group placement, but the child's intellectual level, emotional maturity, and social adaptability. The public school should attempt a more flexible program of promotion for the blind student, so that he is carefully moved in academic standing according to his progress. The public school could profit from the advantages afforded by the residential school's smaller classes. Most public schools need to enlarge their supplies of braille materials, large print texts, and special equipment, such as the auditory and tactile academic aids that are considered necessary adjuncts to a school program. Public schools must consider the implementation of special facilities and teaching methods for extracurricular activities. Sports programs, physical education facilities, industrial arts programs, metal, electrical, woodworking shop, art instruction, music braille programs, arts and crafts, dramatics, and scientific field trips should be provided for the blind in a public school setting. The public school needs within its program integrated services that include medical services, readers for the blind, and mobility instruction. Both residential and public schools need increased emphasis on special training for the blind in the social amenities of grooming, dressing, and eating skills.

The public school could profit from a public information program designed to help their sighted students understand the needs and limitations of blind students as well as their similarities to the sighted, so that the blind can be better accepted at all education levels.

COMPETITION BETWEEN PUBLIC AND RESIDENTIAL SCHOOLS MUST BE ELIMINATED

It is most important that the severe competition and rivalry that currently exists between many public and residential schools be eliminated in the interests of what is best for the blind child rather than on the basis of chauvinistic protection of a particular regime. Thus, if a blind child does not fare well in public school and it is more appropriate for him to return to residential school, it should not be interpreted as a loss of face to the child and his parents and a failure for the integrated public school program. This will make it difficult for the child's parents to countenance returning him to a residential school. The residential school should not guard its territory so zealously that, if a residential child shows sufficient intellectual potential and social adaptability as well as no formidable additional handicaps, it can relinquish him and allow him to continue his education within a public school setting.

REFERENCES

Abel, G. "Problems and Trends in the Education of Blind Children and Youth," *Concerning the Education of Blind Children*, American Foundation for the Blind, New York, 1959.

Davis, A. "Special Education in Atlanta," *The New Outlook for the Blind*, December, 1961.

Frampton, M. "The Tragedy of Modern Day Education for the Blind as Practiced in the Integrated Public Day School Classes," The New York Institute for the Education of the Blind.

Hunter, P. "Education of Handicapped Children in Residential Schools," *School Life*, U.S. Department of Health, Education, and Welfare, Office of Education, 1964.

Sibert, K. "An Itinerant Teacher's Aims," *The New Outlook for the Blind*, March, 1961.

"The Perkins Program," Perkins School for the Blind, Perkins Publication 24, Mass., June, 1964.

"The Pine Brook Report," National Work Session on the Education of the Blind with the Sighted, American Foundation for the Blind, No. 2, Group Reports, New York, 1954.

Wolman, M. "Preschool and Kindergarten Child Attitudes Toward the Blind in an Integrated Program," *The New Outlook for the Blind*, 52, 4, 1958.

** 16 **

Merits of Special Class, Resource, and Itinerant Plans for Teaching Partially Seeing Children

THOMAS M. STEPHENS AND JACK W. BIRCH

This review is concerned with organizational accommodations used in the special education of partially seeing children. It first deals briefly with the history of fulltime special classes, the resource teacher approach, and the itinerant teacher approach as organizational patterns. Opinions about organizational patterns and their purposes and relative effectiveness are then summarized. Finally, research evidence is presented on the contributions of various organizational patterns to attaining the educational objectives for partially seeing children.

Partially seeing children are defined as visually handicapped children who use ink print as a major mode of construction. They are children who have visual acuity between approximately 20/70 and 20/200 after optimum correction or who have other visual disabilities and, in the opinion of a vision specialist, can benefit from special instruction.

ORGANIZATIONAL SCHEMES

Three distinct day school organizational plans used for the special education of partially seeing students (Jones, 1963) are:

1. The fulltime special class in which all academic instruction is with a special teacher in a classroom containing only visually limited children.
2. The resource teacher plan in which partially seeing students are enrolled in a regular classroom and obtain most of their instruction within the regular class; the students go to the resource teacher in the special room for instruction and to use special materials as determined by individual requirements.
3. The itinerant teacher plan in which a specialist in teaching partially

∗ From *Exceptional Children* 1969, *35*, pp. 481–485. Reprinted by permission of the senior author and the publisher.

seeing children travels from school to school in order to provide parttime individual instruction to students and to offer consultant services to regular classroom teachers who have partially seeing students in their classes.

Provisions for partially seeing children in public schools in the United States began in 1913 when day classes for such children were started in Boston and, later that same year, in Cleveland. The class in Boston was housed in a special building separate from normal children. In Cleveland, a cooperative plan was devised whereby partially seeing children engaged in activities requiring special materials and techniques in the special class but participated with normally seeing students in activities not requiring close visual work (Hathaway, 1953).

As educators developed programs for partially seeing youth, some used the Boston special day school plan as a model and others emulated Cleveland's cooperative scheme. No evidence has been found, however, to link those historical events with theoretical positions or educational research findings to that era.

Educators have devised many procedures, through the years, to provide for intellectual, academic, and physical differences of students. While present innovations in organizational modifications for instruction are made primarily to facilitate learning, Goodlad (1960) has noted that other purposes also are served. These include financial considerations, administrative ease, and teacher satisfaction. The present authors would add the influence of individuals who have strong views and who are in leadership positions as another factor to consider when attempting to account for the organizational patterns which have developed in the education of partially seeing children and youth.

OPINIONS—ITINERANT AND RESOURCE PLANS

A survey of the literature concerned with administration of special education for the visually handicapped reinforced Dunn's (1963) conclusion that there appear to be no studies concerned with the advantages or disadvantages of one plan of organization or concerned with comparisons among plans up to the time of his publication. Only one seems to have been made since 1963 (Stephens, 1966) and it will be referred to later in this review.

However, without a basis in specific research, many arguments have been offered in support of itinerant teacher plans and resource teacher approaches in preference to special classes. Jones (1963) cited five of what he stated are the most frequently reported advantages:

1. *Similarities.* Emphasis is placed on the child's abilities and likeness to other children rather than on his differences.

2. *Resources.* The wealth of resources within the regular school program is made available to these children by including them in most general school activities.

3. *Multihandicaps.* The services of specially prepared teachers may be made available more easily to visually handicapped children who have additional major handicaps, and to both blind and partially seeing children when they are not kept together in the special class during the entire school day. The mentally retarded child who is also visually handicapped, for instance, can be enrolled in a special class for mentally retarded children, but still be served by resource or itinerant teachers specially prepared to instruct visually handicapped children.

4. *Individualized.* Under these plans teachers of the visually handicapped devote fulltime to individualized instruction of children. . . .

5. *Social.* The visually handicapped child is educated in a setting more nearly approximating that which he will encounter in adult life [pp. 35–36].

The advantages of itinerant and resource plans reviewed by Jones are presumably less likely to be available to partially seeing children in fulltime special classes. Clearly, these arguments imply that the itinerant and resource plans permit more flexibility than does the special class plan.

Ashcroft (1963) believed that the itinerant plan was often characterized by sound educational practices. He described the direct services to students performed by the teachers as tutorial and remedial in nature. Usually, the direct services take the form of assistance to students in the use of equipment and special materials and in counseling services. Itinerant plans seemed more desirable to him at the secondary level after the students had instruction in programs similar to resource teacher plans where more services are available.

Ashcroft reasoned that as partially seeing students become more proficient in basic skills they can function effectively with less comprehensive help. The earliest statement of that line of reasoning the present authors found was presented 27 years ago by Pintner (1942). He found what appeared to be a decline in median IQ scores between the ages of 10 and 12 years in students in "sight conservation" (fulltime day) classes. The 1937 Revised Stanford-Binet was used; the total group included 602 partially seeing children. A median IQ score of 97 was found for the 10 year olds in his sample. The 12 year olds had a medial IQ score of 90. Pintner attributed this difference to a belief that the more intelligent partially seeing subjects were returned to regular classes between the ages of 10 and 12. Unfortunately he did not report a test of the significance of the difference between the median IQ scores for the two age groups. When the present authors applied a chi square test to his data, the difference in median IQ scores between the two age groups was not significant at the .01 level of confidence. Thus if a criterion of the rigor of the .01 level of confidence is used, there is no ground for considering the observed difference a real one, since chance factors could have contributed to the difference in median IQ's.

Morin (1960) credited an itinerant plan with two noninstructional advantages: (a) reduced transportation costs because the students were able to attend their neighborhood schools, and (b) the itinerant teacher being able to serve more visually limited children. No evidence was reported as to the effectiveness of this plan in relation to academic achievements.

Sibert (1960) described an itinerant teacher program in which the students were seen individually by the teacher for one hour a week. Consultant services were provided by the itinerant teacher to regular classroom teachers regarding proper seating, lighting, and use of special materials and equipment. No data concerning the effectiveness of the program were reported.

The Chicago Public Schools use a resource room placement for children with severe vision impairments who need an intensive program of special teaching. Placement in an itinerant program is made for visually handicapped children with impaired vision at the lower limits of the range for special education services (Powers, Schall, & Welsch, 1965). Again, no evidence was presented to support the differential use of facilities.

Bertram (1958) stated that the itinerant plan can accommodate children from a wide range of ability levels, while the resource plan tends to require intellectual functioning within the average range. But she provided no evidence to suport her contention.

Taken together, the arguments presented favor both itinerant and resource approaches, with nothing said in support of the special class. Differential use of organizational patterns is recommended by many, with the implication that a school system should include both the itinerant and resource plans. They should be accessible to all children so that those who would profit more from one or the other may be so placed. It is important to note that the above summary statements are neither supported nor refuted by research.

RESEARCH EVIDENCE

Bertram's (1958) claim implies that the itinerant plan allows for more flexibility of instruction than the resource teacher plan. If she is correct, the mean score on intelligence measures for pupils in itinerant plans should be less than for pupils in resource plans, since more partially seeing children of lower intelligence would be found in itinerant plans. Also, the span of pupil intelligence found in itinerant programs, as indicated by such measures as range and standard deviation, should be greater than those found in resource plans. However, a comparison study (Stephens, 1966) of 768 subjects in itinerant and resource plans yielded the reverse, a significant difference in mean IQ scores ($p < .01$) in favor of the itinerant group; the same study showed no significant difference between standard deviations of the IQ scores for the two groups.

Opinions have been expressed to support the belief that partially seeing children who are served by itinerant teachers may have acquired higher levels of academic skills than those provided for through the other plans, with the result that the itinerant teacher needs to have less contact with the students (Ashcroft, 1963). Those who are unable to keep pace academically with only the brief, infrequent contacts with an itinerant teacher would, presumably, be taught by a resource teacher or placed in a special class. If Ashcroft's observations are correct, students in itinerant plans should demonstrate higher academic achievement than those partially seeing children in special classes or resource plans. That position does have some research support. Stephens (1966) found a significant difference when mean scores on the Metropolitan Achievement Test were compared among the three organizational plans, with subjects in itinerant plans having a higher mean score than the children in the other two plans.

Jones and Collins (1965) found that only 16 percent of the programs in a national survey use the fulltime special class plan. But it should not be assumed that only 16 percent of partially seeing children are in fulltime classes. In a recent study of national scope Birch, Tisdall, Peabody, & Sterrett (1966) found that most partially seeing children in the elementary grades are in fulltime special classes. Apparently the districts which enroll large numbers of partially seeing students also tend to use many fulltime special classes. Special class plans do continue to be used. One can surmise that financial considerations may determine when a special class plan will not be used, since it requires a group of partially seeing children in the same building in order to justify the assignment of a teacher.

Another possible reason for the continued use of special classes for partially seeing students may be that regular teachers are reluctant to have these children in their classrooms (Murphy, 1960). When this reluctance exists, isolating these children from regular classes would probably serve to perpetuate unwillingness on the part of regular teachers to receive partially seeing students in their classes.

Historically, there seems to be no theoretical or research based rationale which has guided the development of resource, itinerant, or special class programs. The available opinions are sometimes consistent and sometimes inconsistent with the limited research information available. All things considered, the literature is inconclusive as to the contributions various organizational plans make to the school achievement of partially seeing children.

REFERENCES

Ashcroft, S. C. Blind and partially seeing children. In L. M. Dunn (Ed.), *Exceptional children in the schools*. New York: Holt, Rinehart and Winston, 1963. Pp. 413–461.

Bertram, F. The education of partially sighted children. In W. M. Cruickshank & G. O. Johnson (Eds.), *Education of exceptional children and youth.* Englewood Cliffs, N.J.: Prentice-Hall, 1958. Pp. 265–294.

Birch, J. W., Tisdall, W. J., Peabody, R. L., & Sterrett, R. *School achievement and effect of type size on reading in visually handicapped children.* Pittsburgh, Pa.: University of Pittsburgh, 1966.

Dunn, L. M. An overview. In L. M. Dunn (Ed.), *Exceptional children in the schools.* New York: Holt, Rinehart and Winston, 1963. Pp. 1–51.

Goodlad, J. I. Classroom organization. In C. W. Harris (Ed.), *Encyclopedia of educational research.* New York: MacMillan, 1960. Pp. 413–461.

Hathaway, W. An historical view of the education of partially seeing children. *Sight Saving Review,* 1953, 23, 148–156.

Jones, J. W. *The visually handicapped child.* Washington: US Department of Health, Education and Welfare, 1963.

Jones, J. W., & Collins, A. P. Trends in program and pupil placement practices in the special education of visually handicapped children. *The Education of the Blind,* 1965, 14, 97–101.

Morin, A. Waukegan finds advantages in the itinerant teacher plan. *Sight Saving Review,* 1960, 30, 31–35.

Murphy, A. T. Attitudes of educators toward the visually handicapped. *Sight Saving Review,* 1960, 30, 31–35.

Pinter, R. Intelligence testing of partially sighted children. *Journal of Educational Psychology,* 1942, 33, 265–272.

Powers, M. H., Schall, S. M., & Welsch, R. A. Utilization of medical information in school planning for visually handicapped children. *Exceptional Children,* 1965, 32, 5–14.

Sibert, K. N. Instructional materials and procedures for the partially seeing. *Sight Saving Review,* 1960, 30, 162–165.

Stephens, T. M. Organizational plans for partially seeing children in grades five and six relative to language achievement and individual differences. Unpublished manuscript, University of Pittsburgh, 1966.

** 17 **

Multiple Disabilities—
An Old Problem with a New Challenge:
A Review of the Literature

JAMES M. WOLF

Historically, children with two or more disabilities have been described as doubly afflicted, doubly-defective, dual handicapped, doubly handicapped, multi-handicapped, multiple handicapped, multiply handicapped, additionally handicapped, multiply exceptional, and multiple disabled. In recent years these descriptive terms have been used to designate children with two or more disabilities so severe as to make it impossible for them to profit satisfactorily from an educational program established for any one of the disabilities. Much confusion stems from terminology currently in vogue to describe these children, and this quandary makes it difficult for educators to plan and organize special programs. It also complicates the collection of incidence and prevalence data. From the origin of the special education movement the problem of multiple disabilities has beseiged educators and medical specialists. For over a century and a quarter educators have expressed concern for children with multiple disabilities, but little progress has been made in finding solutions, even after a hundred and twenty-five years of "viewing with alarm."

Current interest in multiple disabilities is stimulated by the increased number of such children in the population. Medical science has reduced the infant mortality rate and has also extended life by more effective control of acute infection and disease. Many children who years ago would have died as a result of infection or disease are alive today because of modern medical practices. A large number of these children must live out their remaining years under handicap of one or more disabilities.[1] Professional and public awareness of disabilities is reflected in the increased identification of children with such conditions in the rapidly expanding child population.

Kirk[2] recommended the initiation of research projects to determine the

* From *The New Outlook for the Blind* 1965, 59, pp. 265–271. Reprinted by permission of the author and the publisher.

most desirable ways to provide for children with multiple disabilities. Goodenough [3] indicated that "even with the best of training, only a few of the children who suffer from more than one major defect can become capable of complete self-support in a world of normal people." Cruickshank and Trippe [4] write that there are few educational problems which are more complex, or which require more immediate thought, than does the problem of multiple disabilities in children. Wishik [5] reports that since the majority of handicapped children have multiple disabilities, consideration should be given to ways of meeting this situation more efficiently.

Although there is recognition of a higher incidence of multiple disabilities among exceptional children, there exists neither accurate census data as to the kinds of these additional disabilities nor effective methodology for teaching such children. Farber has stated that "Perhaps further investigation of the problem of multiple handicaps (disabilities) as an exceptionality will indicate directions for developing special education programs." [6]

INCIDENCE AND PREVALENCE STUDIES

Wishik, [5, 7] in a study of prevalence, disability, needs, and resources of handicapped children in the State of Georgia, found that handicapped children had an average of 2.2 disabilities each. Only 29 per cent of the handicapped children had one disability; 39 per cent had two disabilities; 17 per cent had three; and 10 per cent had four.

Farber, [6] in an extensive census of exceptional children in Illinois, found in ages seven to seventeen a total multiple disability prevalence rate of eleven per 1,000 children. He also found that 18 per cent of the exceptional children ages seven to sixteen not attending school had multiple disabilities.

An investigation of ten school districts of Westchester County, New York, revealed a high incidence of children with multiple disabilities in an economically and culturally favored population. [8]

Mackie, et al., in reporting statistics on education for exceptional children states that many exceptional children have more than one disability, which creates a dilemma regarding how they should be classified:

> Many of them, (children with multiple disability) furthermore, receive more than one kind of special education service, for example, speech correction and special teaching for the hard of hearing or cerebral palsied. The solution which has been used is to request that each child be counted once only according to his major disability. [9]

The authors do not suggest a rationale by which the primacy of one disability should be selected over another. Mackie's position is illustrative of professional preoccupation with classification schemes that lean heavily on medical systems which categorize children by pathological descriptions. In such classifications a priority is assigned to the extant disabilities and the professional worker deals with handicap in a unitary fashion, and in the case of two (or more) disorders, a priority is established. Arbitrary decisions are made in regard to which disabilities are primary and which are secondary. Cleft palate, cerebral palsy, orthopedic disorders, and heart abnormalities are usually primary. Mental retardation that exists with cerebral palsy is considered secondary, the cerebral palsy primary. The terms impairment, disability, and handicap are used loosely in such classification schemes and many times interchangeably.

Stevens,[10] in conceptualizing a taxonomy in special education for children with body disorders, considers these terms strategic and gives them definition: *impairment* is defined as defective (diseased or disordered) tissue; *disability* is the term intended to convey the meaning of general loss of body organ function—it is, in fact, a synonym for organ dysfunction; *handicap* is the term intended to convey the concept of the personal and social burden which is imposed on the person when confronted with a situation which cannot be resolved by reason of body dysfunction or impairment. Only recently is more concern being shown for making a distinction between these terms.[11, 12]

It is Steven's view that the dilemma involved in classifications of multiple disabilities can be resolved by standardizing classification language, since it provides the rationale for shifting the emphasis to the handicapping consequence of the two (or more) disabilities. For example, deafness and blindness is the partial basis for the ensuing handicap:

> The educator will view the communication deficit as being of primary importance and translates the disability data language to mean he cannot build communication skills in visual or auditory modalities. The handicap is to be viewed as a description of the behavior phenomena and the description of the disability becomes the etiological explanation.[10]

This same logic applies equally well to other combinations of disability and provides a concept of multiple disability from which educational significance can be deduced which dictates the educational processes within predictable limits.

Other investigators studying one particular disability category of exceptionality have noted, as has Mackie, that these children seldom have a unitary disability. For example, a census conducted of children referred because of a presumptive diagnosis of mental retardation in Onondaga County, New York, found accompanying disabilities in one-third of the mentally retarded children enumerated.[13] In another study of 412 handicapped children, Stifler, et al.,[14] found that only 3 per cent of these children had one disability while 70 per cent had three to six additional disabilities. Quibell, et al.,[15] in a study of crippled children, noted that 90 per cent of these patients had two or more disabilities. Fouracre[16] found that 80 per cent of 171 crippled children had multiple disabilities.

MULTIPLE DISABILITIES AND CEREBRAL PALSY

The cerebral palsied child with multiple disabilities has been the subject for numerous investigations. Cruickshank [17] has formulated a functional classification of eight distinct types of multiple handicapped cerebral palsied children. Cardwell [18] reports that multiple disabilities are common in children with cerebral palsy; 50 per cent of these children have visual defects; 25 per cent have hearing impairments; 50 to 75 per cent have speech defects; and 50 per cent have convulsive disorders.

Asher and Schonnel, [19] Holloran, [20] and Heilman [21] have conducted incidence studies of the extent of mental retardation among cerebral palsied children and concur that approximately 75 per cent of these children are below average in intelligence and at least 50 per cent are seriously retarded or mentally defective. Their findings are inconsistent with earlier studies and statements of McIntire [22] and Phelps, [23] who found that 70 per cent of all cerebral palsied children were of normal intelligence.

MULTIPLE DISABILITIES AND IMPAIRED HEARING

Doctor [24] has emphasized the seriousness of multiple disabilities in the field of deafness. Incidence and prevalence reports by Frisina, [25] Doctor, [26] Leonhouts, [27] Hoffmeyer, [1] and Weir [28] reveal discrepancies in the number of disabilities reported among deaf children. These estimates range from 4.5 per cent to 15 per cent.

Investigations by Birch and Matthews, [20] Schlanger, [30] Johnston and Farrell, [31] Siegenthaler and Kryzwicki [32] show a high incidence of hearing impairment in mentally retarded children, and estimates range from 13 to 49 per cent depending upon the criteria used. The estimates range from 3 to 10 per cent in public school children. [33]

DEAF-BLIND DIAD

Concern for the deaf-blind in the United States emerged early in the history of special education and had its origin with the tutoring of Laura Bridgman by Samuel Gridley Howe. [34] The most instrumental force in developing interest in the deaf-blind was the successful education of Helen Keller by Anne Sullivan Macy. [35] Helen Keller undoubtedly has had great influence on calling attention to multiple disabilities. She has described the deaf-blind disability as, "a comparatively few people surrounded by a multitude of cruel problems." [36]

The register of the American Foundation for the Blind shows 372 deaf-blind children in the United States as of January 1, 1960. There are relatively few children in the deaf-blind group compared to other multiple disability groups. The National Study Committee on the Education of Deaf-Blind Children provides the following definition which has educational implications:

> A deaf-blind child is one whose combination of handicaps (disability) prevents him from profiting satisfactorily from educational programs provided for the blind child or the deaf child.[37]

This definition implies that children with two or more disabilities so severe as to make it impossible for them to profit from a program established for any one of the disabilities are in need of special facilities and services. A recommendation for research on this topic was made at a Conference of Educators of Deaf-Blind Children held at Perkins School in 1953.

MENTALLY RETARDED-BLIND

For years the mental retardation-blind diad has received special attention of educators of the blind. A paper was read on the subject of the feeble-minded blind child at the International Conference on the Blind in 1906. It was concluded that feeble-minded blind children when admitted to schools for the blind "not only absorb undue energy from caretakers and teachers but also exert a deteriorating influence on the rest; hence, they should not be received into a school for the blind." [38]

Early proceedings of the American Association of Instructors of the Blind (1918) [39] record serious questions of "what to do with the feeble-minded blind child." Through the years terms have changed, but the question— what to do with the mentally retarded blind child—still remains largely unanswered.

The problem is becoming more critical today with the increased number of blind children. There was spectacular growth in enrollments of blind children in local public school programs between 1948 and 1958. Mackie, et al.,[9] reports a 448 per cent increase in this period. The gain did not result from a loss of enrollments in residential schools, for these enrollments also increased during the period by 34 per cent.

Fraenkel [40] states, "with few exceptions, blind-retarded persons live in a socialized 'no-man's land.' Too often they are shunted between agencies or persons who can provide little or no assistance."

Long,[41] concerned over the lack of resources available to blind children with multiple disabilities, attempted to study the problem through a questionnaire returned from fifty-nine institutions for the blind and fifty-five institutions for the crippled. Her findings indicate that a little more than half of the cerebral palsy-blind children applying for admission to institutions for the blind and/or institutions for the crippled were accepted for placement between the years 1942 and 1952. Long strongly recommended coordinated services for the blind child with multiple disabilities.

The American Printing House for the Blind [42] reported the results of a survey of multiple disabilities among children in residential schools and day classes for the visually impaired. The study revealed that 19.6 per cent of visually impaired children included in the study had one or more disabilities in addition to blindness. Residential school programs had fewer (18.5 per cent) multiple handicapped children than day school programs (24.4 per cent). Mental retardation was found in 7.9 per cent of the blind children.

Paraskeva,[43] in a survey of twenty-nine residential schools for the blind, found that approximately 15 per cent of the blind students were also mentally retarded. A trend was noted that more residential schools for the blind were willing to take more mentally retarded blind children into residential schools. In the past most of these schools excluded blind children with multiple disabilities. Long and Perry[44] surveyed forty-three residential schools for the blind and found a total of one thousand mentally retarded blind children. The report emphasized the need for research on the methodology for teaching mentally retarded blind children.

Norris, et al.,[45] in a five-year study of approximately 300 blind preschool children in the Chicago area, noted that some blind children committed to institutions received psychological ratings which were average or above. The fact that 84 per cent of these children had other disabilities in addition to blindness was thought to be a major factor in the placement. DiMichael indicates that 10 to 14 per cent of blind children in the age range five to seventeen are retarded. He wonders, however, about the validity of the intelligence score:

> The basic question is whether the IQ and MA guides given for the educable and trainable apply without change to the retarded-blind. We would expect that they would not because the individuals have two disabilities; in fact, it would be more correct to say that most of them have multiple disabilities.[46]

Additional disorders such as cleft palate or crippling conditions in blind children are easily detected. Many blind children have additional disabilities of an intangible behavioral nature. These children have been diagnosed as being autistic, mentally retarded, psychotic, aphasic, emotionally disturbed, and brain injured. Moor, in discussing this type of blind child, writes that "many of them have been denied admission to or have been dismissed from educational programs as being too immature, not fitting into the school, uneducable, unable to talk, or in need of more individual attention."[47] A variety of complex and interrelated factors are associated with multiple disabilities. Assessment instruments and methods are many times inadequate with this group of children (Zwarensteyn and Zerby,[48] Hepfinger,[49] Davis,[50] Root,[51] Donlon,[52] Komisar and MacDonnell[53]).

Several reports (American Printing House for the Blind,[42] American Foundation for the Blind,[54] Norris, et al.[45]) indicated that mentally retarded-blind children are frequently commited to institutions where very limited educational and training programs are provided for them. Boly and DeLeo[55] conducted a survey of educational provisions for the mentally retarded blind in fifty-two of the 104 state institutions for the mentally re-tarded, and found great variations between institutions in terms of the number of blind and educational provisions for them. The median number of blind persons in residence at each institution was twenty-three, and limitation of educational programs for the retarded blind was noted.

Winschel [56] surveyed the facilities for the education and care of retarded blind in the United States and found that the main facilities providing service to this disability group were: classes within institutions for the mentally retarded; public school classes; private schools; educable classes within schools for the blind; and foster homes. The study did not indicate the extent of services available. The National Association for Retarded Children (NARC) [57] also attempted to find out what provisions are available for the mentally retarded blind child. NARC surveyed 393 of its chapters in the United States and found that school programs were utilized most frequently.

The information available concerning the incidence of speech problems of the blind is inconsistent. Stinchfield [58] found that 49 per cent of the blind children tested at the Overbrook School for the Blind in Philadelphia and the Perkins School for the Blind in Watertown had some form of speech problem. Rowe [59] surveyed the blind child in the Northern California area and found that 6.7 per cent of the blind children would benefit from speech correction. Miner [60] attempted to investigate the incidence of speech deviations among children at the Michigan School for the Blind and the Illinois Braille and Sight Saving School. Two hundred and ninety-three children were tested and 33.8 per cent were found to have some sort of speech deviation. Different populations used different admission standards to the schools included in the survey, and differences in testing procedures may account for the variations in findings.

Because of an unpredicted increase in the number of blind children in New York State and the lack of resources to handle them, a comprehensive study was completed. It revealed that approximately one third of all blind persons studied have additional disabilities. Local schools reported 23.3 per cent of their blind children as having multiple disabilities; residential schools reported 35.8 per cent of their enrollees had multiple disabilities. The residential schools for mentally retarded indicated that 75 per cent of the mentally retarded blind children had additional complicating disabilities.[4]

A recent survey (1962–63) by the U.S. Office of Education, Division of Handicapped Children and Youth, indicates that there has been a substantial increase in recent years in special school services for visually impaired children with multiple disabilities. Almost 80 per cent of the programs in the United States served visually handicapped children who also had one or more additional disabilities. The report states that research exploration is clearly indicated on almost every aspect of special education programs for visually impaired children who have other major disabilities. The particular process of classification and placement needs much study.[61]

A NEW CHALLENGE

Danwalder found that the majority of State Departments of Education anticipated that enrollments will continue to increase slightly in residential and day school programs for the blind. "However, the percentage increase will be material in the multi-handicapped (disability) group while an actual decrease will probably occur in the enrollments of blind and visually handicapped students who do not have other physical or mental disabilities." [62]

Cruickshank has raised the question regarding which agency is best equipped to serve the child with multiple disabilities. Although public schools and community clinics play an important role, it is his opinion that the problem can be best handled by the residential school. "One of the important considerations in urging residential schools to assume the problem of the multiple handicapped blind child is that of the research potential in such a center." [63] Ashcroft expresses a similar idea when he states:

> With increases in day school provision and with the reduced incidence of retrolental fibroplasia and the increased use of optical aids for low-vision children, this trend may lead residential schools to enlarge their function in providing specialized service for children with complex problems. [64]

Frampton and Kerney, [65] in an analysis of the history, contributions, and future of the residential school for the blind, apply the following measures as a standard of social utility to institutions for the blind: 1) time and endurance; 2) social adaptation; 3) demand; and 4) product. The authors make the following point in regard to social adaptation:

> As an organization it has changed with the changing demands of the whole social structure. . . . Few social investigations can point to any item of social importance in the long history of the residential school for the blind which has remained static long enough seriously to affect the continuing high-quality service to the blind child through the passing decades. As in all social organizations, necessary changes are sometimes delayed, sometimes not as completely realized in action as their proponents would have wished. But the end result has been a steady, continuously vital, living social organization, alert and sensitive to the specific needs of its clients in its generation, a social organism destined to continue as long as this fundamental law of survival is observed in theory and practice.
> Specific needs of its blind clients in this decade appear to indicate expanded research and services to blind children with multiple disabilities. Before plans can be formulated additional data are needed concerning the problems presented by children with multiple disabilities. [65]

SUMMARY

A review of related research from epidemiological surveys and other sources on multiple disabilities, specifically the mentally retarded-visually impaired diad, reveals the following:

1) Lack of a theoretical concept concerning the syndromes of multiple disabilities.

2) Confusion and lack of agreement on definitions, classifications, and terminology.

3) Inadequacy of a rationale by investigators in assigning priority to a disability.

4) Conflicting viewpoints concerning which facilities are most appropriate and the extent and availability of such facilities.

5) Inconsistencies in reported incidence and prevalence rates.

6) Lack of a precise methodology for teaching children with multiple disabilities.

The educational problem presented by children who have multiple disabilities is as old as man's attempt to provide services to exceptional children. For far too many years special educators have been dealing with handicapped children in a unitary fashion. Special classes have been organized, classified, and categorized according to a primary schema of disabilities which has little meaning for educational planning and remediation. There is urgent need for additional research in all aspects of multiple disabilities. The results of this research will have immediate and serious implications for organizing instruction and teacher training in the rapidly growing field of special education.

REFERENCES

1. Hoffmeyer, Ben E. "The Multiple Handicapped Child: A Product of Improved Medical Care," *Medical Times* (Aug. 1961), 89:807–815.

2. Kirk, Samuel A., "Needed Projects and Research in Special Education," Chapter XVII, in *The Education of Exceptional Children*, Part II, The Forty-Ninth Yearbook, National Society for the Study of Education. University of Chicago Press, Chicago, 1950, p. 326.

3. Goodenough, Florence L., *Exceptional Children*. Appleton-Century-Crofts, Inc., New York, 1956, p. 389.

4. Cruickshank, William M., and Matthew J. Trippe, *Services to Blind Children in New York State*. Syracuse University Press, Syracuse, 1959, p. 80.

5. Wishik, Samuel M., *Georgia Study of Handicapped Children*. Georgia Department of Public Health, 1964.

6. The Illinois Census of Exceptional Children. *The Prevalence of Exceptional Children in Illinois in 1958*, Report of the 1958 Illinois Census of Exceptional Children, Circular Census 1A. Superintendent of Public Instruction, State of Illinois, Springfield, 1959, p. 9.

7. Wishik, Samuel M., "Handicapped Children in Georgia: A Study of Prevalence, Disability, Needs, and Resources," *American Journal of Public Health* (1956), 46:195–203.

8. Cruickshank, William M., and Orville G. Johnson (Editors) *Education of Exceptional Children and Youth*. Prentice-Hall, Inc., Englewood Cliffs, New Jersey, 1958. pp. 6–8.

9. Mackie, R., et al., *Statistics of Special Education for Exceptional Children and Youth,* 1957–58 (Final Report). United States Department of Health, Education, and Welfare, Office of Education, Washington, D.C., 1963, p. 5.

10. Stevens, G. D., *Taxonomy in Special Education for Children with Body Disorders.* University of Pittsburgh, Department of Special Education and Rehabilitation, Pittsburgh, 1962.

11. Wright, Beatrice A., *Physical Disability—A Psychological Approach.* Harper and Brothers, New York, 1960.

12. Mayo, Leonard W., and Maya Riviere, "An Investigation into the Feasibility of Developing a System of Codes for Use in Rehabilitation," *Association for the Aid of Crippled Children,* New York, 1957, p. 35 (Mimeo).

13. New York State Department of Mental Hygiene, Mental Health Research Unit, 1955. *A Special Census of Suspected Referral Mental Retardation, Onondaga County, New York.* In: Technical Report of the Mental Health Research Unit. Syracuse University Press.

14. Stifler, J. R., et al., "Follow-up Study of Children Seen in the Diagnostic Centers for Handicapped Children," *American Journal of Public Health* (Nov. 1963), 53:1743–1750.

15. Quibell, E. P., et al., "A Survey of a Group of Children with Mental and Physical Handicaps Treated in an Orthopaedic Hospital," *Archives of Disease in Childhood* (Feb. 1961), 36:58–64.

16. Fouracre, Maurice H., "Educational Abilities and Needs of Orthopedically Handicapped Children," *Elementary School Journal* (Feb. 1950), 51:331–338.

17. Cruickshank, W. M., "The Multiply Handicapped Cerebral Palsied Child," *Exceptional Children* (1953), 20:16–22.

18. Cardwell, Viola E., *Cerebral Palsy: Advances in Understanding and Care.* Association for the Aid of Crippled Children, New York, 1956.

19. Asher, P., and F. E. Schonnel, "A Survey of 400 Cases of Cerebral Palsy in Childhood," *Archives of Diseases of Children* (1950), 25:360–379.

20. Holloran, I. M., "The Incidence and Prognosis of Cerebral Palsy," *British Medical Journal* (Jan. 1952), 4751:214–217.

21. Heilman, A., "Intelligence in Cerebral Palsy," *The Crippled Child* (1952), 30:11–13.

22. McIntire, J. T., "The Incidence of Feeble-Mindedness in the Cerebral Palsied," *American Journal of Mental Deficiency* (April, 1946), 50:491–494.

23. Phelps, W. M., "Characteristic Psychological Variations in Cerebral Palsy," *Nervous Child* (1948), 7:10–13.

24. Doctor, P. V., "Multiple Handicaps in the Field of Deafness," *Sixth Annual Conference on Problems of Hearing and Speech,* Syracuse University, 1951.

25. Frisina, D. R., "A Psychological Study of the Mentally Retarded Deaf Child," *Dissertation Abstracts* (1955), 15:2287–2288.

26. Doctor, P. V., "Multiple Handicaps in the Field of Deafness," *Exceptional Children* (Nov. 1959), 26:156–158.

27. Leonhouts, M. A., "The Mentally Retarded Deaf Child," *Report of the Proceedings of the Thirty-Ninth Meeting of the Convention of American Instructors of the Deaf.* Colorado School for the Deaf, Colorado Springs, Colorado (June 1959), United States Government Printing Office, Washington, D.C., 1960, pp. 55–64.

28. Weir, R. C., "Impact of the Multiple Handicapped Deaf on Special Education," *The Volta Review* (June 1963), 65:287–289.

29. Birch, J., and J. Matthews, "The Hearing of Mental Defectives," *American Journal of Mental Deficiency* (1951), 55:384–393.

30. Schlanger, B. B., and R. H. Gottlesben, "Testing the Hearing of Mentally Retarded," *Journal of Speech and Hearing Disorders* (1956), 21:487–493.

31. Johnston, P. W., and M. J. Farrell, "Auditory Impairments Among Resident School Children at the Walter E. Fernald State School," *American Journal of Mental Deficiency* (1954), 58:640–644.

32. Siegenthaler, B. M., and D. F. Krzywicki, "Incidence and Patterns of Hearing Loss Among an Adult Mentally Retarded Population," *American Journal of Mental Deficiency* (1959), 64:444–449.

33. Kodman, F., "Sensory Processes and Mental Deficiency," Chapter XIV in *Handbook of Mental Deficiency*, N. R. Ellis, Editor. McGraw-Hill Book Co., Inc., New York, 1963.

34. Elliott, M. H., and F. H. Hall. *Laura Bridgman, Dr. Howe's Famous Pupil and What He Taught Her.* Little Brown and Co., Boston, 1903.

35. Braddy, Nella, *Anne Sullivan Macy, The Story Behind Helen Keller.* Doubleday, Doran and Co., Garden City, N.Y. 1933, p. 365.

36. Keller, Helen, Letter to Peter J. Salmon, dated April 3, 1959 in World Council for the Welfare of the Blind Report of Committee on Services for the Deaf-Blind to the World Assembly, Rome, Italy, July 1959. Brooklyn, N.Y., The Industrial Home for the Blind, 1959, p. 152.

37. National Study Committee on Education of Deaf-Blind Children, *Report.* (Meetings, Washington, D.C., July 12, 1953, and Council Bluffs, Iowa, Jan. 25–26, 1954), p. 30.

38. Allen, Edward E., "The Feeble-Minded Blind," in *Proceedings of the National Conference of Charities and Correction*, Alexander Johnson, editor, Thirty-Third Annual Session, Philadelphia, Pennsylvania, 1906, pp. 259–261.

39. American Association of Instructors of the Blind, *Proceedings*, 1918, p. 100.

40. Fraenkel, William A., "Blind Retarded—Or Retarded Blind?" *New Outlook for the Blind* (June 1964), 58:165–169.

41. Long, Elinor H., *The Challenge of the Cerebral Palsied Blind Child.* American Foundation for the Blind, New York, 1952.

42. American Printing House for the Blind. Report: *The Survey of the Multiple-Handicapped, Visually Handicapped.* Louisville, Kentucky, May 1955.

43. Paraskeva, Peter C., "A Survey of the Facilities for the Mentally Retarded-Blind in the United States," *The International Journal for the Education of the Blind* (May 1959), 8:139–145.

44. Long, Elinor and J. Perry, "Slow Learner and Retarded Blind Child," 43rd Biennial Convention, *American Association of Instructors of the Blind*, 1956.

45. Norris, Miriam, et al., *Blindness in Children.* University of Chicago Press, Chicago, 1957, p. 3.

46. DiMichael, Salvador G., "Meeting the Needs of Retarded Blind Children," 43rd Biennial Convention, American Association of Instructors of the Blind, *Proceedings*, 1956.

47. Moor, P., "Blind Children With Developmental Problems," *Children* (January–February 1961), 8:9–13.

48. Zwarensteyn, S. B., and M. Zerby, "A Residential School Program for Multi-Handicapped Blind Children," *New Outlook for the Blind* (June 1962), 56:191–199.

49. Hepfinger, Lucy M., "Psychological Evaluation of Young Blind Children," *New Outlook for the Blind* (Nov. 1962), 56:309–316.

50. Davis, Carl J., "The Assessment of Intelligence of Visually Handicapped Children," *International Journal for the Education of the Blind* (Dec. 1962), 12:48–50.

51. Root, Ferne K., "Evaluation of Services for Multiple-Handicapped Blind Children," *International Journal for the Education of the Blind* (Dec. 1963), 13:33–37.

52. Donlon, Edward T., "An Evaluation Center for the Blind Child with Multiple Handicaps," *The Education of the Blind* (March 1964), 13:75–78.

53. Komisar, David and Marian MacDonnell, "Gain in I.Q. for Students Attending a School for the Blind," *Exceptional Children* (1955), 21:127–129.

54. American Foundation for the Blind, *Services for Blind Persons in the United States.* Nov. 1960.

55. Boly, L. F., and DeLeo, G. M., "A Survey of Educational Provisions for the Institutionalized Mentally Subnormal Blind," *New Outlook for the Blind* (1956), 50:232–236.

56. Winschel, James F., *Facilities for the Education and Care of Mentally Retarded Blind Children*, University of Pittsburgh, March 1960.

57. National Association for Retarded Children, *Survey on Blind Retarded Children*, 1960.

58. Stinchfield, S. M., *Speech Pathology.* Expression Company, Magnolia, Mass., 1928.

59. Rowe, Emma Dorothy, *Speech Problems of Blind Children: A Survey of the North California Area.* New York, American Foundation for the Blind, 1958.

60. Miner, L. E., "A Study of the Incidence of Speech Deviations Among Visually Handicapped Children," *New Outlook for the Blind* (Jan. 1963), 57:10–14.

61. Jones, John Walker, *Educational Programs for Visually Handicapped Children.* Office of Education, U.S. Department of Health, Education, and Welfare, Washington, D.C., (in press).

62. Danwalder, Donald D., *Education, Training and Employment of the Blind.* The Western Pennsylvania Scohol for Blind Children, June 1964, p. 11.

63. Cruickshank, William M., "The Multiple-Handicapped Child and Courageous Action," *International Journal for the Education of the Blind* (March 1964), 13:65–74.

64. Ashcroft, S. C., "The Blind and Partially Seeing," in *Review of Educational Research* (Dec. 1959), 29:519–28.

65. Frampton, Merle E., and Ellen Kerney, *The Residential School: Its History, Contributions and Future.* The New York Institute for the Education for the Blind, New York, 1953.

* PART FOUR

Speech and Hearing Impaired

This section treats problems and issues in the areas of speech and language impairment, and deafness.

In the area of speech impairments as in all areas of exceptionality there are a variety of unresolved problems and issues. There are, for example, questions about the practice of centering speech correction activities in the first and second grades, about the relative merits of various speech therapy techniques, and about the excessive attention given to articulation defects as compared with other speech impairments. These are issues and problems of speech practitioners and, while relevant for special education, are outside the scope of the present volume. Teacher identification of children with speech impairments is of great interest and concern to special education, and a piece dealing with this problem is reprinted here ("Accuracy of Teacher Referrals of Speech Handicapped Children"). The James and Cooper article is a report of research. The authors studied the ability of third grade elementary teachers—given written instructions—to identify speech handicapped children. As had been found in related investigations, teachers were not skilled in identification even when given some information describing categories of speech impairment. Teachers were most accurate in identifying stutterers and least accurate in identifying those with voice disorders. The results point to the inescapable conclusion that teachers cannot accurately identify children with speech impairments. The large problem remains, i.e., how to develop techniques which enable teachers to more accurately identify speech handicapped children. Work in this area has not been undertaken.

A second article reprinted here deals with the language handicapped child ("The Language Handicapped Child and Education"). Problems with such children are likely to be of a more serious nature than are the problems of those children described by James and Cooper in the first article of this section. Indeed, the critical point of this article revolves around difficulties encountered in the differential diagnosis of children with delayed language. McWilliams goes beyond these questions, however, to talk about implications of the findings for teaching and educational practice.

In no area of special education have controversies raged with such intensity and for so long as in the area of the deaf. Indeed, problems and issues of a decade ago are alive and kicking. Moores (1969) has written an interesting commentary on the state of the field:

> For all intents and purposes, the history of education of the deaf in our country has been and continues to be a chronicle of frustration, failure, and bitter controversy.
>
> . . . Neither our methods nor results have changed appreciably since the 19th century. With the exception of mechanical advances in equipment, the teaching of the deaf reflects unimaginative, dated concepts for the most part unaffected by improvements, breakthroughs, and new insights achieved in related areas. While educators of the deaf busy themselves with internecine strife over issues that should have been buried generations ago, deaf children with normal intelligence are leaving programs after 12, 15, or 18 years of training with reading achievement of fifth grade level or below and exhibiting exactly the same inadequate and insufficiently developed language patterns as hearing impaired children in 1818 or 1868. The uninterrupted history of failure, however, has led to no significant changes in emphasis or philosophy; on the contrary, it has had the effect of intensifying efforts along lines that have already produced unsatisfactory results and of producing individuals who draw lines and advocate rigid, unyielding commitments to one position or another and who effectively stifle any exchange of ideas.

Some of the issues and problems alluded to by Moores are taken up in the article "The Handicap of Deafness," from the report *Education of the Deaf*, which presents an overview of problems inherent in the handicap of deafness and a discussion of critical variables which must be considered in describing a deaf population, and, finally, takes up the variety of arguments surrounding the methods controversy.

The methods controversy in the area of education of the deaf is one of the most persistent in special education. The issues in this controversy have been highlighted by Vernon (1969):

> Nobody advocates a manual education. This is not the issue. The issue is between a combined use of oral and manual methods of communication as contrasted to an approach that is limited to oral modalities only. Despite the failure of just using oralism, despite the evidence of Stuckless and others on the value of early manual communication, and despite the common sense self-evident lack of logic in trying to teach a child through a method that emphasizes his weaknesses (speech and hearing) and minimizes his assets (vision), deaf children continue to be denied the right to learn in an efficient way that meets their needs. (p. 3)

Only recently (Birch and Stuckless, 1966; Meadows, 1968; Morkovin, 1960) has empirical evidence bearing on the methods controversy been accumulated, but some of this writing is itself the subject of controversy (Di Carlo, 1966). With respect to finger spelling, Morkovin (1960) called attention to certain Russian experiments which demonstrated that this technique combined with oral methods facilitated the progress of preschool deaf children in speech and lipreading. This widely quoted article, however, is not a pure test of the value of finger spelling, since it was combined with oral methods; the unique contribution of finger spelling to speech and lip reading is unknown. However, a British committee (Lewis, 1968), constituted specifically "to consider the place, if any, of finger spelling and signing in the education of the deaf," calls attention to the fact that finger spelling has been particularly advantageous in teaching deaf Russian children because of the highly phonetic nature of the Russian language (i.e., words are pronounced as spelled). The value of the procedures for English-speaking children, the committee points out, needs additional study.

The first article on deafness took into account, at a relatively broad level, certain factors that must be considered in describing deaf populations. The second article reprinted in this subsection on deafness extends the discussion to differential diagnosis of young children with communication disorders ("Differential Diagnosis of Auditory Deficits—A Review of the Literature"). The authors summarize and assess various stimuli, modes of presentation, and methods of indicating response "from the point of view of how they may relate to and affect the characteristic of consistency of threshold response." The critical need for "investigation of the relative effectiveness of various stimuli and techniques in evaluating the hearing of children with CNS auditory and language disorders" was emphasized.

A second section from the report *Education of the Deaf* takes up factors to be considered in selecting educational programs for deaf persons. Although there is general agreement that the deaf should be educated in their home community, a variety of factors conspire against such programs. In the past, most of the deaf were educated in residential institutions. There were then, and are now, several kinds of programs and arrangements for the education of the deaf: residential school programs, the day school, the day class, and the integrated class with hearing students. The problem becomes not which education program is best, but rather what educational program is best for what deaf person? The chapter reprinted here takes up advantages and disadvantages of the above educational programs in objective fashion. It is important to note, however, that in spite of the well-reasoned arguments for and against various educational plans, little empirical evidence is available to support any given arrangement with any circumscribed group of deaf children.

The status of post-high school programs for the deaf is evaluated in a third section from *Education of the Deaf,* and a number of problems are highlighted: the need for a wider range of career choices, the need for more adequate provisions for technical and vocational education and training, and the need for more enlightened programs of adult education.

In a final article, Doctor ("Multiple Handicaps in the Field of Deafness") takes up general problems of multiple handicaps among deaf populations, giving some attention to incidence and reporting.

REFERENCES

Birch, J. W. and E. R. Stuckless, "The Relationship Between Early Manual Communication and the Later Achievement of the Deaf," *American Annals of the Deaf* 1966, 111, pp. 444–452, 499–504.

Di Carlo, L. M., "Much Ado About the Obvious," *Volta Review*, 1966, 68, pp. 269–273.

Lewis, M. M. (Committee Chairman), *The Education of Deaf Children: The Possible Place of Finger Spelling and Signing* (London: Her Majesty's Stationery Office, 1968).

Meadows, Kathryn P., "Early Manual Comunication in Relation to the Deaf Child's Intellectual, Social, and Communicative Functioning," *American Annals of the Deaf* 1968, 113, pp. 29–41.

Moores, D., "Psycholinguistics and Deafness," *American Annals of the Deaf* (in press).

Morkovin, B. V., "Experiment in Teaching Deaf Preschool Children in the Soviet Union," *Volta Review*, 1960, 62, pp. 260–268.

Vernon, M., "The Failure of the Education of the Deaf," *Illinois Advance*, 1963, 101, pp. 1–4.

** 18 **

Accuracy of Teacher Referrals of Speech Handicapped Children

HARRIET P. JAMES AND EUGENE B. COOPER

Public school speech therapists frequently rely upon teacher referrals to locate children with speech and hearing problems. Teacher accuracy in identifying and referring children with hearing losses has been studied (Curry, 1950; Geyer and Yankauer, 1959; Kodman, 1956). Diehl and Stinnett (1959), pointing out the lack of research in the area, investigated the efficiency of teacher referrals of children with speech defects. The study was conducted in school systems which had never had speech correction programs. Second grade classroom teachers were asked to fill out a questionnaire for each of their students. The information requested consisted of the child's name, age, grades failed, and whether or not the child possessed a speech or voice defect. The writers did not define or describe speech or voice defects for the teachers, and the purpose of the study was not revealed until after the teachers had completed the questionnaires.

A followup survey by speech therapists showed that the teachers had identified 57 percent of the children rated as speech defectives by the clinicians. A breakdown according to disorder indicated that the teachers had identified 61 percent of the articulation problems, 37 percent of the voice problems, 70 percent of the children with both articulation and voice problems combined, 44 percent of the rhythm problems, and 67 percent of the combined articulation and rhythm problems. Teachers located 82 percent of the articulation problems which the clinicians ranked as severe (four or more sound errors) and only 43 percent of those rated as mild articulation disorders. It was concluded that elementary teachers with no speech therapy orientation can be expected to locate speech defective children with less than 60 percent accuracy; they fail to locate 2 out of 5 children with speech disorders. The results of their study led Diehl and Stinnett to suggest that inservice training programs in speech therapy for all classroom teachers seem to be justified.

The purpose of this study was to investigate the ability of classroom teachers, given the aid of a written statement defining and describing speech

* From *Exceptional Children* 1966, *33*, pp. 29–34. Reprinted by permission of the senior author and the publisher.

■ TABLE 1 *Performances of Individual Subjects in Referring Children with Speech Problems*

Subject	Number of Children Screened	Number of Speech Problems	Number of Accurate Referrals	Number of Inaccurate Referrals	Percentage of Accurate Referrals
1	28	7	3	2	42.8
2	27	11	3	0	27.2
3	29	5	2	0	40.0
4	31	14	5	3	35.7
5	32	9	2	0	22.2
6	28	13	4	3	30.7
7	31	12	3	0	25.0
8	37	9	2	1	22.2
9	36	17	8	0	47.0
10	37	10	3	0	30.0
11	11	5	3	0	60.0
12	9	5	2	0	40.0
13	37	9	6	2	66.6
14	22	8	3	1	37.5
15	30	13	7	1	53.8
16	18	5	3	0	60.0
17	25	7	3	3	42.8
18	25	6	6	3	100.0
19	26	10	3	3	30.0
20	10	2	1	2	50.0
21	14	7	2	1	28.5
22	10	3	1	1	33.3
23	27	13	5	0	38.4
24	7	3	3	0	100.0
25	6	5	5	1	100.0
26	32	7	0	3	00.0
27	34	8	2	1	25.0
28	17	6	3	0	50.0
29	20	9	3	1	33.3
30	27	5	2	0	40.0
Totals	718	242	98	32	40.4

handicaps, to identify speech handicapped children. A secondary purpose of this study was to determine the extent to which the teacher's ability to identify speech handicapped children was related to the type and/or severity of the speech disorder.

METHODS

Thirty third grade teachers employed in city and county schools in southern Ohio were subjects. Schools which had never had speech therapy programs

■ TABLE 2 *Teacher Referrals of Types of Speech Disorders*

Type of Disorder	Total Number	Number of Accurate Referrals	Number of Undetected Problems	Percentage of Accurate Referrals
Articulation	184	76	108	41.4
Voice	22	2	20	10.1
Stuttering	5	4	1	80.1
Voice and Articulation	23	12	11	52.1
Stuttering and Articulation	8	4	4	50.0

■ TABLE 3 *Teacher Referrals of Severities of Speech Disorders*

Severity Rating	Total Number	Number of Accurate Referrals	Number of Undetected Problems	Percentage of Accurate Referrals
2	51	15	36	29.4
3	81	23	58	28.3
4	78	34	44	43.5
5	24	19	5	79.1
6	5	4	1	80.0
7	3	3	0	100.0
Mild (2 and 3)	132	38	94	28.7
Moderate (4 and 5)	102	53	49	51.9
Severe (6 and 7)	2	7	1	87.5
Moderate and Severe (4, 5, 6, and 7)	110	60	50	54.5
Mild to Moderate (2, 3, and 4)	210	72	138	34.2
Moderate-Severe to Severe (5, 6, and 7)	32	26	6	81.2

were selected in an attempt to control the variable of the subjects' past exposure to speech therapy principles and practices. Each teacher was asked to read a one page statement describing various speech and voice defects and to list the names of the children in his classroom suspected of having speech defects. All children in these classrooms were then given a speech screening test. Those children who were diagnosed as having a speech problem were seen later for a detailed speech examination and were rated on a seven point scale of severity. A linear scale was devised for rating severity of general defectiveness of oral communication, ranging from 1 (normal speech) to 7 (severe disorder).

The children were evaluated by an experienced speech therapist, who had six years' professional experience, five of which had been in public school speech therapy programs. The relative credibility of the investigator to judge the severity of the communicative disorder using the seven point scale was established by comparing his judgments with those of two university staff members with doctorates in speech pathology. Comparisons of judgments were based on the administration of 50 speech screening tests and 15 diagnostic tests.

RESULTS

A total of 718 children was screened. Of these, 242 were diagnosed by the examiner as having speech irregularities. Of these children, 98 were referred by their classroom teachers. The percentage of accurate referrals for the group of teachers was 40.4 percent. Thus, the classroom teachers overlooked three out of every five children with speech problems. Table 1 reveals a wide range of accuracy in reporting speech problems.

Table 2 presents the accuracy of teacher referrals of the various types of speech problems. Teachers referred 76 of the 184 children with disorders of articulation only. The percentage of articulatory disorders which were referred (41 percent) approximated the total percentage of accurate referrals (40 percent). In the present study 22 children, or 3 percent of the total sample, had voice disorders only. Two of these children were referred, yielding a 10.1 percent accuracy score. An additional 23 cases were included in the combined articulation and voice group. This brought the total number of children manifesting some vocal deviation to 45, or 6.2 percent of the total sample of third graders. Twelve of the 23 combined articulation and voice disorders (52.1 percent) were referred by the teachers.

Only 13 stuttering cases were encountered in the present study, comprising 1.8 percent of the total number of children screened. Eight of the children were included in the category of combined articulation and stuttering. Four from this latter group, or 50 percent, were referred. Four of the remaining five stutterers (80 percent) were referred by the classroom teachers.

Table 3 presents the grouping of speech disorders according to the rating of severity. Inspection of this table reveals that the percentage scores of accurate referrals increased as the severity of the problems increased. One hundred thirty-two of the total 242 speech disorders were rated as mild; teachers referred 38 (28.7 percent) of these mild problems. Fifty-three of the 102 moderate problems (51.9 percent) were referred; and 7 of the 8 severe problems (87.5 percent) were referred.

DISCUSSIONS

No attempt was made to determine the significance of difference between the results of this study and the results of the Diehl and Stinnett (1959) study. It is interesting to note, however, that even with the aid of a statement describing and defining speech problems, teachers in this study were consistently less accurate in their referrals than were the teachers in the Diehl and Stinnett study. One explanation for this might be that the criteria used in this study for what constituted a mild speech problem were more severe than those in the Diehl and Stinnett study.

This conclusion is supported by further comparison. Of the 242 children in this study who were judged as having defective speech, 132 were rated as mild. These cases were those children who, in the opinion of the examiner, were likely to respond well to help from the classroom teachers. Problems rated as moderate and severe were designated as cases which would seem to warrant the attention of a specialist. Of the 110 children grouped in the moderate and severe categories, 60 (54.5 percent) were referred by the classroom teachers. Eliminating the large group of children rated as 4 on the severity scale (lowest scale score in the moderate range), it was found that the teachers' percentage of accurate referrals rose to 81.2 percent. This latter group includes those children who would be most eligible for speech therapy services. Diehl and Stinnett concluded that teachers in their study located severe articulatory defectives with slightly better than 80 percent accuracy. In both studies, then, teachers referred four out of every five children who would be the most likely candidates for speech classes.

The finding that teachers were least accurate in referring children with voice disorders is consistent with the Diehl and Stinnett results, as well as with Frick's (1960) conclusions. Because voice disorders frequently do not affect speech intelligibility, teachers may tend to accept unusual voice qualities as normal individual differences. Speech clinicians, however, are aware of the frequently unfavorable medical implications of voice disorders and are, therefore, more alert to what might seem to a layman a relatively unimportant symptom.

The results which indicated that teachers were most accurate in referring stutterers are perhaps the only major difference between the findings of this study and Diehl and Stinnett's results. The number of stutterers found in this study was relatively small and any generalization, of course, must be guarded. However, it would seem that interruptions in speech fluency (hesitations, sound prolongations, and/or repetitions) and the accompanying mannerisms would tend to interfere with the communication process to a greater extent than do irregularities of vocal quality or of pronunciation (unless disorders of the latter types are relatively severe).

The results of this study, when compared with previous studies, do not indicate that teachers refer speech handicapped children with more accuracy when provided with a statement defining and describing speech problems. However, subjective evaluations of the procedure by the teachers indicated that secondary benefits existed. Many teachers reported that the descriptions of speech problems assisted them in making referrals. Although it apparently did not increase their accuracy, they felt more comfortable. Also, the descriptive material appeared to be a time saving device.

Many questions which typically are asked concerning speech and voice problems were answered in the statement given the classroom teacher.

Studies of this nature have shown that teachers fail to refer a significant number of children who are classified as speech handicapped by speech specialists. Newman (1961) reported that a national health survey, based on the judgment of lay persons, revealed that the incidence of speech problems in the population under 25 years of age was .97 of 1 percent. Speech specialists consistently indicate that between 5 and 10 percent of this population are speech handicapped. Newman suggested that speech pathologists might be too discriminating in their judgments. Teachers, involved very closely with communication, can hardly be termed lay persons, and yet speech pathologists have consistently found them inadequate in identifying communication disorders. Perhaps in interpreting results such as those found in this study, speech therapists should consider that not only might teachers overlook speech handicapped children, but the therapists might have lost perspective in what constitutes a speech problem.

REFERENCES

Curry, E. T. The efficiency of teacher referrals in a school hearing testing program. *Journal of Speech and Hearing Disorders,* 1950, 15, 211–215.

Diehl, C., and Stinnett, C. Efficiency of teacher referrals in a school speech testing program. *Journal of Speech and Hearing Disorders,* 1959, 24, 34–36.

Frick, J. The incidence of voice defects among school age speech defective children. *Pennsylvania Speech Annual,* 1960, 17, 61–62.

Geyer, M., and Yankauer, A. Teacher judgment of hearing loss in children. *Journal of Speech and Hearing Disorders,* 1959, 24, 482–486.

Kodman, F. Identification of hearing loss by the classroom teacher. *Laryngoscope,* 1956, 66, 1346–1349.

Newman, P. Speech impaired? *Asha,* 1961, 3, 9–10.

** 19 **

The Language Handicapped Child and Education

The language handicapped child has been called by many names according to the manner in which he has been viewed by the many disciplines concerned with him. Aphasia, brain injury, psychosis, mental retardation, deafness, environmental deprivation, developmental delay, auditory apathy, and idiopathic language delay have all been applied to this confusing and often misunderstood child who eventually finds his way into one educational facility or another. There he is likely to meet teachers who have been so often warned about the need to meet the special and unique requirements of all children that they have grown reluctant to tackle that which they view as a problem for the "experts." The purposes of this paper are (a) to discuss the language handicapped child as he actually exists and as he is viewed by clinicians who are called upon to examine him and to recommend comprehensive treatment for him and (b) to present a philosophy for his education understandable to those teachers who meet him in the classroom.

DIFFERENTIAL DIAGNOSIS

A review of the literature devoted to children with language impairment suggests that the failure to develop expressive and receptive language is usually the result of deafness, mental retardation, brain damage, emotional disturbance, or some variation or combination of these disorders (Kastein and Fowler, 1954; Kastein, 1961; Monsees, 1959). While the literature is not always consistent in describing the symptomatology related to these various problems and the reader is acutely aware of much overlapping in behavioral characteristics, it is, nonetheless, clear that the initial clinical problem is to decide into which broad classification a given child falls. The process of making this decision is called differential diagnosis (McWilliams, 1959). By definition, diagnosis is the art of recognizing disease from its symptoms. As has been pointed out, in problems of delayed language, the

* From *Exceptional Children* 1965, 32, pp. 221–228. Reprinted by permission of the author and the publisher.

symptoms are often complex, poorly differentiated from one etiological group to another, and peculiarly prone to subjective alteration. While an honest attempt is made to diagnose differentially, in reality, the process is more nearly akin to "ruling out," which is both practically and philosophically different from diagnosing.

If a nonverbal child does not present a conflicting picture of response to auditory stimuli and shows no reduction in auditory threshold, we can conclude that he is not deaf. If he relates well to the examiner and if his history is not unusually loaded with psychodynamic material, we tend to think that he is probably not severely emotionally disturbed. If the child does reasonably well on nonverbal psychological tests and has considerable discrepancy between performance and verbal measures of intelligence, we tend to conclude that he is not mentally retarded. In actual practice, the decision that he is *not* mentally retarded is often erroneously made on flimsy evidence or on no evidence at all. The ruling out of severe hearing loss, emotional disturbance, and mental retardation (Barry, 1961) leaves the clinician with only two additional possibilities—brain damage, which so often cannot be proved, resulting in "disturbance in symbolic language formulation" (Wood, 1964) or delayed language of unknown origin. If, however, we look at his symptom complex and see distractibility, visual and auditory perceptual deficits, hyperactivity, perseveration, disinhibition, compulsivity, or disturbances in body imagery, there is a tendency to think of brain injury even though neurological study may not support the clinical observations. If the child with these symptoms also (a) relates poorly to people, (b) enters into repetitive and patterned behavior, (c) adopts bizarre and compulsive response patterns, (d) has motility disturbances, and (e) has well educated but reserved and "rejecting" parents, we tend to call him psychotic.

It may be that we are not yet sufficiently mature in our basic knowledge and in our evaluative methodology to enter into definitive differential diagnosis in language handicapped children and that the best we can do, in many cases, is to describe the symptoms and to attempt to understand them within our own limitations. Mimi is an example of this kind of child and of our kind of dilemma. The writer thought of Mimi as a brain injured child with language deficits similar to those seen in the so-called aphasic child. An examining psychiatrist called her symbiotic. She was later diagnosed as mentally retarded and, still later, as having a character disorder. The dozens of procedures through which this child went were not particularly helpful because clinician bias colored interpretation. There was, however, general agreement that Mimi was indeed a problem child.

It would appear that much of the confusion which exists in relationship to the language handicapped child results from dogmatism in the absence of truth. If, on the other hand, we are able to accept our lack of total information as truth, we shall perhaps set the language handicapped child and ourselves free to seek the most reasonable help available. Without preconceived notions, we can operate with what we know and seek after that which we do not understand.

The facts suggest that our information is woefully impoverished and that differential diagnosis which we have wanted to believe in is often impossible. This does not mean that we cannot *study* children with language handicaps in an effort to understand them as individuals and to provide treatment that is custom created to meet their particular pattern of deficits and to help them function at the upper limits of their abilities rather than at the lower limits of their disabilities. We speak now of patient evaluation, investigation, and study. We speak of a diagnostic process that carries through the child's entire period of treatment and that ceases only when he has shown us that he has reached his full potential to the extent that we are able to recognize potential. This kind of diagnostic attitude destroys any professional need we may feel to defend our position that a child is aphasic against the equally strong opinion that the same child is psychotic or deaf. We now speak in descriptive terms rather than in evaluative ones and in so doing we alter the course of the child's clinical and educational experience.

PROCESS OF EXAMINATION

This kind of study begins upon the child's initial contact with the clinic. At this time, usually a disturbed mother is evident; but with our new philosophy we are not compelled to label her defensive, rejecting, unaccepting, denying, resistant, or overprotective. Instead we describe as best we can her relationship with her child, her understanding of what the child's problem is, her own particular human self apart from her child, and her interaction with the other members of her family. We look at this complex for clues that will help in the management of the child in question. It becomes less important to decide that a mother is rejecting when one is able to decide instead that her relationship with her language handicapped child is in one way or another an influencing factor in the etiology or in the persistence of the problem. We look carefully at the child's entire background in an effort to understand how his life began from the moment of conception and how it has proceeded up to the day of his clinic visit. We must learn to know this child and the things that have happened to him as if we had lived them with him and with his family. As we assign ourselves this task, we must accept also the responsibility for the reservation of judgment, for our role is now that of detective or seeker for truth. There is no room at this stage in our clinical experience for the emergence of personal attitudes toward the mother, the child, or his history which might endanger our vision of the things that are to come.

OBSERVATION

As we look at the child and his mother, and, hopefully, his father and siblings, we attempt to watch them together in the waiting room, in the examining room, or in an informal play area. The way in which he and his family interact becomes of major concern to us. Three examples of this come quickly to mind. One mother interrupted her two year old every time he began to babble to compliment him for trying to talk. The surprised child would stand and stare at her as if he could not understand this strange world of adults in which he found himself. A second example is that of a mother who sat with a nonverbal child in a room filled with toys forbidding him to touch, criticizing his every more, and saying in a half hour period not one positive thing to her little boy. A third example was a mother, who sat for an equally long period of time without saying a word to her child or entering in any way into his activity. This is not to say that these maternal attitudes caused the language problem. It is to say only that they were factors to be considered in planning treatment.

TESTING

The next phase of an examination of a language handicapped child is to study the child himself in terms of his ability to deal with various kinds of test situations. With every child who does not talk probably by the age of 30 months, there is the question of hearing deficit. These children vary tremendously in their responsiveness to sound and in their ability to use auditory stimuli. Some few will be deaf children or will have hearing losses sufficient to prevent their acquisition of speech in the normal way. When a child has a straightforward loss of hearing, we can enter into differential diagnosis because we can demonstrate the hearing loss and understand ways of approaching it. However, a certain percentage of these children will not respond in a typical way to hearing examinations and will show variability in responsiveness to auditory stimulation. These are the children who may hear a whisper but fail to respond to a clap of thunder. These are the children who may understand ten words and hear them when they are spoken but who will be unresponsive to unknown words or to sounds to which they have not learned to listen. These are the children who dwell in an area of auditory mystery. These are the children whom we call centrally deaf as opposed to the more straightforward and more easily understood peripherally deaf. Again, where confusion exists, it seems wise to describe the confusion and to test the child's ability to utilize what we recognize as an imperfect sensory pathway in the process of learning language and of learning to live in a world with other people.

Some few of these children respond well to hearing aids temporarily and then discard them when they have learned to listen. Some, when aids are tried experimentally, reject them and seem not to profit from them. Others do not reject them but react as to an unnecessary encumbrance. In this group of children we must describe auditory behavior lest we fall into the trap of deciding that they do or do not hear and then treating them according to our diagnostic biases. Our knowledge relative to the auditory process is limited, and children with unusual response patterns have taught us what we do not know and in turn, challenge us to understand them better. The one thing of which we can be sure is that the child who shows auditory perceptual deficits, regardless of what caused them, is a child who will need training in auditory perception. His learning process may proceed at a faster pace if sensory avenues that are less impaired can be utilized in training and teaching while attempts are made also to build and strengthen the impaired sense.

This leads into discussion of another important sensory avenue—vision. We do not understand well how to test visual perception in small children. Certain tests have been developed and used widely. Subtest items from many intelligence tests give us certain information. In many cases we cannot be sure whether the child with whom we are dealing has poor visual perception or poor eye-hand coordination. There is a difference in these functions. The one has to do with the perception of form. The other has to do with the ability to direct the hand to do what the eye perceives. Some clinicians have found that the matching of forms from the Merrill-Palmer test helps them understand a little about perception as does color matching and other such items that do not require the copying of a form. Many clinicians have learned that the child with poor eye-hand coordination will frequently show dissatisfaction with his performance but will not know what to do to correct it, while the child with poor perception is satisfied that he is performing well. Children with disturbances in visual perception often appear quite normal. Some even talk and develop verbal language at the usual time and encounter language difficulties only when they encounter reading. We recently examined a ten year old boy who was unable to read a preprimer, who had lost his father at a crucial period in his life, whose mother was overprotective, and who had many malfactors in his case history. However, after a year of psychiatric treatment, he showed no change in his ability to deal with the public school situation. The psychiatrist requested language evaluation at which time profound reduction in visual-motor behavior was found. In addition, an intention tremor was noted which made it difficult for him to do the fine motor tasks required, probably especially difficult when he was forced to try at the age of six when maturation of these skills was even poorer than at age ten. In this case the psychiatrist and the speech clinician working together speculated that this might be organic brain damage but they did not feel compelled to label it as such. Instead, both recognized that the goal of psychiatric treatment would have to be that of helping a child to accept very real limitations and that specific remedial education was indicated and had been since the boy had entered school. A new approach to reading would have to be tried and it would become essential to teach this boy through a sense mechanism that played down his visual handicap and utilized instead his good auditory capacity. It mattered very little at this point whether the primary etiology of his deficit lay in the structure or function of the central nervous system or whether it lay in his own concept of himself. He still required assistance that would help him make use of the abilities which he had. The child psychiatrist who worked with this boy indicated quite specifically a deep concern for programs that did not take into account the very real and ongoing educational difficulties which constitute at least a part of the problem of many either damaged or disturbed children.

One of the ways of looking at visual perception is to test a child for body imagery. We point to a case where the child drew a complete man, the parts of which were not connected in any way or even appropriately related one to the other. An arm, an eye, a foot, a head, and an ear were liberally scattered over the page. This little girl had no verbal language. She was distractible, hyperactive, and difficult to manage. Training in body imagery, in visual perception, and in language resulted in a child who at age ten is functioning in a normal school at the appropriate grade level. This little girl was diagnosed as psychotic at the age of three, as mentally retarded by the age of four, and as brain damaged by the age of five. At the age of six she demonstrated severe hypernasality in speech with no movement in the soft palate or pharyngeal wall. She presented a syndrome of symptoms which have been described elsewhere (McWilliams and Musgrave, 1965). She responded well to pharyngeal flap surgery which made the speech that she had quite intelligible. This child still deals almost entirely on a concrete level, but she is intelligent enough to compensate for her deficits and to function relatively adequately in her peer group.

When we talk about perception we speak of a totality of function which in some way must be broken down if it is to be understood. For example, one child may not perceive because he has not received the sensation. This is true in deafness in relation to auditory stimulation. It is true in blindness in relation to visual stimulation. Another child may receive an imperfect message as would be the case in partial hearing loss or in partial blindness. His perception is, therefore, determined by the capacity of the sense organs to respond. If the image is distorted the perception will be distorted. On the other hand certain other children appear to have a sensory end organ that is capable of normal response but the breakdown occurs somewhere in the sensory tract or at the level of the central nervous system. These children have trouble with interpretation and with understanding the signal that is received. This may occur for many reasons, and a certain kind of ruling out must take place in connection with these disorders.

We can probably say with relatively little qualification that psychological testing is an essential part of the study of and the experience with language involved children. Perception does not exist as an entity apart from intelligence. It is related to intelligence and yet is separate from it. It is for this reason that we view it as an erroneous examination procedure when pieces and snatches of many different psychological tests are utilized in the evaluation of language involved children. A mentally retarded child always shows reduction in perception. His reduction, however, is commensurate with his reduced abilities in other areas of functioning. If these other areas of functioning are not explored and comparisons made, we are in a poor position to determine whether true perceptual deficit exists or whether it is merely an understandable part of depressed intelligence. There is no particular magic in one psychological test as opposed to another. Much depends upon the skill, the training, and the preference of the clinician who utilizes these tools. However, there must be some uniformity of procedure and some recognition of relationships among subtests. When asked, a mentally retarded child may point to the cup on the Stanford-Binet. He may fail to point to "the one we drink out of" on the same test, indicating that he has a breakdown in abstract ability and suggesting that he can deal with the concrete but has trouble when he is asked to handle more abstract concepts. This breakdown is an important distinguishing characteristic in the child who then goes on to perform tasks at his chronological age so long as they do not involve his understanding or his dealing with verbal concepts. It is equally differentiating for the child who stops at this level in all areas of functioning. The latter child appears to be mentally retarded. The former gives evidence of a youngster who has specific deficits, for whatever reason, in dealing with language but who can operate successfully when language is not demanded.

It becomes evident that the child whose functioning is fairly evenly distributed and who does not present discrepancies is the child for whom an IQ can probably be computed with a degree of safety. For the child whose performance is uneven and widely scattered, who shows wide subtest variations, the IQ becomes a meaningless concept. So much depends upon the pattern of behavior that entered into the acquisition of the score. With language involved children, the skill of the examiner is not mathematical skill but interpretative. These children require that their testing be handled by someone well acquainted with communication barriers and with children who have them. We see too many boys and girls with at least average ability in most areas of development being forced to live their lives as retarded children; but we also see too many with remnants of what was once good intelligence being overestimated and frustrated by the demands of a society that understands too little about their limitations.

Neurological study is also essential. While these examinations frequently do not reveal the focus of trouble, there are some few cases where actual tragedy may be averted by neurological intervention. In some instances medication can control hyperactivity to a miraculous degree. Unfortunately in many cases it cannot; but for the few who can benefit from drug therapy it seems worth the investment. Because a child is progressing in diagnostic language therapy does not necessarily imply that he has no active pathology. A case in point is a child whose hyperactivity was well controlled during therapy, who progressed from a nonverbal to a verbal level in a matter of weeks in a nursery school, but whose impoverished vocabulary and associated behavior suggested organicity. The removal of a brain tumor of long standing resulted in the child's retention of only rudimentary, vegetative behavior.

Psychiatric evaluation of children with language handicaps is not always possible. There are too few psychiatrists available to meet the needs of an ever expanding patient load, and too often these children are found in communities where there is no access to psychiatric diagnosis and care. It would be fair to say, however, that the psychiatric group in many cases has little to offer the child who cannot talk. This child is as poorly understood by this group as he is by all the other professional disciplines which attempt to help him. One child psychiatrist said, "We're turning him back to the speech clinic. If you can make him talk, we can then deal with his psychosis." Our answer was, "If we can make him talk, he may not need to have his psychosis treated." This of course is not always true. Many psychotic children respond to speech therapy and to teaching techniques. As the years pass, however, we learn that their responses are stereotyped, unconventional, bizarre, both predictable and unpredictable, and not socially useful. In some psychotic children speech serves to accentuate the problem by the very nature of the speech end product.

CLINICALLY ORIENTED TEACHING

The evaluation of a child in a clinic is meaningful only if the results of the studies can be integrated and interpreted for the future management of the child. It is incumbent upon the clinic to be communicative with and to serve as a consultant to the school program into which the child eventually must go. It is incumbent upon the school to make use of clinical resources in planning educational programs and in developing inservice training for teachers who are to provide the highly specialized teaching required by children with language handicaps. The entire process of clinical-teacher communication would be simplified if it were possible to outline a "system" of education which could be prescribed and then applied for all children with language handicaps. In reality, it is not possible to provide teachers with specific and foolproof recipes. Each child with a language deviation will provide his own model and his own system of educational needs based upon the extent to which he is atypical in his language development as well as upon the manner in which his problem is typical of the classification into which it fits.

Insightful teaching of children with language problems demands teachers who can recognize that academic achievement must always come after the child is helped to a position where it is reasonable to expect him to learn. For example, a highly distractible child may need help first of all with his distractibility. He may need to be taken out of the clutter and confusion of the classroom and permitted the luxury of aloneness. A teacher may find that the child with auditory perceptual disturbances will never carry out an instruction given to him behind his back. He may cooperate only when given visual clues and when the teacher stops to show and do with him, all the time explaining in simple terms what is happening and why. Teachers of these special children learn that there are no group techniques for teaching them to read, for teaching them arithmetic, or for teaching them any of the academic subjects. Sometimes a skillful teacher can devise small group instruction which takes into account the individual abilities and disabilities of each child in the group. The language handicapped child needs individual teaching often, and he needs to travel at his own pace. This kind of programing is hard to come by when he is so often educated in classrooms originally designed for the orthopedically handicapped, the mentally retarded, or the hard of hearing. It is time for people concerned primarily with study, evaluation, treatment, and research in language problems to recognize with classroom teachers that their job is a difficult one and that adequate settings have too frequently not been established.

For all children with language deficits the setting of consistent and understandable limits both in the classroom and at home appears to be of major significance. In fact, it has often appeared that some children who have not responded well to therapy while they remained at home responded better in a residential setting. There the staff was able to maintain a schedule, to be consistent in demands, and to give the child, primarily through experience, a clear understanding of what was expected of him and, more important, of those things which were not socially acceptable. Consistency implies repetition, and repetition of stimuli appropriately presented can sometimes constitute the secret password to the mind of a language disturbed child, particularly if his understanding is impaired. In short, he must be consciously *taught* to live and to do those things which other children acquire by living alone.

With both deaf children and language involved children from other causes, we are finding that a major drawback to their learning from experience and to their gaining better language concepts is that either people do not talk to them or they talk in terms much too complex. These children must be talked to; they must be read to and shown pictures. They must learn as much as possible through concrete experience. One child learned the word *diamond* by pointing to my ring and looking questioningly. I answered simply, "Diamond," pointing to the stone, and "Ring," pointing to the band. She looked and felt and said the words. She then looked at her own ring and said, "Diamond." I said, "No, ring." Pointing to her band, I said, "Ring." I then said, "Diamond," and showed her my stone and, "Ruby," and showed her hers. Later, she came to me, pointed to my stone, and said, "Diamond." She then pointed to her own and said, "Ruby." She had learned new words through a multiple sensory approach. Visual, auditory, and tactile senses were utilized, and they all added up to a positive incidental learning experience. This is a little girl who seems to hear none of the words she does not know but appears to hear at normal levels of intensity those words which she has learned. Speechreading has been an important aid to her education. Language came faster when she was placed in a classroom situation and taught to read.

We must point out that for the severely involved child, language treatment becomes the central goal of his education. It becomes, as it is for all children, the hinge upon which all future learning swings. It is true, therefore, that our educational goals for the language handicapped child must of necessity be different from those goals which we have for the normal child who enters school for the express purpose of acquiring academic skills, making social adjustments, and taking his place in the world. Some of our language handicapped children will do sufficiently well that they probably can handle higher education and again, within limits, assume a responsible place in life. For other children, because we are talking of multiple handicaps, almost never of a single problem, the goals will be more limited. We will look toward habilitation that permits the child to make use of those abilities that are at his disposal and that takes into account those abilities which are essentially absent. We cannot mislead parents into believing that some magic system of education will solve their child's problem and will return him untarnished to a normal place in society. When this occurs, we celebrate along with the parents; but, because we are realistic and look at these children and at ourselves honestly, a part of our ethical responsibility in education becomes the careful and compassionate guidance of parents who must in all probability accept the reality and the limitations of language deprivation in children. If we as professional people are overly optimistic about the outcome, then we lead parents to heartbreak. We must be willing to wait and see. Time is the best prognosticator and, in some cases, the best clinician. We have no magic formula; we have no system of treatment to offer. We have only an eclectic view that says, "Children fail to talk for many different reasons, and they probably require as many different approaches to learning as there are etiologies for their problems." Magic lies in persistence, in understanding, in careful planning, in the earliest possible intervention, and in fine cooperation among clinicians, teachers, and parents.

The language involved child remains at least a partial enigma. No one can provide the final answers except the child himself. This means that a well qualified and knowledgeable teacher need not quake in her shoes in the presence of "experts." Education is the only lifeline we can extend when language fails. Teachers should start where the child is and do what they are trained to do—*teach*.

REFERENCES

Barry, Hortense. *The young aphasic child.* Washington, D.C.: Alexander Graham Bell Association for the Deaf, Inc., 1961.

Kastein, Shulamith and Fowler, E. Differential diagnosis of communication disorders in children referred for hearing tests. *Archives of Otolaryngology,* 1954, **60**, 468–477.

Kastein, Shulamith. The different groups of disturbances of understanding langauge in children. *The Nervous Child,* 1961, **9**, 31.

McWilliams, Betty Jane and Musgrave, Ross H. Differential diagnosis and management of hypernasal voices in children. *Transaction, American Academy of Ophthalmology and Otolaryngology,* 1965.

McWilliams, Betty Jane. The non-verbal child. *Exceptional Children,* 1959, **25**, 420–423, 440.

Monsees, Edna K. Aphasia and deafness in children. *Exceptional Children,* 1959, **25,** 395–399, 409–410.

Wood, Nancy. *Delayed speech and language development.* Englewood Cliffs, New Jersey: Prentice-Hall, 1964.

** 20 **

The Handicap of Deafness

ADVISORY COMMITTEE ON THE EDUCATION OF THE DEAF

For a child who is born deaf, or becomes deaf in his early years before the acquisition of language, there are hurdles to be overcome that stagger the imagination. Most such children are normal in other ways—in native intelligence, in vocal apparatus—but they cannot hear the spoken language which is absorbed and spoken relatively effortlessly by hearing children. Language is the indispensable tool of learning acquired with little effort by the hearing child, but it is acquired only after great effort and determination by deaf children and their dedicated teachers.

For a deaf child to learn to speak and to read speech on the lips and the expressions of others is a minor miracle—but a miracle that is happening every day in hundreds of classrooms for the deaf throughout the country. Most persons deaf from birth or early childhood have somewhat distorted speech, not as a result of any defect in their speech apparatus, but because their deafness denies them the opportunity to hear their own speech and to monitor its quality against the speech of others.

The doggedness and courage of the deaf person and the dedication of his teachers as together they battle to achieve communication—the use of language—and to use this vital tool in the learning process are deserving of the best that our society can offer in the form of understanding, of help, and of ingenuity in finding ways to make the task easier.

* From *Education of the Deaf.* Washington: U.S. Department of Health, Education and Welfare, 1965, pp. xxv–xxxi.

THE DEAF POPULATION

It is recognized that the deaf person must be described in terms of a number of variables which may interact with each other to varying degrees. Some of these variables are:

1. The degree of hearing loss. This is the traditional psycho-acoustic variable for measuring deafness. The deaf individual can be described in terms of his degree of loss of awareness of sound. A loss of at least 75 or 80 decibels in the better ear is often considered to be a dividing line between the deaf and the hard of hearing so far as degree of loss is concerned. It should be remembered, however, that individual differences are of great importance.

2. Age at onset of hearing loss. The age at which an individual's hearing becomes impaired is of crucial importance in the educational process. Two individuals might have exactly the same hearing loss as measured in decibels with an audiometer; yet, if one individual were born deaf and the other became deaf at the age of 15, there likely would be profound differences between them in such factors as educational achievement, language development, and speech and speechreading ability.

3. The site of the lesion. This refers to the part of the hearing apparatus in which damage occurred to cause loss of hearing. If the damage is in the middle ear, the individual usually will have what is termed a conductive hearing loss. This type of loss is only partial and usually can be helped greatly with the use of a hearing aid. If the damage is in the inner ear it is referred to as sensory-neural and often cannot be helped greatly with an aid. If the damage is in the cerebral cortex it is referred to as central deafness. Most of the people whom we refer to as deaf have sensory-neural hearing loss caused by destruction of parts of the inner ear.

4. Method of communication used by the deaf individual. There is variation in the methods used by deaf persons to communicate with each other and with hearing persons. Some deaf persons rely almost exclusively on speech and speechreading for communication. Others use mostly the language of signs. Stll others depend largely upon the use of finger spelling. Probably the majority use various combinations of these methods as well as written communication.

5. The deaf person's attitude toward his deafness. The reaction of the deaf person to his deafness has important implications for his psychosocial and educational adjustment. He may react by striving to become a member of the hearing community and by refraining from participation in the deaf community. He may react in exactly the opposite manner and shun participation in the hearing community. He may endeavor to function as well as possible in both the deaf and the hearing communities.

These are only a few in the complex of variables which must be considered when attempting to describe the deaf population. Each of the variables should be considered as a continuum along which deaf persons may be distributed. It is difficult, therefore, to describe or define the "typical" deaf person. Individuals who are termed deaf may vary widely in degree of hearing loss, in age at onset of hearing loss, in methods of communication used, in their attitudes toward their deafness, and in many other factors. For example, an individual might be classified audiometrically as being hard of hearing on the basis of his decibel loss and yet be considered sociologically as deaf on the basis of his acceptance of, and gravitation to, the deaf community rather than the hearing community. Similar interactions are possible among the other variables.

In spite of the wide variation among deaf persons on the dimensions described, some factors are common to most deaf individuals and serve to some extent to describe the deaf population. Thus deaf persons have hearing losses severe enough to produce serious disorders of communication and must be taught language and communication by special educational procedures. Deaf persons also have in common the fact that they are coupled to the world visually. Although recent technological advances in the design and construction of hearing aids, in addition to increased emphasis on auditory training procedures, have undoubtedly improved the utilization of residual hearing by deaf persons, it is likely that most of them still depend primarily on their vision for communication and for the acquisition of information. If one had to select a single factor as being descriptive of deaf people in general it would be this factor of being linked to the world visually. The deaf person receives communication primarily through his eyes: whatever hearing he may have left is a supplement to his visual perception.

There is no reliable census of the deaf population. Estimates, however, place the number of profoundly deaf persons at between 200,000 and 250,000. These estimates refer to persons whose hearing is "nonfunctional" with or without a hearing aid—those who are linked to the world primarily through their eyes. The estimates reflect a prevalence rate commonly encountered in the literature—1.2 to 1.4 per thousand—which seems to remain reasonably constant.

This report addresses itself to the problems of education of the *deaf*, to the extent that it is possible to separate them from the hard of hearing. It should be borne in mind, however, that there are many times as many hearing-impaired children who are classified as hard of hearing. These children also require special attention in varying degrees.

THE METHODS CONTROVERSY

Educators of the deaf differ on the most useful method of communication for the deaf—the oral or the manual.

Advocates of the purely oral method of instruction concede that speech and speechreading, aided by auditory training to take advantage of even small residual hearing, may be more difficult and take longer to learn than manual methods. They maintain, however, that it prepares the deaf child for wider horizons and greater opportunities in the hearing world culturally, socially, and economically. It prepares the child to take advantage of a wider range of educational opportunities than are likely to be offered by special programs for those who can easily communicate only manually. Furthermore, they consider that it makes possible a fuller, more satisfying life. Those who favor the oral method also point out that manual communication is more easily acquired, and that a child who is taught manually is less likely to put forth the extra effort required to achieve speech and speechreading.

Those who favor the employment of manual methods are less likely to be purists. In fact, in the course of hundreds of discussions by the staff, not a single person was encountered who did not agree with the desirability of oral instruction for young deaf children. The difference appears really to hinge on how readily one gives up on oral instruction. The advocates of manual methods emphasize that inevitably some children will be unable to acquire usable speech or to learn speechreading well enough to communicate effectively. They maintain that a child should not be denied the opportunity to learn a form of communication within his capabilities. They contend that it is easier to communicate subject matter in the classroom by manual methods. Some advocate the combination of oral methods with finger spelling, a combination that keeps the English language as the symbol system of instruction and communication. Others favor employing all methods—oral, finger spelling, and the language of signs—in an effort to make the learning process easier. They also maintain that it is less of a strain on the deaf person to communicate manually, and point to the fact that most deaf adults prefer to use manual communication among persons —deaf or hearing—who know it.

This Committee, recognizing that it cannot resolve a question that has been a lively one for the past hundred years in this country, feels, however, that a point of view with respect to the question is essential in setting goals for the education of the deaf and in evaluating the effectiveness of educational programs. It has therefore arrived at this consensus:

A clear difference is recognized between primary reliance on a restrictive means of communication in the educational process and such reliance in later life. It is generally agreed that primary emphasis should be placed on teaching speech and speechreading to young deaf children. The Committee does not rule out the employment of finger spelling as an adjunct to oral methods in language teaching if the combination proves more effective, since the symbol system of the spoken and written language is retained. In order to encourage keeping open as wide a range of subsequent choices as possible for deaf young people, the Committee urges that educators of the deaf continue to place emphasis on oral methods, but that manual methods be employed in individual cases when it is clear beyond a reasonable doubt that success by oral methods is unlikely.

There will continue to be failures in the oral method, and facilities for teaching in the language of signs should therefore be retained. Furthermore, many deaf adults will prefer the use of the language of signs and the company of the deaf as an easier and more relaxing social experience. They have a perfect right to make that choice, and no aura of failure or opprobrium should surround it. The Committee believes, however, that the option should be kept open for deaf children to make such a choice as responsible adults. The choice should not be made for them in the schools unless it is clear after careful professional analysis on an individual basis that the choice cannot be kept open.

THE EDUCATIONAL INSTITUTION

Educators also differ on the setting in which deaf children should be taught. Feelings are perhaps not as strong on this question as on the methods question, but there are distinct differences. Some favor special residential schools, which were the first setting for formal education of the deaf in this country, and which remain the predominant facility today. Others see distinct advantages in special day schools for the deaf in communities large enough to support them. Both groups, however, are inclined to join in criticism of special day *classes* for the deaf unless there are enough deaf children to warrant an adequate program of progressive graded classes. Most day school advocates look with favor on secondary school classes in which deaf children are integrated with hearing children (but with specialized help made available as needed), while most residential school advocates generally oppose such integration, except in the case of the most gifted deaf children.

The Committee feels that there is a proper place in a good system of education of the deaf for each of the facilities—specialized residential schools, day schools, and day classes and for the use of classes in which deaf and hearing children are integrated. Local conditions and needs, as well as the needs and abilities of individual deaf children, will inevitably play a part in decisions with respect to facilities designed to serve the deaf children of each community.

21

Differential Diagnosis of Auditory Deficits—
A Review of the Literature

JEROME REICHSTEIN AND JOSEPH ROSENSTEIN

A serious challenge to clinical audiologists and other workers in the area of speech and hearing is posed by the problem of differential diagnosis of young children with communication disorders. Differential diagnosis has been identified by the Committee on Research of the American Speech and Hearing Association (1959) as a primary area of research concern to those who work with language disordered children.

The first comprehensive and detailed discussion of differential diagnosis of children with auditory disorders is presented by Myklebust (1954) and is a compendium of procedure and technique as well as an exposition of symptomatology, according to diagnostic category. He notes that auditory disorders and accompanying language retardation are due to, or are associated with, four basic conditions: impairment of the peripheral hearing mechanism, central nervous system involvement (such as aphasia), emotional disturbance, and mental deficiency. He points out that the diagnostic workup—a joint effort by a team which may include an otolaryngologist, pediatrician, neurologist, child psychiatrist, psychologist, audiologist, speech pathologist, and educator—includes a differential history taking, comprehensive medical examination, and clinical observation and testing of auditory capacity, language development, social maturity, mental development, motor capacity, and emotional adjustment.

Early reports (Anderson, 1945; Fromm, 1946; Karlin, Youtz, and Kennedy, 1940) on the evaluation of individual children with communication disorders appear in the literature. Nance (1946), however, is one of the first to have written about the procedure of differential diagnosis of children with retarded language development. She briefly discusses measures that could be standardized and used objectively in the evaluation of case history, hearing, social maturity, emotional development, mental ability, and language development. Strauss and Lehtinen (1947), Kastein and

* From *Exceptional Children* 1964, *31*, pp. 73–82. Reprinted by permission of the authors and the publisher.

Fowler (1954), and Hardy and Bordley (1951) are among others who contributed to the development of techniques for differential diagnosis.

Kastein and Fowler (1954), McHugh (1961), Filling (1962) and Di-Carlo, Kendall, and Goldstein (1962) have indicated that the communication disorders of many children are caused by a combination of two or more of the basic conditions outlined by Myklebust. Filling reports that 25 percent of the children she examined resulted from multiple causal conditions, while McHugh finds the incidence in his clinic to be 42 percent.

CNS COMMUNICATION DISORDERS

Central nervous system (CNS) disturbances as a causal factor in communication disorders in children have only recently been discussed in detail. Of all the various CNS language and auditory disorders, the concept of aphasia and the term "aphasia" have received the most attention. There is, however, disagreement on the very existence of the group or diagnostic category and on the characteristics of children with aphasia.

The definition of aphasia offered by McGinnis, Kleffner, and Goldstein (1956) is used by some workers in the field:

> Aphasia . . . may be regarded as an inability to express and/or to understand language symbols, and it is the result of some defect in the central nervous system rather than the result of a defect in the peripheral speech mechanism, ear or auditory nerve, defect in general intelligence or severe emotional disturbance (p. 239).

The child whose predominant disability is understanding language has sensory or receptive aphasia; the child whose predominant disability is expressing language has motor or expressive aphasia. Both McGinnis, Kleffner, and Goldstein (1956) and Myklebust (1954) point out that because of the interdependence of language functions, children with receptive aphasia also have expressive deficiencies as a consequence of not understanding language.

Kleffner (1959) narrows the concept of aphasia with respect to the larger constellation of neurological disorders:

> The term "aphasia" refers to a specific kind of deficit in language ability. The term "brain-injured" is very general and may include individuals with problems ranging from severe cerebral palsy to abnormal EEG patterns without other obvious defects. (p. 414); and:
> Although aphasia was defined . . . as resulting from a deficit in the central nervous system, evidence of a pathological condition in the central nervous system . . . is *not* (italics not in the original) essential to our classification of a child as aphasic (p. 413).

Support for Kleffner's approach concerning pathology is available in the observations and evidence presented by other authorities. At least three neurologists (Catholic University, 1962; Douglass, Fowler, and Ryan, 1961;

Institute on Childhood Aphasia, 1962) indicate that the absence of classical neurological signs does not necessarily rule out central nervous system involvement. According to Karlin, "physical examination in congenital aphasia is usually negative. There are no specific neurological signs" (Institute on Childhood Aphasia, 1962, p. 22). While Nielsen (1959) holds that only severe bilateral brain damage can cause aphasia in children, others state that the CNS disturbance may be either minimal or severe and may involve either cerebral damage or dysfunction (Institute on Childhood Aphasia, 1962).

On the other hand, the very existence of aphasia in children has been questioned. DiCarlo (1960) states that the congenitally aphasic child presents a multiplicity of disturbances which can no longer be considered "a clear-cut, single, clinical or pathological entity" (p. 361). Bender (in Brown, 1959) reports that upon re-examination at later dates, "all the children" she originally considered as "congenitally aphasic" appeared to be cases of "emotional disturbance."

Bender's re-examination approach is especially risky in the diagnosis of children with CNS disturbances. Karlin and Michal-Smith (1962) explain that behavioral symptoms of a CNS disorder may wane as a child grows and that secondary emotional disturbances may develop. Ewing (1962) and Berry and Eisenson (1956) suggest that the late development and maturation of the CNS is a cause of language and hearing disorders. A third factor to be considered is educational treatment. A child who was basically aphasic at a younger age may, after training, appear clinically as a predominantly emotionally disturbed individual at a later date.

The American Academy of Ophthalmology and Otolaryngology (1960) has recently suggested "dysacusis," a term which has already been used by some as a replacement for such terms as "central auditory problems" (Hardy and Pauls, 1959, p. 124) and "agnosia . . . (and) receptive aphasia" (Douglass, Fowler, and Ryan, 1961, p. 43). Dysacusis, as defined by the AAOO, is an "impairment of hearing that is *not* primarily a loss of acuity," but a "dysfunction of either the nervous system, the auditory nerve or the cochlea." It includes discrimination loss, recruitment, and aphasia. In contrast, *Rehabilitation Codes* (Association for the Aid of Crippled Children, 1962) specifically excludes receptive aphasia from the framework of dysacusis. Another term, "central dysacusis" (Davis and Silverman, 1960, p. 82), encompasses psychogenic deafness and phonemic regression. Although the term dysacusis is being used to describe children with CNS communication disorders, it is still a term that requires further amplification.

Myklebust (1954) delineates four CNS communication disorders: aphasia, central deafness, auditory agnosia, and auditory imperception. He describes aphasia as a disorder in the use of language symbols; central deafness as a deficiency in transmitting auditory impulses along the auditory pathways to the auditory cortex; auditory agnosia as a generalized inability to understand verbal and nonverbal auditory sensations; and auditory imperception as a deficiency in structuring and appropriately attending to auditory stimuli. He acknowledges that the behavioral characteristics of these various conditions are frequently very similar to each other.

Hardy (1956) discusses three types of disorders related to CNS disturbances: transmission (similar to central deafness); perception (which appears to be similar to Myklebust's auditory imperception and auditory agnosia); and verbal-symbolic association (aphasia). He associates the first condition with the central pathways, the second with the temporal lobe, and the third condition with other cortical areas.

A number of workers have questioned the validity of very fine diagnostic differentiation. After pointing out that organic involvement may cause a wide variety of "language-hearing-behavioral disorders," Levine (1960) calls attention to the availability of only scant evidence for supporting the use of neat diagnostic labels. Goldstein (1958) states that there is a continuum in communication disorders, ranging from deafness, a peripheral loss of sensitivity, to aphasia, a disturbance in language learning because of an impairment in the CNS.

A report by DiCarlo (1960) dramatically reflects the differences of opinion and lack of standardization of terminology and practice discussed above. He describes the re-evaluation of 67 children previously diagnosed as aphasic by a number of other diagnosticians and finds that 20 of these children were emotionally disturbed; 15, peripherally deafened; 28, mentally retarded in various degrees; and only four, "aphasoid." Eisenson recently notes, ". . . about 90 percent or more of the youngsters brought to me are relieved of their congenital aphasia immediately by my rediagnosing them . . ." (in Institute on Childhood Aphasia, 1962, p. 21).

Techniques in Differential Diagnosis

In an effort to discover differential diagnostic indicators, Goldstein, Landau, and Kleffner (1960) examined 183 children educationally confirmed as aphasic or deaf at the Central Institute for the Deaf with a battery of tests, including neurologic examination, EEG, skull X rays, audiometric studies, psychometric tests, vestibular function tests, and the medical history. They conclude that only gross neurologic abnormalities and a few etiologic categories help to distinguish one group from the other. Thirty-two percent of the aphasic population had no neurologic abnormalities and about 40 percent of both the aphasic and deaf children had abnormal electroencephalograms. Hardy (in Institute on Childhood Aphasia, 1962) has commented that he does not place too much confidence in etiology as a clue in diagnosis. No difference was noted in the language behavior and educational progress of the neurologically normal and neurologically impaired aphasic children.

Although the deaf group in the CID study showed greater hearing losses, the authors state that a serious hearing loss does not preclude aphasia in the same child. Twenty-one aphasic children and 13 deaf children had flat U-shaped audiograms; 43 deaf and 32 aphasic children had gradually sloping curves; and 54 deaf and one aphasic child had very severe, residual type audiograms.

With respect to shape of pure tone audiometric curves, Merklein and Briskey (1962) assessed the hearing, frequently after extended training, of 25 children suspected of central neuropathology and suggested that, in at least some cases, severely sloping, high-frequency, peripheral hearing losses, and not central neuropathology, may have caused the language disorders of the subjects. Ewing (1930) made a similar observation, also after having examined children suspected of having aphasia.

Landau, Goldstein, and Kleffner (1960) report the first educationally and clinically diagnosed case of childhood aphasia with accompanying pathologic data. A ten-year-old child with aphasia and near-normal hearing died after an attack of mumps. A neurologic autopsy revealed bilateral degeneration of the sylvian regions (auditory areas) of the temporal lobes and of the medial geniculate nuclei. The authors caution their readers, however, that such gross lesions are not to be necessarily anticipated in most cases of congenital aphasia, "for a large portion of the congenital aphasic population shows no collateral clinical or laboratory evidence of such extensive lesions" (p. 920).

Rubin, Lieberman, and Bordley (1962) offer what they consider to be the first factual validation of central deafness in children. They measured the cochlear and VII nerve action potential produced at the round windows of 15 children assumed to have central deafness. Three children indicated cochlear potential responses and three children gave both cochlear and VII nerve action potential readings. Their results suggest that in the six latter cases, the organ of Corti was functioning and the apparent deafness was caused by retrocochlear factors.

Behavioral evaluations have been given an increasingly larger role in differential diagnosis. Myklebust (1954) lists the following general characteristics as typical of the behavior of aphasic children: distractability, disinhibition, perseveration, failure to grasp the true meaning of their surroundings and experience, and hyperactivity. Hardy and Eisenson (in Institute on Childhood Aphasia, 1962, pp. 20, 54) have made observations similar to those of Myklebust. Kleffner (1959) states that the aphasic children he has known were relatively normal in all respects except for their inability to learn language. He feels that most abnormal behavior can probably be traced to the confusion and frustration of the child-parent relationship. It must be noted that Kleffner's observations were based on extended study of children in a residential school setting.

McConnell and McClamrock (1961) report on research in which the degree of social or group participation was investigated as a technique for differential diagnosis, and find no marked difference in the level of peer interaction between children with peripheral hearing loss and children with "central dysacusis." Bangs (1961) reports on a standardized language evaluation battery incorporated into her diagnostic workup, selecting language subtests from a variety of instruments such as the Stanford-Binet Intelligence Scale.

The Illinois Test of Psycholinguistic Abilities (ITPA) was developed by Kirk and McCarthy (1961) and Sievers (1955) as a tool for differential diagnosis. The test consists of a battery of nine subtests, each of which probes a different aspect of language development. Administering the ITPA to the deaf and aphasic populations at the Central Institute for the Deaf, Olson (1960) found significant group differences in the scores of four subtests (visual-motor association, auditory decoding, vocal encoding, and auditory-vocal automatic) which he had predicted would distinguish between the groups. Although it has not yet been validated for individual differential diagnostic purposes, the ITPA is used for planning and evaluating educational therapy (Kirk and Bateman, 1962).

Diagnostic teachings is an increasingly crucial factor in the diagnosis of children with communication disorders. Reed (1961) explicitly states that aphasia can be established only after a child has been in a teaching situation. On the basis of some of the evidence discussed above, Kleffner (in Catholic University, 1962) concludes that no pattern of characteristics or test results has been able to differentiate deaf from aphasic children conclusively except the ability to learn language and information that is gleaned from diagnostic teaching. Connor (1959) explains the cogent diagnostic potential of educators when he pointed out the unexcelled opportunities the teacher has to observe children day after day under a wide variety of circumstances.

AUDIOLOGICAL ASPECTS OF DIFFERENTIAL DIAGNOSIS

Hardy states that one of the goals of testing the hearing of young children with language disorders is "to differentiate among several possible reasons for the lack of development of speech and language" (in International Conference on Audiology, 1957, p. 219). Goldstein reaffirms in the same *Proceedings:*

> In all our hearing tests we look for at least two things: one, the weakest sound to which a child will respond, that is, his threshold; two, the manner in which he responds to sound . . . We should find out from our hearing tests whether a child's auditory disorder results primarily from a serious reduction in auditory sensitivity or primarily from a deficit in auditory perception and linguistic development (p. 222).

A great deal of attention has been devoted to developing techniques of testing and evaluating the auditory capacity and auditory behavior of children (Barr, 1955; Derbyshire and McDermott, 1958; Ewing and Ewing, 1944; Hardy and Bordley, 1951; and Lowell, Rushford, Hoversten, and Stoner, 1956). Although this body of knowledge is part of the armamentarium used in auditory evaluation, the discussion focuses on studies concerned with subjective audiological techniques that relate to differential diagnosis.

Myklebust (1954) has indicated that the testing of auditory behavior in young children, especially those with auditory disorders, is a difficult task that must be approached with caution and skill in order to insure validity. Wood and Frisina (in Catholic University, 1962) and Myklebust (1954) have discussed types of audiological tests necessary for the purposes of differential diagnosis that are supplemental to tests of auditory sensitivity. Among these are: tests of language understanding, auditory discrimination, localization, foreground-background perception, scanning, memory span, imitative ability, and vocal monitoring.

Consistency of Response

On the basis of test findings and observations, various workers have described patterns of auditory behavior that are differentially characteristic of children with peripheral hearing loss, mental retardation, aphasia, and emotional disturbance. The consensus is that children with peripheral hearing loss, on the one hand, use their residual hearing in a consistent, integrated, and meaningful manner (Myklebust, 1954; Whitehurst, 1961) while, in contrast, aphasic children are characterized by disintegrated, inconsistent auditory behavior (Douglass, Fowler, and Ryan, 1961; Hardy and Pauls, 1959; International Conference on Audiology, 1957; Monsees, 1961; and Myklebust, 1954). Mentally retarded children seem to respond better to test stimuli that are more meaningful and genetically suitable to them than to the more abstract pure tone (Myklebust, 1954; Wolfe and MacPherson, 1959). Aphasic children are harder to condition to auditory stimuli than are those with peripheral hearing losses (in International Conference on Audiology, 1957). These patterns of auditory behavior are frequently supported only by casual evidence based on clinical observation and not by systematic experimental data or statistical analysis.

At least two interacting clusters of factors contribute to the differentiation of behavior patterns: one, the responses and specific auditory behavior; and two, the stimuli and techniques employed to elicit these responses. In order to increase understanding and clinical applicability, the following are some of the specific factors that need to be stated precisely: exact definition of the auditory dimension or characteristic under discussion; the exact stimuli used; the method of stimulus presentation; the motivation to respond; the method of indicating response; complete description of responses; and adequate description of subjects. All or most of this information has not usually been supplied when patterns of auditory behavior are under consideration.

Observations and reports repeatedly note that children with language and auditory disorders associated with central nervous system involvement respond inconsistently to auditory stimuli in both the natural environment and test situations. In measuring auditory threshold, inconsistency is noted by fluctuations in successive threshold responses. Myklebust (1954) suggests that aphasic children respond inconsistently not because of shifts in sensitivity but because of deficiencies in their ability to attend and to integrate.

Myklebust (1954), and Hardy and Pauls (1959) report contradictory responses within a single test session. Goldstein (in International Conference on Audiology, 1957) describes intratest fluctuations of 30 to 40 db in pure tone audiometry. In their case report, Landau, Goldstein, and Kleffner (1960) observe a type of inconsistency related to a time factor. After testing the second ear of a child, the tester returned to the first ear, where the responses had previously been consistent, and found they were now inconsistent. Monsees (1961) discusses inconsistency in terms of intertest pure tone threshold variability.

Although considerable and fruitful efforts have been devoted to the development of auditory tests and techniques, there appears to be relatively little systematic experimentation or study of the relationship between differentiating characteristics such as inconsistency and various test techniques. A review of the literature from the point of view of stimuli, mode of presentation, and method of indicating response is called for in order to seek indications of their influence on the dimension of threshold consistency.

Stimuli

Pure tone. Myklebust (1954) questions the validity of pure tone as a stimulus in routine subjective pure tone audiometry for young children, in which the average response level of normally-hearing children improves from approximately 15 db re Audiometric 0 at age three to approximately 5 db at the age of five. The introduction of conditional play audiometry helps to ameliorate this problem. Many observations about the test inconsistency of aphasic children are based on their responses to pure tones. Warbled pure tone, however, has been found to be more effective than steady tone with "dysacusic" children (Douglass, Fowler, and Ryan, 1961). Hardy (in International Conference on Audiology, 1957) observes that warbled tone is an attention-getting device, essential for children who have difficulty in attending because of CNS involvement.

Speech. Several workers report on the efficacy of speech as a stimulus in testing the level of awareness in children. A number of special techniques and word lists (Keaster, 1947; Siegenthaler, Pearson, and Lezak, 1954) have been prepared for determining the speech reception threshold of children. Dale (1962) describes the popular "Go-Game," in which children respond by a simple motor act when they hear the word "Go!" Solomon (1962) finds that the threshold of overt responses was better for speech sounds than for toy sounds and/or pure tones with normally hearing children between 20 and 33 months of age. Similarly, Wolfe and MacPherson (1959) note that more mentally retarded children responded to speech signals than to pure tones. Sortini (1960) reports that speech is a more effective stimulus than the more abstract pure tone for many brain-injured children.

Complex stimuli. Other sounds frequently used as stimuli are music, noisemakers, and animal sounds (O'Neill, Oyer, and Hillis, 1961; Streng, Fitch, Hedgecock, Phillips, and Carrell, 1958). Many of these stimuli are employed in warm-up periods to make preliminary assessment of children's hearing. In the Solomon study (1962), music was one of the more effective stimuli for obtaining overt reactions from her young subjects. Whitehurst (1961) points out that peripherally hard-of-hearing children usually respond consistently to these complex stimuli. Morgan (in Douglass, Fowler, and Ryan, 1961) notes as well that complex sounds such as these are more effective in testing "dysacusic" children. Earphone thresholds are frequently better than sound field thresholds. The earphones help the "dysacusic" child to focus on the presence of sound and the descending method is often more effective with "dysacusic" children.

Method of Indicating Response

In subjective audiometry, the variety of methods by which children indicate response may be grouped in the following manner: reflex-localization; direct voluntary indication; complex-play conditioned response; and simple-play conditioned response. Although some response methods overlap, they have been arbitrarily categorized for purposes of discussion.

The use and analysis of reflex response and localization of sound have been frequently reported (DiCarlo and Bradley, 1961; Ewing and Ewing, 1958) as an aid to hearing evaluation and differential diagnosis in infants and very young children. Downs (1960) formulated some rules by which she infers thresholds for infants from the intensity of the stimuli to which there are reflex responses.

Myklebust (1954) states that direct voluntary responses (saying something, raising a hand) may not be valid for determining pure tone thresholds in children younger than five years. For children with communication disorders, the minimum chronological age at which this technique becomes valid is probably higher.

Conditioned response methods based on learning theories described by Thorndike, Hull, and Skinner (in Hilgard, 1956; and Miller and Dollard, 1941) have made it possible to test children subjectively as young as two and a half years of age. Most subjective audiological procedures require the testee to sustain attention and to respond each time he hears. Audiologists have created techniques in which children are conditioned to reach for or do something pleasant each time they perceive an auditory stimulus. Reward-response techniques have succeeded in mobilizing interest and providing motivation to listen and to respond repetitively.

The peep show of Dix and Hallpike (1947) and the pediacoumeter (Guilford and Haug, 1952) were among the first in a series of complex play conditioned response techniques involving a hear-and-do combination. With the peep show, children look into a darkened house, and when they hear a tone, push a button which illuminates the interior and revolves a group of dolls. Investigators, working with mentally retarded (Wolfe and MacPherson, 1959) and young, normally hearing children (Sills, 1961) have pointed out that complex toys such as these were less effective than other simpler ones. Apparently the coordination and actions involved were either too complex or the situation too distracting.

On the other hand, Meyerson and Michael (1960) have built an elaborate Skinnerian operant-conditioning apparatus combining a two-lever operation and 100 percent candy and knick-knack reinforcement, for the purpose of testing the hearing of mentally retarded children. Although not all the 67 experimental subjects were amenable to operant-conditioning techniques, Meyerson and Michael feel that the apparatus and procedures were effective and merit further experimentation.

The Ewings (1944) and Lowell and his team (1956) have developed and described some of the simple-play conditioned response techniques employing simple toys and activities. Children are taught that when they hear a signal, they should perform a simple motor act such as putting a peg in a pegboard or putting a ring on a stick. The Lowell group conditioned normally hearing children as young as two and one half years of age to respond with blocks and other simple toys to pure tones at levels less than Audiometric 0. They also validated the play audiometry thresholds of young severely deaf children against routine audiograms made several years later on the same children. The audiograms were very similar.

Candy has been used as the reward-reinforcer in both complex and simply conditioning methods. In the Meyerson and Michael study (1960), it was an important motivating factor. Costa, Mandel, and Rapin (1962) report on the use of candy coated chocolate pellets as a reinforcer in an experimental study of reaction time to visual and auditory stimuli. Both normally hearing children and deaf children, whose responses were rewarded with candy pellets, performed significantly better than nonreinforced children.

Discussion

The attempt has been made to summarize and assess various stimuli, modes of presentation, and methods of indicating response from the point of view of how they may relate to and affect the characteristics of consistency of threshold response. There has not yet been an investigation of the relative effectiveness of various stimuli and techniques in evaluating the hearing of children with CNS auditory and language disorders similar to the Wolfe and MacPherson experimental study (1959) with trainable retarded children.

While it has been observed and noted that aphasic children respond inconsistently to sound as compared to the consistency of children with peripheral hearing loss, there has been no experimental attempt to study inconsistency in and of itself, nor its relationship to various audiological techniques. One may speculate that, possibly, by more efficient selection of stimuli, mode of input, method of indicating response, and motivation, the amount of inconsistency of aphasic children in response to threshold tests may be reduced. While such findings might not disprove the inconsistent nature of the aphasic child, they might have some bearing on various aspects of the diagnostic process.

REFERENCES

American Academy of Opthalmology and Otolaryngology. *A guide to the care of adults with hearing loss*. Rochester, Minnesota: Whiting Press, 1960.

American Speech and Hearing Association Committee on Research. Research needs in speech pathology and audiology. *Journal of Speech and Hearing Disorders*, Monograph Supplement 5, September, 1959.

Anderson, Jeanette O. Eighteen cases of aphasia studied from the viewpoint of a speech pathologist. *Journal of Speech Disorders*, 1945, **10**, 9–33.

Association for the Aid of Crippled Children. *Rehabilitation codes*. New York: The Association, 1962.

Bangs, Tina E. Evaluating children with language delay. *Journal of Speech and Hearing Disorders*, 1961, **26**, 6–18.

Barr, B. Pure tone audiometry for pre-school children. *Acta Otolaryngologica* Supplement 121, 1955, 1–84.

Berry, Mildred F., and Eisenson, J. *Speech disorders*. New York: Appleton-Century-Crofts, Inc., 1956.

Brown, S. F. (Editor) The concept of congenital aphasia from the standpoint of dynamic differential diagnosis. Washington, D.C.: American Speech and Hearing Association, 1959.

Catholic University of America, Workshop on Speech and Language Therapy with the Brain-Damaged Child. *Speech and language therapy with the brain-damaged child*. Washington, D.C.: The University, 1962.

Connor, L. E. Diagnostic teaching—the teacher's new role. *Volta Review*, 1959, **61**, 311–315.

Costa, D., Mandel, I. J., and Rapin, Isabelle. Visual and auditory reaction time under reinforcement conditions in children at a school for the deaf. *Asha*, 1962, **4**, 415.

Dale, D. M. C. *Applied audiology for children*. Springfield, Illinois: Charles C Thomas, 1962.

Davis, H., and Silverman, S. R. (Editors) *Hearing and deafness*. (Revised edition) New York: Holt, Rinehart, and Winston, Inc., 1960.

Di Carlo, L. M. Differential diagnosis of congenital aphasia. *Volta Review*, 1960, **62**, 361–364.

Di Carlo, L. M., and Bradley, W. H. A simplified auditory test for infants and young children. *Laryngoscope*, 1961, **71**, 628–646.

Di Carlo, L. M., Kendall, D., and Goldstein, R. Diagnostic procedures for auditory disordered children. *Folia Phoniatrica*, 1962, **14**, 206–264.

Dix, M. R., and Hallpike, C. S. The peep show. *British Medical Journal*, 1947, **2**, 719–723.

Derbyshire, A. J., and McDermott, M. Further contributions to the EEG method of evaluatory auditory function. *Laryngoscope*, 1958, **68**, 558–570.

Douglass, Frances M., Fowler, E. P., Jr., and Ryan, Genevieve M. *A differential study of communication disorders*. New York: Columbia-Presbyterian Medical Center, 1961.

Downs, Marion P. *The auditory development of the normal child and its relation to testing and therapy for the hearing handicapped child.* Tel Aviv: Micha Society, 1960.

Ewing, A. W. B. *Aphasia in children.* London: Oxford University Press, 1930.

Ewing, A. W. B. Central deafness pedagogy. *International Audiology,* 1962, 1, 106–111.

Ewing, Irene R., and Ewing, A. W. B. The ascertainment of deafness in infancy and early childhood. *Journal of Laryngology and Otolaryngology,* 1944, 59, 309–333.

Ewing, Irene R., and Ewing, A. W. B. *New opportunities for deaf children.* London: University of London Press, Ltd., 1958.

Filling, Sonja, Differential diagnosis of hearing and language disturbance in children. *International Audiology,* 1962, 1, 88–94.

Fromm, Erika O. Study of a case of pseudo deaf-muteness (Psychic deafness). *Journal of Nervous Mental Disease,* 1946, 103, 37–59.

Goldstein, R. Differential classification of disorders of communication in children. *American Annals of the Deaf,* 1958, 103, 215–223.

Goldstein, R., Landau W. M., and Kleffner, F. R. Neurologic observations in a population of deaf and aphasic children. *Annals of Otolaryngology, Rhinolaryngology, and Laryngology,* 1960, 69, 756–767.

Guilford, F. R., and Haug, C. O. Diagnosis of deafness in the very young child. *Archives of Otolaryngology,* 1952, 55, 101–106.

Hardy, W. G. Problems of audition, perception, and understanding. *Volta Review,* 1956, 58, 289–300, 309.

Hardy, W. G., and Bordley, J. E. Special techniques in testing the hearing of children. *Journal of Speech and Hearing Disorders,* 1951, 16, 123–131.

Hardy, W. G., and Pauls, Miriam D. Significance of problems of conditioning in GSR audiometry. *Journal of Speech and Hearing Disorders,* 1959, 24, 123–126.

Hilgard, E. R. *Theories of learning.* (2nd edition) New York: Appleton-Century-Crofts, Inc., 1956.

Institute on Childhood Aphasia. *Childhood aphasia.* Edited by Robert West. San Francisco: California Society for Crippled Children and Adults, 1962.

International Conference on Audiology. Proceedings . . . May 13 through 16, 1957. *Laryngoscope,* 1958, 68, 209–698.

Karlin, I. W., Youtz, C., and Kennedy, Lou. Distorted speech in young children. *American Journal of Diseases of Children,* 1940, 59, 1203–1218.

Karlin, I. W., and Fowler, E. P., Jr. Differential diagnosis of communication disorders in children referred for hearing tests. *Archives of Otolaryngology,* 1954, 60, 468–477.

Karlin, I. W., and Michal-Smith, H. *The special child.* Seattle: New School for the Special Child, 1962.

Kastein, Shulamith, and Fowler, E. P., Jr. Differential diagnosis of communication disorders in children referred for hearing tests. *Archives of Otolaryngology,* 1954, 60.

Keaster, Jacqueline. A quantitative method of testing the hearing of young children. *Journal of Speech Disorders,* 1947, 12, 159–160.

Kirk, S. A., and Bateman, Barbara D. Diagnosis and remediation of learning disabilities. *Exceptional Children,* 1962, 29, 73–78.

Kirk, S. A., and McCarthy, J. J. The Illinois test of psycholinguistic abilities—An approach in differential diagnosis. *American Journal of Mental Deficiency,* 1961, 65, 399–412.

Kleffner, F. R. Teaching aphasic children. *Education,* 1959, 79, 413–418.

Landau, W. M., Goldstein, R., and Kleffner, F. R. Congenital aphasia: A clinicopathologic study. *Neurology*, 1960, 10, 915–921.

Levine, Edna S. *The psychology of deafness.* New York: Columbia University Press, 1960.

Lowell, E. L., Rushford, Georgina, Hoversten, Gloria, and Stoner, Marguerite. Evaluation of pure tone audiometry with preschool age children. *Journal of Speech and Hearing Disorders*, 1956, 21, 292–302.

McConnell, F., and McClamroch, Margaret. Social participation levels of non-language children. *Journals of Speech and Hearing Disorders*, 1961, 26, 354–358.

McGinnis, Mildred A., Kleffner, F. R., and Goldstein, R. Teaching aphasic children. *Volta Review*, 1956, 58, 239–244.

McHugh, H. E. The brain-injured child with impaired hearing. *Laryngoscope*, 1961, 71, 1034–1057.

McHugh, H. E. Hearing and language disorders in children. *Postgraduate Medicine*, 1962, 31, 54–65.

Merklein, R. A., and Briskey, R. J. Audiometric findings in children referred to a program for language disorders. *Volta Review*, 1962, 64, 294–298.

Meyerson, L., and Michael, J. L. *The measurement of sensory thresholds in exceptional children: An experimental approach to some problems of differential diagnosis and education with special reference to hearing.* Houston, Texas: University of Houston, 1960.

Miller, N. E., and Dollard, J. *Social learning and imitation.* New Haven: Yale University Press, 1941.

Monsees, Edna K. Aphasia in children. *Journal of Speech and Hearing Disorders*, 1961, 26, 83–86.

Myklebust, H. R. *Auditory disorders in children: A manual for differential diagnosis.* New York: Grune and Stratton, Inc., 1954.

Nance, Lorna S. Differential diagnosis of aphasia in children. *Journal of Speech Disorders*, 1946, 11, 219–223.

Nielson, J. M. Disturbances of language. *Education*, 1959, 79, 404–407.

Olson, J. L. A comparison of sensory aphasic, expressive aphasic, and deaf children on the Illinois test of language ability. Unpublished doctoral dissertation, University of Illinois, 1960.

O'Neill, J. J., Oyer, H. J., and Hillis, J. W. Audiometric procedures used with children. *Journal of Speech and Hearing Disorders*, 1961, 26, 61–66.

Reed, M. Hearing and speech disorders. *Cerebral Palsy Bulletin*, 1961, 3, 52–56.

Rubin, R. J., Lieberman, A. T., and Bordley, J. E. Some observations on cochlear potentials and nerve action potentials in children. *Laryngoscope*, 1962, 72, 545–554.

Siegenthaler, B. M., Pearson, J., and Lezak, R. J. A speech reception threshold test for children. *Journal of Speech and Hearing Disorders*, 1954, 19, 360–366.

Sievers, Dorothy J. Development and standardization of a test of psycholinguistic growth in pre-school children. Unpublished doctoral dissertation, University of Illinois, 1955.

Sills, Sandra. An evaluation of two techniques for screening the hearing of pre-school children. Unpublished masters thesis, Hunter College, 1962.

Solomon, Sandra. Evaluation of hearing acuity in very young children. Unpublished masters thesis, Hunter College, 1962.

Sortini, A. J. Hearing evaluation of brain-damaged children. *Volta Review*, 1960, 62, 536–540.

Sortini, A. J., and Flake, C. G. Speech audiometry testing for pre-school children. *Laryngoscope*, 1953, 63, 991–997.

Strauss, A. A., and Lehtinen, Laura E. *Psychopathology and education of the brain-injured child.* New York: Grune and Stratton, Inc., 1947.

Streng, Alice, Fitch, J., Hedgecock, L. D., Phillips, J. W., and Carrell, J. A. *Hearing therapy for children.* (2nd revised edition) New York: Grune & Stratton, Inc., 1958. 63, 430–432, 463.

Whitehurst, Mary W. Testing the hearing of pre-school children. *Volta Review,* 1961, 63, 430–432, 463.

Wolfe, W. G., and MacPherson, J. R. *The evaluation and development of techniques for testing the auditory acuity of trainable mentally retarded children.* Austin: University of Texas, 1959.

** 22 **

Factors in the Selection of Types of Educational Programs for Deaf Persons

ADVISORY COMMITTEE ON THE EDUCATION OF THE DEAF

Four types of organized educational programs for the deaf are offered in the school systems of the country: residential schools, day schools, day class programs, and classes for hearing children into which deaf children are integrated, usually with the provision of a resource teacher who is available to assist the deaf child as difficulties arise. Other programs also play an important part in the education of the deaf child, including home programs for teaching speech to very young deaf children; a few specialized programs for the child with two or more handicaps, one of which is deafness; and a number of centers, both public and private, which offer diagnostic services or speech training. For the purposes of this chapter, however, the discussion is concerned with those resources of subject matter education which can be said to be a part of an educational system.

Many factors deserve consideration in the selection of one of the several types of programs, some obvious, some not so obvious—and some about

* From *Education of the Deaf.* Washington: U.S. Department of Health, Education and Welfare, 1965, pp. 31–41.

which present knowledge is insufficiently advanced to justify unequivocal conclusions. The following discussion deals with the advantages and disadvantages of each of the kinds of programs.

RESIDENTIAL SCHOOLS

The first organized programs in this country were started in residential schools. These have remained the main resource for over a century, despite recent more rapid growth in the other programs. A statement of the advantages and disadvantages of such programs will not meet with unanimous agreement, but the following points are consistent with the objectives set forth in the introduction to this report.

Advantages

1. The residential schools offer the most satisfactory solution to the geographical problem—that of offering an organized educational program to deaf children whose homes are in rural areas or in communities too small to support a specialized program.

2. From the standpoint of organization and administration, residential schools enjoy the advantage of having reasonably full responsibility for direction fixed in a superintendent or headmaster, who by virtue of his position is concerned solely with the objective of educating deaf children.

3. The residential schools permit a sufficiently large number of deaf children to be brought together to justify the acquisition of specialized auditory examination and training facilities and equipment. It must be conceded that this factor is not a completely consistent one. Twenty-one out of a total of 87 public and private residential schools have enrollments of less than 100, while 9 of 15 public day schools and 15 of 297 day class systems have enrollments of more that 100. Nonetheless, residential schools do generally have larger enrollments.

4. The larger average size of residential schools also makes feasible a larger and more diversified faculty and the consequent offering of a wider range of subjects taught.

5. A residential school provides an "around-the-clock" school environment for dealing with language-learning and related problems of deaf children.

6. Surrounded as he is by deaf companions, the deaf child can lead a less strained life in out-of-school hours. (Some will dispute that this is an advantage, contending that it may encourage at an early age the segregation of the deaf in our society.)

7. For many deaf children from economically disadvantaged families, the residential school offers better physical surroundings, better nutrition, and an environment more conducive to after-school study than would be provided at home.

Disadvantages

1. The deaf child in a residential school is necessarily removed from the many daily attentions of his family—family affection and interest and the "give and take" of family life—which our society generally prizes.[1]

2. The child is in most cases isolated to a considerable degree from the kind of life and society to which he will have to adjust on emerging from the residential setting.

3. Even though the program of the school attempts to counteract this isolating tendency by facilitating contacts with the surrounding community, too many residential schools are located in very small communities. Our country is experiencing a rapid trend to urbanization, and the adult deaf in particular generally prefer to congregate in urban centers, but residential schools generally do not prepare students adequately for urban living.

4. Many factors in residential schools operate to encourage the segregation of the deaf in our society. The children do not have opportunities to play and associate fully with hearing children or the challenge of finding ways to communicate effectively with them. The reliance on manual methods of communication at least outside of the classroom in the majority of such schools tends to fix a habit of such relatively easy communication for social purposes and thus to dull the motivation to surmount the more difficult obstacles to oral communication. (Some will point out, on the other hand, that many deaf children who are psychologically and socially handicapped as well suffer a greater degree of isolation in a hearing environment at home and that it is only in a segregated setting that they find the social satisfaction of communicating with their peers.)

5. Most residential schools provide less opportunity for the movement of deaf students on an individual basis to other systems than do day schools and day class programs. The latter more often seek to prepare students to be integrated into classes of hearing children and to effect such transfers on an individual basis when the child is considered ready. In residential schools, the objective is more likely to be the completion of the residential school program.[2]

6. As with any institution—educational or otherwise—in which teen-aged boys and girls are housed, problems of adolescence and sexual maturing arise and must be handled by school personnel in a nonfamily environment.

---

[1] A few residential schools in densely populated areas recognize and counteract this to a degree by requiring that the children return to their families on weekends. Others permit it where possible.

[2] Here again, others will see this as an advantage rather than a disadvantage, contending that the uprooting of the deaf child from a setting in which his progress makes him stand out and placing him in a setting where his achievement is likely to be below average is a psychological and social shock which may be harmful to his development.

It should be noted also that several residential schools—those which are purely "oral" in approach—have as their objective the preparation of all students for transfer to hearing classes at either the junior high school or the high school level.

Such problems might be more constructively prepared for and handled in the more normal environment of home, church, and day school.

DAY SCHOOLS FOR THE DEAF

Fifteen day schools for the deaf located in nine states operate as parts of the public school systems of the cities or school districts in which they are located. All use only oral methods of instruction. Only one of them offers 12 grades of instruction, most of them seeking the progression of students to either special classes for the deaf or integrated classes at either the junior high school or the high school level.

The establishment of a day school is generally controlled by population considerations since it must serve an area in which there are enough deaf children to justify a specialized school with graded classes, trained teachers, and adequate teacher supervision.

Advantages

1. The day school for the deaf permits the special instructional needs of the deaf child to be met without separating him from his family.

2. Day schools are, virtually by definition, located in large urban areas and thus offer to the children the advantages of growing up in the familiar environment in which most of them will spend their lives and of becoming familiar with urban institutions.

3. Day schools permit deaf children to enjoy as much of a normal growing-up environment as their personalities and inclinations seek. After-school play and associations are likely to involve hearing children to a degree that will make easier the deaf child's active participation in society in later years. (Some contend, however, that it is the exceptional deaf child who is able to enjoy a full and satisfying relationship with hearing companions and that the lot of most individual deaf children in groups of hearing children is one largely of isolation and frustration.)

4. Like residential schools, day schools are generally large enough to justify specialized equipment helpful in the education of the deaf, as well as the employment of trained teachers of the deaf with adequate subject matter specialties.

5. Day schools enjoy an advantage over day class programs for the deaf in that each day school has a principal whose administrative and educational concern is focused on the instruction of deaf children.

6. Because the school is located in districts where the students live, it is possible to involve the children's parents more deeply and directly in the children's educational problems and progress than is the case generally with residential schools.

7. There are easier opportunities than are found in residential schools to move the more advanced students to integrated classes with hearing

children when they are considered ready. (But see footnote, page 207 for the *contra* argument.)

Disadvantages

1. The day school cannot control the out-of-class environment of the students to meet the extraordinary language-learning needs of deaf children. (Some will contend, however, that the natural curiosity of the children can be so stimulated in school and nourished at home that language-learning achievement is superior to that of children in residential schools.)

2. In some cases, residential schools are able to be more selective in intake, with the result that day schools must take more of the lower achievers, the emotionally disturbed, and the multiply handicapped. In such cases, unless it is feasible to organize special classes, all suffer—the slower students, the teachers, and the "normal" deaf students. (This is a problem in nearly all schools and classes for the deaf to a greater or lesser degree. In some day schools, however, the problem is particularly acute.)

3. The day schools do not enjoy the same degree of identity in the educational system that residential schools do. The day school for the deaf must compete with many other schools for the time and attention of officials of the school system.

DAY CLASS PROGRAMS FOR THE DEAF

The number of day class programs for the deaf in this country has more than doubled in the past 15 years. Such programs are organized and housed within the same school buildings as accommodate hearing children. In cases where there are many graded classes taught by trained teachers of the deaf under qualified supervisors, a day class program can be more like than unlike a day school for the deaf. Much of the day class growth, however, except in the large urban centers, has been in the establishment of classes to serve a relatively small number of deaf students in a wide age range. This has led many educators of the deaf to view with alarm what they refer to as a "return to the little red schoolhouse" in education of the deaf.[3] In such cases, the educational needs of deaf children are obviously

---

[3] While there is reason to believe that the information is not in all cases complete or fully descriptive of the programs, the listing of day classes for the deaf in the *American Annals of the Deaf*, January, 1964, shows 142 schools having graded class systems with fewer than 20 deaf students enrolled. Of these, 83 supplied information on the number of grades offered and the number of teachers assigned. Grades offered ranged from 1 to 12 and teachers assigned from 1 to 6. In only four cases did the number of teachers equal or exceed the number of grades covered. Nearly half of the schools in the group (35) reported 6 grades offered, and half of these (17) reported only 2 teachers covering the 6 grades. Seventy-one reported teachers covering 2 or more grades, and 39 reported only 1 teacher who was responsible for from 3 to 12 grades.

not being served nearly as well as in either residential schools or day schools.

Most advantages and disadvantages cited above for day schools are equally applicable to those day class systems with distinct graded classes having at least one teacher each. In addition, the following are peculiar to day class programs:

Advantages

1. The point is made by some that day classes offer opportunities superior to day schools for structured relationship between deaf children and hearing children. While classroom instruction is segregated to permit specialized attention to the educational needs of deaf children, other school activities and facilities are integrated. Others contend that the advantage is more apparent than real, since on the playground and in the lunchroom there seems to be an invisible wall between most deaf and hearing children.

2. There is even greater opportunity than in the case of day schools to place students who make rapid progress in integrated classes with hearing students, since it is often possible to arrange trial transfers for one or two classes a day. In such cases, the break is not as complete.

Disadvantages

1. The day classes are organized within schools for hearing children, and the deaf children constitute a distinct minority in such schools. The problems confronting the principal of such a school are likely to be predominantly those concerning the hearing students and their program, and the time and attention devoted to the operation of the classes for the deaf may be minimal. It is essential that the education of the deaf be more closely supervised than that of the hearing because of the additional learning problems involved. This particular disadvantage may be overcome by special provision for such supervision within the individual school.

2. There is one additional potential difficulty in the larger day class systems where several schools have classes for the deaf and special provision is made in the central office of the system for supervision of such classes. This inevitably involves dual lines of supervision to the classes for the deaf, one from the central unit concerned with the education of the deaf and the other from the principal of the school. In many cases—probably most cases—this presents no serious difficulty, but it is always a potential source of trouble, since individual interests and personalities are involved. In the case of day schools for the deaf, this danger is avoided.

INTEGRATED CLASSES WITH THE HEARING

Integrated classes with hearing students do not constitute the same kind of alternative program for the education of deaf children as do the residential schools, day schools, and day class programs. In order to succeed in integrated classes, deaf children must have received in one way or another intensive, specialized instruction in speech and speechreading. Integrated classes are therefore a progressive step in the education of the deaf, and the advantages and disadvantages are not listed in the same form as for the other types of programs.

With the present state of our knowledge of and provision for the education of the deaf, we may expect only a minority of deaf children to have a good chance of educational success in integrated classes, even with facilitative services and help. The lower achievement levels of most deaf students attributable to their early and continuing language and reading difficulties pose insurmountable obstacles for most of them in integrated classes.

For the substantial minority who are able to register satisfactory achievement, however, and to whom such placement does not create serious psychological and social difficulties, placement in integrated classes is eminently to be desired. It serves to keep more fully open to them the choices in later life which are important to deaf adults and is likely to enhance their further educational opportunities. To increase the likelihood of success in such a setting, special counseling and help is normally made available to deaf students in integrated classes as long as it is needed.

DIFFICULTIES IN RELATING PROGRAMS TO TYPES OF DEAF PERSONS

It would be convenient if it were possible to develop neat categories of deaf persons by type and to suggest the development of individual types of educational programs for each. The basic fact, however, is that each deaf person is an individual endowed with a complex of talents and limitations, just as is the case with hearing people. There are wide ranges of native intelligence, personality characteristics, aspirations, physical abilities in other respects than hearing, talents, skills, and aptitudes, including those for language learning. To these differences that characterize the general population must be added such differences among the deaf as the degree of hearing loss, the site of the lesion, and the age of onset of hearing loss.

All of these differences interact on each other in ways that defeat attempts to develop an orderly classification for purposes of such vital decisions as those involving types of educational programs. While certain groupings can and must be tentatively attempted, the system must never be allowed to obscure the basic concern with the individual deaf child or to lessen in any way the importance of being alert to desirable modifications in the program planned for him.

With these strictures kept prominently in mind, it is possible to discuss kinds of programs that may be suitable for deaf children.

At the outset, it must be recognized that there are some deaf children whom it will not be possible to educate in the generally accepted meaning of the term, just as is the case with some hearing children. The most seriously mentally retarded children who have the additional handicap of deafness should be given such training as they are capable of receiving in specialized classes for the deaf retarded. In such cases, the mental retardation should be considered the primary handicap, and the program should be the responsibilty of those providing training programs for retarded children, with specialized teaching developed for the deaf child. A real danger should be recognized here, however—the possibility that educational retardation caused by deafness may be mistaken for mental retardation. Careful and repeated diagnoses and evaluations should be conducted to minimize the likelihood of such confusion.

Early and repeated diagnosis and evaluation should, in fact, be conducted in all cases of suspected deafness. Every possible advantage should be taken of advances in techniques of auditory training or of possibilities of surgical or other corrective measures. When it appears, however, that a child has an apparently uncorrective hearing loss of sufficient severity to constitute a severe obstacle to the learning of language, special instruction should be provided as discussed in Chapter I. With rare exceptions, such instruction should be given in programs that permit the child to live at home at least until he is three to four years of age. If an adequate program is available, it will be in most cases desirable for him to maintain a regular presence and close identification with his family for several more years; but these are the most critical years for the young deaf child in the learning of language, and if circumstances are such that an adequate educational program cannot be offered in a setting that permits him to live at home, the parents should be urged to cooperate in such a program at a residential school.

For children who are profoundly deaf, whose deafness occurred at birth or before language patterns were established, specialized educational programs are indicated. If these can be offered in a day school or day class setting, there are some familial and social advantages to be realized in such a program. However, individual circumstances in such cases should be controlling, and it may well be that psychological or social factors (the home environment, for example) would indicate that a residential school program would be preferable.

If such a child makes satisfactory progress in oral communication, there would be both individual and social advantages in striving to transfer him when ready to an integrated class with hearing children, preferably under circumstances that would permit return to specialized programs without the harmful experience of a sense of failure.

If, after repeated attempts with a good oral program, it becomes clear that a child is not making satisfactory progress, there should be no hesitation in turning to manual communication methods. The key phrase here is "after repeated attempts." The change to a "manual track" in the school program generally preempts a decision which it is normally desirable to leave to the individual when he becomes an adult: whether avenues of communication with the hearing world are to be severely restricted.

In every case, however, important individual differences must be taken into account. If a child for whom a residential school program is indicated is unduly emotionally upset at the prospect of separation from his family, it may be that the consequences of such an emotional wrench could be far more harmful to his educational progress than an otherwise less satisfactory program.

In summary, the generalizations above should always give way to considerations of what is best for the individual, to the extent that "what is best" can be perceived.

CONCLUSION

The Committee concludes that there is a place for the residential school, the day school, the day class program, and the integrated class with hearing students in a comprehensive program of education for the deaf. The skills and insights required to make the best use of alternatives in individual cases cannot be imparted by formula. Such decisions should be the product of the best interdisciplinary talents that can be summoned for careful diagnosis and evaluation on a continuing basis. In all types of programs there should be constant striving for improvement in quality and an eager receptivity to research findings which offer hope of more effective educational techniques.

23

Post-High School Programs

ADVISORY COMMITTEE ON THE EDUCATION OF THE DEAF

The post-high school educational opportunities for young deaf people are extremely limited. Few emerge from their secondary education with speech and speechreading skills adequate to permit them to succeed without special help in an institution for the hearing.

PRESENT STATUS

Liberal Arts

Gallaudet College is the only four-year liberal arts college for the deaf in the country. For the deaf student who emerges from secondary school with major reliance on manual communication, it offers the only hope for a college degree of bachelor of arts or bachelor of science. Moreover, as admission and performance standards are raised for students in colleges for the hearing, more deaf and very hard-of-hearing students who with some difficulty would have been able in the past to earn such degrees in hearing colleges are also turning to Gallaudet College. In 1959, 116 students entered either the preparatory year or the freshman class. Of these, 21 or 18 per cent came directly from schools other than public residential schools. (While not all public residential schools employ the manual method of communication, very few of the day schools and classes do.) In 1964, 246 students entered the preparatory year or the freshman class, of whom 72, or 29 per cent, came directly from schools other than public residential schools. The proportionate increase from these sources is thus over 60 per cent.

Comprehensive source material on deaf students who attend hearing colleges is meager; they become statistically "lost" as they are commingled with hearing students. A survey, reported in the September, 1963, issue

* From *Education of the Deaf*. Washington: U.S. Department of Health, Education and Welfare, 1965, pp. 43–49.

of the *Volta Review,* indicates that not more than 19 students who gradu-ated from secondary schools with hearing students in the preceding year were attending colleges where they might be taking liberal arts courses. It is of course unlikely that the survey achieved complete coverage, but it is a fair conclusion that far more deaf students currently pursuing a liberal arts course in college are attending Gallaudet College than all other col-leges combined.

Professional Education and Training

The opportunities for professional education and training are indeed limited for the deaf student. Aside from the graduate course in education at Gallaudet College leading to the degree of Master of Science in Educa-tion, there is no known professional offering in American colleges and uni-versities available to deaf students unless they have better than average skills in speech and speechreading. Available information indicates that relatively few deaf persons pursue their education along professional lines except to become teachers.

A survey by Lunde and Bigman whose results were published in 1959 showed a total of 528 "professional, technical, and similar workers" among 7,920 respondents. More than half of these (304) were teachers, athletic coaches, or school counselors. Of the remaining 224, the largest groups were to be found in technical occupations (59 draftsmen and cartographers, 21 photographers, 24 technical engineers, 28 natural scientists, 30 technicians—medical, dental, and other, etc.). The rather extensive sample revealed only one lawyer, two social workers, three journalists, and eight clergymen. Even this probably gives an inflated impression of the professional proportion of the deaf, as the authors themselves suggest that the less well-off-economically were probably significantly under-represented in the sample.

On the assumption that the pursuit of advanced degrees does relate to professional education, however, it may be worthwhile to note that some deaf persons do succeed in hearing colleges in earning such degrees. The 162 deaf respondents in a study in progress as the University of Illinois included 25 who had earned their Master's degrees in hearing colleges, as well as 6 with earned doctorates. But with between 1,200 and 1,500 stu-dents over 16 leaving schools and classes for the deaf each year, this rep-resents a very small cumulative total who pursue professional studies to the point of a career.

Vocational Education

Vocational education and training in the traditional secondary-school sense has been more available to deaf students in the past, although here again there is little specialized opportunity at the post-secondary level. Perhaps the greatest success to which specialized schools for the deaf have been able to point is in the vocational education area. Nearly all such schools have offered and continue to offer outstanding programs.[1]

The basic problem is that the requirements of vocational education in general have been dramatically increased in recent years by technological advances. The job requirements in many lines of work that could formerly be met by a good trade or technical training program at the secondary school level now call for a much broader-based foundation in English, mathematics, and science before the technical training requirement can be met. Also, more and more vocational education and training courses must be provided at the post-secondary level to meet changing employment requirements. Recognition of these needs in the whole field of vocational education is evidenced by the provisions of the Vocational Education Act of 1963 and by a growing number of thoughtful studies, analyses, and comments.[2]

For the deaf student there is little specialized opportunity for post-secondary vocational education and training which is characterized by recognition of and compensation for the nature of his handicap. A notable exception is to be found in the program for the deaf at Riverside City College in Riverside, California.

Riverside City College is a two-year junior college in which a special program for the deaf was inaugurated in the fall of 1961. The students were provided special assistance in the form of hearing-student tutors, instructors' notes, and interpretation in the classroom in the language of signs by trained instructors of the deaf. A house provided by the college was used as a Center for the Deaf. Summer courses in English and mathematics were provided to meet the students' needs for additional instruction in these subjects.

The program has been the subject of continuing evaluation. Some of the findings reported by those in charge of the program are:

1. More rigid entrance screening was required to reduce the dropout rate. (Of 41 students who have entered the program, 3 completed their requirements for the Associate in Arts degree, 1 the vocational nursing program, 1 the cosmetology course, and 13 were still enrolled in early 1964. The other 23 had left for a variety of reasons.)

2. The more verbally oriented classes (English and history) required a retreat from the attempted integration with hearing students to separate classes for the deaf.

---

[1] For a more detailed discussion, see Chapter I of the report by the Advisory Committee.

[2] See "Vocational Education: In the High School?" in the *Saturday Review*, August 15, 1964, an editorial which concludes that the needed expansion of technical training should take place not in high school but in junior colleges, adult evening schools, post-high school technical schools, and programs conducted by industry. For a comprehensive current study, see *Man, Education, and Work: Postsecondary Vocational and Technical Education*, by Grant Venn. June, 1964, 184 pp. Published by the American Council on Education, Washington, D.C.

3. The special program is best suited to students who have a profound hearing loss. Students with minimal hearing losses accepted in the special program did not integrate well with either the deaf students or the hearing students.

For the deaf student seeking post-secondary vocational education in other areas of the country, no such specialized program has come to the Committee's attention. Occasionally a residential school for the deaf is able to accommodate one or two postgraduate students, but there is no systematic program for them. The information received from schools and classes for the deaf shows that many students who leave, either as graduates or as having attained the maximum age of eligibility for school attendance (commonly but not uniformly 21 years), go on to regular business, trade, and technical schools for the hearing, often with the assistance of the state department of vocational rehabilitation. Unfortunately, this study was not able to include information on the degree of success or lack of success that attended their efforts there. It is likely, however, that the training received in many such schools is assimilated with somewhat less difficulty than is a liberal arts education in a hearing college, since more of the instruction can be expected to be by demonstration and less by verbal communication.

Adult Education

The growth in adult education programs in America in recent years has not included sufficient programs for the adult deaf. The fact that most adult deaf communicate principally by the language of signs has probably discouraged any significant steps in this direction. A few attempts to initiate such courses have been enthusiastically received by the deaf themselves, but have failed to gain continuing support within the school system.

NEEDS FOR IMPROVEMENT

Aside from the offerings at Gallaudet College and a few isolated programs in other fields, the only post-secondary educational opportunities for the deaf in this country are those which are available to the hearing population —and they are available only as offered to hearing students, without special facilities that recognize the handicap of deafness. Hearing colleges and schools are attended successfully by a few deaf individuals with exceptional qualities. It is clear, however, that without a dramatic improvement in language learning and a correspondingly dramatic improvement in educational achievement at all levels—preschool through secondary—the educational facilities for the hearing will continue to be of real use and value only to a few of the exceptionally gifted deaf, unless some kind of special assistance is provided to counteract the educational deprivation from which the deaf suffer.

In the following paragraphs, the Committee sets forth its judgment on specific areas of need in the provision of post-secondary educational programs to serve the deaf, followed in the next section by recommendations to meet the needs.

A Wider Range of Choices

For most deaf persons the only post-secondary educational experience available is the liberal arts program of Gallaudet College. This means a choice between a trade of limited complexity for which they have received some training in secondary school and a liberal arts college experience.

The deaf, like the hearing, should have an opportunity to exercise the widest practicable selection of careers. Each deaf person should be assisted to achieve to the limit of his abilities, but it is all too often assumed that these are very narrowly restricted for a person who suffers a hearing loss. It is true that the hearing loss makes the learning of language and speech extremely difficult. This in turn creates difficulties in developing innate abilities, but there are many deaf persons who are able with minor special help to overcome these difficulties. Too often, such minor special help is lacking.

In view of the relatively small number of deaf students comprising the potential post-secondary educational market each year, it is obviously impracticable to contemplate an array of junior colleges, liberal arts colleges, engineering and technical institutes, professional courses for advanced degree work, etc., exclusively for the deaf. It is practicable, however, to provide in some of our post-secondary institutions, from junior colleges to the more advanced professional schools, certain special facilitative services to enhance the prospects of deaf students' success in following any of a wide range of choices. Some specific suggestions will be offered at the end of this chapter.

Technical and Vocational Education and Training Needs

Educators of the deaf generally agree that the present provision for technical and vocational education and training is inadequate. This is not surprising in view of the growing recognition of the need to effect great improvements in our system of vocational education and training for all students.

The Vocational Education Act of 1963 (P.L. 88–210) gives practical recognition to the changing needs in this field by extending federally-aided vocational education into post-secondary programs.

We need a new emphasis on post-secondary vocational education programs for the deaf. Such would release present vocational education departments of schools for the deaf for prevocational orientation—a development which has already occurred in many such schools largely because of the increasingly costly and complex equipment required for terminal vocational offerings. Many of the less complicated trades could continue to be taught to the more limited students. For most students, additional time could be devoted to the teaching of those academic subjects in which the deaf need more instruction and to the improvement of communication skills.

Adult Education

The deaf need access to more courses offering opportunities to learn more about insurance, changes in social security programs, tax issues in which they have a vital interest, developments in national and international affairs as well as in state and local government, legal matters (wills, license requirements, deeds, etc.), and the raising of children. In addition, there are many adult education courses with a semivocational application which would enhance the resources that the deaf have to offer.

** 24 **

Multiple Handicaps in the Field of Deafness

POWRIE V. DOCTOR

The problem of rehabilitating persons handicapped with more than one disability is a growing one, and a serious problem in the United States in the present century. Possibly, to an extent, it is being made more serious by the very advancements in science that would tend to alleviate the contributing conditions. A greater number of children and adults suffering from one or more handicaps are today confronting our teachers and our rehabilitation workers than in previous years, mainly, perhaps, because medicine has become so much more adequate that some patients who would

* From *Exceptional Children* 1959, *26*, pp. 156–158. Reprinted by permission of the author and the publisher.

have died 25 years ago are today being saved, but, in many cases, being saved at the price of living out their remaining years under the handicap of one or more major disabilities.

With a few exceptions, we have been oriented to thinking of people as being deaf, or as being blind, or as being crippled, but in this modern twentieth century we must adjust our thinking and our acceptance to include individuals who are both deaf and blind, deaf and aphasic, blind and crippled, and even those who suffer not only from a physical handicap, but also from a mental handicap, and for these groups we need not only schooling, rehabilitation, and social service, but a genuine acceptance of them into our present day scheme of life.

Many of us can recall at almost a moment's notice the founding of the first school for the blind, or the first school for the mentally retarded in the United States, but aside from Helen Keller and Laura Bridgeman in the department for the deaf-blind in the Perkins School in Boston, few of us can name the first school or institution in the United States for the teaching of multiple handicapped children. No doubt the reason for this is that such schools and classes are of comparatively recent origin, and because so very few have been established, and also, possibly, because this is uniquely a twentieth century problem that has been accentuated by our great progress in science.

However, in discussing the broad field of multiple handicaps, we must remember that any single physical handicap often drags with it many other social, educational, and emotional handicaps. In the field of deafness so many tend to think that communication is the one and only difficulty that requires attention. Because of the breakdown in communication in the field of deafness other problems arise, such as the inability to acquire language in the same manner as hearing people do, the difficulty to think in abstract terms, and the consequences on the personality of a deaf person brought about by a communication breakdown with his environment.

All of these byproducts of deafness are being accentuated today as never before by the increased tempo of the times and, in some cases, by the advancement in medical science.

When communication breaks down between a mature deaf person and his environment, handicaps worse than his deafness may occur. Dr. Dohn of Denmark, in explaining the high percentage of deaf persons in mental institutions in Denmark, says it is mainly due to isolation. Thus we should remember that keeping active all forms of communication for the deaf: speech, speechreading, language, use of hearing aids, and manual methods such as the use of the manual alphabet and the language of signs, are of paramount importance in this respect.

Today science is helping in a great measure to diagnose properly those who have a single handicap and those who have an additional handicap. This is being pinpointed quite realistically by designating more accurately those who are deaf, and those who are aphasic, those who are both deaf and aphasic. It is fairly easy to label deafness and cerebral palsy or blindness and deafness, but it is extremely difficult and requires much more scientific technique to label such disorders as aphasia, especially when it involves another handicap.

PROGRESS IN UNDERSTANDING

We have come a long way in the past 150 years. In the early days most schools for the deaf were known as asylums. Calling an institution for the deaf a school for the deaf is a product of the present century. There are a few people even today who believe the deaf are mentally below normal people. It is interesting to note that in New York in 1887 a teacher of the deaf named Greenberg experimented quite successfully with tests for the deaf in an effort to differentiate between those who were deaf and normal and those who were deaf and sub-normal, because, as we all know, a deaf person without language may easily be mistaken for a mentally retarded or a mentally deficient person.

For many years the main double handicap brought to the attention of the layman was deafness with blindness. To an extent, this was because of the very great accomplishments of Laura Bridgeman and Helen Keller, both of whom received much publicity. Today we have the aphasic and deaf person, the aphasic and blind person, the mentally-retarded deaf person, or the mentally-retarded aphasic blind person, the emotionally disturbed deaf and the emotionally disturbed aphasic.

REPORTING THE HANDICAPPED

For the past three years the *American Annals of the Deaf* has been publishing the number of multiple handicapped pupils enrolled in schools for the deaf. We have asked for reports in six categories: the aphasic and deaf, the blind and deaf, the cerebral palsied and deaf, the orthopedic and deaf, the mentally retarded and deaf, and the brain injured and deaf. This does not imply by any means that our list is a complete census of all these categories. It merely means that the reports show the number of school age children so handicapped in all types of schools and classes for the deaf in the United States. In a few instances the classes for the deaf-blind as reported are in schools for the blind. How many more of these children there are of preschool age, I do not know. How many adults suffer from multiple handicaps is another question which I am unable to answer. In 1957 a total of 307 pupils were reported as being aphasic and deaf. This is an increase of 140 over the figure for 1955. In 1957 a total of 102 were reported as being deaf and blind, an increase of 58. Also in 1957 there were 483 reported as being cerebral palsied and deaf, an increase of 164. In 1957 there were 168 reported as being orthopedic and deaf, an increase of 43. In 1957 a total of 212 were reported as being brain injured and deaf, an increase of

105. And lastly, in 1957 there were 910 pupils reported as being mentally retarded and deaf, an increase of 487 in the three-year period.

There is a distinct possibility that we are reporting cases more accurately than before, but essentially the same schools reported in 1957 as reported in 1955. There is a possibility that these figures may be attributed to increased enrollment. However, I doubt very much if the increased enrollments can account for all of them. Perhaps schools and classes are feeling their responsibility toward the multiple handicapped more keenly than before. Again, there is the very distinct possibility that more multiple handicapped children are being born than before. Is this problem of the multiple handicapped child a product of the great scientific advances made in this twentieth century, especially in the field of medicine? Are the new medicines keeping alive many children with multiple handicaps who, even a quarter of a century ago, would not have survived? If this is true we must see that adequate provision is made to have the professionally diagnostic services available with which to ascertain the various handicaps, and to see that educational and rehabilitative services are available for these children. It is unwise to allow one field of service to outstrip all the others. If we give $1000 to medical research, let us also give a similar amount to improving facilities for teaching the multiple handicapped and training them for positions where they may earn all or part of a livelihood.

But even this is not the complete answer. We must also see that society is oriented to the problem of accepting the multiple handicapped. In some ways this in itself is one of the major problems of this mid-twentieth century. We need sources of adequate information about this group of handicapped people. We need to know to an extent the number of persons with various multiple disabilities in the United States. We need to know if the number of trained teachers for the various groups is sufficient. This question, however, can be answered now. There is an alarmingly scarce supply of adequately trained teachers for all fields in *Special Education* and in *Rehabilitation*. It may be that one of the frontiers in science in this country lies in what we will do with these handicapped people that in a measure science has bequeathed to us.

PART FIVE

Emotionally Disturbed

Significant movement in educational programming for emotionally disturbed children is a development of the 1950s and 1960s. As a result, perhaps, most textbooks on the psychology and education of exceptional children have given little attention to this population. Who are the emotionally disturbed? Haring (1963) has given a comprehensive definition:

> The emotionally disturbed child is one who, because of organic and/or environmental influences, chronically displays (a) inability to learn at a rate commensurate with his intellectual, sensory-motor and physical development; (b) inability to establish and maintain adequate social relationships; (c) inability to respond appropriately in day-to-day life situations, and (d) a variety of excessive behavior ranging from hyperactive, impulsive responses to depression and withdrawal. Although there are varying degrees of the above behavioral deviations in emotionally disturbed children, the key to the eventual diagnosis of this condition is the chronicity of these symptoms. (p. 291)

Certain problems and issues in the area of emotional disturbance have not had the history that is to be found in the more established areas, e.g. mental retardation and visual and auditory handicaps. It is against this backdrop that the first two articles of this section were written (Quay's "Some Basic Considerations in the Education of Emotionally Disturbed Children" and Knoblock's "Critical Factors Influencing Educational Programming of Emotionally Disturbed Children"). The authors are attempting to point up the variety of philosophical, conceptual, and organizational problems to be dealt with in planning programs for emotionally disturbed children. Quay reminds us that "in view of our sketchy knowledge about emotionally disturbed children, we should not be too eager to create makeshift special classes since the disproportionate cost of such classes cannot be justified on the basis of the results they are likely to produce." Although written several years ago, these remarks have a contemporary ring. In a similar critical vein Haring has written (1963):

> Although a substantial amount of research is reported in these areas, descriptive studies seemed to predominate. The lack of controlled investigation particularly among the studies involving therapy and education, presents serious limitations to the conclusions that can be drawn at this point.

Among the most serious of the difficulties which complicate the research with emotionally disturbed children are: (a) the lack of information about the specific causes of emotional disturbances; (b) the lack of uniformity of terminology; (c) the varying personality theories and philosophies used as frames of reference influencing treatment methods; and (d) the difficulty encountered in establishing adequate controls. (p. 317)

In his discussion of several critical variables influencing programming for disturbed children, Knoblock gives considerable attention to teacher training, teacher performance, and teacher role confusion. With respect to the latter Knoblock writes, "A teacher of disturbed children quickly finds himself in the position of having to carefully plan and tailor the curriculum to cope with each particular youngster's needs and pathologies; at the same time he must fulfill his needs as a teacher and this involves certain goal directed behaviors on his part."

Problems of role confusion and issues involving the use of specialized sub-professionals are presented in two articles following. In the first, Morse ("Teacher or Therapist") raises the question "How much a teacher, how much a therapist?" in an article written for regular classroom teachers, but with considerable implication for teachers of emotionally disturbed children. Morse marks out some broad areas encompassed by the dilemma and offers guidelines to help the individual teacher in dealing with it. Although this article was written more than a decade ago, the principles, issues and problems, and recommendations have current value, including his final statement that "teachers may need better preparation for the therapeutic aspects of their work."

Fenichel evaluates the teacher-mom program, a program in which a volunteer nonprofessional works with a disturbed child on a one-to-one basis with the responsibility of conducting "the educational and emotional program as prescribed by the professional members of the team." Programs involving mature adults, older students, and a variety of nonprofessionals are developing at a rapid rate. The Fenichel article deals with a program for the emotionally disturbed, but it raises issues critical to the utilization of teacher aides within special education and outside it. Fenichel is particularly critical of the program because it "either ignores or tears down every existing or suggested alternative to the teacher-mom program, including specialized day schools and special classes within a public school setting." In attempting to present alternatives to what is perceived as narrow proscription by teacher-mom proponents, Fenichel hits upon a theme which runs throughout the present volume as a solution to problems concerning various controversies over the relative merits of special educational administrative arrangements. He writes:

In negating every other type of facility the authors do not seem to understand that what is desperately needed is not any one alternative but a vast spectrum of special educational services in regular classes, special classes, specialized schools and day treatment centers as well as residential centers and hospitals to take care of the vastly different needs of children at different times. (p. 49)

Both the Morse and Fenichel articles highlight a variety of problems of role definition and delineation, but in situations in which teachers or their helpers work with disturbed children in fairly conventional ways utilizing concepts from mental hygiene as the principal tools of their work. Within recent years, however, behavior modification has been widely adopted as a strategy for educating emotionally disturbed children. What is behavior modification? Briefly stated, behavior modification is a strategy for influencing behavior and as such keeps company with many procedures of psychotherapy, education, and brainwashing. Behavior modification is characterized by at least two elements: (1) the focus upon overt, observable behavior and (2) the systematic application of concepts drawn from learning theory (Ullman and Krasner, 1965). Among other things, behavior modification techniques have been used in education to increase the emotionally disturbed child's attending behavior, to reduce disruptive behavior in the hyperactive child, and to facilitate the learning of mentally retarded children in reading, writing, and arithmetic.

There are two main behavior modification techniques, one which centers to a great extent around classical or Pavlovian conditioning, and one using primarily operant conditioning and Skinnerian terminology. Pavlovian procedures are considered respondent conditioning, in which the organism is a passive participant; the behavior follows a stimulus, and unless the organism is physically prevented from performing the response, it occurs — it is involuntary. Thus, after many pairings of the meat powder and bell, Pavlov's dogs salivated to the sound of the bell alone. The animals were passive participants in the learning experience; they had no control over their salivation in response to the bell. Not so with operant techniques; the organism is not a passive participant in the learning situation. The term "operant" indicates that the organism is operating on the environment. The basic notion underlying the operant method is that rewards occur as a consequence of the organism's response. Thus when a teacher says "good boy" or gives a child a star when a desirable academic behavior has been emitted, and when, further, it can be demonstrated that the behavior is not emitted in the absence of the rewards, operant methods are being used. Given this basic paradigm, it becomes apparent that certain aspects of the method are used by all of us. However, the important distinction between the operant methods discussed in this section and more pedestrian day-to-day behavior modification efforts, resides in the more systematic observation, measurement, and specification of variables of the former methods (Jones, 1970).

One advantage — among others — seen to accrue to behavior modification is its potential for minimizing problems of role confusion. As Clarizio and Yelon write:

The increasing popularity of behavior therapy and other approaches based on learning now offers teachers opportunities for an integral role in the quest for better mental health for children. Indeed it might well be the mental health specialist who will now assume the supportive role . . . in the treatment of children.

In the application of learning theory principles to the modification of deviant behavior, the emphasis is on the changing of behavior with little attention devoted to the etiology of the behavior. Why should teachers focus on the behavior rather than its causes? There are serveral reasons:

(1) First, teachers by virtue of their orientation are not trained to probe the causes of behavior that even mental hygiene specialists consider obscure and uncertain. Hence is it really helpful to ask the teacher to understand the causes underlying children's disturbed behavior?

(2) Teachers in any case are rarely in a position where they can directly manipulate the causes so as to modify their influence on the child's classroom adjustment. For example, if the problem lies in the parent-child relationship or in a brain lesion, there are few, if any, intervention techniques that the teacher can employ. Yet the child's troublesome behavior persists and must be handled as effectively as possible when it occurs in the classroom.

(3) Even in such occasional cases where the causes can be identified and manipulated directly, the maladaptive behaviors may persist. . . .

(4) Behavior or symptoms or habits may in their own right be incapacitating and disturbing, and current persisting symptoms may themselves be producing emotional disturbance from which the child is suffering. As research indicates . . . it is difficult to disentangle educational and emotional maladjustments in the school age child. . . .

(5) There is little substantial evidence to indicate that if the teacher assists the child in modifying his behavior or symptoms, other undesirable behaviors will inevitably take their place in the form of symptom substitution. . . .

(6) Finally, and most importantly, as already implied, the teacher most commonly has no resort other than to deal with the pupil's behavior as it appears in the here and now. . . .

These are powerful arguments for teacher use of behavior modification with disturbed children. The procedures have not been accepted uncritically, however. MacMillan (1970) has pointed to several problems that have arisen in using behavior modification techniques in education. These problems include the need to consider behavior modification as a technique within the larger context of education, the need to consider what is best for the child—as contrasted with what is most convenient for the teacher, the need to consider individual differences among learners, the need to ensure that pupils are led to function at the highest reinforcement at which they are capable, and the need to recognize that behavior modification constructs are reductionistic in nature. This latter point and others are taken up in the present volume in an article which is critical of certain behavior modification assumptions and practices ("Behavior Modification: Limitations and Liabilities"). It is apparent that the critical points made in the article apply to behavior modification used with the emotionally disturbed as well as with other exceptional children.

Within the past few years programs across the country have integrated emotionally disturbed and brain damaged children into a single special education classroom. In California this grouping is referred to as the educationally handicapped. Mesinger ("Emotionally Disturbed and

Brain Damaged Children—Should We Mix Them?") is critical of this grouping practice and argues that while there are similarities between emotionally disturbed and brain damaged children, "these facts should not be allowed to mask some rather significant differences between the two broad categories of children." A number of arguments are advanced to support this position, arguments that are rebutted by Bower ("The Return of Rumpelstiltskin: Reaction to Mesinger's Article"). Mesinger takes up the Bower reactions in a rejoinder ("A Reply to Dr. Bower's Comments").

It is interesting to note in all of the proposed resolutions of the issue that no mention has been made of the need to develop more refined methods of assessment and a program of research related to issues raised in the articles. Thus it is apparent that we have a long way to go in the resolution of issues dealt with in this debate.

REFERENCES

Clarizio, H. R. and S. L. Yelon, "Learning Theory Approaches to Classroom Management: Rationale and Intervention Techniques," *The Journal of Special Education* 1967, *1*, pp. 267–274.

Haring, N. G., "The Emotionally Disturbed," in Kirk, S. A. and Bluma B. Weiner, *Behavioral Research on Exceptional Children* (Washington: The Council for Exceptional Children, 1963).

Jones, R. L. (Editor), *New Directions in Special Education* (Boston: Allyn and Bacon, 1970).

MacMillan, D., "Ground Rules for Behavior Modification," paper presented at the Annual Meeting of the American Association for Mental Deficiency, Washington, D.C., May, 1970.

Ullman. L. P. and L. Krasner, *Case Studies in Behavior Modification* (New York: Holt, Rinehart and Winston, 1965).

** 25 **

Some Basic Considerations in the Education of Emotionally Disturbed Children

HERBERT C. QUAY

Education for the emotionally disturbed parallels education for the mentally retarded in some significant ways. Johnson's (1962) recent review of research on the efficacy of special class placement for the mentally handicapped cannot be easily dismissed by anyone concerned with any area of exceptionality. The sobering conclusions of this review and, more importantly, the factors that lie behind the failure of special class placement to demonstrate its worth, should be food for thought for special educators in all areas of exceptionality.

LACK OF BASIC KNOWLEDGE

Let us look at the possible reasons why controlled research has failed to demonstrate the efficacy of the special class. One basic reason is clear: we do not really know what the needs of the mentally retarded child are in terms of either a method or a curriculum. We really do not know what he can learn nor how best to teach it to him. We have not fully explored whether the laws of learning are different for IQ 50 than for IQ 100 for all types of learning. We do not know whether the low IQ child fails in input, output, retention, any two of these factors, or all three. As a result of the lack of basic knowledge of learning processes in the retarded, special class programs are not and cannot be clearly defined and scientifically based.

While the foregoing is certainly the basic factor mitigating against special class effectiveness, there is the added problem of pupil selection. While the 120 distinct factors of intellect proposed by Guilford (1959) seem, at best, to lack parsimony, intellective ability is clearly not undimensional. Yet special class placement is generally made on the basis of a score on a test which probably does not measure all of even the major

* From *Exceptional Children* 1963, *30*, pp. 27–31. Reprinted by permission of the author and the publisher.

facets of intellect. In short, it is likely that we are not measuring and describing mental retardation as adequately as we might.

Now let us look at the situation with the emotionally disturbed. In terms of ongoing programs, education for the disturbed is far less advanced than education for the mentally handicapped. However, educators are responding both to their own and to the community's needs and are setting up classes for maladjusted children. There is concern about the problems of definition, identification, curriculum, methods, teacher training, and administrative practices. But for the most part some basic questions are being ignored in the rush to get programs underway. As yet, we do not even have any systematic knowledge of what actually is happening in the creating of programs, but what appears to be taking place leads one to conclude that it is only a matter of time until someone writes an article parallel to Johnson's on the efficacy of special class placement for the emotionally disturbed.

CLASSIFICATION AND PLACEMENT

Classification and placement are both based primarily on an impressionistic basis. Children who do not fall under the rubric of some other area of exceptionality and who are unable to adjust to the regular class are labeled emotionally disturbed and placement is made on that basis. How good a placement procedure is this likely to turn out to be? Are all "not-otherwise-classifiable" non-adjusters emotionally disturbed? Is apparent inability to adjust to a regular class an adequate criterion for classification as disturbed? Are all disturbed children alike, of one and the same kind, behaviorally and psychologically homogeneous? The problem, always a basic one, of description and classification is involved.

We have had enough experience with behaviorally abnormal children to know that the standard psychiatric nomenclature is most often inapplicable to children. A special class made up of children all diagnosed as obsessive-compulsive would be indistinguishable on most educationally relevant variables from a class made up of children all diagnosed as phobics.

There is one thing we do know about problem-behavior children and we know this from a number of empirical research studies. There are certain recurrent, observable symptoms of problem behavior in children and these symptoms tend to cluster into two major syndromes or symptom-clusters. These have been called the acting-out or the "conduct problem" and the withdrawn or "personality problem" (Himmelweit, 1952; Becker, Peterson, Hellmer, Shoemaker and Quay, 1959; Peterson, 1961). It also appears that children with behavior disturbances can be reliably classified as belonging primarily to one group or the other and in the case of the acting-out dimension to one of three sub-dimensions. An important feature of this simple classification scheme is that it has, even at this early stage of our knowledge, implications for the educational process.

CURRENT PRACTICES

What are current practices in regard to curriculum and method? Special class programs for the emotionally disturbed seem generally to be classifiable under three major headings:

1. "Holding actions" which try to exert a minimum of achievement and performance demands while waiting either for some form of therapy to deal with the emotional disturbance or for the coming of the age at which the child can leave school. Methods here are too varied to be describable.
2. A quasi-therapeutic program in which the educative process is seen as primarily therapeutic in its aim. The methods here are likely to be dictated by the assumptions of some theory about psychotherapy rather than any theory of learning or education.
3. The focus is on education and academic achievement rather than on therapy. However, the method still tends to be dictated more by a theory of personality than by a theory of learning. There is generally the assumption that the educative process will also foster better emotional adjustment.

While this classification may not be exhaustive, it does appear to cover the vast majority of present programs. If the primary business of the school is to educate, what is needed is a special class program designed to meet the special learning characteristics of the kinds of emotionally disturbed children contained in it. While we need much more research into both the classification schemes themselves and the principles of learning for the two kinds of maladjustment, there are at present a few guidelines available.

EDUCATING THE "PERSONALITY PROBLEM" CHILD

The withdrawn or personality problem child is most likely to be anxious, either overtly or covertly. Taylor and Spence (Taylor, 1951, 1956; Spence, 1958) have presented both theory and substantiating research bearing on the relation of anxiety to learning. Basically, their theory is that anxiety facilitates the acquisition of simple conditioned responses but interferes with complex learning. That is, the anxious person fixates a simple response, particularly if he has made it from time to time before, more rapidly than a non-anxious person. At the same time, complex responses (and this includes most academic skills unless they are made simple on purpose) are acquired with more difficulty by the anxious. There are a number of ramifications of this hypothesis.

First of all, the already anxious child is quick to learn (by simple conditioning) additional fear and anxiety responses. Stimuli contiguously associated with stimuli causing fear and unpleasant emotion quickly come to have the capacity to elicit the same fear. "Guilt by association" has real meaning in this situation. Since stimulus generalization seems to be facilitated by anxiety, the anxious child's fear and avoidance over-generalize. All of this means that unpleasant and fear-producing experiences are apt to have results quite beyond the immediate setting and such experiences should be minimized for this type of child whenever possible. Unpleasant experiences with one type of academic material quickly generalize to other types. Fear and avoidance of one teacher soon becomes fear and avoidance of many. There is, however, a positive side. The rapid acquisition of conditioned responses applies to "positive" responses as well as negative ones and these positive responses can be appropriate responses to academic problems if they are presented in such a way as to qualify as simple or to fit a conditioning paradigm.

The foregoing has certain useful implications. The early stages of special class placement for these children might well be devoted to making the academic situation and some academic materials less unpleasant. One way to do this might be to do one's best to associate the classroom, the teacher, and the learning materials with pleasant stimuli. Interest can then turn to making appropriate academic responses simple. It appears that programmed instruction may be one approach to this; complex materials are broken down into simpler sequences so that a conditioning model is approximated. Programmed instruction also seems to minimize the opportunity for wrong answers to occur. This is important because one of the basic effects of anxiety seems to be to produce wrong answers as well as right ones when there is a multiplicity of possible responses—hence anxiety hinders complex learning. For the anxious child it seems better if the right answer is the first one with which he responds; allowing the anxious child to make mistakes seems to hinder the efficiency with which he will eventually fixate the correct response.

As a by-product it is also quite likely that the de-sensitization procedures plus the experiences of academic success may also serve to reduce the anxiety of the disturbed child although this "therapy" is not the primary purpose of the educational program. It seems worthwhile to point out, however, that the current behavior therapy approach to the treatment of emotional disorders emphasizes just such deconditioning procedures and tends not to concern itself with hypothetical underlying complexes and conflicts.

EDUCATING THE "CONDUCT PROBLEM" CHILD

The child of the "conduct problem" variety requires a different approach. There is considerable evidence to indicate that personalities of acting-out children are of three major dimensions (Peterson, Quay and Cameron, 1959; Peterson, Quay and Tiffany, 1961; Quay, in press) all of which may look alike to the untrained observer because they all manifest acting-out, if not frankly delinquent behavior. One major category of conduct problem child, and the group which tends to be perhaps the most persistently troublesome, is that group of children referred to as unsocialized aggressive or psychopathic. There are really few of these youngsters, even among the legally delinquent, but their behavior can be so disconcerting and annoying if not actually dangerous that one may seem like many. The British psychologist H. J. Eysenck (1957) has theorized that these individuals are persons who are highly "extroverted" (by constitutional predisposition) and as such they learn conditioned reactions very slowly and with difficulty. The failure of these children to acquire conditioned fear and avoidance reactions does seem to provide a meaningful explanation for their persistent failure to benefit from experience in learning to hold their impulses in check. This poor conditionability, which is hypothesized to be present from the very first, has many ramifications. Consider for a moment how the average child comes to learn to respond to verbal praise and punishment; it is certainly through the process of pairing these verbal stimuli with more primary rewards and punishments. We do have experimental evidence that this psychopathic or unsocialized person fails to respond to verbal reward in the same way that others do (Johns and Quay, 1962).

What can be done educationally about these children? First of all, it appears that learning some fear and avoidance so that impulses can be controlled may be a requisite for doing anything else with them. The first step with these children may be to establish some impulse inhibition and behavioral control in the school situation. This will no doubt be a painful process to both teacher and student but it can be best accomplished by a system of definite rules for behavior with immediate rewards and punishments administered time and time again. These positive and negative reinforcers may have to be rather rudimentary in the beginning (e.g., physical restraint and isolation) but at the same time a determined effort should be made to pair them with the more verbal social reinforcers to which the child must eventually learn to respond.

Academic material, once some behavioral control has been established, should also be presented in such a way that problems and their answers are presented more repetitiously than would be the case with the ordinary child. There are suggestions that these unsocialized children tend to be "novelty seekers" (Fairweather, 1953; Petrie, McCulloch, and Kazdin, 1962) so that novel and unexpected rewards may succeed where other things fail. I have entertained the notion of teaching these children via teaching machines which provide not only the correct answer as the reinforcer but at the same time light up, ring bells, and perhaps even shoot fireworks.

The second major category of acting-out child seems to be primarily a phenomenon of the urban socially deteriorated area. This child comes from a subculture in which aggressive behavior and "conning" ability are valued and in which academic achievement and middle class behavior standards are not highly esteemed. There is a special point to be made about these children. It is probably inappropriate to consider them emotionally disturbed since in a very real sense they are only behaving in a way which is appropriate to their own world. There are currently educational programs for these children which try to show them a little of what the world is like outside the slum and at the same time try to provide them with skills which they can see as enabling them to participate in the larger world.

The third category of conduct problem children encompasses those children whose acting-out behavior seems to reflect a more or less neurotic condition; that is to say, beneath it all these children are anxious, insecure, and unhappy and actually regretful of their overt transgressions. If their acting-out tendencies are not too strong, it might be best to treat them as similar to the withdrawn child in terms of educational method, as suggested previously.

SUMMARY

The foregoing provides only the briefest outline for program operation. It does suggest, however, that all children now called emotionally disturbed are not alike for educational purposes and should not be so considered. While we have only a rudimentary knowledge of educational approaches for the different categories of disturbed children it seems certain that a hodgepodge approach to a mixed group of maladjusted youngsters is not likely to be successful.

A final point merits consideration. In view of our sketchy knowledge about emotionally disturbed children we should not be too eager to create makeshift special classes since the disproportionate cost of such classes cannot be justified on the basis of the results they are likely to produce. If at all possible we should proceed slowly, select children carefully, group at least according to the basic withdrawal and acting-out dichotomies, and structure the special class experience as primarily educational, taking advantage of what we do know about the learning characteristics of the particular kinds of emotional disturbance.

REFERENCES

Eysenck, H. J. *The dynamics of anxiety and hysteria.* New York: Praeger, 1957.

Fairweather, G. W. Serial rote learning by psychopathic, neurotic and normal criminals under three incentive conditions. Unpublished doctoral thesis, University of Illinois, 1953.

Guilford, J. P. Three faces of intellect. *American Psychologist,* 1959, 14, 469–479.

Johns, J. H., and Quay, H. C. The effect of social reward on verbal conditioning in psychopathic and neurotic military offenders. *Journal of Consulting Psychology,* 1962, **26,** 217–220.

Johnson, G. O. Special education for the mentally handicapped—a paradox. *Exceptional Children,* 1962, **29,** 62–69.

Peterson, D. R. Behavior problems of middle childhood. *Journal of Consulting Psychology,* 1961, **25,** 205–209.

Peterson, D. R., Quay, H. C., and Cameron, G. R. Personality and background factors in juvenile delinquency as inferred from questionnaire responses. *Journal of Consulting Psychology,* 1959, **23,** 295–399.

Peterson, D. R., Quay, H. C., and Tiffany, T. L. Personality factors related to juvenile delinquency. *Child Development,* 1961, **32,** 355–372.

Petrie, Asenath, McCulloch, R., and Kazdin, Phoebe. The perceptual characteristics of juvenile delinquents. *Journal of Nervous and Mental Disease,* 1962, **134,** 415–421.

Quay, H. C. Dimensions of personality in delinquent boys as inferred from the factor analysis of case history data. *Child Development,* in press.

Spence, K. W. A theory of emotionally based drive (D) and its relation to performance in simple learning situations. *American Psychologist,* 1958, **13,** 131–141.

Taylor, Janet A. The relationship of anxiety to the conditioned eyelid response. *Journal of Experimental Psychology,* 1951, **41,** 81–92.

Taylor, Janet A. Drive theory and manifest anxiety. *Psychological Bulletin,* 1956, 303–321.

** **26** **

Critical Factors Influencing Educational Programming for Disturbed Children

PETER KNOBLOCK

Within the last five years there has been a perceptible increase in published articles of a professional and popular nature dealing with the education of emotionally disturbed children. That increasing attention is being directed toward this area is also apparent from a recent U.S. Office of

* From *Exceptional Children* 1963, *30,* pp. 124–129. Reprinted by permission of the author and the publisher.

Education study (Mackie and Robbins, 1961) which shows that between the years 1948 and 1958 special education enrollment of disturbed children in public schools approximately doubled. Professional workers in this area are finding a need to formalize their status and share common experiences by forming professional groups. The most recent attempt is the organization of the Council for Children with Behavioral Disorders, a division of The Council for Exceptional Children.

The formation of the Joint Commission on Mental Illness and Health under the Mental Health Study Act of 1955 is viewed as a positive measure. The scope of this project was perhaps indicative of society's willingness to allocate financial resources as well as technical and professional skills to include as one aspect of the Commission's function the study of the role of the public school as a therapeutic agent of society (Allinsmith and Goethals, 1962).

While there is some cause for optimism when considering the above trends, they are to be sure only trends. Professional workers involved in educational programs for these children are finding much to be concerned about in matters directly related to the development of their programs. At best, progress in terms of the adoption of state certification laws for teachers of disturbed children has been slow. A survey conducted by the U.S. Office of Education (Mackie and Dunn, 1954) indicated that nine states have special certification requirements for teachers of disturbed children. Actually, four of those states are certifying visiting counselors and not classroom teachers. This writer recently conducted a survey in an effort to bring such information up to date. Information obtained from forty-three state departments of education revealed that only nine of those states have such certification laws. Thus between the years of 1954 and 1962 the list of states with such specific certification laws has grown at a minimal rate. It should be noted, however, that a dozen states are in the process of investigating the desirability of adopting such legislation.

The situation in the public schools also presents some cause for concern. In the opening paragraph of this article, figures from a recent U.S. Office of Education study (Mackie and Robbins, 1961) were cited to show that enrollment of disturbed children in special programs had doubled between the years 1948 and 1958. It is necessary to point out, however, that the base line for such enrollment in 1948 was very low in relation to the number of students now being serviced in special programs and that only 500 communities out of 5,000 sampled in 1958 had provisions for emotionally disturbed children. Also, the rate of growth in this area was comparatively lower than the development of special programs in other areas of exceptionality. In the 500 communities cited above, 28,500 emotionally disturbed children were being provided special educational opportunities. The inadequacy of such provisions is highlighted rather dramatically in the findings of the first nationwide survey of seriously disturbed children conducted by The National Organization for Mentally Ill Children (1960). This study reported that there are at least 500,000 seriously disturbed children in this country. It seems reasonable to assume that this figure would more than double when one considers children who are not psychotic or borderline schizophrenic but who manifest signs of having emotional handicaps and who would also benefit from special provisions.

It is the writer's belief that before substantial progress can be made in this area in both educational and community spheres, we must attempt to delineate clearly those factors operating to impede progress in designing educational opportunities for these children.

REALNESS OF PATHOLOGY

Basic to a discussion of possible factors accounting for delayed progress in the development of educational programs for emotionally disturbed children, as Redl and Wattenberg (1959) point out, is the tendency to gloss over the realness of pathology. Many of the problems with which children confront us in the school setting can be handled without the necessity of planning around the specific difficulty or disrupting the routine. With many disturbed children, however, such techniques and approaches are often only minimally effective.

The educator's task in accurately recognizing the scope and depth of emotional problems is complicated by the puzzling array of symptomatic behavior which disturbed children present (Berkowitz and Rothman, 1960). In addition to the fact that many problems may be subtle and covert, the classroom teacher is further confronted with the inconsistencies in behavior which many disturbed children exhibit. This inconsistency of behavior, which frequently takes the form of darting back and forth from acceptable to disturbed and disturbing behavior, not only complicates diagnostic evaluations by teachers and clinicians but may also account for the minimizing of problems in the identification and special programming for emotionally handicapped children.

In many situations we have been content to label the problem and ignore the child who has the problem. As Kvaraceus (1962) points out, the very process of labeling a youngster may in itself evoke unique reactions on his part. Also it would seem that, aside from the false sense of security which many workers gain from engaging in such a practice, there is also an element of resistance involved. By labeling a child or his problem, it may thus be possible, in part, to maintain distance both professionally and emotionally.

It is also quite possible that school personnel and others have been content to leave a problem at the labeling stage for lack of any clear operational frame of reference. There is some attempt on the part of states with certification laws (Michigan, Minnesota) and some school systems (Syracuse, New York) to define clearly the types of youngsters they consider emotionally disturbed and to devise programs to deal specifically with the defined groups. Many educators are employing a recent framework by

Bower (1960) which spells out the types of youngsters and problems for which programs can be devised.

ROLE CONFUSION

The difficulties which center about the classroom role of the teacher are not unique to teachers of disturbed children (Morse, 1956). In the framework of present day education, the classroom teacher is being deluged by multifarious demands, not only in terms of her time and energy but also as these demands relate to the skills and approaches she uses with children.

Historically, the question of the proper role of the classroom teacher received extensive scrutiny with the publication of a study by Wickman (1928). This study was an attempt to compare the perceptions or attitudes of teachers and clinicians toward symptomatic behavior of children. The Wickman study stated rather directly that teachers were not attending to the important behaviors. The implication and interpretation was that teacher attitudes should be molded so as to approximate more closely those of clinicians.

The Wickman study dramatically highlighted the confusion, in this writer's opinion, which existed in the public's conception of just how the mental hygiene role of the classroom teacher and school should be defined (Kotinsky and Coleman, 1955). A recent critical evaluation of the Wickman study (Beilin, 1959) attempted to analyze the roles of teachers and mental hygiene workers in terms of role theory. It was Beilin's conclusion that the attitudinal hierarchies of teachers, as opposed to those of clinicians, dictated different orientations and concerns and that it is doubtful if teachers could or should be pressured or encouraged to depart to any great extent from their task-oriented approach.

The encouraging of such broad roles has not clarified the classroom teacher's role as far as the teachers themselves are concerned. A field study conducted under the auspices of the Joint Commission on Mental Illness and Health (Wilson and Goethals, 1962) sampled a group of teachers, and the results clearly highlighted the confused values operating in the public schools.

It would seem reasonable to conclude that the problems of role definition are made even more complex when one considers a teacher of disturbed children (Long and Newman, 1961). A teacher of disturbed children quickly finds himself in the position of having to carefully plan and tailor the curriculum to cope with each particular youngster's needs and pathologies; at the same time he must fulfill his needs as a teacher, and this involves certain goal-directed behaviors on his part. A good example of the present concern in this area can be discerned from a U.S. Office of Education study (Mackie, Kvaraceus, and Williams, 1957) which dealt with an evaluation of a list of teaching competencies by teachers. The sample was composed of teachers of disturbed children who were asked to rate a list of competencies, both as to importance and as to their own proficiency in these particular competencies. One outstanding finding was that these teachers, as a group, felt most proficient in areas they considered of less importance. Specifically, they felt less proficient in areas requiring knowledge and application of definite skills and techniques for working with disturbed children.

TRAINING OF TEACHERS

It is important to approach the problem of developing adequate programs of teacher training both critically and with some degree of caution when interpreting the present situation. Until a few years ago, teacher training institutions were unable to find job placements for the few students they had trained to deal with the educational development of emotionally disturbed children. Also many institutions were, and still are, awaiting the findings of various demonstration and research projects which have recently been initiated to validate the efficacy of different educational approaches for disturbed children. With these two conditions as important factors, training institutions have been reluctant to develop specialized training programs for teachers of disturbed children.

It is hypothesized that a considerable upsurge of interest in this area could be effected by the greater involvement of institutions of higher learning. While many colleges offer one or two courses in the education of the disturbed child, the advantages of a complete and intensive training program are many. First, many of the educational problems and approaches encountered in dealing with the emotionally disturbed child are unique and often not manifested in the study of retarded, physically handicapped, or other specialized groups. Second, for the student-in-training, the availability of such coursework in his special field materially fosters an atmosphere of professionalism and identification with his teaching as a skill area. Third, research into educational problems, programs, and techniques will be promoted by having students-in-training focus their thinking and work onto this special group of children.

If we are to operate on the premise that intensive and organized training programs for prospective teachers of emotionally disturbed children are essential, then it is necessary to consider several problems directly related to the satisfactory development of such training programs.

Teacher Selection

With the current interest in five-year teacher training programs, the question of the feasibility of undergraduate versus graduate training in this area is no longer a burning issue. Of far more importance is the selection of candidates for this particular type of training program. While it is generally recognized that the demands made upon a teacher of disturbed children are enormous and that she must function with some sort of implied "saintliness" if she is to be effective, there has been virtually no attempt to isolate important variables related to selection of prospective teachers of disturbed children and their subsequent effectiveness. Admittedly, this is an extremely thorny problem to investigate (Barr, 1958), but the success of university training programs and ultimately the quality of educational programs depends most directly on the initial screening procedure. It has been this writer's experience that the choice of this particular teaching area is not, in a large number of cases, a capricious one. It is hoped that within the next few years investigators will direct their attention to selection studies grounded in theoretical frameworks and away from the unreliable methods which are generally employed, such as the clinical interview and obtaining of autobiographical information.

One pitfall, although there are many others, which has consistently plagued studies of teacher selection and effectiveness has been the largely unrewarding search for the "ideal" teacher. In a teaching area in which the syndromes of emotional disturbance are conceptually confusing entities, it is reasonable to assume that we are seeing many different types of teachers operating effectively with various groups of disturbed children.

Breadth of Training

A problem exists in recognizing the need to build into such a training program coursework and experiences in many different areas and university departments. It is unrealistic to assume that one specific focus or orientation will be sufficient in such training. There are those who maintain that many of the courses in fields outside education to which we expose our trainees are basically anti-educational in content and philosophy. Implicit is the fear that such students will be diverted from their primary interests and concerns. On the other hand, a well-rounded training program should introduce the student to many diverse frames of reference and points of view in an effort to help him perceive the complexities involved. Another benefit which could possibly accrue from such a broad exposure to other areas and philosophies would be the opportunity for prospective teachers to gain a clearer realization of their role as compared to and contrasted with the approaches of other disciplines.

Field Experience

In this teaching area which is plagued by a multitude of philosophical and methodological problems, there is one aspect of training which receives consistent recognition. There is strong support for the inclusion of field experiences in the training programs for teachers of disturbed children (Kuenzli, 1958). The problem arises in our attempts to implement such experiences. The striking feature of this problem has to do with the dearth of facilities available. Coupled with this is the recognition that a field experience is only as good as the supervisory personnel available to the students (Rabinow, 1960). A recent evaluation of the mental health manpower shortage in the United States (Albee, 1959), when considered along with the sparsity of public school programs for disturbed children (Mackie and Robbins, 1961), points up the clear need to capitalize on existing quality programs and personnel. Although residential treatment centers handle considerably fewer disturbed children than the public schools, many of our treatment centers have carefully programmed educational opportunities into the life experience of the child in residence (Reid and Hagan, 1952). It is recommended that closer working relationships be established between university training programs and residential treatment centers which emphasize educational programs. While some will contend, with a degree of justification, that the approaches and skills required in a residential center differ from those needed in a public school program, the intensity and scope of training received in a total living situation, such as is simulated in residential centers, would serve as valuable training when combined with experiences in a public school program.

Leadership Training

Implicit in our concern for the development of adequate training programs is an emphasis upon preparing teachers to staff special classes. While the use of the special class as one organizational pattern has gained wide acceptance, it is by no means the most beneficial approach in many situations. The high incidence of disturbed children in the public schools alone argues against the feasibility of training sufficient numbers of teachers to fill positions in special classes if such an approach is to be used exclusively. It is hoped that training programs will in time turn some of their emphasis toward preparing supervisory teachers carefully trained to work in consultative capacities within the public schools (Newman, Redl, and Kitchener, 1962). Such individuals would be in a position, for example, to aid the regular classroom teacher and school administrator in planning for the educational growth of disturbed children who remain in the regular classroom or for whom some modifications are made, but which would not necessarily include special class placement (Mackie and Robbins, 1961).

An equally pressing need has to do with the desirability of developing doctoral programs which would channel highly qualified individuals into much neglected areas (Kirk, 1957; Gallagher, 1959). For example, if college programs are to develop, it will be necessary to staff them with competent special educators experienced in the educational needs of emotionally disturbed children. Such highly trained individuals could also be employed as coordinators of public school programs and be in positions to focus on important research needs and encourage creative program planning.

REFERENCES

Albee, G. W. *Mental health manpower trends.* New York: Basic Books, 1959.

Allinsmith, W., and Goethals, G. W. *The role of schools in mental health.* New York: Basic Books, 1962.

Barr, A. S. Problems associated with the measurement and prediction of teacher success. *Journal of Educational Research,* 1958, **51,** 695–699.

Beilin, H. Teachers' and clinicians' attitudes toward the behavior problems of children: a reappraisal. *Child Development,* 1959, **30,** 9–25.

Berkowitz, Pearl H., and Rothman, Esther P. *The disturbed child: recognition and psychoeducational therapy in the classroom.* New York: New York University Press, 1960.

Bower, E. *Early identification of emotionally handicapped children in school.* Springfield, Illinois: Charles C Thomas, 1960.

Gallagher, J. J. Advanced graduate training in special education. *Exceptional Children,* 1959, **26,** 104–109.

Kirk, S. A. A doctor's degree program in special education. *Exceptional Children,* 1957, **24,** 50–52.

Kotinsky, Ruth, and Coleman, J. V. Mental health as an educational goal. *Teachers College Record,* 1955, **56,** 267.

Kuenzli, A. E. A field-experience program with emotionally disturbed children. *Exceptional Children,* 1958, **25,** 158–161.

Kvaraceus, W. C. Helping the socially inadapted pupil in the large city schools. *Exceptional Children,* 1962, **28,** 399–408.

Long, N. J., and Newman, Ruth G. The teacher's handling of children in conflict. *Bulletin of School of Education, Indiana University,* 1961, **37.**

Mackie, Romaine P., and Dunn, L. M. *State certification requirements for teachers of exceptional children.* U.S. Department of Health, Education, and Welfare, Office of Education, Bulletin 1954, No. 1. Washington, D.C.: Superintendent of Documents, Government Printing Office, 1954.

Mackie, Romaine P., Kvaraceus, W. C., and Williams, H. M. *Teachers of children who are socially and emotionally maladjusted.* U.S. Department of Health, Education, and Welfare, Office of Education, Bulletin 1957, No. 11. Washington, D.C.: Superintendent of Documents, Government Printing Office, 1957.

Mackie, Romaine P., and Robbins, Patricia P. *Exceptional children and youth: special education enrollments in public day schools.* U.S. Department of Health, Education, and Welfare, Office of Education. Washington, D.C.: Superintendent of Documents, Government Printing Office, 1961.

Morse, W. C. Teacher or therapist. *School of Education Bulletin, University of Michigan,* 1956, **27,** 117–120.

National Organization for Mentally Ill Children. *The mentally ill child in America.* New York: National Organization for Mentally Ill Children, Inc., 1960.

Newman, R., Redl, F., and Kitchener, H. *Technical assistance in a public school system.* Washington, D.C.: Washington School of Psychiatry, School Research Program, P.H.S. Project OM-525, 1962.

Rabinow, B. A training program for teachers of the emotionally disturbed and the socially maladjusted. *Exceptional Children,* 1960, **26,** 287–293.

Redl, F., and Wattenberg, W. W. *Mental hygiene in teaching.* (2nd ed.) New York: Harcourt, Brace, 1959.

Reid, J. H., and Hagan, Helen R. *Residential treatment of emotionally disturbed children.* New York: Child Welfare League of America, 1952.

Wickman, E. K. *Children's behavior and teachers' attitudes.* New York: Commonwealth Fund, 1928.

Wilson, W. C., and Goethals, G. W. A field study: sources of potential tension in the public educational system. In W. Allinsmith and G. W. Goethals, *The role of schools in mental health.* New York: Basic Books, 1962. Pp. 175–302.

** 27 **

Teacher or Therapist

WILLIAM C. MORSE

One anticipated consequence of the mental hygiene approach in modern education is the current confusion over the proper role of a teacher. Time was when teaching rested securely and singly on the capacity to teach the content areas and basic skills. But we have expanded the perimeters of teaching to include the responsibility for the socialization and adjustment of the pupil. This expansion was not requested; it represented rather a community expectation for the school. Surveys show that this expectation is now firmly rooted in the mind of parents: they see the fostering of adjustment not in place of, but in addition to, the traditional skill and content teaching.

Recognizing the increased heterogeneity of the clientele, to a certain degree schools are trying to help pupils, children and adolescents who would be a challenge to a detention home or psychiatric institution. Even when special referral services are adequate and available, some children are very difficult to help. In many instances the teacher has no referral services available. When teachers discuss the known emotional problems of their charges, they reveal case after case of very disturbed and difficult youngsters attending school. Teachers realize that fostering adjustment

* From *School of Education Bulletin* 1956, 27, pp. 117–120. Reprinted by permission of the author and the publisher.

requires new teaching skills, and frequently implies the invasion of some of the hitherto private psychological world of the pupil. The latter alone is enough to make any serious and perceptive teacher anxious. Yet, for the teacher there is no legitimate escape. Tomorrow children with their problems will again slip into their seats facing the desk. In truth, the conscientious teacher today is in a very trying spot.

Some teachers do escape, it is true, by denying the mental hygiene approach and retreating to the narrow rigidity of the teacher of yesterday. But the vast majority of teachers try to face the responsibility of helping each pupil: it is common indeed to see evidence of deep-seated desire to assist, somehow, even the most wayward. To do this a teacher may convert to a semitherapeutic approach. Others experiment with projective processes, as they are encouraged to do in courses and in the literature.[1] They often find themselves involved in counseling situations which are overwhelming. Love and acceptance are the sacred passwords of mental hygiene; since they represent only part of the appreciation of depth psychology which we need, their application applied at random may produce confusion as often as solution. The modern teacher then faces the dilemma: how much a teacher, how much a therapist? To re-evaluate this situation with any completeness is beyond the scope of this paper. The propositions offered here may serve as guidelines to help an individual teacher to find his own working level and to feel secure at it.

1. *When we work with pupils, we should operate within the confines of our own psychological understandings.* Dealing with complicated emotional areas requires not a casual knowledge about, but an extensive understanding of, depth psychology. And it requires a thorough knowledge of one's self, motivations, assets, and limitations. For example, to know what anxiety is by definition does not mean one understands its workings. Nor does it follow that one is able to manage one's own anxiety in the process of helping a child.

The most glaring deficiency, fostered by the mental hygienists themselves, is the identification of the mental hygiene attitude with permissiveness. Current dynamic psychology recognizes that without deep acceptance for children there is nothing, but that love alone is not enough. There is no single mode of teacher behavior which will be sufficient to help all pupils toward adjustment and maturity. The problem of how to limit and control children through hygienic discipline is very much a concern of mental hygiene in education; in fact, the study of this process bids well to replace the naive permissiveness as the core of the new mental hygiene. Teachers in general have a suspicion of theory, since most theory is borrowed from nonschool settings and is not related to the classroom. We need theory derived from our own reality, and as teachers we need always to deepen and re-examine our theory.

[1] See, for example, the devices suggested in *Mental Health in Modern Education.* Fifty-fourth Yearbook of the National Society for the Study of Education, Part II. Chicago: The University of Chicago Press, 1955. Pp. xi + 397 + lxxiv.

To say that we as teachers should operate within the confines of our psychological understanding is not a negative statement. There is enough for us to do that we do understand. And we can come to understand more. But we do not expect to be able to do everything and we do not feel guilty when we operate in a limited way.

2. *Often we find ourselves restricted, too, by the condition of limited access.* Current practice in many child guidance clinics is to be selective in deciding who is to be accepted for treatment. For example, certain patterns of behavior are amenable to treatment, while other syndromes are not treatable. Or, it may be requested that, before a child is accepted for help, both parents agree to come for related treatment. In another case, it may be felt that only in a closed institution, apart from his family influence, can a child achieve adjustment. Teachers face all types of cases, but have—regardless of their psychological understanding—limited access to the factors in need of control. A teacher is able to monitor class behavior and work with it, but such corrective influence may be unproductive without managing part of the home relationship.

This is not to suggest that we give up when we realize we are doing a "holding effort," rather than a remedial one. For some children this will turn the tide. For others, it will provide areas of normal acceptance as some compensation for the overall negative atmosphere. Having no illusion of a solution, teachers can still give their best supportive effort. We cannot expect rewards in signs of change. We are relaxed in expectations without diminishing our concern for the child.

3. *Since teachers are group workers, many of the procedures of the therapist cannot be incorporated into a school situation.* To most child therapists, a group means two beings, one adult and one child. This provides a freedom to adopt limits to this child's needs. A teacher sees, say, thirty at one time. The pupils did not select him, nor he them. Each must have at least a minimal capacity to function as a group member. The therapist works with a hostility to authority; some ability to use authority is necessary for a pupil in a classroom. Adjustments can be made in subject matter and allowances made for atypical needs, but only to a point. The balance of concentration on the needs of one child at the expense of others requires astute judgment and skill even beyond that of the usual therapist.

4. *Tasks of the teacher and therapist are complementary and may to a degree overlap, but the emphasis and methods differ.* The tasks of the school are designed for relatively normal egos, able to withstand tension and inhibit impulses and to obtain gratification from the teacher, the group, and the learning experiences. Essentially the teacher helps the normal toward better integration. It is the world of reality tempered with flexibility and provision for delays and regressions from modal behavior. The human relationship is warm and friendly. While a teacher recognizes and responds to the unconscious feelings and wishes of pupils, these feelings are not a matter of interpretation and insight. The therapist deals with the

subjective world of the child which reflects the emotional warp. To straighten this warp he utilizes his close rapport, so that interpretation and insight may be forthcoming. He controls the flow of the data the child presents, and patiently anticipates the time needed for essential relearning. For example, play therapy replaces for the unhappy child the play activity of the normal. The blend of emotional sensitivity in reading therapy a step beyond remedial reading is a skill experience alone. A counseling interview with an adolescent differs from a paper the same pupil writes in English class, "How I feel about myself." The setting and purpose is seen by the pupil as different. The reader differs in this instance from the listener. But these very examples illustrate the present lack of any clear point of demarcation between the work of the therapist and that of the modern teacher. No doubt there must be considerable overlapping, and that suggests that teachers may need better preparation for the therapeutic aspects of their work.

** 28 **

Mama or M.A.?:
The "Teacher-Mom" Program Evaluated

CARL FENICHEL, ED. D.

During the past decade we have witnessed a growing community interest and concern in providing educational services and trained teaching personnel to help the deviant child. Mental health agencies and school systems over our nation are earnestly searching for new ways and means to help disturbed children hitherto excluded from our public schools. *Teaching the Troubled Child* by George T. Donahue and Sol Nichtern is the story of the "teacher-mom" program of the Elmont (N.Y.) school system, widely publicized and heralded as a "radically new approach to the education of hundreds of thousands of emotionally and mentally handicapped children through existing community facilities (book jacket)."

* From *The Journal of Special Education* 1966, *1*, pp. 45–51. Reprinted by permission of the author and the publisher.

This book attempts to demonstrate that (a) "The one-to-one relationship is the only method" (p. 199) to educate the troubled child; (b) Since no community can afford one professional for one child, the teacher-mom program presents the ideal solution.

Just what is a teacher-mom? She is a volunteer who works with a disturbed child on a one-to-one basis and whose "responsibility would be to conduct the educational and emotional program as prescribed by the professional members of the team" (p. 5) under their direction and supervision. What are her qualifications? Just take the endearing and enduring virtues of "motherhood and abiding love" (p. 17); then add a blend of the most precious ingredients found in the ideal teacher, "warm, empathic, mature, emotionally stable, dedicated" (p. 52), and you have the teacher-mom, who brings to the child "her own emotional climate—that of an affectionate, understanding mother" (p. 55).

Now I deeply treasure many warm and wonderful memories of my own mother and yield to no one in my reverence for motherhood. But after reading and hearing all about the Elmont teacher-mom program, I am still thoroughly unconvinced that motherhood in and of itself qualifies one to be a teacher of disturbed children any more than it qualifies one to be a psychiatrist, psychologist, or social worker. And yet Donahue and Nichtern, who, I believe, would not suggest that successful parenthood is adequate or sufficient preparation or qualification to make one a "psychiatrist-pop" or a "psychologist- or social-worker-mom" are ready to believe:

> "They (teacher-moms) are successful and professional because they have been trained by life to be successful child rearers and *by the very nature of this task, teachers. So they are professionals in child-rearing in every sense of the word—maybe sometimes more successful than the technical professionals*" (p. 44, italics ours).

I am not going to assess or pass judgment on the remedial or therapeutic effects of "motherliness and abiding love." So much would depend on one's definition of the term and on its particular meaning, relevance and application for a particular child. What I do believe most firmly, however, is that while tender, loving care may make one a good baby sitter, it doesn't qualify one to be a teacher—let alone a teacher of disturbed children. What such a teacher needs is not just some free time and personal motivation to help a disturbed child, but *professional* concern, *professional* interest, *professional* preparation, *professional* involvement, *professional* dedication and *professional* skills in working with disturbed children's specific problems and needs.

No one would deny that much of education—like so much of psychotherapy is—an art in which the personality of the teacher or therapist and such positive attributes as insight, sensitivity and intuition have valuable contributions to make. But what Donahue and Nichtern appear to have done in their Elmont project and in their book is to ignore or fail to recognize those basic areas of teacher competency and skill which are not only desirable but mandatory, and which come not from pregnancy and parenthood but from professional preparation and practice. The authors assure us again and again that since these teacher-moms "all had reared their own children it was felt they had the basic experience to deal with most of the problems which might arise" (p. 144). It is hard to conceive how bringing up a normal child successfully qualifies one to work with a deviant child, whose behavior the authors (p. 48) admit is "unpredictable," who is "compulsive," "anxiety-ridden," "aggressive" and who suffers from impulsivity, learning deficits, communication disorders, maturational lags and disorganized behavior.

Every special educator can name some gifted, well-trained professional teachers who are "warm, empathic, mature, emotionally stable, dedicated" (p. 52), and who are extremely successful in working with normal children, despite the fact that they have basic teaching experiences and skills which the teacher-mom lacks. I believe that teachers who work with deviant children must understand not only normal but abnormal child development and feel comfortable with the pathology of the abnormal. Thy must have at their command a wide repertory of teaching approaches, techniques and curriculum contents for children with all kinds of perceptual and behavioral disorders; sequential steps in the learning process; remedial skills appropriate for individual and group teaching; the planning and organization of lesson plans; and an awareness of when and how to depart from these plans in order to accommodate the unpredictable learning and behavior patterns of the deviant child.

While the teacher-mom is given teacher status and is considered a professional "in child-rearing in every sense of the word" (p. 44), when a principal in the Elmont school system warns that "the use of volunteers can be dangerous if they are allowed to make a professional's decisions" (p. 169), the authors reassure him and the reader that this is not permitted.

This obvious contradiction reveals what would seem to be a lack of awareness of the teaching process with normal and, even more so, with deviant children. The fact is that every minute a teacher (or teacher-mom) is with a child she is making professional decisions.

No teacher can stop the clock and wait for orders or instructions from supervisors or clinicians to determine what techniques and procedures are appropriate for a given child in any given situation. Through cues and clues derived from her ongoing feed-back circuit with a child, she must know when and how to modify her program and plans to meet each changing situation and need as it arises.

We are told that most professionals who originally had raised objections to the non-professional teacher-moms were satisfied with the explanation that the teacher-in-charge is always somewhere in the building in an advisory and supervisory capacity and that "she has been given 20 additional pairs of hands, the teacher-moms, to help her in her work" (p. 184). Now the authors cannot have it both ways. A teacher-mom whose "responsibility would be to conduct the educational and emotional program" (p. 5) needs more than her hands to do the job.

Donahue and Nichtern appear to be confused about a most basic and critical distinction between the role of a non-professional teacher-aide and the Elmont teacher-mom.

Professionals in the mental health field recognize and welcome the tremendously important contributions that volunteers can make. The volunteer can and does play a most important role as a teacher-aide when she works under the constant and ever-present direction and supervision of a professional teacher who, in turn, must be ready and available at all times to move in and take over. The teacher-aide *is* that extra pair of hands which can relieve the teacher of many tasks, routines and specific assignments so that the teacher is free to devote herself to the professional job of individual and group teaching. Teacher-aides can help in the self-managing skills of dressing, feeding and toileting, in taking care of materials and supplies, in helping a child work on a specific academic or learning assignment—all of which have been carefully planned and clearly defined by the teacher and which require no professional decisions by the teacher-aide.

The one-to-one teacher-mom relationship, Donahue and Nichtern constantly remind us, "is the only method which can accommodate the unconventional pedagogic techniques required by these youngsters" (p. 199) who need a program "custom-made for each child" (p. 48).

One reads the book carefully to discover how this highly individualized program operates and comes across many surprising examples of this "custom-made" program in action.

Two teacher-moms are assigned to a particular child two mornings a week and work alone with that child approximately two hours each morning.

> "By design, they had been given very little indoctrination and training for the task. This was done, in part, in order to encourage a maximum degree of participation and to avoid the passive role that so frequently becomes the part of the volunteer worker" (p. 144).

Since when does the training of anyone—professional or volunteer—make for an increase in passivity and a decrease in participation? If it does, why not eliminate *all* training in every field?

Here is how the teacher-mom is instructed to help a child suffering—let us remember—from all kinds of perceptual, learning and behavioral disorders and deficits learn how to read:

> "She (the teacher-mom) is encouraged to *follow the teacher's manual more closely than a professional teacher* because the manuals are well-developed guides and *provide comprehensive directions on how to teach the series with which she is working.* From reading she moves on to other subject areas, such as arithmetic, spelling, language skills, social studies, science. . . ." (p. 54, italics ours)

Is this what Nichtern and Donahue mean by getting away from "the mass approach" (p. 49) through "the successful adaptation of the educational process to the needs of these children" (p. 198)? I know of no reputable educator, principal or supervisor in any public school system with 35 relatively normal children in a class—let alone a special class of deviant, handicapped children—who, in the year 1966, would encourage a teacher to "follow the teacher's manual more closely."

The authors would find it hard to explain how teacher manuals, prepared specifically for use with regular readers and textbooks in regular classes with normal children, can "provide comprehensive directions on how to teach" deviant, unpredictable and disturbed children, each with learning and behavior disorders uniquely his own. Are they attempting to rationalize and conceal the hard, cold fact that the teacher-mom—untrained, unskilled and uncertain—would stumble and fall flat on her face without the crutches of teacher manuals?

The reader is confronted by many other glaring inconsistencies in explaining away some of the program's deficiencies and shortcomings.

One questions, for example, how the Elmont program can justify its lack of contact, guidance or counselling with the child's parents. "Under no circumstances," it is decreed, "would the parents be permitted to contact the teacher-moms or visit the project" (p. 152). We are told that originally the parents were invited to a meeting with the clinical team; that "the meeting was a total and complete failure and a waste of everyone's time" (p. 152), serving to "confirm what all the professionals knew anyhow" (p. 152): that many parents had no understanding of their child's pathology, didn't want to understand it or—if they did—refused to face it.

This does not agree with observations made earlier in the book (which, in my experience, are much closer to the truth): that parents usually suspect the child's pathology very early; that family physicians and pediatricians often tell the parents that the child will "outgrow it;" that parents then start making the rounds from one doctor to another, searching desperately for help but "getting little or no advice or direction" (p. 9).

On another page we are told that "almost all the families which bred and nurtured these children" (p. 193) demonstrated pathology; that professional efforts to modify this pathology rarely succeeded; that many families functioned as if they needed to preserve this pathology. One page later we are informed that all these children suffered from disabilities which "extended into nearly every area of motor and perceptual organization" (p. 194) and that the behavior of most of them was "suggestive of diffuse damage to the central nervous system" (p. 194). Could Nichtern and Donahue be confusing cause and effect? Are they perhaps revealing occupational prejudices against parents by perpetuating the old wives' tale that disturbed parents make disturbed children? Does not the very name "teacher-mom" imply the inadequacy of the disturbed child's mother and the need for a substitute figure who will be both mom and teacher?

I believe that the Elmont project started out as an honest attempt by good people to help disturbed children for whom no other facilities were available. It certainly was far better than having these children vegetate in some custodial setting or waste away in the isolation of their own homes.

At one point in their book Donahue and Nichtern tells us: "The authors do not suggest that this (the Elmont project) is the only approach or the best (p. 37)." But the book either ignores or tears down every existing or suggested alternative to the teacher-mom program, including specialized day schools and special classes within a public school setting.

Nichtern and Donahue disapprove of legislation recently passed in New York State making it mandatory for boards of education to provide special classes in the public schools for disturbed children. This legislation has been widely hailed by professionals and parents who have struggled for years and finally succeeded in getting these excluded children back into our public schools. Donahue and Nichtern, however, reject the legislation as a "process of internal exclusion" (p. 35). Specialized schools and facilities as well as special classes in our public schools are denounced as "holding units" (p. 35); a holding unit "spews forth its poisonous toxins" (p. 35) of "segregation" (p. 35) by a "policy of exclusion and removal" (p. 36).

The writer cannot comprehend how Donahue and Nichtern see exclusion and isolation as taking place in special classes within the public schools and yet ignore or deny the obviously greater exclusion of those Elmont children who are removed from the regular Board of Education building and made to spend most of their time isolated and alone with only four walls and a teacher-mom.

In negating every other type of facility the authors do not seem to understand that what is desperately needed is not any *one* alternative but a vast spectrum of special educational services in regular classes, special classes, specialized schools and day treatment centers as well as residential centers and hospitals to take care of the vastly different needs of different children at different times.

Not one of the children presented or described in their book appears to have the degree of behavior disturbance or intellectual or learning impairment to preclude his having been able to function and to make as much if not more progress in specialized schools or special classes with specially trained teachers within a public school setting. *Teaching the Troubled Child's* major premise—on which the writer believes the Elmont Project must stand or fall—is its major assumption "that the one-to-one relationship is the *sine qua non* for the successful adaptation of the education process to the needs of these children (p. 198).

The field of special education recognized a long time ago that every deviant and handicapped child needs a curriculum unto himself—one that will meet his unique needs, deficits and potentials. But Donahue and Nichtern—with a dogged hangover from the pattern of individual psychotherapy—base their whole program on the assumption that this cannot be developed in a group setting.

The fact is that while there is no magic ratio to govern how many of these children a trained teacher can work with effectively, we do know that superb jobs are being done today, with children sicker than those in the Elmont program, in special classes of anywhere from 3 to 6 children, depending on the pathology of the children, the educational and behavioral make-up of the group, and the skills, resources and capacities of the teacher.

I believe that with few exceptions disturbed children can benefit more from a group than from an individual setting. With many of these isolated and withdrawn children, a one-to-one relationship would only feed their very pathology and need to cling to a dependency figure that each child wants all to himself.

Many of these children's major problems are problems in interpersonal relationships and group living. In teacher-planned and teacher-directed group activities and interactions in the classroom, these children can and do help each other develop the capacity to work and play and live together—something they must achieve if they are to remain within the community. This can take place only in a group setting. Social relationships are lived—not taught.

Donahue and Nichtern appear to be ignoring the field of special education and the rapidly growing number of teachers specially trained and qualified to work with deviant children. They charge instead that teachers generally are trained to deal with the intellectual and not with the emotional, social and physical needs of children and that most of today's educators accept responsibility for the teaching process but overlook the child who is being taught.

For those readers who are not completely sold on the teacher-mom program, the authors devote the closing pages of *Teaching the Troubled Child* to listing the many unique advantages of the untrained teacher-mom volunteer over the trained professional teacher:

1. "They (teacher-moms) have no preconceived set of standards by which to gauge learning expectancies" (p. 199).

2. They can accept and relate to the child regardless of his academic level.

3. "Their lack of sophistication in educational techniques" (p. 199) makes them receptive to applying "basic pedagogical approaches in a direct, forceful and uncluttered manner" (p. 199).

4. "The absence of the self-image of professional teacher permits the volunteer to experience positive satisfaction from improvement in any area of the child's development, not solely the educational" (p. 199).

5. Professional teachers may become anxious if traditional academic growth doesn't take place. The teacher-mom can more readily accept a limited measure of progress.

The only conclusion one would seemingly draw from these anti-intellectual and anti-professional arguments is that we must stop training professional teachers, scrap special education programs and encourage all teacher aspirants to raise families, instead, in the hope that someday they might qualify as successful teacher-moms.

To anyone who knows or wants to know about the problems and programs of "teaching the troubled child," Nichtern and Donahue have little to offer.

REFERENCES

Donahue, G. T., & Nichtern, S. *Teaching the Troubled Child*. New York: Free Press, 1965.

** 29 **

Behavior Modification: Limitations and Liabilities

DONALD L. MACMILLAN AND STEVEN R. FORNESS

Within recent years the application of behavior modification techniques in classrooms of exceptional children has increased greatly. One can scarcely find a recent issue of a periodical concerned with exceptional children which does not include an investigation utilizing behavior modification strategy. Periodicals abound with evidence regarding the efficacy of behavior modification with retardates (Bijou & Orlando, 1961), learning disability children (Hewett, 1965; Lovitt, 1968), autistic children (Ferster & DeMeyer, 1961; Hewett, 1964; Lovaas *et al.*, 1965), emotionally disturbed (Levin & Simmons, 1962a; Levin & Simmons, 1962b), brain damaged (Patterson, 1965), and assorted behavior problems in the classroom (Hively, 1959; Hewett, 1966; Valett, 1966; Whelan & Haring, 1966). Hence, the contention that behavior modification is an effective technique with atypical children appears to be well documented.

Hewett (1968) contends that behavior modification assigns the teacher to the role of the *learning specialist;* the role she is best prepared to assume. Alternate strategies (i.e., psychoanalytic, sensory-neurological) place the teacher in the role of psychotherapist or diagnostician, roles which teachers are generally ill-prepared to assume. In light of successes in teaching atypi-

* From *Exceptional Children,* in press. Reprinted by permission of the senior author and the publisher.

cal children with behavior modification techniques, Bijou (1966) contends that one can no longer categorically explain the failure to learn in terms of their deficiencies, but rather must consider the tutorial inadequacies of the teacher. The combination of the factors above (i.e., teachers in roles of competence and the emphasis on what the child *can* do if material is properly sequenced and correct responses reinforced) provides a more positive approach to the education of exceptional children than previous approaches which attributed the failure to learn to the child's defect.

By focusing on the effects of consequences in altering and maintaining behavior, certain long-standing assumptions of educators have been questioned. One such assumption is that certain rewards, i.e., letter grades and teacher approval, have universal applicability. For certain children, the above rewards are ineffective. In attempts to identify consequences which are rewarding for children who do not respond to the traditional rewards used in school, investigators have utilized rewards considered unconventional by some (e.g., candy, check marks, tokens) with considerable success. Research has further sensitized teachers to the power of their attention, and how their attending to misbehavior may have the effect of increasing its occurrence (Zimmerman & Zimmerman, 1962). Premack (1959) describes the use of activities the child prefers (high probability behavior) as an accelerating consequence for less preferred behavior (low probability behavior). Hence, if the child enjoys building model planes, the teacher can use this behavior as a reward for performing tasks the child enjoys less. Such evidence has had an impact on the ongoing practices in the special education classroom.

Enthusiasm over the reported successes of behavior modification with atypical children coupled with teachers' desperation for something that works may blind us to what behavior modification does not, or cannot, do. Mann and Phillips (1967) point out that a number of practices presently operative in special education are designed to fractionate global or molar areas of behavior. While their discussion did not include mention of behavior modification, their contention may also be valid with regard to this strategy. It is important that behavior modification be put in perspective with respect to the overall picture of education. This paper discusses three limitations in the application of behavior modification to exceptional children. Some of the limitations to be discussed are inherent in the theoretical paradigm itself; others lie in the application, or misapplication, of that theory by practitioners. Specifically, the three limitations to be discussed are:

1. Learning theory does not guide the teacher in determining educational goals.

2. A view of motivation as exclusively extrinsic in nature is limiting in scope.

3. The operational definition of reinforcement ignores certain cognitive aspects of reinforcement.

EDUCATIONAL GOALS

Behavioral Goals

Ullmann and Krasner state that the first question asked by the behavior analyst is, "What behavior is maladaptive, that is, what subject behaviors should be increased or decreased?" (1965, p. 1) To the experimental psychologist this is a question answered only through objective analysis of behavior. Too often, however, the real question that gets answered is "What behavior manifested by the child most annoys me as his teacher," regardless of whether or not that behavior is interfering with the child's learning or development.

The behavior modification strategy does not determine educational goals for the child. This is not to suggest that the behavior modification strategy claims to determine goals, but in its inability to do so may lie the reason for its lack of acceptance in public school programs. Hewett *et al.* discuss the lack of balanced emphasis on goals and methods. They write:

> In general, selection of these goals is based on a desire to aid the child in changing maladaptive behavior to adaptive behavior. At best, these concepts of "maladaptive" and "adaptive" provide only the broadest of guidelines for selection of specific behavioral goals. In this sense the powerful methodology of the behavior modification approach is not matched by concern with goals in learning. Teachers are provided with an efficient means of taking emotionally disturbed children someplace but are not substantially aided in the selection of where to go.
>
> It is this lack of balanced emphasis on goals and methods that may preclude the acceptance of behavior modification in the field of education, particularly in the public school, and thereby may greatly limit its usefulness. (1969, p. 523)

Once the teacher has determined what the child is to be taught, the behavior modification techniques can be employed to achieve that end. Alternate developmental theories (e.g., Erikson, Piaget) may be more helpful for determining goals in that they suggest to the teacher the developmental tasks that the child must master, and what skills he must acquire in order to achieve subsequent levels. Lacking a developmental framework, the teacher rather arbitrarily decides what the child must learn.

Wood (1968) expressed concern over the possibility that teachers are provided with a powerful tool (i.e., behavior modification techniques) without simultaneously developing an understanding of its implications and potential misuse. In light of evidence suggesting that teachers, in general, are more concerned with maintaining power over students than in knowledge and skill transmission, his concern seems well-founded (Eddy, 1967; Henry, 1957; Landes, 1965; Moore, 1967). Implicit in the application of behavior modification techniques with children is the right of the behavior modifier to define what represents "adaptive" or "appropriate" behaviors. Wood (1968) described the teacher's role in such a relationship as follows:

having defined the child's present behavior as "inappropriate" *he* plans to shape it toward behavior *he* has defined as "appropriate." In describing the teacher most likely to misuse this tool without considering the child's rights to participate in defining the goal behavior, Wood states:

> These teachers may often be those against whose already abusive application of their authority pupils have the greatest need to be protected. Like many "tools," behavior modification techniques are themselves morally blind. Like a stout sword, they work equally well in the hands of hero or tyrant. Any person of moderate intelligence can, with assistance if not independently, apply them with great effectiveness for good or ill (1968, p. 14).

In the case of many exceptional children, a number of their rights were abridged at the time of classification or labeling, thus making them more susceptible to abuse than had they not been so labeled.

Academic Goals

When the educational goal is related to the teaching of subject matter, and the teacher employs a strict behaviorist strategy to achieve this goal, certain limitations inherent in the paradigm should be realized. The usual learning situation is much more complex than is suggested by the behavioristic paradigm. Enthusiastic proponents of behaviorism tend to be blinded by the framework and deny other possible explanations for human learning. The analysis of human learning in terms of discrete, operational steps may ignore or violate the inherent logic in the material to be learned. For example, Piaget (Flavell, 1963) theorizes that schemata (organized information) develop as a consequence of "assimilation" and "accommodation" and the learning is facilitated by presenting materials in a manner amenable to reorganization of previously existing cognitive structures (schemata). In addition, Gagné (1962), operating within a different theoretical framework than Piaget, states that the nature and structure of the task which is to be learned is of greater importance than the behavioristic principles of learning (e.g., reinforcement, practice).

It may be that behavior modification strategy fails to adequately consider the goals to which the shaped behavior is related. Determination of goals is left to the individual in control (i.e., the teacher), who may, or may not, be a good judge of appropriate behavior. When the principles of behavior modification are applied to the teaching of subject matter the reductionistic conception of the learning process is a definite limitation. Autoinstructional techniques suffer from many of the same limitations, which are elaborated upon by Stafford and Combs (1967).

MOTIVATION

From the behavioristic point of view, motivation is seen as extrinsic to learning. Bijou and Baer (1961) stress the importance of behavioral scientists concerning themselves only with events which can be observed and quantified. In the application of reinforcement theory to behavioral management an attempt has been made to observe the suggestions of Bijou and Baer. In attempts to get children to read, sit in their seats, attend to materials and develop other school appropriate behaviors, the emphasis has been placed on the use of tokens, check marks, and candy in association with the desired behavior. In programs developed to shape behavior through extrinsic rewards, or consequences which are observable and able to be quantified, it is postulated that the child will ultimately want to engage in these "appropriate" behaviors because the social rewards (e.g. teacher approval, peer approval) have been paired with the extrinsic rewards used during the shaping program. Inherent in such an approach is the belief that desire or motivation can be manipulated by simply applying consequences when the organism behaves in a desired fashion. The theoretical approach described above is extremely limited and ignores much available evidence, presented in summary below, and discounts alternative explanations of motivation.

Piaget describes the equilibration process, wherein cognitive adaptation and growth result from the dynamic functioning of the processes of assimilation and accommodation. Exploratory behavior is inherently interesting and rewards the child if it relates to the child's existing mental structures (schemata). Not only is it important to present material in a fashion commensurate with the child's previous level of cognitive development, but material thus presented can become a source of intrinsic motivation to the child (Hunt, 1961). There is no observable or quantifiable "pay off" for such behavior; however, when a "match," between existing schemata and task, exists the child finds the task inherently interesting.

Stimulation-seeking behavior appears to be another source of intrinsic motivation in higher order organisms. Festinger's (1957) "theory of cognitive dissonance," concludes that when incoming stimulation differs from existing perceptions or conceptions one is motivated to resolve the discrepancy. Festinger (1957) postulated that cognitive incongruities are a primary source of motivation in human beings, a source which is intrinsic in nature, and one which cannot be observed or quantified.

While working outside of the two preceding theoretical frameworks, Harlow (1949, 1953) suggests that there may be an innate drive of curiosity, which is more likely to operate when the learners' primary needs have been satisfied (Maslow, 1943). Harlow (1953) explained that children and monkeys can enjoy exploration for its own sake. He cites the monkey who continues to solve problems despite the fact that his cheeks are full of food with which he can "reward" correct or incorrect responses. Despite such unsystematic schedules of reinforcement, the monkeys increased their ability to learn how to learn (Harlow, 1949).

White (1965) offers another framework within which one can consider motivation. He contends that it is in studying the satiated child that one is truly able to understand "human nature." In his paper critical of the traditional Freudian position which views motivation in terms of need reduction, White suggests that such a framework (i.e., Freudian) is unable to explain satisfactorily the apparent play behavior of the infant, or the one year old who tries to spoon feed himself despite the fact that he could gain greater oral satisfaction by allowing his mother to feed him. It may be added, neither can reinforcement theory explain this behavior in terms of the observable events. Rather, White contends, the child is concerned with achieving mastery over his environment. Regarding play behavior, he writes:

> It is directed, selective, and persistent, and it is continued not because it serves primary drives, which indeed it cannot serve until it is almost perfected, but because it satisfies an intrinsic need to deal with environment (White, 1965, p. 15).

The goal of behavior which White sees as an attempt to achieve competence may be to effect familiarity with the environment, or in more global terms, autonomy. In other words, the "pay off" is a feeling or sense of competence.

The point to be made with regard to motivation is that the behavioristic viewpoint is not the only framework within which one can consider motivation. In fact, the behavioristic paradigm is unable to explain adequately the behaviors described by Piaget, Festinger, Harlow and White. One is unable to observe the consequences for behaviors that result from exploration, cognitive dissonance, curiosity and competence as motives. Yet, these sources of motivation must not be ignored or discounted as one attempts to reach the atypical child, or any child for that matter. Certain programs, which are essentially behavior modification oriented (e.g., Hewett, 1968) have altered their initial approaches and attempt to utilize intrinsic sources of motivation. To the extent that this is practiced, however, such programs violate the pure approach suggested by Bijou and Baer (1961).

REINFORCEMENT

Within the behavior modification framework, reinforcement is commonly defined as "a stimulus which increased the probability of a response." The reinforcement does not have to be directly related to the behavior, and often the separation is intentional. An example of this separation is the use of candy to reinforce problem solving or seat sitting. Theoretically, such a definition does not adequately explain the verbal confirming response discussed by Jensen (1968). In addition, certain practical ramifications should be considered by the practitioner prior to the application of reinforcers which are unrelated to the behavior they are reinforcing.

Jensen (1968) describes the "verbal confirming response" (V_c) or feedback, which is a type of self-reinforcement or symbolic reinforcement used by humans. It is extremely limited in lower forms of animals and young children. V_c is more than merely a secondary reinforcement. A secondary reinforcer is a previously neutral stimulus which has gained reinforcing power through being paired with a primary or biologically relevant reinforcer. Secondary reinforcers are known to extinguish very rapidly in animal studies. Such is not the case with V_c which has the effect of strengthening behavior even though the verbal confirmatory response itself has no reinforcing properties in a biological sense. "The V_c response is most often covert, especially in adults, and may even be unconscious. It consists, in effect, of saying to oneself *Good* or *That's right* or *wrong* (Jensen, 1968, p. 124)." The function of language in the above manner has been demonstrated by several Russian psychologists (Razran, 1959). An interesting feature of the V_c is that it must be self-initiated. To the extent that it is necessary in efficient problem-solving, the use of extrinsic reinforcers that are unrelated to the specific behavior they are reinforcing precludes the necessity for developing the V_c. In depriving the child of the opportunity of this V_c, are we hindering his development as a problem-solver?

Turning to more practical considerations, Ferster (1966) distinguished between *arbitrary* and *natural* reinforcers in a paper on aversive stimuli. He pointed out that arbitrary reinforcers differ from natural reinforcers in two ways: (1) when arbitrary reinforcers are used, the performance that is reinforced is narrowly specified rather than broadly defined, and (2) in the case of arbitrary reinforcers, the individual's existing repertoire of responses does not influence his behavior nearly as much as is the case with natural reinforcers. Therefore, natural reinforcers lead to more integrated, general learning.

In the first case, a positive consequence is promised for a specific behavior (e.g., seat sitting), and the child can obtain that consequence only by conforming to specific demands. He sits in his seat to obtain the reward, but learning does not necessarily generalize to global behaviors (i.e., adequate classroom behavior). In the second case, arbitrary reinforcers benefit the controller, not the controlled. The teacher who says, "If you sit in your seat, I'll give you 5 check marks" is arbitrarily reinforcing seat sitting, which is reinforcing to the teacher for employing the strategy. But the child is not being reinforced by a consequence that naturally exists in his environment. His natural environment has never reinforced his sitting in his seat with a check mark, nor is it likely to in the future. In fact non-sitting has probably been rewarded through satisfying the curiosity drive.

While check marks, tokens, M&Ms, etc. may be justifiable as initial means of bringing behavior under control, they must not represent an end in themselves. In several instances, teachers employing the behavior modification strategy (as they interpret it) have had their children on check marks for an entire year. When asked the reason the children were still functioning at this low reward level, the teacher indicated that "I'm not about to change something that is working." This teacher has failed in her responsibility to bring the child's behavior under the control of reinforcers that will exist in the child's natural environment (e.g., social praise). Whelan and Haring

(1966) distinguished between the acquisition of behavior and its maintenance. The arbitrary reinforcers are useful in the acquisition stage, but in the maintenance stage they suggest:

> When the behavior needs to be maintained, then it is no longer necessary to provide accelerating consequences to each behavioral response. Maintaining behavior requires that the teacher reduce considerably the number of accelerating consequences provided; indeed, it is a necessity if a child is to develop independent learning skills and self control. It is during this maintenance process that appropriate behavior is accelerated by consequences which are intrinsic to completion of tasks, social approval, feelings of self-worth, and the satisfaction of assuming self-responsibility. Therefore, dependence on numerous teacher applied consequences gradually loses significance to a child. (Whelan and Haring, 1966, p. 284)

It is interesting to note that the above authors, two of the most commonly cited behavior modification advocates, refer to intrinsic consequences, feelings of self-worth and satisfaction of assuming self-responsibility. It may be that it is with the practitioner who has learned the *how* of behavior modification and rigidly adheres to its doctrines that the problem lies. In training teachers to utilize the strategy, it seems essential that the instruction should include a heavy dosage of the possible misuse of this potentially useful strategy.

In conclusion, the behavior modification strategy has tremendous potential for work with atypical children. Its use with these children is promising; however, its misuse could be terrifying. It is not a panacea. It gives no direction in determining educational goals, it reduces certain constructs of learning, motivation and reinforcement to simplistic terms on occasion. To the unsophisticated practitioner, it may blind them to broader frames of reference regarding the constructs listed above. Furthermore, it may preclude children from learning how to learn and thus becoming independent of teachers, as such, a major goal of education. It is time we admitted the shortcomings and limitations of the approach as well as extolling its virtues. In an address to a group of autoinstructional techniques enthusiasts, Howard Kendler at the 1964 American Psychological Association Convention said the following: "You have a system called Socrates, but you don't have one called God." This statement applies to the present discussion, and should be heeded by the rigid behaviorist.

REFERENCES

Bijou, S. W., and Baer, D. *Child development, Vol. I.,* New York Appleton-Century-Crofts, 1961.

Bijou, S. W., and Orlando, R. Rapid development of multiple-schedule performance with retarded children. In Ullmann, L. P., and Krasner, L. (Eds.) *Case studies in behavior modification.* New York: Holt, Rinehart and Winston, 1965, pp. 339–347.

Bijou, S. W. A functional analysis of retarded development. In N. R. Ellis (Ed.),

International review of research in mental retardation, Vol. I. New York. Academic Press, 1966.

Eddy, Elizabeth M. *Walk the white line: a profile of urban education*. Doubleday Anchor, 1967.

Ferster, C., and DeMeyer, M. The development of performance in autistic children in automatically controlled environments. *Journal of Chronic Diseases,* 1961, 25, 8–12.

Ferster, C. B. Arbitrary and natural reinforcement. Paper delivered at the 1966 Meeting of the American Assn. for the Advancement of Science, Washington, D.C.

Festinger, L. *A theory of cognitive dissonance*. Evanston, Ill. Row, Peterson, 1957.

Flavell, J. H. *The developmental psychology of Jean Piaget*. Princeton, N.J.: Van Nostrand, 1963.

Gagné, R. M. Military training and principles of learning. *American Psychologist*, 1962, 17, 83–91.

Harlow, H. The formation of learning sets. *Psychological Review*, 1949, 56, 51–65.

Harlow, H. Mice, monkeys, men, and motives. *Psychological Review*, 1953, 60, 23–32.

Henry, J. Attitude organization in elementary school classrooms. *American Journal of Orthopsychiatry*, 1957, 27, 117–133.

Hewett, F. A hierarchy of education tasks for children with learning disorders. *Exceptional Children*, 1965, 31, 207–214.

Hewett, F. Teaching reading to an autistic boy through operant conditioning. *Reading Teacher*, 1964, 17, 613–618.

Hewett, F. The Tulare experimental class for educationally handicapped children. *California Education*, 1966, 3, 608.

Hewett, F. M. *The emotionally disturbed child in the classroom*. Boston: Allyn & Bacon, 1968.

Hewett, F. M., Taylor, F. D., and Artuso, A. A. The Santa Monica Project: Evaluation of an engineered classroom design with emotionally disturbed children. *Exceptional Children*, 1969, 35, 523–529.

Hively, W. Implications for the classroom of B. F. Skinner's analysis of behavior. *Harvard Educational Review*, 1959, 29, 37–42.

Hunt, J. McV. *Intelligence and experience*. New York: Ronald Press, 1961.

Jensen, A. R. Social class and verbal learning. In M. Deutsch, I. Katz, and A. R. Jensen (Eds.), *Social class, race, and psychological development*. New York: Holt, Rinehart and Winston, 1968.

Landes, Ruth. *Culture in American education*. New York: John Wiley & Sons, 1965.

Levin, G., and Simmons, J. Response to food and praise by emotionally disturbed boys. *Psychological Reports*, 1962, 11, 539–546. (a)

Lovaas, O. I., *et al*. Experimental studies in childhood schizophrenia: analysis of self-destructive behavior. *Journal of Experimental Child Psychology*, 1962, 2, 67–84.

Lovitt, T. C. Operant conditioning techniques for children with learning disabilities. *The Journal of Special Education*, 1968, 2, 283–289.

Mann, L., and Phillips, W. A. Fractional practices in special education: A critique. *Exceptional Children*, 1967, 33, 311–317.

Maslow, A. H. A theory of human motivation. *Psychological Review*, 1943, 50, 370–396.

Moore, G. A. *Realities of the urban classroom: observations in elementary schools*. New York: Doubleday Anchor, 1967.

Patterson, G. R. An application of conditioning techniques to the control of a hyperactive child. *Behavior Research and Therapy,* 1965, 2, 217–226.

Premack, D. Toward empirical behavior laws: I. positive reinforcement. *Psychological Review,* 1959, 66, 219–233.

Razran, G. Soviet psychology and psychophysiology. *Behavioral Science,* 1959, 4, 35–48.

Stafford, R. R., and Combs, C. F. Radical reductionism: A possible source of inadequacy in autoinstructional techniques. *American Psychologist,* 1967, 22, 667–669.

Ullman, L., and Krasner, L. *Case studies in behavior modification.* New York: Holt, Rinehart and Winston, 1965.

Vallett, R. A. social reinforcement technique for the classroom management of behavior disorders. *Exceptional Children,* 1966, 33, 185–189.

Whelan, R. J., and Haring, N. G. Modification and maintenance of behavior through systematic application of consequences. *Exceptional Children,* 1966, 32, 281–289.

White, R. W. Motivation reconsidered: The concept of competence. In I. J. Gordon (Ed.), *Human development: Readings in research.* Glenview, Illinois. Scott Foresman and Company, 1965.

Wood, F. H. Behavior modification techniques in context. *Newsletter of the council for children with behavioral disorders,* 1968, 5, No. 4, 12–15.

Zimmerman, E. H., and Zimmerman, J. The alteration of behavior in a special classroom situation. *Journal of the Experimental Analysis of Behavior,* 1962, 5, 59–60.

** 30 **

Emotionally Disturbed and Brain Damaged Children—Should We Mix Them?

JOHN F. MESINGER

There appears to be a trend in recent literature to consider behavioral characteristics to be of prime importance in assigning children to classes for emotionally disturbed children. The presence or absence of identifiable areas of brain damage is correspondingly downgraded in importance. While this appears to be consistent with a more extensive trend in accord-

* From *Exceptional Children* 1965, 32, pp. 237–238. Reprinted by permission of the author and the publisher.

ing specific etiologies less importance in planning remediation, the mixing of brain damaged and functionally emotionally disturbed children seems to me to do a disservice to both groups of children as well as the staff who will teach them.

It is true that many exogenous children exhibit most, if not all, of the characteristics of the Strauss syndrome: extreme distractibility, hyperactivity, visual and temporal sequential learning impairment, inadequate perception of laterality, and figure-ground phenomena. It is also true that the behaviors of such children usually irritate teachers and pupils of conventional classrooms.

Many seriously socially and emotionally disturbed children exhibit both learning disabilities and irritating behavior in manner similar to that of exogenous children. Current practice has indicated that some emotionally disturbed children will respond with the growth desired when an academic milieu is organized in a manner following the model created to serve the needs of exogenous children. These facts however should not be allowed to mask some rather significant differences between the two broad categories of children.

When there has not been a long term exposure to hostile adults, the typical brain damaged child seems to show neither highly developed defenses against learning nor intense hostility toward teachers and other adults. When damage occurs at birth, children often do have trouble learning how to learn. Programs experiencing substantial success with Strauss syndrome type children have included limitations of distractions, reduction of stimuli, involvement of multiple sense modalities, the introduction of sequential, minute increments of abstraction levels, and brief intervals of instruction. This approach is not new. Similar procedures are utilized in the successful training of puppies and the young of other species.

The typical seriously socially and emotionally disturbed child who has reached the point of acceptance in an emotionally disturbed class has, however, usually strongly intrenched defenses against academic accomplishments as a result of successful though aberrant learning. Usually these children harbor extreme hostility toward teachers and other adults whether explicit or concealed. In addition, when two or more psychotic children are placed with others who are mentally retarded or exogenous they seem able to identify each other as deviant from the group, and practically destroy the academic efforts of the teacher and the others in the class.

The rather high degree of structure applied within a pleasant social milieu seems efficacious for exogenous children. Rarely, however, does this lead to dramatic educational development or remediation. With much more flexible applications of learning theory, however, emotinally disturbed children are observed to make gains that are in some instances quite dramatic.

I submit that the quiet, repetitive, long term approach to the education of the exogenous child is neither needed nor desirable for most emotionally disturbed children. The types and frequency of deviation from curriculum likely to be effective with emotionally disturbed children are more often than not likely to interfere with the process of learning by exogenous children.

The burden of proof that the procedure will serve both exogenous children and emotionally disturbed children equally well should be on the educator before this procedure is widely emulated.

The Return of Rumpelstiltskin:
Reaction to Mesinger's Article

ELI M. BOWER

Without any prodding by the proverbial Walrus but helped along by Mesinger's paper, the time has come, it seems to me, to take the magic phrase of the twentieth century out of the hat and examine it realistically. The phrase I refer to is "brain damaged" or "minimally brain damaged" or "neurologically impaired" or any of the other abracadabras used to explain learning or behavior disorders in children in one mystical phrase.

As a child I was particularly enthralled and impressed by the fairy tale about the miller's daughter and her difficulties with the *der kleines Maennchen*, Rumpelstitskin. However, I considered the deal entered into by the girl and the dwarf fair and aboveboard. Rumpelstiltskin promised to help weave straw into gold in return for the first child of the future queen. When our little friend appeared ready to collect, the situation looked foreboding and hopeless *until* our heroine discovered the magic word and with one happy utterance solved everything.

In my perusal of large city telephone directories I have yet to find a Mr. or Mrs. Rumpelstiltskin. This lack seemingly has not discouraged the seekers of present day magic words. Let me be the first to admit that I have used a few of my own in my day. The verbal genii can be extremely powerful and helpful; they cannot, however, be made to do all the work of the world.

If we follow Mesinger down his yellow brick road, we come to such notions as: (a) The grouping together of brain damaged and functionally

---

∗ From *Exceptional Children* 1965, 32, pp. 238–239. Reprinted by permission of the author and the publisher.

emotionally disturbed children tends to do a disservice to both groups. (b) Emotionally disturbed children usually harbor extreme hostility toward teachers and other adults whereas the typical brain damaged child seems to show neither highly developed defenses against learning nor intense hostility toward teachers. (c) The grouping of children for educational services ought to be made on medical or psychiatric etiologies.

With our limited but increasing knowledge of human behavior, it seems clear that man's personality contains an active ingredient called ego processes which serve to define, interpret, and mediate stimuli from the inner and outer environments. Between stimulus and response stands a scanning, organizing, protecting, selecting, and acting component of the organism. By what magic then do we deprive so-called "brain injured children" of these human qualities? Certainly tissue destruction wherever present in any organism affects behavior most probably by lowering the homeostatic capacity of the organism. But this lowered capacity to adjust may be managed in a variety of ways and result in a multitude of different behaviors. Let me suggest an analogous position in the so-called functional disorders. Since we are in a conjuring mood, conjure up a test to identify all problem children rejected by their parents at the .05 level of significance. Because all these children have a common etiology, parental rejection, let us place them all in one learning group. But, you say, these children do not all have the same specific learning problems as do the "brain injured." Consider then for a moment why rejected children do not come out with similar behavior and learning problems and brain injured children do.

It seems probable that when we separate a group of distractable, hyperactive, perceptually impaired, figureground-confused, confabulated children, the roads by which each child travelled to his destination may have been varied and selective. Many of us have sat in on clinical teams of physicians, psychologists, nurses, and teachers loaded with neurological, EEG, and developmental histories trying to decide whether or not the child did or did not have cerebral disrhythmia or lesions. Have we considered the "why" of such deliberations? What truth is revealed by a six to four vote deciding that the child is "brain injured" or a seven to three vote that he is not? Or if drugs are indicated for hyperactivity, does a positive or negative vote affect the prescription either way?

There is little doubt that brain or nervous tissue can be injured or damaged and that such damage can affect the learning and behavior of human beings including children. It is also probable as many obstetricians and pediatricians have pointed out that almost every baby suffers some brain injury at birth as a result of the physical strain and pressure changes during the birth process. If "minimal brain injury" is a unitary, singular, and exclusive cause of specific learning and behavior disorders, I suspect we are dealing with a highly selective and unique group of Homo sapiens.

To say anything of much certainty in the matter of grouping children with learning problems suggests wild courage or a high degree of ESP. Primarily the notion of special groupings for children with special problems has been based on educational needs rather than any specific etiology or derivation of the learning difficulty. We place mentally retarded children together because they lack the ability to handle abstract symbols with the speed and effectiveness of others. I know of no programs where such children are grouped on the basis of medical or psychosocial etiology of the retardation. While I suspect that classes for cerebral palsied children with normal learning potential may have been justified in the past, their presence in today's schools are anachronistic and historical.

In the matter of grouping you "pays your money and takes your choice." I believe that groups ought to be made up of a wide variety of children able to function within each other's limits. To argue that brain damaged, aggressive, withdrawn, delinquent or cerebral palsied children ought to be grouped together is to lose sight of the goals of education. In addition, where there may be some brain damaged children who show less developed defenses and less hostility toward children, I can not see how brain damage protects a child's ego processes from the frustrations of human failure and inadequacy while his nonbrain damaged, emotionally disturbed classmate develops in his normally abnormal way.

There is probably as much heterogeneity in the personalities and educational needs of children diagnosed as "brain injured" as those diagnosed "neurotic." In all cases what the teacher will be striving to change are the mediating or data processing components of the child's personality—those aspects of the child's self which interpret, modify, utilize, and react to stimuli from within and without the person.

If educational diagnosticians insist on getting into the school game, they must find ways of helping teachers and parents make effective decisions about children. I have no objection to placing "suspected brain injury" in the array of facts about a child; I do object to its selection as a magic phrase which reduces the individual child to an automated nervous system and helps remove the more sticky human factors from messing up the neat solution.

I would very much like to believe in fairy tales but unlike Peter Pan I fall on my face every time I try to fly.

A Reply to Dr. Bower's Comments

JOHN F. MESINGER

I have always felt at a disadvantage in discussing topics with lawyers, semanticists, and poets, however much I may admire their metaphors. Unlike Alice's egg, words do not always mean (to others) what we intend. However, "brain damage" and "emotionally disturbed" do not mean entities to me either. Only as we share similar experiences can we omit qualifying phrases. To have discussed my topic in full with proper qualifications would have filled the journal.

My years of work with exceptional children, parents, teachers, and administrators have caused me to be concerned with a general tendency to take tentative classifications and codify them too soon and without allowing leeway for variation or modification for individual needs. To the extent that many programs for brain damaged tend to be long term affairs, fewer children are served per teacher. These programs are not cheap to operate. Hence alternate models (such as resource rooms for the blind) involving materials and concepts combining several levels of abstraction should be explored. They are not now receiving the university blessing that would over-influence their use.

Dr. Bower's notion of how special classes are founded and children placed conjures visions of Valhalla with gods and goddesses for teachers and administrators. It has been my observation that the ideal textbook myth is seldom honored in practice outside of the campus' ivy walls. The realities far too often would make knowing persons make any effort to keep their children out of special classes.

The objection to the use of medical or psychiatric etiologies in their current forms is, in part, well founded. Perhaps, tired of the position of "fourth member of a trinity," educators have discovered learning theory. This is good (though as a panacea it may prove as illusory as the medical model). However, the dialogue with clinicians should not be dismissed because clinicians disagree. The members vary in skill within their professions as much as do educators. Contrary to popular thought, the happy situation of sustained interaction of competent, experienced psychologist and teacher is and always has been a rarity in any country. Research data or private opinion formed from other than the best of conditions hardly lend confidence to the scientific minded.

* From *Exceptional Chidren* 1965, 32, pp. 239–240. Reprinted by permission of the author and the publisher.

However, progress does continue. Even now, for example, such knowledge as the reversed effects of tranquilizers and dexidrine on post-encephalitic children can make the difference between the remediation of one child and chaos for a room.

While I, perhaps, hold a higher brief for the value of a competent diagnosis than does Dr. Bower (many I have seen have discouraged me too), we probably agree that our own prime concern should be with children's behavioral repertoire and our skills in melding them. I believe that certain syndromes of behavior are mutually antagonistic, that some have greatly different prognoses for remediation, and that these are within man's capacity to understand. I believe that competent diagnosticians can significantly help teachers through grouping of compatible children able to progress at reasonably similar rates.

I fear the results of disenchantment with differential diagnosis in the past may result in premature "hardening of the categories." My point is: try the new, but with judicious restraint which will permit yet other innovations to be tried as well. For a thorough discussion of the issues raised by Dr. Bower, I would suggest the reader see Milton's *Behavior Disorders,* Lippincott Company, 1965.

PART SIX

Learning Disabled

How shall learning disabilities be defined, how shall learning disabled children be diagnosed, and how shall they be educated? These are the problems of this section—and problems indeed! Chalfant and Scheffelin (1969), in an impressive summary of the research on problems of learning disabled children, point to a need for research in the following areas: (1) precise descriptions of specific observable behaviors related to dysfunctions in learning; (2) procedures for recording those behaviors; (3) procedures for educational assessment and diagnosis; (4) prevalence and incidence; (5) effective remedial or compensatory methods of intervention; (6) the efficient delivery of services to children; (7) prevention; (8) the nature of learning.

In a similar vein, with respect to problems and needs, Bateman (1967) has written:

> A field which has experienced the phenomenal upsurge in growth and interest that has characterized learning disabilities in recent years is bound to be beset by diverse terminology, procedures and views. To describe learning disabilities today is quite probably an understatement. . . . (p. 1)

And further,

> While there is little substantial agreement on definition, incidence, or remedial procedures, there is almost universal agreement on the need for diagnosis of children with learning problems. But agreement on the need for diagnosis does not produce conformity in the diagnostic procedures used. There has been striking divergence among the diagnostic philosophies and techniques seen in recent years. (p. 1)

With respect to terminology, Clements ("Nomenclature") points to the myriad terms, 38 in all, used to describe this population. Because of the diverse groups involved in work with learning disabled children— educators, psychologists, physicians, speech pathologists, and others—it is not surprising that such a large number of definitions has arisen. Clements has stated a preference for the term minimal brain dysfunction— as contrasted with learning disabilities or one of the 36 other terms used to describe the population—on the grounds that disturbances in behavior, in many instances, extend further than the learning situation or the classroom.

In spite of Clements' reasoned view, the term learning disabilities is adopted for the present volume because it is meaningful to educators, and for educational purposes. Even so, it must be noted that several definitions of this term have been offered (Chalfant and Scheffelin, 1969, pp. 147–148). One of the most widely accepted, and that adopted for communication in the present volume, is that given by the National Advisory Committee on Handicapped Children, which states:

> Children with special learning disabilities exhibit a disorder in one or more of the basic psychological processes involved in understanding or in using spoken or written languages. These may be manifested in disorders of listening, thinking, talking, reading, writing, spelling, or arithmetic. They include conditions which have been referred to as perceptual handicaps, brain injury, minimal brain dysfunctions, dyslexia, developmental aphasia, etc. They do not include learning problems which are due primarily to visual, hearing, or motor handicaps, to mental retardation, emotional disturbance or to environmental disadvantage. (Chalfant and Scheffelin, 1969, p. 148)

The large number of terms used to describe learning disabled children have, of course, carried with them a variety of symptoms descriptive of the syndrome. Clements ("Symptomatology—Identification of the Child") presents a catalog of symptoms attributed to "children with minimal brain dysfunction" resulting from his summary of over 100 recent publications. Capobianco ("Diagnostic Methods Used With Learning Disability Cases") argues for attention to symptomatology rather than etiology, and points to the many problems involved in the diagnosis of children with learning disabilities. The Capobianco and Clements articles certainly highlight some of the complexities of this area—particularly in diagnosis and description.

Having given some idea of definitional and diagnostic concerns, it is appropriate to turn to another area of complexity, that of the variety of broad theories and diverse points of view used to describe and remediate learning disabled children. In the first article in that area ("Learning Disabilities—Yesterday, Today, and Tomorrow"), Bateman surveys certain major contributors to the learning disabilities field "in terms of an integrative approach to the various disciplines which have been concerned with the etiology, diagnosis, and treatment of children with communication problems, reading problems, and sensory-motor disturbances." In a related article ("Toward a Clarification of Central Issues") Clements discusses several basic issues which impede agreement on concepts of brain dysfunction, and the child with minimal brain dysfunction—two of many synonyms for the learning disabled child.

The Bateman article presents the Doman-Delacato theory within the perspective of several other learning disability theories. Because of the great controversy surrounding it, however, the Doman-Delacato theory is singled out for special attention, and two relevant articles are reprinted here. The first ("Doman-Delacato Philosophy") is the authors' statement of their program and its underlying rationale. In other publications (Doman, *et al.*, 1960; Delacato, 1959, 1963, 1966) the authors have claimed remarkable results with brain damaged children. Freeman, in the second article ("Controversy Over Patterning As a Treatment for Brain Damage in Children"), summarizes the main lines of the Doman-Delacato theory, techniques, and evidence used to support them. He concludes that the validity of the claimed results cannot be established at present.

Each of the articles presented in this section has assumed that learning disabilities exist in children. The problems—as one would infer from these writings—are those of terminology, of classification, of symptomatology, and of remedial methods to be used. The existence of learning disabilities—by whatever name—is itself the object of close scrutiny, however, as witnessed by the Siegel view, reprinted as the final article in this section ("Learning Disabilities: Substance or Shadow"). Siegel, while not disavowing the term completely, does call attention to some of its possible pitfalls (seven) and a few advantages (two).

REFERENCES

Bateman, Barbara, "Three Approaches to Diagnosis and Educational Planning for Children With Learning Disabilities," *Academic Therapy Quarterly* 1967, 2, 215–222.

Chalfant, J. C., and Margaret A. Scheffelin, *Central Processing Dysfunctions in Children: A Review of Research* (Bethesda, Maryland: U.S. Department of Health, Education, and Welfare, 1969).

Doman, C. H., *The Treatment and Prevention of Reading Problems: The Neuro-psychological Approach* (Springfield, Illinois: Charles C. Thomas, 1959).

Doman, C. H., *The Diagnosis and Treatment of Speech and Reading Problems* (Springfield, Illinois: Charles C. Thomas, 1963).

Doman, C. H., *Neurological Organization and Reading* (Springfield, Illinois: Charles C. Thomas, 1963).

Doman, R. J., E. Spitz, Elizabeth Zucman, C. H. Delacato, and G. Doman, "Children with Severe Brain Injuries," *Journal of the American Medical Association* 1960, *174*, pp. 119–124.

** 31 **

Nomenclature

SAMUEL D. CLEMENTS

Nomenclature is essential to facilitate communication. Its purpose is to engender mutual understanding. To this end, terminology must define accurately and, in so doing, distinguish clearly one condition from another. To be understood readily, the term must describe the condition.

The task of terminology selection might be simplified if endorsement were required by one group only, e.g., pediatric neurologists. In the case of children with minimal dysfunction the designation must attempt to satisfy the diverse demands of at least four groups:

1. The clinicians (usually involving several disciplines) who diagnose, outline, and execute treatment.

2. The researchers who are concerned with descriptive accuracy, validity, and preciseness of the CNS deviations.

3. Other professional groups who deal with the children and fulfill portions of the treatment plan, e.g., educators.

4. Parents and others who are personally involved with the child.

Disagreement has developed over the use of the term "minimal brain dysfunction" as either a diagnostic or descriptive designation. Historically, the terms "brain-crippled," "brain-injured," and "brain-injured child," were selected by Strauss, Werner, Lehtinen, and others, to describe and account for particular learning and behavioral aberrations in certain children. Other writers, in contributing to or expanding the concept or in describing the condition, used such transitional terms as "brain damage," "brain-damaged child," "brain dysfunction," or "cerebral dysfunction."

Judging from frequency of appearance in the literature, "brain damage" and "brain-damaged child" seem to be the most popular. Although these two terms are the most widely employed, most writers agree that they are unfortunate in that they connote specific demonstrable brain alterations, are unclear, erroneous, too inclusive, or represent a "limited" Straussian view. A proposal for the resolution of the terminology problem was offered several years ago by Stevens and Birch (1).

* From Minimal Brain Dysfunction in Children. Washington: U.S. Department of Health, Education and Welfare, 1966, pp. 8–10, 16–17. Reprinted by permission of the author.

Over the years, the designation "brain-damaged" has been applied to most children determined to be in the "organic" classifications regardless of responsible agents or symptoms. Thus, if the major overt manifestations of a dysfunctioning brain appear in the motor areas (the cerebral palsies); sensory areas (visual or auditory impairments); mentation or intellect (the mental subnormalities); or as seizures (the epilepsies); the "brain-damaged" label has frequently been applied to the child, especially when related specific learning and behavioral deviations accompany the other primary symptoms. This situation has given rise to the frequent complaint that the term has evolved into an all-embracing "wastebasket" designation.

The problem compounds itself when one considers a partial list of other diverse characteristics which have been attributed to brain variations: infantile autism; childhood schizophrenia; superior intellect; specific talents and abilities in music, art, language, athletics; the aphasias; specific dyslexia; or early and superior reading ability.

In an attempt to establish a continuum of dysfunctioning in any of the areas of brain function, and to distinguish severity of symptoms in one or a combination of these areas, many later authors prefixed the adjective "minimal" to the terms "brain damage," "brain dysfunctions," or "cerebral dysfunction." In the main, these terms were used by their authors to describe milder, borderline, or subclinical abnormal manifestations of motor, sensory, or intellectual function, and to indicate specific kinds of learning, thinking, and behavioral sequelae.

Of major significance is the use of "minimal brain dysfunction" to designate a large group of children whose neurologic impairment is "minimal" (as on a continuum), subtly affecting learning and behavior, *without* evident lowering of general intellectual capacity.

Strauss and Lehtinen (2, p. 108 and p. 128) use the terms "minor brain damage," and "minimal brain injury," for this same condition, stating: "Behavior and learning, it is now beginning to be recognized, may be affected by minimal brain injuries without apparent lowering of the intelligence level." The volume by Strauss and Kephart (3) is primarily devoted to this group of youngsters. Gesell and Amatruda (4, p. 240), using the term "minimal cerebral injury," describe the counterpart in infants and young children.

These terms have been criticized by Birch (5, p. 5). Yet the authors using "minimal brain damage" or "minimal brain dysfunctions" apparently have done so in an honest effort to characterize categories of children. These children are *different* in certain learning and behavioral patterns, but when tested individually and comprehensively achieve within the near average, average, or above average ranges of intellectual functioning. The vital implication is that educational programing and rehabilitation for these children must be different than for the brain-damaged mentally subnormal groups.

Response to the cardinal questions: "What shall it be called?" and "Whom shall it include?" will depend upon the acceptance of two basic premises:

1. Brain dysfunction can manifest itself in varying degrees of severity and can involve any or all of the more specific areas, e.g., motor, sensory, or intellectual. This dysfunctioning can compromise the affected child in learning and behavior.

2. The term *minimal brain dysfunction* will be reserved for the child whose symptomatology appears in one or more of the specific areas of brain function, but in mild, borderline, or subclinical form, without reducing overall intellectual functioning to the subnormal ranges. (Note: The evaluation of the intellectual functioning of the "culturally disadvantaged" child, though perhaps related, represents an equally complex, but different problem.)

A review of selected literature revealed a total of 38 terms used to describe or distinguish the conditions grouped as minimal brain dysfunction in the absence of findings severe enough to warrant inclusion in an established category, e.g., cerebral palsies, mental subnormalities, sensory defects. Several methods of grouping these terms are possible, such as:

Group I — Organic Aspects

Association Deficit Pathology
Organic Brain Disease
Organic Brain Damage
Organic Brain Dysfunction
Minimal Brain Damage
Diffuse Brain Damage
Neurophrenia
Organic Drivenness
Cerebral Dysfunction
Organic Behavior Disorder
Choreiform Syndrome
Minor Brain Damage
Minimal Brain Injury
Minimal Cerebral Injury
Minimal Chronic Brain Syndromes
Minimal Cerebral Damage
Minimal Cerebral Palsy
Cerebral Dys-synchronization Syndrome

Group II — Segment or Consequence

Hyperkinetic Behavior Syndrome
Character Impulse Disorder
Hyperkinetic Impulse Disorder
Aggressive Behavior Disorder
Psychoneurological Learning Disorders
Hyperkinetic Syndrome
Dyslexia

Hyperexcitability Syndrome
Perceptual Cripple
Primary Reading Retardation
Specific Reading Disability
Clumsy Child Syndrome
Hypokinetic Syndrome
Perceptually Handicapped
Aphasoid Syndrome
Learning Disabilities
Conceptually Handicapped
Attention Disorders
Interjacent Child

With few exceptions, the most striking omission throughout the literature was the lack of attempt at a definition of the terms used or the condition discussed. Although there is a more than ample supply of terminology and characteristics, there is a shortage of interpretative elucidation.

Notable among so-stated definitions is that of Strauss and Lehtinen (6). Others have approached definition by extensive description (7).

MINIMAL BRAIN DYSFUNCTION SYNDROME DEFINITION

The term "minimal brain dysfunction syndrome" refers in this paper to children of near average, average, or above average general intelligence with certain learning or behavioral disabilities ranging from mild to severe, which are associated with deviations of function of the central nervous system. These deviations may manifest themselves by various combinations of impairment in perception, conceptualization, language, memory, and control of attention, impulse, or motor function.

Similar symptoms may or may not complicate the problems of children with cerebral palsy, epilepsy, mental retardation, blindness, or deafness.

These aberrations may arise from genetic variations, biochemical irregularities, perinatal brain insults or other illnesses or injuries sustained during the years which are critical for the development and maturation of the central nervous system, or from unknown causes.

The definition also allows for the possibility that early severe sensory deprivation could result in central nervous system alterations which may be permanent.

During the school years, a variety of learning disabilities is the most prominent manifestation of the condition which can be designated by this term.

The group of symptoms included under the term minimal brain dysfunction stems from disorders which may manifest themselves in severe form as a variety of well-recognized conditions. The child with minimal brain dysfunction may exhibit these minor symptoms in varying degree and in varying combinations.

Classification Guide, Brain Dysfunction Syndromes

Minimal (minor; mild)	Major (severe)
1. Impairment of fine movement or coordination.	1. Cerebral palsies.
2. Electroencephalographic abnormalities without actual seizures, or possibly subclinical seizures which may be associated with fluctuations in behavior or intellectual function.	2. Epilepsies
3. Deviations in attention, activity level, impulse control, and affect.	3. Autism and other gross disorders of mentation and behavior.
4. Specific and circumscribed perceptual, intellectual, and memory deficits.	4. Mental subnormalities.
5. Nonperipheral impairments of vision, hearing, haptics, and speech.	5. Blindness, deafness, and severe aphasias.

REFERENCES

1. Stevens, G. D. and J. W. Birch, "A Proposal for Clarification of the Terminology Used to Describe Brain-Injured Children," *Exceptional Children,* 23 (1957), pp. 346–349.

2. Strauss, A. A. and L. Lehtinen, *Psychopathology and Education of the Brain Injured Child* (Grune & Stratton, 1947), serves as vol. I.

3. Strauss, A. A. and N. Kephart, *Psychopathology and Education of the Brain Injured Child.* Vol. II, Progress in Clinic and Theory (Grune & Stratton, 1955). Cataloged under Strauss and Lehtinen.

4. Gesell, A. and C. Amatruda, *Developmental Diagnosis* (Paul B. Hoeber, 1941).

5. Herbert G. Birch (ed.), *Brain Damage in Children—The Biological and Social Aspects* (Williams and Wilkins, 1964).

6. Strauss, A. A. and L. Lehtinen, *Psychopathology and Education of the Brain Injured Child* (Grune & Stratton, 1947).

7. Bender, L., "Psychological Problems of Children with Organic Brain Disease," *American Journal of Orthopsychiatry,* 19 (1949), pp. 404–441; Birch, Herbert G. (ed.), *Brain Damage in Children—The Biological and Social Aspects* (Williams and Wilkins, 1964); Bradley, C., "Characteristics and Management of Children with Behavior Problems Associated with Organic Brain Damage," *Pediatric Clinics of North America* (November 1957), pp. 1049–1060; Clements, S. D. and J. E. Peters, "Minimal Brain Dysfunctions in the School-Age Child," *Archives of Genetic Psychology,* 6 (1962), pp. 185–197; Doll, E. A., "Behavior Syndromes of CNS Impairment," in J. Magary and J. Eichorn, *The Exceptional Child* (New York: Holt, Rinehart & Winston, 1960); Eisenberg, L., "Psychiatric Implications of Brain Damage in Children," *Psychiatric Quarterly,* 31 (1957), pp. 72–92; Paine, R., "Minimal Chronic Brain Syndromes in Children," *Dev. Med. Child Neuro.,* 4 (1962), pp. 21–27; Knobloch, H. and B. Pasamanick, "Syndrome of Minimal Cerebral Damage in Infancy," *Journal of the*

American Medical Association, 170 (1959), p. 1384; Silver, A. A., "Behavioral Syndrome Associated with Brain Damage in Children," *Pediatric Clinics of North America*, pp. 687–698; Clements, S. D., L. E. Lehtinen, and J. E. Lukens, "Children with Minimal Brain Injury—A Symposium," National Society for Crippled Children and Adults, 1964).

Symptomatology—Identification of the Child

SAMUEL D. CLEMENTS

In a search for symptoms attributed to children with minimal brain dysfunctioning, over 100 recent publications were reviewed.

Many different terms were used to describe the same symptom, e.g., excessive motor activity for age might be referred to as any one of the following: hyperactivity, hyperkinesis, organic drivenness, restlessness, motor obsessiveness, fidgetiness, motor disinhibition, or nervousness.

A large number of terms were too broad for other than limited value, e.g., "poor academic achievement"; others were more specific, e.g., "reading ability two grade levels below grade placement." A few are mentioned one time only, e.g., "inclined to have fainting spells." Others are too general (or judgmental) to classify, e.g., "often good looking." Opposite characteristics are common: "physically immature for age"—"physically advanced for age"; "fearless"—"phobic"; outgoing"—"shy"; "hyperactive"—"hypoactive."

These examples represent some of the difficulties encountered in developing a scheme for classification of the symptoms, and indicate the variety of syndromes contained within the primary diagnosis of minimal brain dynfunctioning. The following represents an attempt to classify some of the descriptive elements culled from the literature.

PRELIMINARY CATEGORIES OF SIGNS AND SYMPTOMS

A. *Test Performance Indicators*
1. Spotty or patchy intellectual deficits. Achievement low in some areas; high in others.
2. Below mental age level on drawing tests (man, house, etc.).
3. Geometric figure drawings poor for age and measured intelligence.
4. Poor performance on block design and marble board tests.

* From *Minimal Brain Dysfunction in Children.* Washington: U.S. Department of Health, Education and Welfare, 1966, pp. 11–13.

5. Poor showing on group tests (intelligence and achievement) and daily classroom examinations which require reading.

6. Characteristic subtest patterns on the Wechsler Intelligence Scale for Children, including "scatter" within both Verbal and Performance Scales; high Verbal—low Performance; low Verbal—high Performance.

B. *Impairments of Perception and Concept-formation*
   1. Impaired discrimination of size.
   2. Impaired discrimination of right-left and up-down.
   3. Impaired tactile discriminations.
   4. Poor spatial orientation.
   5. Impaired orientation in time.
   6. Distorted concept of body image.
   7. Impaired judgment of distance.
   8. Impaired discrimination of figure-ground.
   9. Impaired discrimination of part-whole.
   10. Frequent perceptual reversals in reading and in writing letters and numbers.
   11. Poor perceptual integration. Child cannot fuse sensory impressions into meaningful entities.

C. *Specific Neurologic Indicators*
   1. Few, if any, apparent gross abnormalities.
   2. Many "soft," equivocal, or borderline findings.
   3. Reflex assymetry frequent.
   4. Frequency of mild visual or hearing impairments.
   5. Strabismus.
   6. Nystagmus.
   7. High incidence of left, and mixed laterality and confused perception of laterality.
   8. Hyperkinesis.
   9. Hypokinesis.
   10. General awkwardness.
   11. Poor fine visual-motor coordination.

D. *Disorders of Speech and Communication*
   1. Impaired discrimination of auditory stimuli.
   2. Various categories of aphasia.
   3. Slow language development.
   4. Frequent mild hearing loss.
   5. Frequent mild speech irregularities.

E. *Disorders of Motor Function*
   1. Frequent athetoid, choreiform, tremulous, or rigid movements of hands.
   2. Frequent delayed motor milestones.
   3. General clumsiness or awkwardness.
   4. Frequent tics and grimaces.

5. Poor fine or gross visual-motor coordination.
6. Hyperactivity.
7. Hypoactivity.

F. *Academic Achievement and Adjustment* (Chief complaints about the child by his parents and teachers)
1. Reading disabilities.
2. Arithmetic disabilities.
3. Spelling disabilities.
4. Poor printing, writing, or drawing ability.
5. Variability in performance from day to day or even hour to hour.
6. Poor ability to organize work.
7. Slowness in finishing work.
8. Frequent confusion about instructions, yet success with verbal tasks.

G. *Disorders of Thinking Processes*
1. Poor ability for abstract reasoning.
2. Thinking generally concrete.
3. Difficulties in concept-formation.
4. Thinking frequently disorganized.
5. Poor short-term and long-term memory.
6. Thinking sometimes autistic.
7. Frequent thought perseveration.

H. *Physical Characteristics*
1. Excessive drooling in the young child.
2. Thumb-sucking, nail-biting, head-banging, and teeth-grinding in the young child.
3. Food habits often peculiar.
4. Slow to toilet train.
5. Easy fatigability.
6. High frequency of enuresis.
7. Encopresis.

I. *Emotional Characteristics*
1. Impulsive.
2. Explosive.
3. Poor emotional and impulse control.
4. Low tolerance for frustration.
5. Reckless and uninhibited; impulsive then remorseful.

J. *Sleep Characteristics*
1. Body or head rocking before falling into sleep.
2. Irregular sleep patterns in the young child.
3. Excessive movement during sleep.
4. Sleep abnormally light or deep.
5. Resistance to naps and early bedtime, e.g., seems to inquire less sleep than average child.

K. *Relationship Capacities*
1. Peer group relationships generally poor.
2. Overexcitable in normal play with other children.
3. Better adjustment when playmates are limited to one or two.
4. Frequently poor judgment in social and interpersonal situations.
5. Socially bold and aggressive.
6. Inappropriate, unselective, and often excessive displays of affection.
7. Easy acceptance of others alternating with withdrawal and shyness.
8. Excessive need to touch, cling, and hold on to others.

L. *Variations of Physical Development*
1. Frequent lags in developmental milestones, e.g., motor, language, etc.
2. Generalized maturational lag during early school years.
3. Physically immature; or
4. Physical development normal or advanced for age.

M. *Characteristics of Social Behavior*
1. Social competence frequently below average for age and measured intelligence.
2. Behavior often inappropriate for situation, and consequences apparently not foreseen.
3. Possibly negative and aggressive to authority.
4. Possibly antisocial behavior.

N. *Variations of Personality*
1. Overly gullible and easily led by peers and older youngsters.
2. Frequent rage reactions and tantrums when crossed.
3. Very sensitive to others.
4. Excessive variation in mood and responsiveness from day to day and even hour to hour.
5. Poor adjustment to environmental changes.
6. Sweet and even tempered, cooperative and friendly (most commonly the so-called hypokinetic child).

O. *Disorders of Attention and Concentration*
1. Short attention span for age.
2. Overly distractible for age.
3. Impaired concentration ability.
4. Motor or verbal perseveration.
5. Impaired ability to make decisions, particularly from many choices.

Several authors note that many of the characteristics tend to improve with the normal maturation of the central nervous system. As the child matures, various complex motor acts and differentiations appear or are more easily acquired.

Variability beyond that expected for age and measured intelligence appears throughout most of the signs and symptoms. This, of course, limits predictability and expands misunderstanding of the child by his parents, peers, teachers, and often the clinicians who work with him.

Ten characteristics most often cited by the various authors, in order of frequency:

1. Hyperactivity.
2. Perceptual-motor impairments.
3. Emotional lability.
4. General coordination deficits.
5. Disorders of attention (short attention span, distractibility, perseveration).
6. Impulsivity.
7. Disorders of memory and thinking.
8. Specific learning disabilities:
   a. Reading.
   b. Arithmetic.
   c. Writing.
   d. Spelling.
9. Disorders of speech and hearing.
   regularities.
10. Equivocal neurological signs and electroencephalographic irregularities.

The "sign" approach can serve only as a guideline for the purpose of identification and diagnosis.

The protean nature of the disability is the obvious conclusion from the approach to symptomatology and identification taken above.

The situation, however, is not as irremediable as it might appear. Order is somewhat salvaged by the fact that certain symptoms *do* tend to cluster to form recognizable clinical entities. This is particularly true of the "hyperkinetic syndrome," within the broader context of minimal brain dysfunctioning. The "hypokinetic syndrome," primary reading retardation, and to some extent the aphasias, are other such examples.

Recognition and acceptance of these specific symptom complexes as subcategories, within the general category of minimal brain dysfunctioning, would facilitate classification and the development of appropriate management and education procedures.

32

Diagnostic Methods Used With
Learning Disability Cases

R. J. CAPOBIANCO

Perhaps the one irrefutable characteristic attributed to children with learning disabilities is their wide variability of behavior. Considerable time, effort, and money has been expended in attempts to describe, measure, diagnose, and remedy the learning problems which are commonly regarded as the aftereffects of brain injury. Efforts to group these children into categories variously termed neurologically impaired, exogenous, cerebrally dysfunctioned, and the like, have complicated the interpretation of research findings rather than providing a basis for operational definitions. With the intensity of effort to "pigeonhole" or classify these youngsters as one clinical entity, the behavioral descriptions which resulted have grown far out of proportion to functional diagnosis. Indeed, if the exhaustive list of behaviors attributed to neurologically impaired children were accepted at face value, then it would be difficult, if not impossible, to imagine a child who could not be labeled brain injured on the basis of one set of behaviors or another.

Modern educators and psychologists have attempted to skirt the problem of diagnostic difficulty by coining a new phrase for the old list of names— children with learning disorders (or disabilities). This new phrase provides for the inclusion of all youngsters with a syndrome of behaviors which interfere with the learning process and yet eliminates the inherent difficulty in establishing the existence of a brain injury. Hence, the modern special class for children with learning disabilities may be composed of youngsters who are brain injured, emotionally disturbed, visually impaired, auditorially handicapped, intellectually subnormal, or suffering from some motor imbalance—perhaps any one individual may be hampered by a combination of these handicaps. The apparent heterogeneity of these children according to the multiplicity of labels is deceiving. They are no less homogeneous than groups of students collected together merely be-

* From *Exceptional Children* 1964, *31*, pp. 187–193. Reprinted by permission of the author and the publisher.

cause they have been categorized as brain injured. Nevertheless, it is suspected that for some time to come, classes for children with learning disabilities will still be composed predominantly of youngsters who meet the psychoeducational criteria established for the brain injured—the only difference being that they will not be labeled brain injured.

Candidates for these special classes are selected primarily on the basis of the overt display of certain characteristics such as underachievement, hyperactivity, distractibility, poor motor coordination, impulsivity and short attention span and secondarily on their performance on selected psychological tests of perceptual processes. There is no intent here to argue for or against this approach; indeed, this author has suggested years ago that teachers should deal with symptomatology rather than etiology. Similar notes of caution have been voiced by Barnett, Ellis, and Pryer (1960), Gallagher (1957), Kirk and McCarthy (1961) and Newland (1963) among others. In the final analysis, the worth of the program will rest upon the adequacy with which specific methods tend to alleviate identifiable learning impairments without respect to causation.

Clinical-educational techniques have been devised which purport to lessen the difficulties in learning, characteristic of brain injured, or "Strauss syndrome" children. Varying degrees of success have been reported by psychologists and educators employing these methods. But who is to say that all children with learning disabilities need to be exposed to this intensive program of special education to insure learning? Certainly there would be less expenditure of time and effort and fewer demands for extensive professional training on the part of teachers if some of these children could learn without recourse to rigorous programs of education suggested by some professional educators. Hence, the importance of an exhaustive psychoeducational diagnosis to determine the need for specific clinical-educational techniques and devices which would eliminate or remedy certain behaviors detrimental to learning. Kirk and McCarthy (1961) have already differentiated between classification and diagnosis, as has Newland (1963) between testing and assessment. Mere classification and/or testing does not necessarily prescribe treatment—complete diagnosis or assessment implies a course of remediation with prognosis.

The diagnosis of brain injury is difficult to formulate. Even with identification, the problem is not so readily resolved; for the neurologically impaired do not follow any typical, preconceived set of behaviors. In fact, the behaviors exhibited vary so greatly that the differences observed are as variable intra-group as between brain-injured and normal populations. To complicate the situation further, many of the neurologically impaired children do not present any specific learning problem in the classroom whereas non-brain injured children with supposedly organic behaviors do have difficulty.

One attempt to isolate and refine some subpopulations of brain injured mental retardates according to behavior was described by Capobianco and Funk (1958). The Rorschach test was administered to exogenous and endogenous subjects representing both sexes. A pathology gradient was established, based upon electroencephalographic tracings, which isolated four groups: endogenous-normal, endogenous-convulsive, exogenous-convulsive and exogenous-focal. Omitting the first group, the remaining three may be considered brain injured. Although there may seem to be an apparent contradiction within the category, endogenous-convulsive, let it be known that the original endogenous-exogenous dichotomy was based upon the Riggs and Rain (1952) classification system before administration of the electroencephalogram (EEG). Thus, convulsive tracings were found in records of children who had originally been diagnosed as familial retardates (endogenous) without evidence of brain damage. Although the EEG is admittedly not a foolproof test, the proportion of abnormal tracings (58%) found within the familial population far exceeded the expected error.

The emerging patterns on the selected Rorschach variables, followed closely the hypothesized gradient, reversals occurring occasionally between the endogenous-normal and endogenous-convulsive categories. Results were interpreted by the authors as follows: "If this function of pathology and etiology is 'real', the exogenous-focal end of the distribution reflects more conceptualizing; more outward-directed affect; more interest in people; less immature, stereotyped thinking; more feelings of negative self-appraisal; less negativism; and more perceptual difficulty . . ." (Capobianco and Funk, 1958, p. 68). The authors caution that this pathology gradient is based upon the results of a very small sample of familial and brain injured retardates but that it should promise to be a fertile area for research in the future.

Similar attempts to refine sub-populations of children according to specific kinds of brain damage and EEG tracings have been reported by Burns (1960) and Sievers and Rosenberg (1960).

DIAGNOSTIC PROCEDURES

The asserted preponderance of learning difficulties exhibited by organically impaired children has been the mainstay of the argument presented by those professionals who view the education of these children as a distinct and separate process. The fact that some of the neurologically impaired children do not experience difficulties in the learning process and that some nonimpaired children do, is not sufficient justification to eliminate special teaching methodology. Insofar as the teacher is concerned, the disturbing behaviors demonstrated by these children, brain injured or not, must be eliminated or modified. The teacher will find no difficulty in recognizing that all is not well with a child who:

• Follows no logical pattern in his behavior.
• Never sticks with anything over a long period of time.

- Wanders aimlessly about the room apparently concerned with everyone else's business.
- Never sits still for a minute—always runs never walks.
- Acts before thinking—seldom considering the consequences of his behavior.
- Repeats, excessively, a task or movement.
- May be able to read but not comprehend the significance of what has been read.
- Experiences difficulties in arithmetic, performing at a level far below expectancy.
- Demonstrates visuomotor difficulties.
- Seems at times to be out of contact—does not hear you.
- Rapidly changes his mood or temperament.
- Performs inconsistently and with marked variability in the various school subjects.

These behaviors do not comprise a total list of indicators of potential organicity, however, they serve as specific examples of the many factors comprising the learning difficulty syndrome. It is not within the province of the school teacher's responsibility to make the diagnosis, but rather it is his duty to utilize techniques and methodologies which prove to alleviate the condition responsible for the inadequacy of the child's functioning. When the techniques at the teacher's disposal do not improve the situation, then it is time to request a diagnostic workup by the school psychologist.

It is a rare school system indeed which has available to its students the services of a neurologist. Hence, the problem of identification of the brain injury usually falls into the hands of the school psychologist. Working in collaboration with the classroom teacher and the school physician or nurse, a screening process is effected. If the evidence obtained is sufficient to warrant a referral to a neurological specialist, it is based upon the collective information gleaned from behavioral descriptions, medical evidence and psychological assessment. Strauss and Lehtinen have established four criteria for a complete diagnosis of minor brain damage: (a) a history of trauma before, during or after birth, (b) neurological (or "soft") signs are present, (c) evidence that the child comes from normal familial stock and (d) indicative evidence gleaned from psychological tests (1947). In recent years the trend in diagnosis of brain injury has been to rely more and more upon the results and interpretation of psychological tests. Complete neurological examinations, including the administration of the electroencephalographic test, often fail to discover positive evidence of injury, and, perhaps equally often, may discern an injury which is nonexistent. Positive identification through the utilization of multitudinous tests of perceptual and conceptual disturbances are equally questionable—but considerably less expensive and time consuming. Oftentimes, the behavior described by the classroom teacher may overtly appear to be an indicator of brain damage but may actually be the result of some emotional upheaval recently affecting the child. Other characteristic behaviors may be "read in" by the referring teacher, often in good faith, but without basis in fact. The failure of his particular teaching methods with the child in question may lead to a request for diagnostic information out of sheer desperation in not knowing what next to do. Whatever the reason for the request for further information on the child, the psychologist must serve as the first recourse for the teacher in the total assessment process.

The diagnostician is often forced to make a decision regarding the role he must play—to serve as an ancillary aide to the neurologist or to provide some practical suggestions for the teacher. Usually, the suspected degree of impairment serves to decide the course of action. Mild cases are groomed for the educator; more severe suspects are assessed for future referral to the neurologist. For education purposes, the psychologist is better equipped than the neurologist to offer recommendations regarding remedial techniques. Only for cases requiring medical treatment, such as post-encephalitis or tumors, would the referal to the neurologist be of subsequent help to the educator.

Armed with an array of information on the child which includes his cumulative record and the behavioral description prepared by the teacher, the psychologist then selects the particular instrument or battery of tests to administer in his search for diagnostic evidence. A multitude of tests are already available which purport to be of unique value toward the diagnostic evaluation of brain injured behaviors. Many clinicians prefer to utilize various subtests from standardized instruments seeking to arrive at qualitative evidence in addition to quantitative scores. This type of assessment, a "cafeteria" approach has been described by Newland (1963) as an effective approach in the absence of individual devices suitable for use. This method of diagnosis is only as proficient as the clinician who employs it. In the hands of an inexperienced clinician or untrained personnel, the method would be relatively useless and perhaps dangerous.

Scatter patterns on some tests of intelligence have been investigated to determine characteristic performance of brain damaged patients. Unfortunately, the results of research efforts in this area of diagnosis are often misleading and confusing—indeed, the results of one investigator may be directly contradictory to the conclusions formulated by another. Reitan (1955), in his very comprehensive work on Wechsler-Bellevue patterning, found that brain damaged subjects generally exhibited characteristic patterns based upon the extent and localization of the brain insult. Verified left hemisphere damage usually resulted in lower Verbal than Performance IQ's while the reverse was true of right hemisphere lesions. Subjects with diffuse damage performed approximately equally well on both scales. Morrow and Mark (1955) reported characteristically low performance by brain injured subjects on Digit-Symbol, Digit-Span and Arithmetic in support of Reitan (1955) and Wechsler (1944). On the other hand, Beck and Lam (1955) found no characteristic subtest patterns for their brain damaged subjects and Taterka and Katz (1955) reported that Coding, as a subtest, was affected adversely by brain damage. In an extensive comparative study of exogenous and endogenous subjects, Capobianco and Funk (1958) found similar patterns on the Wechsler Intelligence Scale for Children for both groups and both sexes. The differences between groups was in the predicted direction on the Arithmetic, Block Design, and Coding subtests; however, these differences were not statistically significant.

Many workers in the field have reported varying degrees of success in diagnosis of brain injury using perceptual organization tests such as the Rorschach, Bender-Gestalt, Graham-Kendall, Ellis Visual Design and a variety of cube, stick, marble, and mosiac tests. The results are inconclusive. Even though many of the studies demonstrated differences in performance between brain damaged and nondamaged subjects, individual children who scored poorly on one of these tests did not necessarily score correspondingly on another. Many known cases of brain injury are not isolated by these instruments and the number of over referrals is overwhelming.

Even if the reader were willing to accept the diagnostic patterning of test scores and/or inferior performance on perceptual tests as truly characteristic of brain injured functioning, he would still be at a loss to explain why these deficiencies apparently do not hamper educational progress. Research reports by Bensberg (1958), Capobianco (1956), Capobianco and Miller (1958), Capobianco and Funk (1958) and Gallagher (1957) among others, have failed to discern any significant differences in performance between brain damaged and nondamaged subjects on a number of educational and psychological variables. In an exhaustive investigation of psychological and psychophysical abilities displayed by organic and familial retardates, Clausen found that of 51 variables measured, only one (critical flicker frequency) obtained significance at the .05 level (Personal communication, 1964). Although other investigators have reported poorer performance by brain injured subjects on this test (but not consistently), this one significant difference out of 51 comparisons could easily have occurred on a chance basis. Barnett, Ellis, and Pryer (1960) suggest that the term "brain injury" be dropped since it has been demonstrated that all Ss so labeled do not exhibit distinct behaviors nor do they necessarily demand special modes of instruction.

The one significant finding pervading this research is the characteristic variability of performance by brain damaged subjects, far in excess of the performance exhibited by the control subjects—mean performances, however, remained relatively consistent. Attempts to subgroup populations of brain injured subjects along an ordered continuum [pathology gradient proposed by Capobianco and Funk (1958)], and new methods of differential diagnosis (Illinois Test of Psycholinguistic Abilities) recently developed by Kirk and McCarthy (1961) appear to offer keys to future success in the bothersome area of brain injured functioning.

CLASSROOM BEHAVIOR

One cannot expect the teacher to be proficient in the administration and interpretation of projective techniques, intelligence tests and tests of perceptual organization. The responsibility of the teacher in the total assessment process is far removed from the one to one clinical setting. First and foremost, the teacher is expected to keep complete records, including achievement tests, samples of school work, anecdotal reports and rating scales. One incidence of unpredictable behavior in the classroom is not sufficient reason to trot the child to the nearest psychologist. But periodic outbreaks of unexplainable behavior, short attention span and hyperactivity, coupled with poor scholastic performance, would warrant genuine concern on the part of the teacher. Unlike the consistently poor achievement characteristic of the mentally retarded child, the brain injured child displays an irregular pattern of performance. He may be very proficient in reading and far below capacity in arithmetic. He may excel in verbal facility but experience considerable difficulty in reasoning. He may display superficial charm in initiating social acquaintances yet "wear off" with the passage of time. He may learn quickly some skills which emphasize rote but fail miserably in tasks which require independent thinking. These inconsistencies should be noted in the teacher's anecdotal records.

The periodic use of sociograms within the classroom often gives significant information to the teacher. The hyperactive, disinhibited youngster is seldomly accepted by his classmates. The individual's own choices of peers on the sociogram give some clue as to the personality he himself may desire to be. Gross distortions in the child's art work serve to implement further the informal diagnosis within the classroom. The child at play exhibits behaviors which oftentimes yield more information regarding his problem than actual classroom performances. All too often the teacher does not take note of this particular fertile area for study. Obviously, the teacher cannot keep a complete, up to date, ongoing record on every child in his room but behaviors of note should be included in the anecdotal record. Trusting to memory, the teacher often fails to record significant behaviors which occur during the school day. The practice of attempting to record all pertinent information at the end of the school day should be abandoned in favor of immediate recording—not total descriptions of the incident but a word or two to identify the behavior, who was involved, and the time it occurred. Later, the more complete description may be recorded. With information as complete as described, the teacher not only systemizes his own interpretation of the youngster's behavior but also preserves diagnostic information which would be an invaluable asset to the psychologist who may ultimately be responsible for the complete assessment of the child.

Rating scales, such as described by Gallagher (1957), force an orderly account of the children's behavior. These instruments provide insurance against the tendency, on the part of many observers, to record only the negative aspects of behavior.

SUMMARY

The term brain injury has failed to serve any practical function. It is an etiological concept which offers little to the educator, psychologist, or other specialist who is interested in the behavioral symptomatology of the child with learning disabilities. The generic term adds more confusion to a field in which specialists are constantly seeking to differentiate sub-populations through newly formulated diagnostic systems. The term itself offers no help to the specialists engaged in the development of sound educational and therapeutic programs to ameliorate the problems demonstrated by children with special learning disabilities. Some investigators have proposed new titles for the general area of brain damage without essentially dismissing the criticisms leveled above. One of the effects of the newer terminology was to instill in the minds of the regular classroom teacher a greater fear of those youngsters labeled cerebral dysfunction, neurophrenia or organically impaired. In the eyes of the teacher these newer diagnoses quickly joined those originally labeled brain injured as youngsters "who cannot learn." Some attempts to isolate specific subgroups of brain injured youngsters in accordance with differential characteristics are more rewarding. Differential diagnosis within this field, however, is still at the infancy stage of development.

Recently, parents of these children have established organizations which seek to collect and distribute information in an attempt to educate the layman regarding the disabilities of brain injured children. This movement has been directly or indirectly responsible for the establishment of many public school special classes for these children. Psychologists and educators have collaborated with neurologists and pediatricians in helping the parent groups to present professional programs to their membership. Research and demonstration projects are currently on the upswing in this field. Specialists representing the allied areas of emotional disturbance, mental retardation, orthopedic handicaps and remedial instruction have sought a reciprocal interrelationship with authorities in the field of neurological impairment to consolidate their respective gains made to date. State departments of education have included special classes for the brain injured within their structure of reimbursement, special aids and transportation allowances. The growth within the field is constantly supplemented by new discoveries in the areas of neurology and psychology. Clinical educational techniques which have proven value in the training of brain injured youngsters are periodically described in the literature. Hence, in spite of the large gaps which exist in our knowledge of this area, the infant field of brain injury is starting to grow up.

Diagnostic procedures, at this writing, are still somewhat spotty. It is difficult, at best, to expect the classroom teacher to succeed in the technical aspects of diagnosis when the instruments of the neurologists and psychologists are still subject to gross errors. Whereas one particular clinician may experience a high degree of success with one battery of tests, a similarly trained specialist may question its validity. The research literature compounds the confusion by presenting conflicting results often within the same issue of a specific journal.

The burden of action, nevertheless, remains with the teacher. Keeping complete records on learning disability cases is one of his major responsibilities. Armed with an organized series of reports, including tests results, rating scales, sociograms, anecdotal records, and personal impressions, the teacher is in an excellent position to discuss the particular problem with the school psychologist. Prescriptions for teacher reaction to the child's behavior are supplied by the psychologist. He may recommend firm control for the hyperactive, disinhibited child and more permissiveness for the withdrawn, apathetic youngster. Gallagher (1960) describes a system of tutoring which was successful with brain injured, mentally retarded children. Perhaps the new movement to establish special classes for children with similar learning disabilities may reduce some of the frustrations suffered by the diagnostician who no longer will find it necessary to "prove" that a brain injury exists.

REFERENCES

Barnett, C. D., Ellis, N. R., and Pryer, M. W. Learning in familial and brain-injured defectives. *American Journal of Mental Deficiency*, 1960, 64, 894–901.

Beck, H. S., and Lam, R. L. Use of the WISC in predicting organicity. *Journal of Clinical Psychology*, 1955, 11, 154–158.

Bensberg, G. J., Jr. The relation of academic achievement of mental defectives to mental age, sex, institutionalization and etiology. *American Journal of Mental Deficiency*, 1953, 58, 327–330.

Burns, R. C. Behavioral differences between brain-injured and brain-deficit children grouped according to neuropathological types. *American Journal of Mental Deficiency*, 1960, 65, 326–334.

Capobianco, R. J. Quantitative and qualitative analyses of endogenous and exogenous boys on arithmetic achievement. *Monograph of Society for Research in Child Development*, 1956, 19, 101–141.

Capobianco, R. J., and Funk, Ruth A. *A comparative study of intellectual, neurological, and perceptual processes as related to reading achievement of exogenous and endogenous retarded children.* New York: Syracuse University Research Institute, 1958.

Gallagher, J. J. A comparison of brain-injured and non-brain-injured mentally retarded children on several psychological variables. *Monograph of Society for Research in Child Development*, 1957, 22, (2).

Gallagher, J. J. *The tutoring of brain-injured mentally retarded children.* Springfield, Illinois: Charles C Thomas, 1960.

Kirk, S. A., and McCarthy, J. J. The Illinois test of psycholinguistic abilities—an approach to differential diagnosis. *American Journal of Mental Deficiency*, 1961, 66, 399–412.

Morrow, R. S., and Mark, J. C. The correlation of intelligence and neurological findings on 22 patients autopsied for brain damage. *Journal of Consulting Psychology*, 1955, 19, 283–289.

Newland, T. E. Psychological assessment of exceptional children. In Cruickshank, W. (Editor), *Psychology of exceptional children and youth* (Second Edition). Englewood Cliffs, New Jersey: Printice-Hall, Inc., 1963.

Reitan, R. M. Certain differential effects of left and right cerebral lesions in human adults. *Journal of Comparative and Physiological Psychology*, 1955, 48, 474–477.

Riggs, Margaret M., and Rain, Margaret E. A classification system for the mentally retarded. *Training School Bulletin*, 1952, 49, 151–168.

Sievers, Dorothy L., and Rosenberg, C. M. The differential language facility test and electroencephalograms of brain-injured mentally retarded children. *American Journal of Mental Deficiency*, 1960, 65, 46–50.

Strauss, A. A., and Lehtinen, Laura E. *Psychopathology and education of the brain-injured child.* New York: Grune and Stratton, Inc., 1947.

Taterka, J. H., and Katz, J. Study of correlations between electroencephalographic and psychological patterns in emotionally disturbed children. *Psychosomatic Medicine*, 1955, 22, 62–72.

Wechsler, D. *The measurement of adult intelligence.* (Third Edition) Baltimore: Williams and Wilkins, Inc., 1944.

** 33 **

Learning Disabilities— Yesterday, Today, and Tomorrow

BARBARA BATEMAN

The child with special learning disabilities has recently become the subject of numerous conferences and conventions, books, and articles. Interest in his problems is shared by the fields of general medicine, psychology, special education, neurology, psychiatry, and education. And above all, his problems concern his teachers, parents, and himself. Who is the child with special learning disabilities? He belongs to a category of exceptional children which, like many other categories, is easier to describe than to define. Unlike other types of exceptional children, however, he is often described in terms of characteristics he does not possess; e.g., his learning

* From *Exceptional Children* 1964, *31*, pp. 167–177. Reprinted by permission of the author and the publisher.

problems are not due to mental retardation, deafness, motor impairment, blindness, faulty instruction, etc. The children who do have special learning disabilities might be described by some clinicians as educationally retarded, autistic, dyslexic, perceptually handicapped, minimally brain injured, emotionally disturbed, neurologically disorganized, dysgraphic, aphasic, interjacent, or word-blind, etc.

Remedial procedures currently recommended by some learning disability specialists include such diverse activities as psychotherapy, drugs, phonic drills, speech correction, tracing, crawling, bead stringing, trampoline exercises, orthoptic training, auditory discrimination drills, and controlled diet.

Regardless of the lack of agreement about etiology, definition, incidence, and treatment of special learning disabilities which is implicit in the various terms given above, the child with learning disabilities is perhaps best described as one who manifests an educationally significant discrepancy between his apparent capacity for language behavior and his actual level of language functioning.

Within this broad concept of learning disabilities, at least three major subcategories can be delineated, although there is certainly much overlap among them.

Dyslexia, or reading disability, is perhaps the most frequent of all types of learning disabilities or language disorders. Estimates of the incidence of dyslexia vary greatly, primarily as a function of the definition used. Those who distinguish "primary" dyslexia as a specific congenital syndrome find fewer cases than do those whose definition is based on a simple discrepancy between apparent capacity for reading and actual level of reading, regardless of etiological or correlated factors. A conservative estimate is that perhaps five percent to ten percent of the school population has severe enough reading problems to require special educational concern and provisions. Disabilities in other academic subject areas such as arithmetic do occur, but much less frequently.

Verbal communication disorders, or difficulties with the comprehension or expression of spoken language, have been labeled aphasic disorders in the past. But the term aphasia is now felt by many to be inappropriate. The term "verbal communication disorders" is used here to designate those children whose comprehension or expressive language problems involve the spoken word.

Visual-motor integration problems have been widely noted, often in conjunction with reading problems. But there are also children who manifest severe spatial orientation, body image, perceptual, coordination, etc., problems and who are not dyslexic.

The appearance of the medical terms dyslexia and aphasia in the categorization is more than coincidence, as physicians were the first professional group to interest themselves in problems of this nature. A parallel development occurred in mental retardation, where the pioneer educators —e.g., Itard, Seguin, Montessori, and DeCroly—were also physicians.

However, as Kirk (1962, p. 30) has stated, "special education as viewed today, begins where medicine stops." Until the time of Orton and his followers, medical interest in learning disabilities had focused almost exclusively on the diagnosis and classification of these problems. Little progress was made in remedial techniques until the focus shifted away from the hereditary and cerebral-pathology correlates of learning problems. The very fact that we cannot exchange parents or repair damaged brains has led to the present-day concern of many with behavioral and symptomatic rather than pathological or etiological factors. Kleffner (in Daley, 1962) suggests that:

> Those who have chosen to concern themselves with the *pathology* underlying language problems have rarely been able to go beyond speculation. From this group come guesses about brain damage, cortical inhibition, hemispheric dominance, cerebral plasticity, synaptic connections. . . There is no practical value in guessing and speculating about the anatomic-physiologic bases. . .
> *Etiologic* investigations . . . have told us little more than that such problems can occur with various etiologic backgrounds or without any significant etiologic factors being apparent. . .
> The *behavioral* approach . . . has been more fruitful in a practical sense than approaches through pathology and etiology (pp. 106–107).

Cohn (in Daley, 1962) points out that the basic reason for the present lack of success in following the neurological pathology or etiological approach is the "lack of definite correlations of brain pathology with inability to learn readily, to retain the meaning of what has been learned, and to recall that which is stored" (p. 34).

From a practical viewpoint one might ask how the remedial specialist would proceed even if there were definite correlations between brain pathology and learning disabilities. If it were known that Johnny couldn't read because (etiology) of a lesion in the angular gyrus (pathology), the remedial reading specialist would still have to plan remediation on the basis of behavioral observations.

This is by no means suggesting that learning disability personnel can ignore the medical-neurological contributions presently offered. Drugs, for example, can sometimes facilitate the learning processes of some hyperactive children by the indirect routes of increasing attention span or decreasing distractibility. Rather than ignoring medical-neurological advances, the field of learning disabilities will do well to utilize all the help presently available and to alertly watch for future developments that promise application. In the meantime, it appears that remediation must still be planned on the basis of observed behavior.

A reasonably thorough overview of work to date in the area of learning disabilities would have to include, as an absolute minimum, a discussion of: (a) etiology or correlated factors; (b) diagnostic procedures, and (c) remedial practices in each of the areas of reading, communication disorders, and visual-motor problems. Each of these topics would be further subdivided by professional orientation—medical, psychological, and educational. Figure 1 suggests the dimensions that would be involved

■ FIGURE 1 *Three Dimensions of Learning Disabilities*

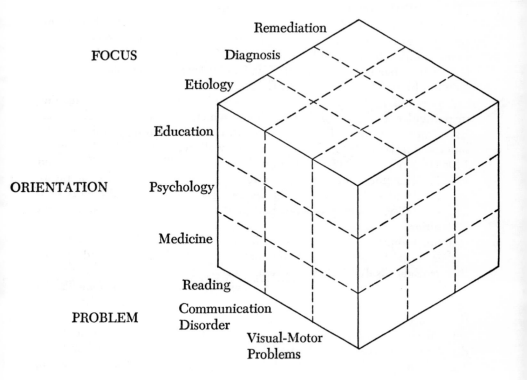

in such an undertaking. The omnipresent fourth dimension of time (past, present, and future) would also have to be superimposed on this model.

Since a complete overview as shown in Figure 1 would require a large volume, some of the terrain of the field today is summarized in the paragraphs that follow.

ETIOLOGY OR CORRELATED FACTORS OF LEARNING DISABILITIES

In all of education it would be difficult to find more voluminous literature than that on causes of reading disability. A large body of literature explores single factors that are believed to cause reading problems. The author wishes to acknowledge reliance on the discussion of single factor etiological theories presented by Corinne Kass (1962). These factors are often physiological and include (a) damage to or dysfunction of certain localized areas of the brain such as the angular gyrus (Hinshelwood, 1917), second frontal gyrus (Wernicke, 1874) as reported by Penfield and Roberts (1959), connection between the cortical speech mechanism and the brain stem centrencephalic system (Penfield and Roberts, 1959), and the parietal and parietaloccipital areas (Rabinovitch, 1959); (b) hereditary or developmental lag factors such as inherited underdevelopment of directional function (Hermann, 1959), hereditary delayed development of parietal lobes (Drew, 1956), slow tempo of the neuromuscular maturation (Eustis, 1947; Harris, 1957), general development (Olson, 1940); and (c) other factors such as lack of cerebral dominance (Orton, 1928; Delacato, 1963), minimal brain injury (Strauss and Lehtinen, 1947), endocrine disturbance and chemical imbalance (Smith and Carrigan, 1959), and primary emotional factors (Blau, 1946; Gann, 1945; Fabian, 1951; Vorhaus, 1952).

A very different approach to the causes of learning disabilities, reading in particular, is the multiple-factor view which emphasizes the characteristics frequently found in groups of children with learning problems. The multiple-factor symptomatology view is well represented by Malmquist (1958), Monroe (1932), Robinson (1946), and Traxler and Townsend (1955). Prominent among the characteristics mentioned in this literature are visual and auditory defects, inadequate readiness, physical factors such as low vitality, speech problems, personality factors, and social adjustment difficulties.

A third approach to causation of learning disabilities is that referred to earlier as the behavioral or symptomatic view in which correlated (rather than causal) disabilities are assessed. This approach is perhaps the newest and is espoused primarily by those whose basic interest is in remediation of disabilities. Deficits in these areas are among the correlates frequently found in cases of learning disability: visual and auditory perception, perceptual speed, strength of closure against distraction, visual and auditory discrimination, phonics skills such as sound blending and visual-auditory association, visual and auditory memory span, kinesthetic recognition, visualization, laterality, verbal opposites, eye-hand coordination, and body image. (e.g., Money, 1962.)

Literature on the etiology of communication disorders has been somewhat limited in extent and scope, when contrasted to that in reading problems. Much of the older work has focused on cerebral pathology and language deprivation with a relatively recent upsurge of interest in the processes of language learning. (e.g., Bateman, 1964a.)

Visual-motor disturbances are quite generally agreed to be a manifestation of organic dysfunction and as such the etiology is primarily a medical concern. However, the recent work of Frostig and Horne (1964) and Witkin, et al. (1962) suggests intriguing relationships between personality and visual-motor functioning.

DIAGNOSIS

General principles of diagnostic procedures for learning disabilities of all types are presented by Gallagher (1962), Haeussermann (1958), Kleffner

(1962), Bateman (1964b), Wood (1962), and many others. Recent work emphasizing the diagnosis of reading disability includes Kolson and Kaluger (1963), Roswell and Natchez (1964), and Strang (1964). In general, authorities agree that diagnosis must include assessment of both the level of performance and the manner of performance and that it must seek precise formulation of specific disability. Development of specific diagnostic tests has enabled diagnosticians to move from global classifications and labels such as reading retardation or delayed language or poor motor development based only on level of performance to more precise diagnostic hypotheses such as body image, spatial orientation, and directionality disturbances underlying reversals in reading or inability to integrate simultaneous visual and kinesthetic stimuli.

The specific tests used in the diagnostic process must vary from child to child, but frequently broad coverage tests such as the Binet, WISC, ITPA, or Kephart Perceptual Rating Scale are given first and followed by more specific tests in those areas of difficulty revealed by the comprehensive tests. Among the specific tests frequently used are visual and auditory acuity measures, articulation tests, tests of visual and auditory memory, discrimination and closure, spatial orientation, laterality and directionality, and visual-motor coordination, etc.

A minor cleavage in philosophies of diagnosis is seen in the "standard battery" versus "individually chosen" test approaches. The former is perhaps more useful in screening and in some research, while the latter (discussed below) is most appropriate for clinical purposes.

One view of the relationship between clinical diagnostic and remedial procedures is diagrammed in Figure 2. The diagnostic process is conceived here as a successive narrowing of the disability area examined until the exact problem can be pinpointed and a diagnostic-remedial hypothesis formulated which is internally consistent and well-supported by objective data. An hypothesis, so stated, leads directly to remedial planning. The remedial process is the inverse of the diagnostic process in that the initial focus is narrowed to the primary area of disability and then gradually broadens.

The first diagnostic step is a comparison of the expected level of functioning with the actual performance of the child. In almost all areas of possible disability, e.g., speech, reading, motor coordination, etc., our estimate of the expected level of functioning is based on some normative combination of mental age, chronological age, and certain experimental factors. Both standardized and informal tests are used in the assessment of the actual level of performance. When a significant discrepancy is found between expected and actual performance (e.g., in reading, a discrepancy between CA and/or MA and the level of difficulty of the misarticulated sounds), a disability exists.

The second step is obtaining as comprehensive and detailed behavioral description of the disability as is possible. If the disability is in reading, e.g., the diagnostician would obtain from a standard diagnostic reading

■ FIGURE 2   *A Schematc Representation of the Diagnostic-Remedial Process*

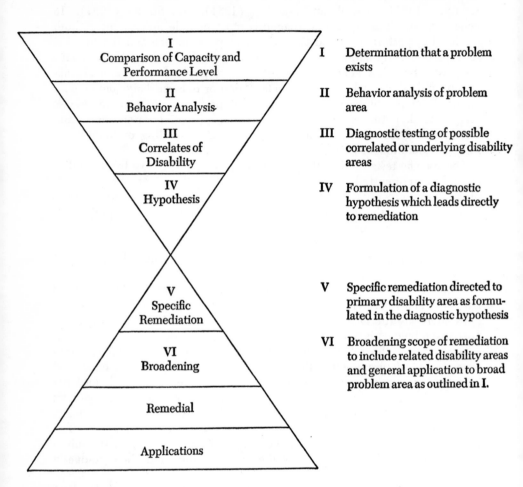

examination (in contrast to a reading achievement test) a behavioral description of how the child reads. He might find an absence of phonic skills, inconsistent word attack, lack of sight vocabulary, hurried and in-accurate oral reading, reversal problems, and so forth. If the disability involved spoken language, rather than reading, this step would involve an exact and full description of the speech problem. An articulation inventory or vocabulary analysis, e.g., might be part of this aspect of diagnosis.

The third step, a most crucial one for planning remedial action, is determining relevant correlates of the disability. The child who is found to have no phonic skills whatsoever, in spite of several years of reading instruction, will probably show deficiencies in auditory discrimination, auditory closure, or a closely related area. The youngster with a limited sight vocabulary will often show visualization and/or visual memory problems. The child who shows the perseverative, perceptual-spatial and hyperactive disturbances often called "Strauss Syndrome" characteristics frequently has weaknesses in interpreting visual information and in expressing ideas motorically. The child with so-called "delayed language development" may show basic deficiencies in incidental verbal learning, i.e., he fails to pick up "automatically" the intricacies of speech.

The number and scope of available standardized and informal diagnostic tests, useful in exploring these factors which underlie and/or accompany language disorders, is already large and growing rapidly. It is at this stage in the diagnostic process that a thorough familiarity with the correlates of learning problems and the available means of testing these functions becomes most important.

On the basis of the information gathered in the preceding three steps an hypothesis is formulated which must be both precise and comprehensive. It must take into account all the relevant factors and yet be so precise that it leads directly to remedial planning. An example of such an hypothesis is quoted from a case report:

A thorough review of Casee's test performances, general behavior, classroom functioning, and prior remediation led to formulating a new diagnostic hypothesis: the normal sensory integration processes, by which vision becomes dominant by about age five, had been interrupted. At this time Casee preferred to operate with her intact auditory-vocal skills, and when she was required to use visual-motor skills she was hindered by "interference" or lack of integration between the visual and tactile stimuli. . .

In summary, Casee showed primary motor encoding and visual decoding disabilities, manifested in these ways:

1. Visual-motor-spatial disturbances . . . (specifically) (a) gross interferences in response attempts to simultaneous visual and tactile stimuli, and (b) lack of body image and accompanying laterality and spatial orientation confusion.

2. Overly developed mechanical verbal skills, which were without full comprehension, seen as an over-all discrepancy of about four years between the auditory-vocal and the visual-motor subtests of the ITPA.

3. Difficulty in everyday tasks such as buttoning, putting a lid on a box, getting into cars, etc.—disabilities presumably related to all of the above specific deficits and which involve substantial motor encoding functions.

Remediation was planned to correspond point for point to this diagnostic hypothesis. When the precise disability areas have been remediated, treatment can be broadened to include a more general focus. In the case described, more daily activities were later used in the further development and refinement of motor skills.

Further illustration of broadening remedial focus could be found in a case of reading disability related, e.g., to a deficit in auditory closure. After this weakness had been strengthened, remediation could progress to an application of phonics, other word attack skills, and finally perhaps even to speed and comprehension.

REMEDIATION

In order to meaningfully relate the great diversity of remedial techniques abroad in the area of learning disabilities, it is essential to have a schema which shows all the possible areas of behavior in which a disability might occur and shows the relationships among those areas.

Figure 3 attempts to schematize language behavior in such a way that all possible remedial foci are included. Language is divided into receptive, intermediate, and expressive processes. Receptive language is further subdivided by the sense modality used in receiving the stimulus; expressive is subdivided into vocal and motor responses; and the intermediate

■ FIGURE 3 *Schematic Model of Selected Contributors to Remediation of Learning Disabilities*

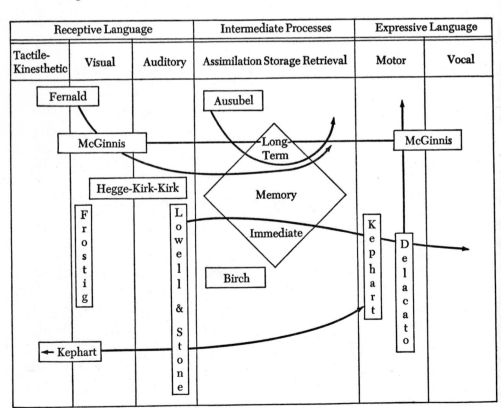

processes are quite arbitrarily called assimilation, storage, and retrieval.

A further dimension is implicit vertically in that the activities at the top of each column involve a high degree of obtaining or conveying the meaning of language symbols, while those near the bottom involve only the perception or manipulation of the symbol, with little regard for meaning. Memory is divided into immediate (rote), intermediate, and long term storage.

Figure 3 indicates only sketchily the areas of primary focus in the work of certain remedial specialists in learning disabilities. Many others could have been chosen—these were selected only to illustrate the diversity of foci which can be encompassed by a schema of this sort. Each of the contributors whose work is represented could quickly and correctly point out that, in fact, he deals with more aspects of language behavior than are shown here.

Some work, such as that of Frostig and Horne can readily be seen as focusing on remediation of visual perception and assimilation with some attention to certain motor responses. Lowell and Stoner's (1960) work in auditory training, with some focus on certain vocal response characteristics, is somewhat parallel to Frostig's contribution, but on the other primary receptive channel.

In the field of assimilation of stimuli, Birch (1963) has contributed significantly to our knowledge of the integration of nonsymbolic material received on one receptive channel with that received simultaneously on another receptive channel. Ausubel (1960) on the other hand, has done extensive investigations of certain relationships among assimilation, storage, and retrieval of highly complex, meaningful (symbolic) language information.

Fernald's (1939) system of remedial reading can be conceptualized as employing the assimilation of simultaneous visual and kinesthetic symbolic stimuli as an aid to retrieval. The emphasis in Fernald's approach are on the meaningfulness of the symbols presented to the child and the facilitation of visual storage and retrieval thereof.

In contrast, the Hegge-Kirk-Kirk (1940) remedial reading system initially emphasizes auditory fusion or sound blending (assimilation with little regard for meaning) and vocal expression in response to the visual stimulus.

And finally, the currently controversial work of Delacato (1963) can be schematized as being centered in neurological (dis)organization and moving through the entire developmental or sequential hierarchy of motor expression. Kephart's (1960) well established program appears to focus simultaneously on visual, receptive, assimilative (integrative) and motor expressive behaviors at the lower levels, with a gradual ascendance to more symbolic behaviors. Although the remedial programs of both Delacato and Kephart contain a large motor expression or motor activity component, this superficial resemblance reflects quite different theoretical formulations and rationale.

Remedial reading systems per se are legion and still multiplying rapidly. Two of the most helpful ways to categorize them as an aid in selecting the best program for a given youngster are: (a) single versus multisensory approach and, (b) specific, eclectic suggestions for special problems such as improving rate of reading versus tightly integrated, comprehensive programs which are sequentially presented. Fernald's system is primarily visual-kinesthetic and is tightly and systematically organized. Gillingham and Stillman's (1960) program is just as comprehensive and systematic, but is thoroughly multisensory. Monroe (1932) and Harris (1956) offer many specific suggestions for particular problems and are not as concerned with channel or sequence.

Remedial offerings in communication disorders have again been limited, in comparison to those in reading. One of the more comprehensive approaches to communication disorders (aphasia) is presented by McGinnis (1963). Interestingly, this system also provides an approach to remedial reading. Further remedial suggestions for children with communication disorders can be found in Agranowitz and McKeown (1964), Myklebust (1954), and Lowell and Stoner (1960). Treatment suggestions for some expressive problems can be found in standard speech correction and pathology texts.

Remedial reading spills over into remediation of visual-motor problems just as it does into communication disorders. Kephart (1960) and Delacato (1963) both offer programs which have an initial primary focus on motor and visual-motor activities followed by a somewhat eclectic reading approach. Teaching methods for children with perceptual disorders are also given by Cruickshank, et al. (1961), Strauss and Lehtinen (1947), Gallagher (1960), and Frostig and Horne (1964).

LEARNING DISABILITIES AND THE FUTURE

Within the field of learning disabilities, there is already evident a healthy trend toward early identification of potential cases of learning disabilities. Much, of course, remains to be done in the refinement of both diagnostic and remedial techniques, but it is not too soon to begin intensive work on prevention through appropriate educational experiences. The day may come when such preventive educational treatment at age five or six will be outmoded by medical prevention at a much earlier age. But that day is not as imminent as the day of educational prevention. This focus on early identification and selection of educational remediation is currently being paralleled by at least one pilot effort in the broader field of elementary education (Highland Park, Illinois) to identify the psychological-cognitive learning pattern of normal first-graders and to differentially gear instructional techniques to those patterns.

Another trend which is apparent in special education is that of more and finer categories. In one school system, e.g., there is already a special program for culturally deprived gifted which differs from the culturally deprived nongifted program and from the nonculturally deprived gifted program! A glimpse into a rose tinted crystal ball might suggest some trends not yet so apparent. For example, in the future, this proliferation of programs will perhaps reverse itself and be replaced by an integrating and unifying application of certain concepts which are now being explored and applied in learning disabilities.

Some of these concepts which the field of learning disabilities will hopefully promulgate are offered here, not as the sole property of this field by any means, but as ideas evolved from many disciplines and belonging to all of education.

The concept of analyzing or evaluating specific cognitive patterns has been furthered by the recent work of Guilford (1956) on the structure of intellect. In the same vein, Gallagher and Lucito (1961) have demonstrated, with the cognitive abilities measured by WISC subtests, that retarded children are relatively stronger in tasks requiring perceptual organization than in those demanding verbal comprehension; the gifted show just the reverse or mirror pattern, being relatively stronger in verbal comprehension abilities than in perceptual organization, and that the average group showed patterns of abilities different from both the retarded and the gifted.

Recent work with the ITPA, which yields a profile of nine separate language abilities, has demonstrated identifiable patterns of language strengths and weaknesses among certain groups of children, e.g., retarded, culturally deprived, athetoid and spastic cerebral palsied, receptive and expressive aphasics, partially seeing, etc. But even more importantly, the individual ITPA profile of psycholinguistic strengths and weaknesses points the way for specific planning of educational techniques appropriate for that child. Similarly, Valett (1964) has recently suggested a clinical profile to be used in showing patterns of cognitive strengths and weaknesses as revealed by items passed and failed on the Stanford Binet L-M.

Educators have long discussed the need for recognizing individual differences among children within a group. The application of these new developments in analyzing patterns of cognitive differences within an individual child is a logical and necessary extension of this interest in inter-individual difference. In spite of this widespread acceptance of educational planning for inter- and intra-individual differences, there has been an equally broad dissatisfaction with many of the traditional grouping techniques. Whether one favors homogeneity or heterogeneity of grouping, a crucial consideration is that such grouping be based on relevant variables. Neither chronological nor mental age has proven entirely satisfactory, since each is a highly global measure. Is it too idealistic to suggest that grouping by shape and level of those cognitive patterns most relevant to the subject or content area to be studied is both possible and worthy of exploration? The field of learning disabilities may become a leader in demonstrating the feasibility of such an approach.

Educators have traditionally been concerned with promoting and developing achievement in specific academic areas. There are, however, certain cognitive abilities upon which academic achievement depends. Through a series of historical accidents American psychologists and educators have belonged to and been primarily influenced by the school of thought which held that intelligence (basic cognitive structures) was innate, hereditary and unchanged by experience. Only in fairly recent years has the concept of the "educability of educability" become even a little popular or respectable. The field of learning disabilities, and perhaps that of reading readiness, stand as primary contributors at the present time to the area of educating cognitive abilities directly. This type of ability training (focused, e.g., on spatial orientation, visualization, retention, or auditory discrimination) is usually employed in a remedial setting after a youngster has evidenced an inability to achieve in an academic area which requires those underlying cognitive skills in which he is weak. If, in this case, an ounce of prevention is worth a pound of cure, it would follow that a broadening of curriculum to include ability as well as achievement training is in order. The work in early identification of children with potential learning disabilities (e.g., Gillingham, 1960; DeHirsch, 1957) mentioned earlier, is closely related to this concept of ability training.

"Meet the child where he is" is oft heard in educational circles—so oft, in fact, one might suspect that if we were better able to do it we might be less compelled to talk about it. A basic premise of remediation in cases of learning disabilities is that one must determine exactly where the child is functioning and begin instruction at or slightly below that point. Diagnostic teaching is a valuable aid in this determination. Recognition of the fact that a child's presence at a desk in the third grade room does not necessarily insure he is ready for a third grade book is widespread, but the actual doing something about it is not so prevalent. Too often we judge performance level by grade placement or mental age, rather than by actual examination of functioning.

When the teacher and child meet, a major part of the teacher's armament must be a knowledge of principles of learning. Many normal children learn readily in spite of repeated violations of learning principles. However, children with learning disabilities cannot do this. By sharpening our awareness of some of these principles, as applied in teaching children with learning disabilities, we can anticipate broader adherence to them.

Some of these major principles of learning include overlearning, ordering and sizing (programing) of new material, rewarding only desired responses, frequent review, and avoidance of interference and negative transfer. (See Bryant, N. D., in press, for an excellent discussion of the principles of remediation.)

Analyses of patterns of cognitive abilities, grouping by these patterns, curriculum planning to include the education of underlying abilities as well as achievements, meeting the child where he really is, and teaching him in accord with known principles of learning—all seem worthy of further exploration.

If the promise of maturity now visible in the gawky, uncoordinated, sprawling adolescence of the field of learning disabilities is fulfilled, we will see one more example of special education's contribution to the education of all children, exceptional and not-so-exceptional.

REFERENCES

Agranowitz, Aleen, and McKeon, M. R. *Aphasia handbook for adults and children.* Springfield, Illinois: Charles C Thomas, 1964.

Ausubel, D. P. The use of advance organizers in the learning and retention of meaningful verbal material. *Journal of Educational Psychology,* 1960, 51, 267–272.

Bateman, Barbara. *The Illinois test of psycholinguistic abilities in current research.* Urbana: University of Illinois Press, 1964. (a)

Bateman, Barbara. Learning disabilities—an overview. Paper read at CEC 42nd Annual Convention, Chicago, April, 1964. (b)

Blau, A. *The master hand; a study of the origin and meaning of right and left sidedness and its relation to personality and language.* New York: American Orthopsychiatric Association, 1946.

Birch, G. H., and Lefford, A. Intersensory development in children. *Monograph of Society for Research in Child Development,* 1963, 28 (5).

Bryant, N. D. Some principles of remedial instruction for dyslexia. *International Reading Association Journal,* in press.

Cohn, R. Neurological concepts pertaining to the brain-damaged child. In Daley, W. T. (Editor), *Speech and language therapy with the brain-damaged child.* Washington, D.C.: Catholic University of America Press, 1962.

Cruickshank, W. M., Benton, F. A., Ratzeburg, F. H., and Tannhauser, Mirian T. *A teaching method for brain-injured and hyperactive children.* New York: Syracuse University Press, 1961.

DeHirsch, Katrina. Tests designed to discover potential reading difficulties at the six-year-old level. *American Journal of Orthopsychiatry,* 1957, 27, 566–576.

Delacato, C. H. *The diagnosis and treatment of speech and reading problems.* Springfield, Illinois: Charles C Thomas, 1963.

Drew, A. L. A neurological appraisal of familial congenital word-blindness. *Brain,* 1956, 79, 440–460.

Eustis, R. S. The primary etiology of specific language disabilities. *Journal of Pediatrics,* 1947, 31, 448.

Fabian, A. A. Clinical and experimental studies of school children who are retarded in reading. *Quarterly Journal of Child Behavior,* 1951, 3, 15–37.

Fernald, G. *Remedial techniques in basic school subjects.* New York: McGraw Hill Book Company, Inc., 1939.

Frostig, Marianne, and Horne, D. *The Frostig program for the development of visual perception.* Chicago: Follett Publishing Company, 1964.

Gann, E. *Reading Difficulty and personality organization.* New York: King's Crown Press, 1945.

Gallagher, J. J. *The tutoring of brain-injured mentally retarded children,* Springfield, Illinois: Charles C Thomas, 1960.

Gallagher, J. J. Educational methods with brain-damaged children. In J. Masserman (Editor), *Current psychiatric therapies.* Volume II. New York: Grune and Stratton, Inc., 1962, Pp. 48–55.

Gallagher, J. J., and Lucito, L. J. Intellectual patterns of gifted compared with average and retarded. *Exceptional Children,* 1961, 27,479–483.

Guilford, J. P. The structure of intellect. *Psychological Bulletin,* 1956, 53, 293–297.

Gillingham, Anna, and Stillman, Bessie. *Remedial training for children with specific disability in reading, spelling and penmanship.* Cambridge, Massachusetts: Educators Publishing Service, Inc., 1960.

Harris, A. J. *How to increase reading ability.* New York: Longmans Green & Company, 1956.

Haeussermann, Else. *Developmental potential of preschool children: an evaluation of intellectual, sensory and emotional functioning.* New York: Grune and Stratton, Inc., 1958.

Hegge, T. G., Kirk, S. A., and Kirk, Winifred. *Remedial reading drills.* Ann Arbor, Michigan: George Wahr Publishing Company, 1940.

Hermann, K. *Reading disability.* Springfield, Illinois: Charles C Thomas, 1959.

Hinshelwood, J. *Congenital word-blindness.* London: H. K. Lewis, 1917.

Kass, Corinne. Some psychological correlates of severe reading disability (dyslexia). Unpublished doctoral dissertation, University of Illinois, 1962.

Kirk, S. A. *Educating exceptional children.* Boston: Houghton Mifflin Company, 1962.

Kleffner, F. R. Aphasia and other language deficiencies in children: research and teaching at Central Institute for the Deaf. In W. T. Daley (Editor), *Speech and language therapy with the brain-damaged child.* Washington, D.C.: Catholic University of America Press, 1962.

Kolson, C., and Kaluger, G. *Clinical aspects of remedial reading.* Springfield, Illinois: Charles C Thomas, 1963.

Lowell, E. L., and Stoner, M. *Play it by ear.* Los Angeles: John Tracy Clinic, 1960.

McGinnis, M. A. *Aphasic children: identification and education by the association method.* Washington, D.C.: Alexander Graham Bell Association for the Deaf, 1963.

Malmquist, Eve. *Factors related to reading disabilities in the first grade of the elementary school.* Stockholm: Amquist and Wiksell, 1958.

Money, J. (Editor) *Reading disability: progress in research needs in dyslexia.* Baltimore: Johns Hopkins Press, 1962.

Monroe, Marion. *Children who cannot read.* Chicago: University of Chicago Press, 1932.

Myklebust, H. R. *Auditory disorders in children.* New York: Grune and Stratton, Inc., 1954.

Olson, W. C. Reading as a function of the total growth of the child. In W. S. Gray, *Reading and pupil development.* Chicago: University of Chicago Press, 1940. Pp. 233–237.

Orton, S. T. Specific reading disability—strephosymbolia. *Journal of American Medical Association,* 1928, 1094–1099.

Penfield, W., and Roberts, L. *Speech and brain-mechanisms.* New York: Princeton University Press, 1959.

Rabinovitch, R. D. Reading and learning disabilities. In S. Arieti (Editor), *American handbook of psychiatry.* Volume 1, Chapter 43. New York: Basic Books, Inc., 1959.

Robinson, H. *Why pupils fail in reading.* Chicago: University of Chicago Press, 1946.

Roswell, Florence, and Natchez, Gladys. *Reading disability: diagnosis and treatment.* New York: Basic Books, Inc., 1964.

Smith, D. E. P., and Carrigan, P. *The nature of reading disability.* New York: Harcourt, Brace and World, Inc., 1959.

Strang, Ruth. *Diagnostic teaching of reading.* New York: McGraw Hill Book Company, Inc., 1964.

Strauss, A. A., and Lehtinen, L. E. *Psycho-pathology and education of the brain-injured child.* New York: Grune and Stratton, Inc., 1947.

Traxler, A., and Townsend, Agatha. *Eight more years of research in reading: summary and bibliography.* New York: Educational Records Bureau, 1955.

Valett, R. E. A clinical profile for the Stanford-Binet. *Journal of School Psychologists,* 1963–1964, **2** (1), 49–54.

Vorhaus, P. G. Rorschach configurations associated with reading disability. *Journal of Projective Techniques,* 1952, 16, 3–19.

Witkin, H. A., Dyk, R. B., Paterson, H. F., Goodeonugh, D. R., and Kapp, S. A. *Psychological differentiation: studies of development.* New York: John Wiley & Sons, Inc., 1962.

Wood, Nancy. Evaluation of language disorders in children of school age. In W. T. Daley (Editor) *Speech and language therapy with the brain-damaged child.* Washington, D.C.: Catholic University of America Press, 1962.

** 34 **

Toward Clarification of Central Issues

SAMUEL D. CLEMENTS

Several basic issues impede agreement on the concepts of "brain dysfunction" and the "child with minimal brain dysfunction." They come from our incomplete knowledge of the human organism, our communication failures, and our personal biases. Any serious attempt at solution must at least acknowledge these issues.

* From *Minimal Brain Dysfunction in Children.* Washington: U.S. Department of Health, Education and Welfare, 1966, pp. 6–7. Reprinted by permission of the author.

THE ORGANICITY-ENVIRONMENT OBSTACLE

One issue is the age-old dilemma: Organicity vs. environment. This conflict, which is reminiscent of the heredity-environment controversy, represents an updating and expansion of its predecessor.

The concept of organicity has been broadened to include all factors which originate in or are inherent in pathology, including genetic variations, biochemical irregularities, perinatal brain insults, or the results of illnesses and injuries sustained during the years critical for the normal development and maturation of the central nervous system.

Included in the organicity concept is the proposition that any condition which alters normal functioning can manifest itself as learning and behavioral irregularities. These irregularities depend upon such factors as causes, loci of the assault, developmental stage of embryo, fetus, or child, and diffuseness or discreteness of the damage to the central nervous system (CNS).

The concept of environment would consider all factors related to the normal life experiences inherent in the social-economic-cultural milieu of the individual, his interpersonal relationships, and his personal psychological traumata and stresses. Included is an appreciative regard for the part such elements could play in the production of learning and behavioral irregularities.

Assuming agreement that the two major determinants of learning and behavior are organicity and environment, the diagnostic team must determine, as accurately as possible, the amount of impairment each is contributing to the chief complaints about the child and to his clinical symptoms.

If the "whole child" approach to diagnosis is deemed essential to the earnest understanding of a "difficult" youngster, then equal weight, in terms of symptom antecedents and investigatory priority, must be given to both organicity and environment.

Although organicity is often recognized as a contributor to symptomatology, it is frequently ignored in the final diagnosis of the child, and in the treatment planning, unless it is grossly obvious. The justification offered is our inability to ascertain exactly the extent of its contribution.

TWO DIFFERING POINTS OF VIEW

A second clouded issue reflects uncertainty regarding the very existence of a condition such as "minimal brain dysfunction" in the *types of children with which we are dealing.* For convenience, the extreme views will be categorized and labeled according to the sentiments of their proponents.

1. The purist point of view is that "minimal brain dysfunction" is in most instances an unproven presumptive diagnosis. Therefore, the concept can have little meaning and acceptance until such time as our

knowledge is greatly increased and our diagnostic skills remarkably refined. Brain dysfunctioning can only be inferred until physiologic, biochemical, or structural alterations of the brain are demonstrated.

2. The pragmatic case might be presented in the following manner: With our limited validated knowledge concerning relationships between brain and behavior, we must accept certain categories of deviant behavior, developmental dyscrasias, learning disabilities, and visual-motor-perceptual irregularities as valid indices of brain dysfunctioning. They represent neurologic signs of a most meaningful kind, and reflect disorganized central nervous system functioning at the highest level. To consider learning and behavior as distinct and separate from other neurologic functions echoes a limited concept of the nervous system and of its various levels of influence and integration.

We cannot afford the luxury of waiting until causes can be unquestionably established by techniques yet to be developed. We cannot postpone managing as effectively and honestly as possible the large number of children who present chronic differences we feel are more related to organicity variables than others.

The above two views represent the extreme versions of the situation. If clinicians' viewpoints could be plotted, the result would most likely take on the shape of a bimodal distribution with overlapping.

** 35 **

Learning and Human Achievement
Philosophy and Concepts

GLENN DOMAN AND CARL DELACATO

PROLOGUE

The conceptual and philosophical statement set forth below is the culmination of more than 20 years experience. It is intended as a simple and straight forward declaration of what the authors believe.

∗ From *Human Potential* 1968, 1, pp. 113–120. Reprinted by permission of the authors and the publisher.

During the decade of the 1930's, Temple Fay, an extraordinary neurosurgeon and scientist, developed certain basic insights concerning malfunction of the human central nervous system and concerning pragmatic treatment techniques. In 1941, Dr. Fay became the mentor of Glenn Doman and in the years immediately following World War II, Carl Delacato and Robert Doman came under his influence.

In the period of the late 1940's, little had been done to fill in between Fay's notable insights and the techniques he had developed. Since 1946, the authors together with Robert Doman and others, have worked to expand Fay's early insights into well founded concepts and the early techniques into successful treatment methods.

Works such as those of David Krech of the University of California, Joseph Altman of the Massachusetts Institute of Technolgy and B. N. Klosovskii in Russia, as well as those of cyberneticist Norbert Wiener, recently of the Massachusetts Institute of Technolgy and of engineer James Reswick of The Case Institute of Technolgy, Cleveland, have provided increasing confirmation of the research findings, and they have led to a greater understanding of why the techniques, methods, principles and concepts fit together to form what can now be considered a general philosophy based on principles of neurological organization.

STATEMENT

This philosophy and alignment of concepts deal with the entire learning process as differentiated from the narrower process of formal education. It extends to include the totality of human behavior.

The learning process of an individual begins in utero. It begins long before the moment of birth and possibly at the instant of conception. The learning process is clearly evident with the birth cry as the baby begins to breathe air for the first time, in the new environment, outside his mother's body.

From the instant of birth onward the learning process takes place at what can be described only as a breathtaking pace.

It is possible that the child learns more, fact for fact, before he enters school than he will learn thereafter in the rest of his life.

By the age of six, seven or eight years, depending on his nationality, when a child enters school he has learned about himself, his relationship with his family, his family's relationship with its community and his community's relationship to the larger world.

He has learned about individual ownership, family ownership, community ownership and national ownership.

He has learned about words, phrases, sentences, and he has learned the better part of an entire language.

He has learned about and how to move his bodily parts, and he has learned about how to crawl, creep, walk and run.

He thinks abstractly and is sophisticated about a world which deals in terms of nuclear energy and space travel.

This very small listing of accomplishments does not begin to touch the scope of the child's learning achievements. It is after all of this, that we normally say he is ready for the process of formal education.

The process of formal education is, in the end, nothing more than the transmission of existing information from the teacher to the pupil, coupled with presentation of a degree of love for the subject—that is, assuming that the teacher has proved worthy of identification as a teacher.

When, in the presentation of this philosophy, we use the term learning, we mean it in the broadest sense, encompassing the entire process. By learning how to hear while in utero, how to distinguish light from dark at two days of age, how it feels to use arms and legs in crawling at one week of age, how to understand spoken sentences at eighteen months of age, how to read and deal with abstractions and thus eventually, how to achieve the highest level of human learning and thereby performance as a consequence.

Development

Learning is a function of the central nervous system. A review of the literature on learning evokes this pronouncement as the only generalized truth about learning on which there is universal agreement. There is also broad agreement on the idea that the more complex the nervous system the greater the ability of the organism to learn more completely and more abstractly.

Phylogenetic Development

The relationship of complexity of function is demonstrated in those creatures of the earth that have developed more complex nervous systems as they developed more complex functions. "You may be sure that first there was a need and then there was a facility. Nature is an opportunist" (Fay).

Man represents the present peak of phylogenetic rise in the size, complexity and organization of the central nervous system, a process which has spanned millions of years. He also represents the present peak among all living creatures in his ability to learn.

As one descends in the animal kingdom through less complex central nervous systems, the successively lower creatures may be said to have successively lower learning abilities as compared with higher forms of life.

The ability to learn correlates directly with development of the nervous system. This relationship results in a high learning ability in well-developed nervous systems and a low learning ability in undeveloped or underdeveloped nervous systems. This is also true *within* a species and nowhere is the difference between individuals as evident as it is in man himself.

A primary function of the brain is to relate the organism to its environment. It is axiomatic that the central nervous system of an organism develops through use. Although the neurophysiological evidence to support this view is manifold, few examples are clearer than that of Klosovskii's newborn kittens and puppies. After 10 to 19 days of rotation in a horizontal plane, the experimental animals showed 22.8 to 35 percent increase in the size of the vestibular areas of the brain as compared with the control animals.

Ontogenetic Development

Development of the brain is a result of interaction of the organism with its environment. Increased interaction produces increased development and decreased interaction results in decreased development. This interaction, which is prerequisite to development, is also prerequisite to learning.

Assuming physical integrity of the brain, we have seen that the brain interacts with its environment through a cybernetic loop which begins in the environment, follows afferent or sensory pathways to the brain and then efferent or motor pathways from the brain back to the environment. Thus, information about the environment, as it reaches the brain through sensory pathways, is the primary prerequisite for development of the central nervous system, and, as a result, for learning.

Human Sensory Growth

Variations of environmental opportunity result in variations of the informational nourishment upon which sensory pathways of the brain grow, are elaborated and are organized. Such variations range from severe sensory deprivation to enormous sensory enrichment. These variations in quantity and quality of the environmental input account for growth of the sensory pathways.

Building and elaboration of sensory engrams takes place as a result of correlation of the myriad stimuli received by the brain as well as a result of the intensity, frequency and duration with which the stimuli are applied.

Therefore growth, elaboration and organization of the sensory pathways may be limited by a lack of stimulation and they are increased in direct relation to the frequency, intensity and duration of sensory input.

Learning is limited to the amount of information which the brain has received and stored and the ability to learn more is limited to the amount of information the sensory pathways can process.

Since it is input that elaborates the sensory pathways and, since the amount of input which can be handled is dependent upon growth of the

sensory pathways, it is obvious that the more input (and therefore learning) which takes place, the more input (and therefore learning) is possible. It is thus evident that the sensory pathways, which are the result of
input, constitute the ability to learn and pure learning is the amount of
information a brain has acquired.

While this kind of learning process has been long understood in a motor
context, it has not been understood in a sensory context. Function determines structures in both sensory and motor terms. Biceps function, for
example, creates a stronger, larger and more effective biceps. More importantly, this stronger, larger and more effective biceps is now capable of greater feats of strength, variety and effectiveness than a less
functioning biceps, which in turn enables it to become still stronger, larger
and more effective. In the same way, sensory input elaborates sensory
pathways and such input contributes not only to the sum total of learning,
which is stored, but, more importantly, it makes the sensory pathways
capable of even greater learning feats. A child who knows more than another child can be taught more than the other child, but more importantly
such a child is *neurologically* more capable than the other child.

If input is non-existent, limited or confused, the sensory pathways (and
therefore learning) will similarly be undeveloped, underdeveloped or
incorrectly developed. As a result, there will be no sensory function, underdeveloped sensory function or incorrect sensory function.

Conversely, if input is multiplied, varied and clearly programmed, the
sensory pathways (and therefore learning) will similarly be developed,
enriched, and organized. As a result, there will be greater sensory function, enriched sensory function and organized sensory function.

Learning is a sensory process.

Human Motor Growth

Information or learning which does not result in performance is obviously
useless.

While learning is dependent upon the sensory pathways, performance
is dependent upon the motor pathways.

It is well understood that motor pathways are developed and elaborated
through use.

What has not been understood is that the building and elaboration of
motor pathways is entirely dependent on the previous creation of sensory
pathways. If sensory pathways are undeveloped, underdeveloped or incorrectly developed, the motor pathways will similarly be undeveloped,
underdeveloped or incorrectly developed. As a result, there will be no
motor function, underdeveloped motor function or incorrect motor function.

The influence of motor function on learning is to reinforce learning. As
a consequence, if motor pathways and thus motor function are undeveloped, underdeveloped or incorrectly developed, learning will not exist.
will be incomplete, or will be incorrect to the same degree.

Development of motor pathways of the brain, and thus reinforcement of learning, takes place as the organism reacts expressively or efferently to stimuli coming from the environment through afferent pathways.

The sensory pathways and the motor pathways taken with their interconnections make up the organ known as the brain.

Learning is a function of the brain.

The Dynamics of Environment

The process of learning is dependent on the complexity of development and on organization of the brain. Development of the brain, in turn, depends upon opportunities of this organ to take in and react to stimuli offered by its environment. Variations in environmental stimulation result in variations in the ability to learn.

Sensory deprivation, and thus lack of expressive opportunity for reinforcement, can be the result of envionmental variations. Therefore, an extremely limited environment creates a virtually zero state or idiot brain.

While a limited environment creates brains limited in both development and function, on the other hand, a highly enriched, a highly varied, a highly organized and a highly dynamic environment results in a highly developed, versatile and highly organized brain. Environment therefore is a factor strongly at play in the development of inferior or a superior brain.

Cybernetic Functions

The effect of environment (or input) upon performance (or output) can be seen clearly when one considers the almost exact functional analogy between the human brain and the computer.

Norbert Wiener developed the entirely new field of cybernetics when he saw this analogy following creation of the first electronic computer.

Henshaw has referred to the human brain as a wet system and the computer as a dry system.

Intensity of Input

If the dry system computer is supplied with no input for storage it will give no answer. Such a computer is said to be in an unprogrammed or zero state. We have learned that the wet system or human brain when supplied with no input for storage will also give no answer and can be said to be in an unprogrammed or idiot state.

Henshaw states that if a dry system computer is given only limited input it will give back limited or unsophisticated information. Such a computer is said to be in a partially programmed state. We have learned that the wet system or human brain when supplied with limited input for storage will produce a child with limited or unsophisticated information. Such a child can be said to be in an unsophisticated or immature state.

An ordinary dry system computer given ordinary input will give back limited heuristic information—that is, information obtained by search and discovery. Such a computer may be said to be in a limited heuristic state. We have learned that the wet system, or human brain, when supplied with average information for storage will produce a child who has average and limited heuristic information. Such a child can be said to be an average one or one with limited heuristic capability.

In order for a dry system computer to give back truly heuristic information a superior computer had to be developed. Such a computer is called an heuristic computer. We have found that a high degree of input into the wet system, which is the child's brain, does in fact create a superior system which will give back heuristic information. Such a child is regarded as a genius. Therefore, in either humans or computers which have physical integrity, the environment or input is an important determinant of performance or output.

However, a limited environment is not the only factor which can interfere with brain development. Lack of physical integrity of the brain is also a factor which can limit brain development. Such lack of physical integrity can result from trauma to the brain prenatally, natally or postnatally. This will also result in lack of performance.

Integrity of Systems

What has just been said of injured wet systems can also be said of a computer which has damage. A computer with extensive damage will give back no information. Such a computer may be said to be in a nonfunctioning state. A child with an extremely damaged brain will give back no information. Such a child may be said to be in a non-functioning or vegetable state.

In a high percentage of cases we can correct damaged computers by making internal repairs or readjustments. When this is done, the computer is made to function. Such a computer is said to be repaired. We have discovered that, in a high percentage of severely brain-injured children, we can correct damage by certain surgical procedures or by neurological reorganization of the child. When this is done, the child is made to function. Such a child is therefore said to be rehabilitated.

A computer which has less extensive damage will take in less information or will take in the information in a garbled way. It will therefore, give back limited information or garbled information. Such a computer may be said to have a learning problem. We have found that a child with less extensive brain damage will also take in limited information or take in information in a garbled way. Such children give back limited performance or garbled performance. Such children are also said to have learning problems.

We can correct such a computer through reorganizing it. When this is done the computer is made to function. Such a computer may be said to be organized. We have discovered that with children who have less extensive damage we often correct the problem through use of certain organizational procedures. When this is done the child is made able to function at his appropriate level. Such a child we say is organized.

In summary, the following statements can be made about wet and dry computers.

1. When supplied with no sensory input, they will remain in an idiot state until information is supplied. Supplying information with increased frequency, intensity and duration will often correct the problem.

2. When they are able to receive no information due to extensive damage or dysorganization, they will be in a non-functional state until extensive reorganization is carried out by supply of information with increased frequency, intensity and duration.

3. When supplied with limited sensory input, they will remain unsophisticated or immature until appropriate information is supplied. Supply of information with increased frequency, intensity and duration will correct this problem also.

4. When they are able to receive only limited information, or information received in a garbled way due to less extensive damage or dysorganization, they will have learning problems until reorganization is carried out and until they are then supplied with the necessary information increased in frequency, intensity and duration.

5. When they have ordinary physical integrity and are supplied with ordinary amounts of informational input, they respond with ordinarily expected performance.

Implications

When a superior computer is created based on the presently existing computer, or a superior brain is created based on enriching the input to the present brain, the result will be a highly heuristic dry system and a genius wet system.

The knowledge now exists to make dry systems highly heuristic.

Where do we stand on making the wet system genius?

After many years of failure it has been learned that the normal level of environmental stimulation is not sufficient to overcome the neurological deficit caused by environmental deprivation or by trauma to the central nervous system. It was therefore our original postulation that it might be possible to modify and heighten development of the underdeveloped or traumatized brain. This obviously could be done surgically where necessary by removal of obstacles to neurological development and organization. It obviously might be accomplished nonsurgically also by enhancing the environment through a myriad of correlated stimuli greatly increased in frequency, intensity and duration.

While knowledge that the environment plays a role in brain growth is not new, the directness of that role and the degree of its importance have been greatly underestimated. The work of David Krech with sensory enriched and sensory deprived rats makes this very clear.

Indeed in the ancient debate between the geneticists and the environmentalists as to which of these factors has the greater bearing on ultimate development of men or of man, it would now appear to the authors that man is falling so far below his environmental ceiling that genetic factors have comparatively little influence. It is our present position that not until man is reaching his environmental ceiling will the genetic differences in man be measurable as a practical matter.

Present Level of Knowledge

This statement reports our present level of knowledge, based upon two decades of clinical research with several thousand "mentally retarded" or frankly brain-injured children.

The unique body of knowledge accumulated has led us to our present position.

The Institutes for the Achievement of Human Potential is now committed to a significant increase in the ability of *all* children to perform in the physical, intellectual and educational realms.

The objective is to be obtained in all children throughout the spectrum of human accomplishment.

The Institutes have devoted much time to researching the problems of childhood behavioral development. Our methodology for this research has included both pathological and clinical deviations from expected norms of development.

Studying children who are lacking developmentally has led to the conclusion that most of the developmental lags are directly correlated with similar lags in development of nervous system. Because children who exhibit such lags progress at a slower rate than do normal children, or indeed not at all, we have been able to ascertain validity the significant developmental sequence without interference from the vagaries of the chronology of development. To this we have added the physiological correlates.

In well human beings the process of brain maturation, which begins at conception and which is clearly evident at birth, is virtually complete by eight years of age.

The speed at which this process takes place varies widely from human being to human being.

By measuring children against the several functional scales which comprise the Doman-Delacato Developmental Profile (the criteria by which it is possible to measure the child's level of progression in this process of brain maturation), we can determine the child's neurological age.

It can easily be established that the process of neurological maturation can be *slowed slightly* by certain cultural factors which prevent good brain organization, that this process can be *slowed considerably* by certain environmental deprivations which create neurological dysorganization, and that this process can be *completely halted* by brain injury.

The *delaying* of neurological maturation is evidenced by the *immature child* or the slow learner.

The dysorganization of neurological growth is evidenced in the *reading problem* or even the *retarded child*.

The *total halting* of neurological growth is seen in the *severely brain-injured child*.

In a neurological sense all children can be embraced in a continuum which ranges from the severely brain-injured child without neurological organization at one end of the spectrum to the superior child with extremely good neurological organization at the other end of the spectrum.

The work of the individual institutes has established clearly, and contrary to popular belief, that children who are far below average in this continuum can be raised to average levels. Indeed, the work has proved that even severely brain-injured children may be raised to average levels by the employment of surgical or non-surgical approaches.

When significant numbers of brain-injured children had been raised to average and, occasionally, far above average brain levels, it became apparent that *the process of neurological maturation can be speeded as well as delayed and that this speeding can be accomplished by certain simple non-surgical procedures.*

The use of these procedures on normal children has enabled us to significantly enhance developmental progress in infancy and childhood.

As a result, we can change human potential which was formerly considered a static and irrevocable fact to a dynamic and ever-changing process. In short, we may be able in the near future to improve universally the very nature of man.

Significance

Such a global concept, together with these simple procedures that are applicable on a universal scale, could be of such significant importance that their continued reassessment and indeed their dissemination to the people, need very careful and judicious scientific and lay direction.

To show the magnitude and the urgency of attention to work in this field, certain comments by Oliver J. Caldwell of the U.S. Office of Education are cited. Following a visit to Moscow in 1963 for interchange of Soviet and American ideas concerning education, programmed learning and the human mind, Dr. Caldwell wrote as follows:

> Since my visit to Moscow, I have discussed with a number of American scholars and scientists the work being done in the United States, in the U.S.S.R., and elsewhere designed to expand the capacity of the human brain and thus to create a "superior man." It is clear that considerable research is being done in

this area. However, as a nonprofessional observer, I have the impression that research in the U.S.S.R. may be more advanced than similar research in the non-Communist world. If this is true, and if the Soviet scientists achieve even a small portion of their stated goals during the next generation, the results could bring about a serious effect on the balance of power.

We were impressed by the Soviet scientists we met on our visit to Moscow and by their generally warm welcome to us. Is it perhaps not time for responsible American leadership to take a new look at the problems involved today in developing human resources? Furthermore, it seems imperative that the United States should devote a larger proportion of its energies and resources to the development of a new generation of Americans, who will have the skills and wisdom necessary for carrying out their responsibilities for leadership and cooperation in a new world of tomorrow.

EPILOGUE

We believe that the implications for Man, and his future, are obvious.

REFERENCES

Altman, Joseph, and Das, G. D. *"Autoradiographic Examination of the Effects of Enriched Environment on the Rate of Glial Multiplication of the Adult Rat Brain."* Nature. 204:1161–1163, 1964.

Caldwell, Oliver J., and Graham, Loren R., *"Moscow in May, 1963: An Interchange of Soviet and American Ideas Concerning Education, Programmed Learning and the Human Mind."* U.S. Department of Health, Education and Welfare, Office of Education. 1964. Supt. of Documents Catalogue No. 5.214:14106.

Henshaw, Paul S. *"Information per se."* Nature. 199:1050–1052, 1963.

Klosovskii, B. N. *"The Development of the Brain and Its Disturbance by Harmful Factors."* Pergamon Press, Oxford, 1963.

Krech, David, Rosenzweig, Mark R., and Bennett, Edward L. *"Environmental Impoverishment, Social Isolation and Changes in Brain Chemistry and Anatomy."* Physiology and Behavior. 1:99–104, 1966.

Wiener, Norbert. *"Cybernetics."* M.I.T. Press. Cambridge, Mass. 1948, 1961.

** 36 **

Controversy Over "Patterning" as a
Treatment for Brain Damage in Children

ROGER D. FREEMAN

Many persons in responsible professional positions who work with handicapped children have been asked to give opinions on the procedures used and promoted by the Institutes for the Achievement of Human Potential in Philadelphia. (The names of the director and associate director, Glenn Doman, RPT, and Carl Delacato, EdD, respectively, have become almost synonymous with the title of the institutes.) Some national, state and foreign organizations have felt it necessary to make cautionary statements because of enthusiastic publicity.[1-4] The need for adequate assessment of results has been noted by many, including the proponents of the system,[5] but nothing definitive has emerged. Meanwhile, the institutes have taken the position that there is with respect to their program that lack of understanding and acceptance which sometimes accompanies the introduction of radical methods which threaten "conventional medicine."[5] No generally accepted or statistically sophisticated proof exists that establishes that either any conventional method of treatment or that of the institutes gives superior results in management of brain damage.[6] In the light of the need, then, to evaluate critically any new methods which bring hope into this area, it would seem appropriate to explore some of the reasons for the controversy which surrounds the methods of the institutes.

THE "PATTERNING" THEORY AND TECHNIQUE

The hypothesis providing the basis for the methods of the institutes follows

* From *Journal of the American Medical Association* 1967, *202*, pp. 385–388. Reprinted by permission of the author and the publisher.
From the Handicapped Children's Unit, St. Christopher's Hospital for Children, and the Department of Psychiatry, Temple University School of Medicine, Philadelphia.

the principle that "ontogeny recapitulates phylogeny" and that failure to pass properly through a certain sequence of developmental stages in mobility, language, and competence in the manual, visual, auditory, and tactile areas reflects poor "neurological organization" and may indicate "brain damage." [7(p1)] Unlike conventional methods which are said to be "symptomatic," "we reach the brain itself by pouring into the afferent sensory system . . . all of the stimuli normally provided by his environment but with such intensity and frequency as to draw, ultimately, a response from the corresponding motor systems." [7(p6)] In the more severe cases of brain damage, patterns of passive movement are imposed which have as their goal "the reproduction of normal activities which would have been the product of the injured brain level had it not been injured." [8] Several people are required to manipulate repeatedly the extremities and head of the child with "brain damage," in positions determined by the theory and which will not be fully presented here. This manipulation is usually carried out for five minutes at least four times each day, seven days a week.

Additional techniques may include: sensory stimulation (not unique with this system of therapy); rebreathing of expired air with a plastic face mask for 30 to 60 seconds once each waking hour (alleged to increase vital capacity and stimulate cerebral blood flow); restriction of fluid intake, salt, and sugar (alleged to decrease cerebrospinal fluid production and cortical irritability); early learning of reading (beginning at age 2, if possible); and techniques which are aimed at establishing uniform cortical hemispheric dominance (latter including restrictions on hand use, eye use, or exposure to music; sleep and rest positioning; and visual and gait training. [7(pp6-7)] A controversial element of the theory is that enhancement of one function will result in improvements in other areas (eg, gains in mobility patterns will, without special attention to speech, lead to improvement in expressive language.) [7(p7),9]

The theory has also been applied to normal development: "The use of these procedures on normal children has enabled us to augment developmental progress significantly in infancy and childhood." [10(p4)]

This brief description does not do justice, of course, to the complexities of theory and practice, but may assist the reader without acquaintance with the system in judging the extent of the changes which may occur in family life when such a regimen is used. For a more complete exposition of the theories involved, the reader is referred to material published by the institutes. [11] The need for large numbers of volunteer patterners has led to appeals for help in newspaper articles, many children requiring as many as 200 or more each week. ("Eventually, David's little army of strangers-turned-helpers numbered 240." [12]) Alternatively, the "Peterson Patterning Machine" (reported to cost between $3,000 and $4,000) may substitute for the patterning team and permit greater frequency of some of the procedures.

THE CONTROVERSY

The institutes have portrayed those skeptical or critical of their methods as "dogmatic"[5] or "conventional"[5] in thinking and fearful both of new ideas and of the possibility that they have actually harmed their patients:

> Why was resistance to the evidence demonstrated by Semmelweis so pronounced and prolonged when it would have been easy for physicians to test its validity in their own practice? Is it not possible that the emotional resentment behind the opposition was caused by an unconscious as well as conscious reluctance to accept not a new theory but the reality that physicians dedicated to healing had been helping to spread illness and death? And is it not possible that the reluctance of modern believers in conventional physiotherapy to investigate methods of treating the brain is due in part to an unconscious fear that some of their methods of symptomatic treatment have been harmful?[5]

We shall avoid speculations about unconscious motivations and confine ourselves to the question: What are some of the sources of objections to the methods of the institutes expressed by informed professional individuals and groups? Some are as follows:

1. *A tendency to ignore the natural clinical course of some patients with brain injuries.* On more than one occasion, the directors of the institutes have stated that when they began their work around 1945 they had never "seen or heard of a single brain-injured child" who had ever gotten well.[9,13] They suggested that conventional methods of treatment were worse than simply leaving the child to creep or crawl on the floor. In actuality, many physicians have observed children with severe brain damage who have achieved partial or apparently complete recoveries of function without either "conventional" physical therapy or the methods of the institutes.[14] Information regarding such recoveries has always been accessible to the institutes, and may account for their statement elsewhere, apparently contradictory to the previous one, that "it is well established that some individuals with brain injuries have recovered functions without treatment."[5] If the impression is given that no brain-damaged children spontaneously recover and that conventional treatment is worse than none, then it appears easy to attribute improvement in children managed by the institutes to their specific methods. There are so many nonspecific variables involved that the assumption of such a causal relationship seems scientifically gratuitous, even if apparently beneficial results could be demonstrated.

2. *Assumption that their methods treat the brain itself, while other methods are "symptomatic."* There is no agreement as to what constitutes a "pattern" nor whether passive movements have a specific central effect, although the latter assumption is reiterated in the publications of the institutes,[5,7(p6),8,9] for example, "by means of such patterning, the brain, the most remarkable computer the world has ever known, is patterned

through its sensory pathways." [7(p6)] Evidence is also lacking that stimulation can raise "the living but functionally depressed cells . . . to their full capability." [7(p6)]

3. *Assumption that because the "full potential of the brain" is not known one can conclude that each child not "genetically defective" may have above average intellectual potential.*[7(pp5-6),9] The diagnosis of mental retardation is a catastrophic disappointment to parents and it is understandable that they may willingly embrace the idea of a remediable condition which gives hope of not just normal but of superior intelligence: ". . . many of the severely brain injured children . . . reached levels of performance which were far above those of the normal average child." [15] Most professionals who work with such children know of mistakes in prognostication in the past and that there may be "a serious danger in too early and too dogmatic a prognosis, especially if this prognosis is used as a basis for limitation of therapeutic effort." [14] When prognostic errors are followed by seeming improvement under whatever therapeutic regimen, it is easy for that regimen to receive undeserved credit. Undue therapeutic or prognostic optimism can combine with parental wish or denial or both and eventually become a serious disservice.

4. *Making parents therapists.* Although others are usually involved in the "patterning," parents have the ultimate responsibility between follow-up visits, which are usually at 60- to 90-day intervals.[7(p7)] Placing the parent in the role of therapist, especially with a very demanding and inflexible regimen, not only changes the nature of the parent-child relationship, but places on the parents the burden of possible failure of treatment, in addition to feelings of guilt and inadequacy which are probably universal with parents of handicapped children.[16] Relative neglect of other important aspects of family life may possibly ensue.[16]

5. *The forceful prevention of self-motivated activities of the child.* Some brain-damaged children who begin to sit or walk before the institutes decide they have properly mastered the preceding stages of mobility are prevented from doing so by a variety of ingenious devices.[17] The long-term effects of such procedures are not known and the parents may become the target of the child's anger and frustration.

6. *Assertions which may increase parental anxiety and concern.* In addition to statements previously mentioned to the effect that conventional physical therapy cannot help and may even be harmful, there are a number of other assertions which deserve some detailed comment.

(*a*) *The threat of death.* The effect on parents of the following unproven statements in material given to them will be left to the reader's imagination:

> Delay [in treatment] not only establishes a widening gap between Neurological Age and Chronological Age but creates additional problems such as complicating illnesses which may eventuate in the death of the individual [7(p5)] Respiratory movement in the brain injured person is usually shallow . . . and the vital capacity reduced. It is on this depression of respiratory function that are based

the frequently recurrent respiratory infections with fevers and commonly fatal pneumonias.[7(P6)]

(b) *The implication that a variety of almost universal child-rearing practices may damage a child's potential.* Of all the criticisms of the publicity emanating from the institutes, perhaps none is felt to be better founded that that directed to a popular article written by Doman and Delacato. Without going into detail, the tenor can be indicated by the title and subtitle: "Train Your Baby to be a Genius: Is your baby in a play-pen? Are his clothes snug? Is his crib near a wall? Then you may be in-hibiting his mental development.[9] Is this kind of communication proper for a group claiming that

> such a global concept, together with these simple procedures that are applicable on a universal scale, could be of such . . . importance that . . . their dissemi-nation to the people, need very careful and judicious scientific and lay direc-tion? [10(P4)]

(c) *The implication that there is a need for absolutely rigid perform-ance of "patterning" to obtain successful results.* Many reports sent to re-ferring physicians by the institutes make essentially the same statement about treatment being carried out "without deviation" or with "religious intensity amounting almost to an obsession." According to a magazine article which has been reprinted and distributed by the institutes, "instruc-tors . . . emphasize the importance of never skipping any part of the daily patterning schedule." [12] Yet this seems to be in contrast to Doman's statement before the American Academy for Cerebral Palsy [18] that the number of times "patterning" must be done a day (four at the start) was *empirically chosen.* Despite the fact that the total program is an extremely demanding one in terms of daily routine, the parents are led to feel they may be interfering with their child's progress if they permit any deviation.

7. *Assumption that improvements are due to specific factors.* The sys-tem involves such a change in family life, possibly involving hope where there may have been none and stimulation where much of this may have been given up, along with the social support and interest of the commu-nity, that these profound influences must be taken into account in any considerations of reasons for possible "improvement." These factors pre-sent major difficulties in designing and carrying out controlled studies.[19]

8. *The test instrument* (*Doman-Delacato Profile*).[20,21] It is alleged that this profile permits simple and conclusive diagnosis of brain damage and other developmental problems [7] which most workers have found to be quite complex and difficult.

> All [children with abnormal behavior] can be classified as belonging to one of three groups. These are (1) the truly brain injured . . . ; (2) the psychotic child whose brain has not sustained organic injury but whose behavior ranges from mildly aberrant to severely abnormal; and (3) the inherently deficient child whose brain was not adequately endowed genetically.[7]

It is by no means decided that psychotic children have no organic involve-ment, nor are children described as "mildly aberrant" ordinarily classified as psychotic. This scheme does not provide, apparently, for neurotic and behavior disorders, nor for mixtures of these categories. The institutes state that "the cause in the vast majority of individuals with behavioral problems is brain injury," [7(p5)] which opinion cannot be regarded as generally acceptable, but "the Institutes deal only with brain-injured individuals since they have found workable and effective solutions only for such people." [7(p5)] There has been no report of studies which adequately relates the profile to any standard methods of assessment of development, although interrater reliability is reported to be satisfactory. [22] The uniqueness of the test instrument renders comparisons with accepted standards difficult.

9. *Statistical defects.* The original publication of the institutes in a medical journal [8] reported an uncontrolled study which yielded encouraging "preliminary results." Three books have been published reporting on the relationship between reading, on the one hand, and dominance and "neurological organization" on the other. [23,25] The studies were done in a number of schools and centers and have recently been subjected to detailed and independent statistical analysis. [26] Glass' critique found them

> exemplary only for their faults. They were naively designed and clumsily analyzed. They suffer from a multitude of sources of invalidity . . . [and] appear to have been executed in thoroughgoing ignorance of the fundamental principles of comparative experimental design which have been known to researchers for thirty years. [26]

In particular, use of matched groups rather than randomization, and failure to take into account the effect of regression toward the mean vitiated the results. (Groups of individuals chosen for the extremeness of their scores on a variable will tend to regress toward the mean of the total group from which they were chosen on subsequent observations on the same or related variables. [26]) Since the claim has been made [10(p4),15] that methods fostering "neurological organization" can help the normal as well as the brain damaged in the area of reading, two independent studies were carried out and failed to confirm theoretical expectations. [27,28] The relationship between cerebral dominance and reading ability has also been questioned. [29,30]

COMMENT

While research workers argue over statistical validity and research design, children with problems require assistance. Parents and therapist are placed in an awkward position and must often feel some resentment toward the researcher who says, or implies, that nothing should be done until a method is proved to be effective. Moreover, current techniques of management are open to valid criticism. They probably do relatively little to assuage parental anxiety.

Although individual professional workers have stated that they have seen instances of therapeutic failure or lack of success with "patterning" techniques, it may be assumed that the patients returning to physicians from the institutes with no manifest improvement might constitute a biased sample.

While the general tone of publicity and communications has been to offer hope and, discounting conventional methods, to claim success for techniques not adequately evaluated, with the implication that a "cure" is possible, the institutes and their affiliated regional centers point out that parents are asked to sign a statement that they have been told some children do not improve.

Material distributed by the institutes which shows graphs of development before and after treatment by their methods dramatizes the hope that slow development may become better than average development as soon as the procedures are instituted: "With therapy . . . the rate of neurological growth changes from an average of 35% of normal to an average of 210% of normal." [7(p9)] Furthermore, somewhat utopian predictions have been made: ". . . we can change human potential. Indeed, we may be able in the near future to change the very nature of man" [10(p4)] and "indeed we may be discussing a means for hurrying the evolutionary process." [23] In these respects, the generally uncritical attitude of the institutes differs from the more scientific approach to methods of treatment of brain damage of other professional groups, albeit in this area, as in the case of psychiatric treatment, opinions differ as to efficacy of therapeutic measures.

Since a well-controlled study which would settle all aspects of the controversy regarding effectiveness of the program of the institutes is probably impossible to design and carry out at this time, physicians and other professionals will have to weigh carefully the recommendation of such treatment.[16,31] Certainly it behooves all involved in work with handicapped children to be informed about the major therapeutic approaches. It is hoped that this brief exposition of the nature of the controversy may provide a basis for informed thought and discussion.

This investigation was supported by US Children's Bureau grant 416, personnel training project for handicapped children.

REFERENCES

1. Executive Board Statement, American Academy of Pediatrics, *Amer Acad Pediat News Letter* 16:1 (Dec 1) 1965.

2. *Statement of Executive Committee*, American Academy for Cerebral Palsy, Feb 15, 1965.

3. *The Doman-Delacato Treatment of Neurologically Handicapped Children, Information Bulletin*, United Cerebral Palsy Association of Texas, ND.

4. Institutes for the Achievement of Human Potential, Canadian Association for Retarded Children, *Ment Retard (Canada)*, fall, 1965, pp 27–28.

5. Thomas, E. W.: *Public Health and the Brain Injured*, Senate Committee on Appropriations, Labor-Health, Education, and Welfare Appropriations for 1966: Hearings Before the Subcommittee on Appropriations, 89th Congress, 2nd Session on H.R. 7765, U.S. Government Printing Office, June 18, 1965, pt 2, pp 2394–2399.

6. Crothers, B., and Paine, R. S.: *The Natural History of Cerebral Palsy*, Cambridge, Mass: Harvard University Press, 1959.

7. *A Summary of Concepts, Procedures and Organization*, Philadelphia: Institutes for the Achievement of Human Potential.

8. Doman, R. J., et al: Children With Severe Brain Injuries: Neurological Organization in Terms of Mobility, *JAMA* 174:257–262 (Sept 17) 1960.

9. Doman, G., and Delacato, C. H.: Train Your Baby to be a Genius, *McCall's*, March 1965, p 65.

10. *Statement of Objectives*, Philadelphia: Institutes for the Achievement of Human Potential.

11. LeWinn, E. B., et al: "Neurological Organization: The Basis for Learning," in Hellmuth, J. (ed): *Learning Disorders*, Seattle: Special Child Publications, 1966, vol 2, pp 48–93.

12. Maisel, A. Q.: Hope for Brain-Injured Children, *Reader's Digest*, October 1964, pp 135–140.

13. Knight, H.: A Fresh Start for Injured Brains, *Sunday Bull Mag* (Philadelphia), June 6, 1965, pp 5–7.

14. Masland, R. L.: Unproven Methods of Treatment, *Pediatrics* 37:713–714 (May) 1966.

15. *Institutes for the Achievement of Human Potential Bulletin*, September 1965, vol 10, p 46.

16. Holt, K. H., in discussion, Presentation of Systems of Therapy, 20th annual meeting of the American Academy for Cerebral Palsy, New Orleans, Dec 5, 1966.

17. *Instruction Sheet—The Harness*, Philadelphia: Institutes for the Achievement of Human Potential, 1964.

18. Doman, G., in discussion, Presentation of Systems of Therapy, 20th annual meeting of the American Academy for Cerebral Palsy, New Orleans, Dec 5, 1966.

19. Delacato, C. H.: *The Diagnosis and Treatment of Speech and Reading Problems*, Springfield, Ill: Charles C Thomas, Publisher, 1963; reviewed by Brown, J. R., *Neurology* 14:599–600 (June) 1964.

20. *The Doman-Delacato Development Mobility Scale*, Philadelphia: Institutes for the Achievement of Human Potential, 1960.

21. *The Doman-Delacato Profile and the Doman-Moran Graphic Summary*, Philadelphia: Institutes for the Achievement of Human Potential, 1963.

22. The Philosophy of the Treatment of Brain-Injured Children Utilizing Principles of Neurological Organization, Institutes for the Achievement of Human Potential, mimeographed, distributed at the 20th annual meeting of the American Academy for Cerebral Palsy, New Orleans, Dec 5, 1966.

23. Delacato, C. H.: *The Treatment and Prevention of Reading Problems: The Neuro-Psychological Approach*, Springfield, Ill: Charles C Thomas, Publisher, 1959.

24. Delacato, C. H.: *The Diagnosis and Treatment of Speech and Reading Problems*, Springfield, Ill: Charles C Thomas, Publisher, 1963.

25. Delacato, C. H.: *Neurological Organization and Reading*, Springfield, Ill: Charles C Thomas, Publisher, 1966.

26. Glass, G. V.: *A Critique of Experiments on the Role of Neurological Organization in Reading Performance*, Urbana, Ill: University of Illinois College of Education, October 1966.

27. Robbins, M. P.: A Study of the Validity of Delacato's Theory of Neurological Organization, *Exceptional Child* 32:517–523 (April) 1966.

28. Robbins, M. P.: A Reply (to a Letter to the Editor by Carl Delacato), *Exceptional Child* 33:200–201 (Nov) 1966.

29. Money, J.: "Dyslexia: A Postconference Review," in Money, J. (ed.): *Reading Disability: Progress and Research Needs in Dyslexia,* Baltimore: Johns Hopkins Press, 1962.

30. Belmont, L., and Birch, H. G.: Lateral Dominance, Lateral Awareness and Reading Disability, *Child Develop* 36:57–71 (March) 1965.

31. Bax, M., and MacKeith, R.: The Results of Treatment, editorial, *Develop Med Child Neurol* 9:1–2 (Feb) 1967.

** 37 **

Learning Disabilities: Substance or Shadow

ERNEST SIEGEL

Recent years have witnessed a growing practice among some educators of classifying certain children as "learning disabilities." This practice undoubtedly came about as a reaction to the many weaknesses inherent in the traditional medical/psychological basis for classification of exceptional children (e.g., "mentally retarded," "brain injured," "emotionally disturbed," etc.). It may also have evolved, in part, because of its implication to positive action (i.e., What do you do for a child suffering from specific learning disabilities? Why, you *teach* him, of course!). It may even be a result of the unconscious desire of educators to demonstrate the importance of their discipline to the psychological and medical professions.

Without systems and patterns, we have no order, only chaos. If man never learned to generalize, each situation would be unique, and one would never profit from experience. In any categorizing model, we conscientiously seek similarities, while deemphasizing individual differences, hence losing some information. It is possible, then, that any classification system will necessarily possess some limitations. That the practice of classifying children according to specific learning disabilities is thought to pos-

* From *Exceptional Children* 1968, *34,* pp. 433–438. Reprinted by permission of the author and the publisher.

sess merits can be seen by the increased literature devoted to that entity. The purpose of this article is to present some of its possible pitfalls.

PITFALLS OF TERM

1. The loose, somewhat open ended nature of the term lends itself to considerable confusion among the professionals regarding the definition of learning disabilities. Kirk and Bateman (1962) offered this definition:

A *learning disability* refers to a retardation, disorder, or delayed development in one or more of the processes of speech, language, reading, writing, arithmetic or other school subjects resulting from a psychological handicap caused by a possible cerebral dysfunction and/or emotional or behavioral disturbances. It is not the result of mental retardation, sensory deprivation, or cultural or instructional factors [p. 73].

Bateman (1964) repeated this theme by again defining learning disabilities as learning problems resulting from only two possible sources—minimal brain injury or emotional disturbances:

. . . his learning problems are not due to mental retardation, deafness, motor impairment, blindness, faulty instruction, etc. The children who do have special learning disabilities might be described by some clinicians as educationally retarded, autistic, dyslexic, perceptually handicapped, minimally brain-injured, emotionally disturbed, neurologically disorganized, dysgraphic, aphasic, interjacent, or word-blind, etc. [p. 167].

(It should be noted that, in the main, the foregoing adjectives are synonyms for, or examples of, minimally brain injured or emotionally disturbed.)

Capobianco (1964), however, in an apparent literal interpretation of learning disabilities, proclaims:

Hence, the modern special class for children with learning disabilities may be composed of youngsters who are brain-injured, emotionally disturbed, visually impaired, auditorially handicapped, intellectually subnormal, or suffering from some motor imbalance . . . [p. 187].

These contradictory views are not only confusing, but may actually hinder any effective educational program (e.g., screening, class placement, curriculum design, etc.) for the children diagnosed as learning disabilities. If there is any validity for this entity, then the professionals who use the term ought to agree on so basic an issue as to which medical diagnoses are included—or excluded!

2. In the swing, by some educators, towards educational rather than psychological and/or medical diagnosis, the neurologist's services are frequently downgraded. Capobianco (1964) states: "Only for cases requiring medical treatment, such as post encephalitis or tumors, would the referral to the neurologist be of subsequent help to the educator [p. 190]." Isn't it likely, though, that even in cases of minimal brain injury (the so called "Strauss child"), the neurologist's training and experience qualify him in

giving the educators and the parent recommendations relevant to the child's education? The neurologist might recommend drug therapy, visual training, communication therapy, or even psychotherapy, if necessary. He might make referrals to camps, after school play groups, or parent associations. He is usually involved in screening and placement, and can make suggestions for specific instructional techniques (e.g., tactual training, visuomotor activities, reduction of stimuli, etc.). Moreover, since education is an ongoing process and since the child is a growing and changing organism, periodic neurological assessment (as part of the generally accepted interdisciplinary approach) can enhance the child's educational experiences. In fact, a leading research neurologist (Cohn, 1964) has stated:

> Neurological practice by precise examination can point out the channels of relatively normal input systems, and thereby indicate the means whereby language can be introduced and developed in the most fruitful way possible for the individual [p. 185].

3. In the enthusiasm for dealing with learning disabilities, the cause of the learning problem is deemphasized. That this might be an inappropriate approach is suggested by various authorities. Even Kirk (Kirk and Johnson, 1951), who is one of the leading proponents of the learning disabilities school, at one time, said:

> When studying and teaching children with low intelligence, it is important for both clinicians and teachers to determine as far as is possible the cause of the intellectual defect in each child. The etiological factors involved sometimes determine the prognosis and educability of the child . . . it is possible that in the future many educational techniques will be based, at least in part, on the etiological factor. Already Strauss and Lehtinen have presented differential techniques for some children diagnosed as brain-injured . . . [p. 15].

Kephart (who is a contributor to the December, 1964 issue of *Exceptional Children*—an issue devoted entirely to the promotion of the practice of classifying children according to their specific learning disabilities, rather than on the basis of their medical or psychological diagnoses) at an earlier date (Strauss and Kephart, 1955), considered the classifying of a child as brain injured (definitely, a medical label) as paramount. In fact, he went so far as to advocate the diagnosing of minimal brain injury, even in the absence of corroborating neurological confirmation.

> We select a group of individuals who behave in a certain fashion. The vast majority of these individuals display definite signs of brain injury. About the few remaining, we do not know one way or the other. It would seem that we are justified in assuming that the factor which is causative in the vast majority is causative in the few remaining especially, in view of the fact that the common neurological examination is known not to be infallible. . . .
>
> The success which has been achieved in the training of brain injured children, identified by neurological or by functional signs, attests to the usefulness of . . . [this] reasoning in the diagnosis of brain injury [p. 42].

Myklebust (1964) also believes in the efficacy of categorizing the minimally brain injured (a medical term) as an educational entity:

In the population with minimal brain damage, it is the fact of adequate motor function, average to high intelligence, adequate hearing and vision, and adequate emotional adjustment together with a specific deficiency in ability to learn that constitutes the basis for homogeneity [p. 355].

Indeed, the learning disabilities enthusiasts often speak in favor of dropping the term "brain injury," inasmuch as all brain injured subjects do not exhibit similar behavioral and learning patterns (Barnet, Ellis, and Pryer, 1960). Is this position justified? Haven't professionals for decades recognized subdivisions within the category of minimal brain injury? Gellner (Epps, McCammon, and Simmons, 1958) recognized four distinct types of minimal brain injury (visual-somatic, visual-autonomic, auditory-somatic, and auditory-autonomic); this recognition of intragroup differences, far from forcing her to scrap the term brain injury, actually served as the basis for the establishment of a meaningful school program based both on these differences as well as on the overall constellation of brain injury.

Then, too, couldn't one argue with similar logic and with equal fervor to drop the term learning disabilities, since the children so classified may exhibit similar educational problems, but for different reasons and therefore very likely require different approaches?

Capobianco (1964) believes that classifying children as clinical entities amounts to pigeonholing. But isn't it just as much a case of pigeonholing to classify youngsters on the basis of their specific learning disabilities, regardless of the cause of their difficulties?

4. By emphasizing learning disabilities, the behavioral aspects of the child are often ignored. Yet Strauss and Lehtinen (1947) have said that brain injured children have perceptual, conceptual, and/or behavioral deficits. It is possible, then, for a brain injured child to manifest behavioral problems even in the absence of learning impairment. Indeed, many such children exist. In fact, there are emotionally disturbed children who, although manifesting aberrant behavior in many situations, manage to perform normally in school work. These children, too, need to be the concern of educators. Is a child's reading reversal more important to the teacher than his poor self concept? Is a child who scores low on motor encoding tasks more within the province of the educator than is the socially immature, impulsive, perseverative child?

5. Enthusiasm, while generally serving as a positive force, can sometimes be misleading (often, quite unintentionally). In the current scientific aura which has gripped education, there has emerged a penchant for finding answers—and we seek them with a vengeance! In this mood, it is quite easy to fall into the trap of believing that a particular approach offers more than it is capable of delivering. For example, The Illinois Test for Psycholinguistic Abilities and The Frostig Program for the Development of Visual Perception have remediation as well as diagnostic guidelines. But learning disability proponents often carry this diagnostic remediation

duo to an extreme, claiming—or perhaps implying—that for every learning disability, there is a known remedy. The error is obvious. It is only 1968 and we do not yet have all the answers. Certainly, at times, children still fail, even under most favorable educational circumstances (Miller, 1965). Then, too, this preoccupation with scientific programming ignores such variables as motivation, personality, stamina, and values; moreover, it makes no provision for the possibility that teaching (and even learning) may be very much of an art.

6. Carrying the thesis of learning disabilities supremacy to its logical conclusion, Capobianco (1964) calls attention to "the new movement to establish special classes for children with similar learning disabilities [p. 193]." This projected placement policy, then, seems to be the heart of the matter (since it constitutes the essential action emanating from the learning disabilities theory), and therefore warrants close examination.

The singular question that rises to the forefront is this: Do children with similar learning disabilities, regardless of cause, learn best by being placed together, and do they require the same remediation techniques? Authorities have generally answered this question negatively.

Myklebust (1954), in considering the educational needs of children suffering from the specific disability of lack of speech development, set up an effective differential diagnostic model which emphasized cause and extracted four distinct medical/psychological categories: peripherally deaf (physically handicapped), psychogenic deaf (emotionally disturbed), aphasic (brain injured), and auditory disorder due to mental deficiency. In explaining his position, he said:

> All language impaired children are not alike; all auditory disorders are not alike. Classification for educational purposes is essential. . . . Programs will develop primarily on the basis of classifying those with peripheral deafness, those with central nervous system damage, and those who are disturbed into separate groups. Educationally, those with peripheral deafness have a non-symbolic type of disorder, whereas those with aphasia do have a basic language disorder; the emotionally disturbed may not be impaired sensorially or symbolically. . . . Each of these groups has different learning and educational needs and the educator will find it most advantageous to develop programs according to their needs . . . [p. 28].

Another example of a specific learning disorder is the inability of some children to duplicate (by drawing) that which they see (e.g., a design, a pattern, a word, etc.). Bender's classical test is dedicated to the importance of not merely unearthing children who cannot copy designs, but of finding out why children are unable to copy designs (Koppitz, 1964). Indeed, many psychologists consider the Bender Gestalt an effective instrument for making differential diagnoses. Cruickshank, Bice, and Wallen (1957) also stressed the importance of differentiating the *cause* of this type of learning disorder:

> Although seldom stated explicitly, perceptual tasks assume competence in making the kind of response called for. For example, an individual who performs

poorly on a design reproduction task because of difficulty in "drawing" would not, on this evidence, be said to have a perceptual impairment. Perceptual differences imply differences in interpretation of stimuli [p. 8].

Even in such broad areas as hyperactivity, authorities have indicated that there is a need for educators to know why (i.e., medical/psychological causative factors) the child presents this specific behavioral and learning disorder. Whieldon (1962) differentiated psychogenic hyperactivity from organic hyperactivity, pointing out that: (a) psychogenic hyperactivity does not generally manifest itself until age ten or twelve, whereas organic hyperactivity generally exists from birth; (b) organically hyperactive children seem to get over their moods more quickly than do emotionally disturbed children, who tend to remain sullen or withdrawn for appreciably long periods of time; and (c) hyperactive brain injured children are basically emotionally labile, whereas the psychogenic hyperactives are essentially emotionally disturbed. Doyle (1962) advocated the identification and separation of three varieties of hyperkinetic children: organic hyperkinetic, emotionally disturbed, and the mentally retarded.

Even the most moderate definitional version of learning disabilities (i.e., problems in learning stemming from only two possible sources: brain injury or emotional disturbance) has been seriously questioned as a valid criterion for educational placement. Mesinger (1965) has challenged the practice of grouping brain injured and emotionally disturbed children in the same class. He points out that: (a) emotionally disturbed children, unlike brain injured children, often show highly developed defenses against learning and are intensely hostile towards teachers and other adults; (b) emotionally disturbed children often perceive themselves as different from brain injured children in their class, and this perceived deviancy then leads them to work against the efforts of the teacher and the class; and (c) structured environment is often advantageous to the brain injured child whereas frequent deviation from curriculum and flexibility are apt to be effective approaches when teaching emotionally disturbed children.

7. At times, even the staunch supporters of the learning disabilities classification system, if for no other reason than sheer communication, are forced to rely on terminology based upon medical/psychological entities. For a moment, Capobianco (1964) himself seems to disembark from the learning disabilities train to explain the essential differences between two medical/psychological categories:

> Unlike the consistently poor achievement characteristic of the mentally retarded child, the brain-injured child displays an irregular pattern of performance. He may be very proficient in reading and far below capacity in arithmetic. He may excel in verbal facility, but experience considerable difficulty in reasoning [p. 191].

School administrators continue to establish classes for minimally brain injured children, not for children designated as having specific learning disabilities. State Departments of Education continue to consider certification requirements for teachers of emotionally disturbed children, not for teachers of children with specific learning disabilities. It is hardly likely that funds can be raised for reading reversals, that legislation will concern itself with auditory vocal automatic disabilities, or that special classes will be established for design copying disorders!

Only recently have parent groups succeeded, to some extent, in their efforts to have legislators incorporate the term brain injured under the heading of physically handicapped, so that greater benefits might accrue to the child; what chance would the term learning disability have had?

Doctors continue to tell parents that their child is brain injured. If this diagnosis becomes subsumed under learning disabilities, how will parents know which services to seek, which literature to read, which parent association to join?

STRENGTHS OF TERM

The chief strength of the emphasis on learning disabilities would seem to be that it makes a renewed plea for good teaching—i.e., teaching based on an understanding of the child's needs as well as an awareness of what the specific task entails and a recognition of its sequential components. Seen in this light, the focus upon specific learning disabilities can, within the framework of (rather than by seeking to displace) the traditional medical/psychological categorization system, give some direction and emphasis to the special educators.

Another purpose served by the term learning disabilities is that it helped solidify various state chapters of parents of minimally brain injured children into a national group. A few years ago, when representatives from the various state chapters met for the purpose of consolidating into a national organization, they were unable to agree upon a common designation, each state having a different nomenclatural title. In the interest of compromise, the brain injured, perceptually handicapped, neurologically impaired, etc., were all welded into The National Association for Children with Learning Disabilities, Inc. In 1965, this association stated that its purpose is:

> to promote the education and general welfare of children and youth, with normal or potentially normal intelligence, who have learning disabilities of a perceptual, conceptual or coordinative nature or related problems [National Association for Children with Learning Disabilities, 1965].

This statement of purpose is printed on the association's official announcements. It seems that the parents are trying desperately to remember what the professionals told them the term learning disabilities means. Can the professionals do less?

REFERENCES

Barnet, C. D., Ellis, N. R., and Pryer, Margaret W. Learning in familial and brain-injured defectives. *American Journal on Mental Deficiency,* 1960, 64, 894–901.

Bateman, Barbara. Learning disabilities—yesterday, today, and tomorrow. *Exceptional Children,* 1964, 31, 167–177.

Capobianco, R. J. Diagnostic methods used with learning disability cases. *Exceptional Children,* 1964, 31, 187–193.

Cohn, R. The neurological study of children with learning disabilities. *Exceptional Children,* 1964, 31, 179–185.

Cruickshank, W. F., Bice, H. V., and Wallen, N. E. *Perception and cerebral palsy: a study in figure-background relationship.* Syracuse, New York: Syracuse University Press, 1957.

Doyle, P. J. A pediatric view of an overactive child in school. Paper read at the Department of Special Education, Board of Education, New York, 1962.

Epps, Helen O., McCammon, Gertrude B., and Simmons, Queen D. *Teaching devices for children with impaired learning.* Columbus, Ohio: The Parent's Volunteer Association, Columbus State School, 1958.

Kirk, S. L., and Bateman, Barbara. Diagnosis and remediation of learning disabilities. *Exceptional Children,* 1962, 29, 73–78.

Kirk, S. L., and Johnson, G. O. *Educating the retarded child.* Cambridge, Massachusetts: Houghton Mifflin, 1951.

Koppitz, Elizabeth M. *The Bender Gestalt test for young children.* New York: Grune and Stratton, 1964.

Mesinger, J. F. Forum: emotionally disturbed and brain damaged children—should we mix them? *Exceptional Children,* 1965, 32, 237–238.

Miller, Nandeen. Learning difficulties in a brain-injured child. In N. J. Long, W. C. Morse, and Ruth G. Newman (Editors), *Conflict in the classroom.* Belmont, California: Wadsworth, 1965. Pp. 430–434.

Myklebust, H. R. *Auditory disorders in children.* New York: Grune and Stratton, 1954.

Myklebust, H. R. Learning disorders: psychoneurological disturbances in children. *Rehabilitation Literature,* 1964, 25, 354–360.

National Association for Children with Learning Disabilities. Announcement of the Second National Conference of the National Association for Children with Learning Disabilities, Inc. Baltimore, Maryland: The Association, 1965.

Strauss, A. A., and Kephart, N. C. *Psychopathology and education of the brain-injured child, Volume II.* New York: Grune and Stratton, 1955.

Strauss, A. A., and Lehtinen, Laura E. *Psychopathology and education of the brain-injured child, Volume I.* New York: Grune and Stratton, 1947.

Whieldon, J. A. Medical implications. In E. C. Grover and Amy A. Allen, *A demonstration program for children in Ohio.* Columbus, Ohio: Department of Education, 1962. Pp. 17–25.

* PART SEVEN

General Problems and Issues

There is considerable dissatisfaction with current labelling and categorizing practices in special education. A primary concern is that the labels do not present guides to educational treatment. Indeed, in some cases they militate against effective education by forcing children into groups that are educationally inappropriate. The need for change is clear, but directions of the change are certainly hazy. Although a clear course has yet to be charted, a variety of intriguing and provocative writings treat this problem, two of which are reprinted in this volume.

The first article, By Lord ("Medical Classification of Disabilities for Educational Purposes—A Critique"), presents an interesting historical perspective on special labelling and categorizing practices. Lord writes, "We have established a fairly rigid grouping of children and . . . many of these labels are not very descriptive of the children in these groups as we find them today." Particular attention is given to forces that maintain current practices—federal legislation which provides support for teacher training based upon traditional categories, state support of programs based upon placement of students in disability categories, and the practice of having a class for each disability category. Finally, Lord looks at some newer models for dealing with the labelling and categorizing problem.

Undoubtedly, many of the problems and issues concerning the validity of various educational methods and procedures for educating exceptional children (e.g., whether deaf children should be taught speech reading or the language of signs, whether blind children should be taught using one procedure or another, etc.) or of various administrative arrangements (e.g., the merits and disadvantages of educating deaf, blind, and retarded children in day schools versus residential schools, etc.) stem from too simple a conception of the educational functioning of exceptional children. The search for a best administrative plan or a best teaching procedure for educating any single group of exceptional children is, at best, a fruitless venture. There simply is too much variation among exceptional children and among the environments in which they are educated to permit generalizations in these areas. Thus there is a certain appeal in a model such as that suggested by Quay ("The Facets of Educational Exceptionality: A Conceptual Framework for Assessment, Grouping, and Instruction") which gives attention to characteristics of individual pupils without regard to the more traditional labels and groupings. The objective is stated succinctly:

> What is needed to produce a truly effective special education is the development of a conceptual framework which permits the assessment of exceptional children on educationally relevant variables, their grouping according to similarities of dysfunction on these variables, and the development of a classroom teaching technology aimed at the correction of these deficiencies.

The Quay model draws heavily from social and behavioral science data already accumulated and thus has a certain empirical foundation. It must be added, however, that this model, and others, have yet to be tested in school settings.

The writings of both Lord and Quay can be interpreted as providing support for the widely held view that many current disability categories have little educational utility. Those subscribing to the view posited by Quay would emphasize—in contrast to current labelling practices—that any meaningful education of pupils, regardless of category of exceptionality, will come only from careful classification of students of a variety of highly specific educationally relevant variables and by remediation of specific areas of dysfunction in individual pupils. Indeed, approaches to education of exceptional children based on the assessment and remediation of specific areas of dysfunction represent an area of great current interest and activity in special education.

Such activities have not been accepted uncritically, however, as witnessed by the Mann and Phillips paper ("Fractional Practices in Special Education"). These authors contend that the fractional practices:

> . . . hold . . . some disturbing portents for special education in their often facile extrapolation of unsettled and controversial experimental and theoretical issues into educational and clinical dicta and practice; in their establishment of techniques of uncertain and, at best, limited validity, as prime diagnostic and treatment instruments; in their seeming disregard of the handicapped child as a unitary, though complex organism; in their approach to him as a collection of discrete and isolated functions.

Mann and Phillips also provide a critical assessment of "this new wave in special education" with the view toward providing "a corrective to the enthusiastic endorsements which are presently appearing in many quarters." Although critical of the practices the authors do not recommend that they be abandoned, only that they be accepted "tentatively and cautiously until they have appropriately proven their worth."

Reynolds, in "A Reaction," takes issue with the Mann and Phillips paper on several grounds, including their theoretical framework (classical measurement theory vs. decision theory), their failure to "place fractional approaches in better perspective" as they had promised, and their tendency to posit general versus fractional approaches as competitive. The debate does not end, however. Mann and Phillips, in "A Reply to Reynolds," play down the importance of the theoretical framework in their criticisms of fractional practices and elaborate upon their central concerns:

. . . (a) the practical value of tests which, with but limited empirical substantiation, are being applied with unwarranted diagnostic panache in special education and (b) the type of faculty training which is their consequence.

Minority group children placed in special education classes are doubly penalized. They are already the victims of discrimination—in many instances—because of their racial background, and the stigma of special education placement places an additional burden on them. Small wonder that in an increasing number of communities lawsuits are being instituted to remove minority children from, and prohibit their placement of in, special classes, particularly those for the mentally retarded and the emotionally disturbed. The arguments are heated indeed—witness the article by Johnson reprinted in this section ("Special Education and the Inner City: A Challenge for the Future or Another Means for Cooling the Mark Out?").

In a similar but broader article, Dunn ("Special Education for the Mildly Retarded—Is Much of It Justifiable?") presents a stinging condemnation of special education practices and procedures. While his remarks are directed primarily toward those classified as mildly retarded, they obviously apply as well to other categories of handicapped children.

In the final article, MacMillan ("Special Education for the Mildly Retarded: Servant or Savant") challenges Dunn on a number of points and suggests several alternate strategies for educating minority and mildly retarded students.

** 38 **

Medical Classification of Disabilities for Educational Purposes—A Critique

FRANCIS E. LORD

Public school classes for handicapped children are roughly 70 years old. However, it has been within the last 40 years that these classes have become a state program in the sense we view developments today. If one considers three types of classes for physically handicapped (deaf, blind, crippled) as a minimum for a state program, then we can say this stage was reached in the twenties in some midwestern and eastern states.

STATES COPIED PLANS

Practices in the first states were copied and applied to other states. What appeared to be a good idea in Michigan soon spread to Ohio. Even the wording of laws in the states resemble each other. Somewhat similar definitions of disabilities were used. So we have arrived at fairly uniform state practices and, along with it, fairly standardized vocabulary. For example, the subgroup referred to as *partially seeing* is a somewhat similar group in state practices. In this case a definition of the disability as set forth in the National Society for Prevention of Blindness has dominated our practices for 40 years. I am stressing the point that we have established fairly rigid grouping of children and I wish to imply now and explain later, that many of these labels are not very descriptive of the children in these groups as we find them today.

Also, states copies from each other the method of support used in financing special classes. The general principle of extra state compensation for districts which operated such classes became established very early—perhaps with our first classes at the turn of the century. No doubt this practice of finance was easy to establish since states at that time were accustomed to paying for education for children who were sent to residential schools.

* From *Fifth Annual Distinguished Lecture Series in Special Education*. Los Angeles: School of Education, University of Southern California, 1967, pp. 48–53. Reprinted by permission of the author and the publisher.

The state had already agreed to assuming an extra financial burden for such children. Financing, like most other practices in the field, was directly related to our labels or disability categories.

The establishment of state support for special classes naturally brought with it the question of eligibility for admission to the class. The state wanted to be sure that all money was spent upon children who really needed the service. Hence, we find our legal definitions of disabilities and the well defined laws relating to eligibility for admission to special classes. These definitions and the stated or implied admission standards became fairly uniform throughout the country. States contemplating legislation read the laws of other states and essentially incorporated the same provision in their proposals. Again the eligibility standards were tied to rather rigid disability categories. A child had to be "in the category" to get services.

Almost from the beginning of state programs in special education, laws were enacted to regulate the requirements relating to teacher preparation. With few exceptions, separate requirements were set up for each of the categories of children. In the early 20's it was clear that credential patterns would be directly related to type of special education classes. Today California, like most other states, prescribes a somewhat separate set of course requirements for each special education program. California has five separate education minors under the new credential pattern. Two special groups have escaped the credential pattern—gifted, and educationally handicapped. We will come back later to some suggestions relating to teacher preparation.

FEDERAL GOVERNMENT FOLLOWS SUIT

Recent Federal legislation which provides support for teacher training programs again are based upon our traditional categories and will be another force to perpetuate our structuring of the field. Today you don't get Federal funds for training teachers unless you can demonstrate that you have a highly specialized program of preparation for the particular category for which you are requesting support. This practice is understandable and a device to control the intent of legislation but it does leave us with another influence which contributes to the structuring of our field. A creative program which departs from tradition would not get support. How do growth and new practices become established under such regulations?

A CLASS FOR EACH GROUP

In the past, we were very particular about keeping our disability group separated in the school program. For example, blind and partially seeing children had separate programs according to the official plans. In practice there was often some mixing, however. One can question the wisdom of such separation especially in the smaller program. It seems obvious that an able resource teacher could handle a variety of special needs of children with varying degrees of visual limitations.

During the past 50 years we have learned a great deal about handicapped conditions of children. Let's look at some illustrations of how we increased our knowledge of children.

The cerebral palsied child is a good example. The medical subclassifications themselves are relatively new and in recent years new medical subgroups have been differentiated. The medical men who identified some of these subgroups are still active in the field.

At the level of classroom problems, we also have learned a lot about education and management. Elaborate teaching procedures have been developed to meet a variety of special needs. So we have made great progress in our knowledge of the CP child and how to serve him.

During the past 40 years we have admitted to the school thousands of cerebral palsied children who would have been excluded 25 years ago because no one knew enough about them to provide a training program. Special education teachers deserve much of the credit for this advance.

A second example of how we have grown in understanding of a disability may be drawn from the increase in the flexibility found in our administrative approaches within the school. For example, the evolution of services for some children from special classes to resource rooms to itinerant teaching is traceable in part to a development of a more realistic insight into the exact nature and needs of the child. We know these children can compete with normal children when they are given appropriate assistance.

ADEQUACY OF GROUP MEDICAL LABELS

Let's examine our categories (or group labels) we are using currently. We tend to use these labels as if they describe a group of children which have significant identical features from an instructional point of view. Look first at the group or classification commonly referred to as *crippled children*. Now we have an exceedingly heterogeneous group of children hiding under this label. Even the crippling condition itself varies greatly from child to child. For a child to have an impaired limb is quite different from having two useless arms. To have a seriously impaired speech as a component in the crippling complex is more significant than many other limitations that may be present. Certainly serious congenital disabilities are more significant than the group of acquired disabilities which respond readily to treatment. Now, to add further to the point being made, note that most disabilities found in the other categories (deafness, visual impairment, retardation) are common among crippled children. So we see the group label never describes the complex of educational problems which characterize the groups.

Let's take another group label: the deaf. On the surface this sounds like a very descriptive term. But when one examines the children in the sub-group, again one finds a heterogeneous lot.

The category of children with visual impairments has always been sub-divided into blind and partially seeing. But these terms have taken on new meaning as we worked with visually impaired children and learned a great deal about them. The 20/200 upper limit of visual acuity has been the practice for years for determining eligibility to special classes. We have known for a long time that these were serious limitations in the use of the arbitrary visual acuity rating. Visual acuity tells very little about a given child's performance in the classroom. We now know, for example, that about 80 per cent of so called blind children are able to read print in school. Of course, the actual amount of print reading done and the circumstances required for reading varies greatly with individual children.

These observations are so obvious that we need not dwell on them fur-ther. All teachers of handicapped children live with and work with a com-plex of disabilities regarding his (her) assignment. These observations are not discouraging to teachers. They know the facts of life and go about their work with strong motivation and show remarkable aptitude for handling a complex teaching assignment.

By way of summary, we can make the following observations:
1. Our categories are largely medical groupings which resulted from the practice of certifying the disability and controlling administration to fulfill legal requirements.
2. Reimbursement practices have tended to use these labels as a device for controlling instructional practices. Administratively the use of group categories is a very helpful tool.
3. On the other hand, we have learned so much about each disability group that we now see the educational limitations of the group labels we have in-herited.

SOME NEWER MODELS

Now let's turn to the other side of the question, what does the future hold for the common labels of the past?

Perhaps one should point out first that most special education teachers really never let the labels get in their way too much. They tended to treat the needs of each child and recognized that these needs varied. They recognized that handicapping is often a complex of limiting conditions and these conditions vary among cases. Consequently, they have adjusted their instructional programs accordingly. There are, however, some interesting signs of change on the horizon. Fortunately, special education is too new a field to become too rigid. We are always prepared for something different. The array of problems we deal with helps to keep us alive professionally.

You have noted that a new grouping of children has appeared lately under the label *learning disabilities*. This is a nice flexible label which comes to us from psychology and education. It is not a medical classification like most of our others. It really doesn't tell us what is wrong with the child, it merely says he has a problem in the area of learning. This label is coming to be used to encompass a variety of problems which are not related to retardation or to cultural deprivation. The term itself (learning disability) seems to be useful in describing a cluster of problems which are clearly recognized by teachers and others who work with children. There is little doubt that the label will prove useful and will continue to take its place along side our other terminology.

California has recently employed the term educational handicapped to refer to children who roughly belong to either of two early established categories-Emotionally Disturbed and Neurologically Impaired. Now again this term (E/H) departs from the medical categories which were developed for the physically handicapped.

One can go back 25 years and note the origin of the term "brain injured." While this term has definite neurological implications it was, however, a term which was related to a definite learning and behavior syndrome. The term when properly applied connoted definite problems of learning and adjustment. In this sense, it was somewhat more descriptive than our older labels.

So perhaps our language is changing and we are gradually acquiring terms which are somewhat more revealing, more descriptive of the child's limitations.

LOOK TO THE FUTURE

Let's look to the future and predict how we will structure our field, and how we will view our roles as educators of the handicapped. There are a number of implications—perhaps predications—we can draw from the 50 years of experience with handicapped children in our public schools.

Implication 1

Teacher preparation must be broadened to include a better knowledge of all the disabilities one finds in each major category.

Teachers of crippled children must know more about retardation, brain injury, emotional problems, speech problems, etc. Teachers of the deaf must be prepared to deal with problems relating to retardation, emotional adjustment, visual impairments.

Speech correctionists must be prepared to deal with the multitude of related problems they encounter in children such as retardation, emotional adjustment, giftedness.

All special teachers need a stronger foundation in the nature and instructional implications of all the major disabilities.

Certainly the rigid credential structure must be reviewed to determine whether the required training is really adequate for the types of classroom problems teachers actually encounter.

Implication 2

Our broader categories such as "learning disabilities" may in time absorb some of the other disability groups. We may even arrive at three of four groupings such as: Intellectual Retardation, Communication Disorders, Learning Disabilities, Visual Impairments.

Implication 3

It is possible that public schools which service handicapped children will in the future be less concerned with the medical diagnosis as a basis for classifying children and be more interested in grouping children in terms of specific educational and remedial needs. For example a school for crippled children, as we now know it, might be organized around special services to the children. The school would be a service centered school. Then the children would be scheduled into services in accordance with their needs. If such an organization prevailed in an institutional center, the center could readily accept any child who could find within the array of services a combination which might assist him in his habilitation. Now the services would be very functional and all would be manned for high level instruction and/ or remedial services. This cafeteria of services would need to be defined in terms of the special developmental needs of the children.

The approach suggested, as you may recognize, parallels that of a rehabilitation center in that the client comes with a set of well defined needs and in turn gets a specific combination of individual services. The center just faces up to the specific needs of the children and organizes itself in terms of these needs.

** 39 **

The Facets of Educational Exceptionality:
A Conceptual Framework for
Assessment, Grouping, and Instruction

HERBERT C. QUAY

It has long been recognized that current programs for exceptional children have at least two basic weaknesses. First, current grouping practices force the educator to deal with children who, while they may be somewhat homogeneous in certain intellectual, physical, and behavioral characteristics, are far from homogeneous in regard to abilities or disabilities crucial to classroom learning. One hardly need point out that cerebral palsy is a medical entity, mental retardation is a psychometric category, and emotional disturbance is a psychiatric-psychological classification.

At the same time, special education programs are rarely designed specifically to improve the academic competence of the child by the application of an instructional technology aimed at improving those aspects of the learning process in which the child may suffer a disability.

A number of approaches have been suggested as correctives. Stevens (1962) has given attention to the development of a taxonomy within the domains of educationally significant somatopsychological variation, educationally significant attributes of body disorders, and special educational procedures. His formulation is much broader than the approach which will be proposed here in that his concept involves many factors outside the classroom (e.g., finance, modification of laws, etc.) and is not based on an analysis of the learning process and the range of individual differences relative to it.

Dunn (1967), in calling into question the current relevance of much special educational practice, argues for the need for developing both tests to measure a child's learning ability (as separate from learning acquisition) and techniques to determine whether special methods or materials will be required to teach him. At the same time, Dunn calls for the design of se-

---

* From *Exceptional Children* 1968, *35*, pp. 25–32. Reprinted by permission of the author and the publisher.

quential step by step programs to move the child from where he is to where he needs to go.

> The first step would be to make a study of the child to find what behaviors he has acquired along the dimension being considered. Next, samples of a sequential program would be designed to move him forward from that point. In presenting the program, the utility of different reinforcers, administered under various conditions, would be investigated. Also, the method by which he can best be taught the material should be determined. Different modalities for reaching the child would also be tried. Thus, since the instructional program itself becomes the diagnostic device, this procedure can be called diagnostic teaching. Failures are program and instructor failures, not pupil failures. . . . This diagnostic procedure is viewed as the best available since it enables us to assess continuously the problem points of the instructional program against the assets of the child. After a successful and appropriate prescription has been devised, it would be communicated to the teachers in the pupil's home school and they would continue the procedure as long as it is necessary and brings results. From time to time, the child may need to return to the center for reappraisal and redirection [Dunn, 1968, pp. 12–13].

The conceptualization offered here attempts to provide a framework for accomplishing what Dunn feels is necessary in both assessment and remediation.

Blackman (1967) has also recently called for the development of a school relevant taxonomy of the psychoeducational characteristics of the mentally retarded to go hand in hand with the description of school tasks "in terms of what psychological and educational 'muscle' a child requires in order to approach that task with a reasonable probability of success [p. 8]."

This paper is clearly directed toward a statement of an educationally relevant taxonomy, at least partially in the belief that the learning parameters to be described are involved in the learning of *any* school relevant task. While it is clear that certain modalities and functions within the framework to be proposed below may be differentially weighted as to their involvement in different tasks, it is not clear that any task can be learned with maximal effectiveness without manipulation of the parameters to be described below.

Finally, the author has suggested thorough study of children grouped according to current practices in terms of their learning characteristics and the peculiar demands which these might make on the instructional process in the hope that some educationally relevant homogeneities might appear (Quay, 1963, in press). While this approach offers some promise and it does not, at least at the outset, require regrouping of children along lines not currently acceptable by custom or by statute, its long range promise is not nearly as good as a more radical approach.

What is needed to produce a truly effective special education is the development of a conceptual framework which permits the assessment of exceptional children on educationally relevant variables, their grouping according to similarities of dysfunction on these variables, and the development of a classroom teaching technology aimed at the correction of these deficiencies.

■ FIGURE 1   *The Parameters, Modalities, and Functions of Classroom Learning*

	PARAMETERS												
	Input				Response				Reinforcement				
	FUNCTIONS				FUNCTIONS				FUNCTIONS				
MODALITIES	Acuity	Orientation	Perception	Failure to Store	Dexterity	Orientation	Organization	Delay	Acuity	Orientation	Effect	Delay	Amount	Ratio
Visual														
Auditory														
Tactile														
Motor														
Verbal														
Primary														
Social														
Information														

The elements of such a system should be those variables related to the learning process *which can be manipulated in the classroom.* While hypothetical constructs may be of value in the construction of theoretical explanations of learning, these are inferred from stimulus response relationships and they cannot be directly manipulated. While defective auditory association may help explain some facet of poor performance in the learning process, only the variables of stimulus, response, and reinforcement can be manipulated to improve auditory association. At least at the outset, then, assessment and remediation should be tied very closely to those facets of the classroom instructional process which can be varied in a systematic way.

The framework which is offered in this paper consists of a set of functions as related to certain modalities involved with the learning parameters of input, response, and reinforcement.

The interaction of these three components provides various areas in which a child may be said to have learning problems or to suffer a dysfunction of ability. Figure 1 presents this framework schematically. There are 41 cells, each of which represents the point of interaction of a function and modality with a parameter of learning; each of these cells also represents a possible condition by dysfunction which can require some intervention (remedial technology) for its remediation.

DEFINITION OF THE FUNCTIONS

Acuity. It should be obvious that problems of sensory acuity may limit or obviate the use of certain receptive channels for stimulus presentation and for the presentation of reinforcing stimuli. We recognize that sensory acuity may be a complex matter, as in the case of the child who has a hearing loss for only certain frequencies in the speech range. However, poor acuity itself may be remediable to some extent under certain circumstances since acuity relates to the use of the modality for learning (Barraga, 1964).

Dexterity. The response counterpart of acuity is the ability, facility, and accuracy with which the child can make responses. The inability of the athetoid cerebral palsied child to make fine motor responses clearly precludes the attachment of such responses to *any* stimulus until the response mechanism itself can be improved.

Orientation. This refers to the basic necessity for the child to be oriented toward the stimulus in order for a response to the stimulus to occur. The hyperactive child who does not even look at his worksheet obviously cannot perceive its contents no matter how good his skills in the perceptual area. Neither can the child respond without orientation; he cannot write the spelling word on the page while looking out the window, nor can he respond orally to a question while talking to his neighbor. Finally, a reinforcer cannot operate unless orientation towards it occurs.

Perception. Orienting to (looking at) a blackboard and perceiving its content are not the same, even though orientation must precede perception. Perceptual differentiation (e.g., discriminating a B from a D) is dependent on both orientation and on the ability to attend to the relevant aspects of the stimuli to be differentiated. This ability to attend to the relevant dimensions of a stimulus is what is meant by perception. For example, studies of the mentally retarded have demonstrated that once they can be taught to attend to the relevant elements of the stimulus presentation, they are able to make the necessary discriminations as well as normals (Zeaman and House, 1963). Perceptual failure may occur due to figure ground reversal, as well as to apparent anomalies in the physical perceptual apparatus.

Organization. On the response side, it can be observed that certain children cannot bring together the components necessary to make a response. For example, some children have difficulty with the integration of the motor and the verbal systems necessary in describing an activity being carried out motorically.

Failure of Storage. This refers to the failure of the stimulus to be retained by the subject so that the stimulus response connection can be made and/or recalled. Ellis (1963), for example, proposes that the retarded suffer from a failure of the stimulus to leave a trace within the organism. Methods can be used to increase the probability that the information will be stored (Adams, 1967).

Delay of Response. Some children may be observed to be unable to inhibit the response to the initial element of a stimulus sequence which then interferes with the ability to respond correctly to the total sequence. The ability to delay in responding appropriately is clearly crucial to effective learning.

Effect. This refers to the capacity of a reinforcer of a certain type or quality to be actually reinforcing. Studies have shown, for example, that knowledge of results is relatively less effective as a reinforcer with lower class children as compared to middle class children (Terrell, Durkin, and Wiesley, 1959; Zigler and Kanzer, 1962), and that social reinforcement is very weak in its effect on hyperaggressive, unsocialized adolescents and young adults (Johns and Quay, 1962; Levin and Simmons, 1962). The failure of a child to respond to social reinforcers can present a serious problem in the classroom.

Delay of Reinforcement. While it has been well demonstrated that immediate reinforcement is most effective in promoting learning, the nature of school organization and society in general requires that some delay in receiving rewards be tolerated with learning still taking place. Research has shown that children differ in the ability to tolerate delay with variations related to both intellectual (Ross, Hetherington, and Wray, 1965) and personality (Mischel, 1966) dimensions.

Amount. The amount and quality of reinforcement necessary to fixate a stimulus response sequence can vary among children (Witryol, Tyrrel, and Lowden, 1965) and can present an educational problem if extremely large rewards are necessary to promote learning. The child who responds only to large doses of attention and praise makes heavy demands on teacher time.

Ratio. It is well known that the frequency with which the correct response is followed by a reinforcer can have a noticeable effect on acquisition and retention. In the classroom it is rare that every correct response can be followed by a reinforcer; children must learn to make a number of correct responses to receive a single reward. Children who do not respond to less than a 100 percent ratio of reinforcement clearly create a special problem.

THE MODALITIES

Sensory Modes. In the main, information reaches the classroom child through the tactile, auditory, and visual modes. Obviously, serious impairment in the function of any one or more of these modalities will require special programing of the stimulus display. In addition, acuity impairment will require modification in the extent to which reinforcing stimuli can be delivered via the impaired modality.

Response Modes. All of the responses of the child can be seen as occurring through either the motor and/or the verbal mode. Impairment of the response functions of either mode will necessitate some remedial approach. For example, the child with expressive aphasia would be said to be handicapped in the dexterity function of the verbal response mode.

Reinforcement Modes. Rewards in the classroom are generally of the primary sensory (food or money—some preferred sensory or motor activity), social (teacher praise, peer approval), or information (knowledge of results) type. The author recognizes that it can be argued that knowledge of results is basically a social reinforcer, but since response to knowledge of results sometimes does not serve as a reinforcer to children who are responsive to direct praise, it has been kept as a separate mode. Failure of any of the reinforcement functions for any of the three modes will usually require some remediation before the child can function most effectively in the regular classroom.

ASSESSMENT

The framework offered above provides a clear-cut guide for the assessment of the exceptional child in terms of learning functions relevant to the classroom. Each of the 41 cells in Figure 1 represents a behavior which can be measured to yield a quantitative estimate for a given child. Measurement will need to be accomplished through direct observation of learning behavior (e.g., orientation, organization) (a) through the use of laboratory type procedures and "miniature situation" tests (e.g., effect and delay in reinforcement), (b) by means of psychometric procedures (e.g., verbal dexterity), and (c) through the employment of tests of sensory (acuity) and motor (dexterity) skills. While it is doubtful that truly adequate measures currently exist for the assessment of the behaviors of all 41 cells (failure to store is perhaps the best example), such tests can be devised because each cell is defined by some observable behavior or behaviors. In fact, such tests would make a much greater contribution to education—and psychology—than the majority of those devised to measure hypothetical constructs.

The framework, as a diagnostic and remedial guide, also has certain properties of a scale. For example, given a complete lack of acuity in a sensory modality, diagnostic study relative to any of the other functions for either input, response, or reinforcement need not be carried out. Given a serious failure of orientation, it is likely that additional diagnostic study would not produce valid results since lack of orientation precludes the operation of the other functions. At the same time, attempts at remediation of perception without correction of orientation failure would be futile. In the reinforcement parameter, questions of magnitude, delay, and ratio are irrelevant if the child fails to respond to a certain type reinforcer. For the child who does not find teacher praise rewarding, manipulation of its quantity and timing are not likely to be effective until his failure to respond to such social reinforcement can be corrected.

DEVELOPMENT OF A CLASSROOM TECHNOLOGY

An additional feature of the conceptual scheme is that it offers a guide to the development of a classroom technology for the modification of the various dysfunctions of the learning process. Since the variables of the framework are closely tied to the empirical facts of learning, procedures designed to facilitate the various functions which have been developed in the laboratory are now directly relevant to the special classroom. There is literature, for example, on the effect of various reinforcers on orientation in the classroom (Patterson, Jones, Whittier, and Wright, 1965; Quay, Werry, McQueen, and Sprague, 1966). Suggestions have also been made, based on experimental evidence, as to how the engineering of the stimulus display can favorably influence organization behavior (Scott, 1966). Many, many other examples could be cited. Further, since the functions of each of the 41 cells are defined behaviorally, they are open to experimentation in regard to remedial methodologies.

GROUPING FOR INSTRUCTION

The use of the proposed framework provides a basis for grouping children according to their special needs in terms of educationally relevant variables rather than according to characteristics related to hypothetical causes (e.g., minimal cerebral dysfunction) or according to variables of concern to fields other than that of education. Thus, children can be grouped because they have orientation defects which can be ameliorated by a particular classroom technology, or because they have defects in their capacity to respond to social reinforcers which can also be corrected. What is likely is that defects in a number of the functions will be correlated so that, for example, a group of children could be formed and placed in a classroom with a program designed to correct orientation, response delay, and reinforcement effect deficiencies, while another classroom might be directed toward helping children with problems in perception, organization, and verbal dexterity.

Ability and Disability. No doubt motivated at least somewhat by a despair of remediating disabilities, there has been considerable concern with capitalizing on abilities—"teach through strength rather than to weakness." While it may be obvious that in certain instances this can occur (e.g., the use of intact auditory modalities instead of impaired visual ones for both input and reinforcement), care must be exercised to see that intact but nonequivalent functions are not substituted in the hopes of circumventing disabled ones. Capitalization on unique storage ability (memory) cannot compensate for orientation failure; in fact, storage cannot occur in the total absence of orientation. Neither is it clear that reliance on unimpaired auditory storage, for example, will not leave holes in the child's achievement that would not be there had the capacity for visual storage been increased by judicious manipulation of the stimulus display.

At the same time it should be recognized that there is likely to be some point at which the disability is so severe that the function in question must be bypassed, either because of absolute necessity or because of cost efficiency considerations.

CURRENT CATEGORIES AND THE PROPOSED CONCEPTUAL FRAMEWORK

It is tempting to compare the profiles of hypothetical children who might be said to typify current diagnostic groups. This is difficult, however, since the abilities of many such children are not clearly understood in terms of the learning relevant functions of Figure 1. For example, the extent to which the retarded child suffers a failure in perception and/or storage is certainly not fully understood. One must also recognize that some cerebral palsied children may have a handicap in the perceptual area while others

■ FIGURE 2   The Parameters, Modalities, and Functions of Learning and the Characteristics of Four Groups of Exceptional Children

						PARAMETERS										
		Input				Response					Reinforcement					
		FUNCTIONS				FUNCTIONS					FUNCTIONS					
	Acuity	Orientation	Perception	Failure to Store	Dexterity	Orientation	Organization	Delay	Acuity	Orientation	Effect	Delay	Amount	Ratio
Visual		MR BD MCD	CP MR MCD	MR										
Audi tory		MR BD MCD	CP MR MCD	MR										
Tactile		MR BD MCD	CP MR MCD	MR										
Motor					MR MCD CP	MR BD MCD	MR CP MCD	MR BD MCD						
Verbal					MR BD	MR BD MCD	MR	BD						
Primary										MR MCD		MR BD		BD
Social										MR MCD	BD	MR BD		
Information										MR MCD	BD	MR BD		

(MODALITIES)

Legend: MR — Mentally Retarded
BD — Behavior Disorder
MCD — Minimal Cerebral Dysfunction
CP — Cerebral Palsy

may not; some emotionally disturbed children suffer from orientation failure while others clearly do not.

With these problems in mind, Figure 2 has been prepared, indicating the functional areas in which certain of the current categories of exceptional children appear to experience difficulties. It is apparent that the profiles of particular groups, assuming that their classical characteristics are in fact correct, are quite similar and thus even now might be effectively combined for certain remedial procedures. For example, orientation dysfunction in both input and response parameters appears to be common to children in the traditional categories of mental retardation, conduct (acting out) behavior disorders, and minimal cerebral dysfunction. Since this is a dysfunction at a basic level, its remediation must occur before one needs to be concerned with dysfunction of perception, organization, delay, and effect. Thus, children of all three categories might be placed *first* in a classroom with a remedial technology directed at improving orientation. The children with minimal cerebral dysfunction, the cerebral palsied, and the mentally retarded could then be grouped in a classroom oriented toward providing remediation for perception deficits, while the conduct problem children would next require a program aimed at correcting dysfunctions in the reinforcement parameter.

CONCLUSION

The conceptual framework offered here has a number of advantages. In drawing upon the empirical facts of the learning process as they operate in the classroom, educationally relevant functions on which children differ widely are made the basis for diagnostic assessment, instructional grouping, and teaching technology. The current state of the art of diagnosis for educational purposes can clearly be improved by attention to these functions and by the development and refinement of measures of them. These same functions can also become the basis for a technology of instruction which can draw on laboratory procedures for effective stimulus display, response control and shaping, and reinforcer manipulation.

Obviously, we do not have a finished product. Additional research in learning will probably reveal functions which will have to be added to the scheme. Perhaps such research will also demonstrate that some of the current functions are special cases of more comprehensive parameters or are altogether irrelevant. Better diagnostic tools are also needed, especially in such functions as perception, effect of reinforcement, and failure to store.

Finally, one cannot help but speculate on the degree to which the entire educational process might be improved if the technology of teaching were directed toward the maximum utilization by normal children of their abilities in the various functions.

REFERENCES

Adams, J. A. *Human memory.* New York: McGraw-Hill, 1967.

Barraga, N. *Increased visual behavior in low vision children.* New York: American Foundation for the Blind, 1964.

Blackman, L. The dimensions of a science of special education. *Mental Retardation,* 1967, **5**, 7–11.

Dunn, L. M. Special education for the mildly retarded—is much of it justifiable? *Exceptional Children,* 1968, **35**, 5–22.

Ellis, N. R. The stimulus trace and behavioral inadequacy. In N. R. Ellis (Ed.), *Handbook of mental deficiency.* New York: McGraw-Hill, 1963. Pp. 134–158.

Johns, J. A., & Quay, H. C. The effect of social reward on verbal conditioning in psychopathic and neurotic military offenders. *Journal of Consulting Psychology,* 1962, **26**, 217–220.

Levin, G. R., & Simmons, J. J. Response to food and praise by emotionally disturbed boys. *Psychology Reports,* 1962, **11**, 539–546.

Mischel, W. Theory and research on the antecedents of self-imposed delay of reward. In B. A. Maher (Ed.), *Progress in experimental personality research.* Vol. 3. New York: Academic Press, 1966. Pp. 85–132.

Patterson, G. R., Jones, R., Whittier, J., & Wright, M. A behavior modification technique for the hyperactive child. *Behavior Research and Therapy,* 1965, **2**, 217–226.

Quay, H. C. Some basic considerations in the education of emotionally disturbed children. *Exceptional Children,* 1963, **30**, 27–31.

Quay, H. C. Dimensions of problem behavior and educational programming. In P. S. Graubard (Ed.), *Children Against Schools.* New York: Follett, in press.

Quay, H. C., Werry, J. S., McQueen, M. M., & Sprague, R. L. Remediation of the conduct problem child in the special class setting. *Exceptional Children,* 1966, **3**, 390–397

Ross, L. E., Hetherington, M., Wray, N. P. Delay of reward and the learning of a size problem by normal and retarded children. *Child Development,* 1965, **36**, 509–518.

Scott, K. G. Engineering attention: Some rules for the classroom. *Education and Training of the Mentally Retarded,* 1966, **1**, 125–129.

Stevens, G. D. *Taxonomy in special education for children with body disorders: The problem and a proposal.* Pittsburgh: University of Pittsburgh, Department of Special Education and Rehabilitation, 1962.

Terrell, G., Jr., Durkin, K., & Wiesley, M. Social class and the nature of the incentive in discrimination learning. *Journal of Abnormal and Social Psychology,* 1959, **59**, 270–272.

Witryol, S. L., Tyrrell, D. J., & Lowden, L. M. Development of incentive values in childhood. *Genetic Psychology Monographs,* 1965, **72**, 201–246.

Zeaman, D., & House, B. J. The role of attention in retardate discrimination learning. In N. R. Ellis (Ed.), *Handbook of mental deficiency.* New York: McGraw-Hill, 1963. Pp. 159–223.

Zigler, E., & Kanzer, P. The effectiveness of two classes of verbal reinforcers on the performance of middle and lower class children. *Journal of Personality,* 1962, **30**, 157–163.

40

Fractional Practices in Special Education: A Critique

LESTER MANN AND WILLIAM A. PHILLIPS

Recent interest and effort in special education have been directed towards the development of techniques designed to fractionate global or molar areas of behavior and functioning for evaluation and educational purposes (Bateman, 1964). A number of new assessment and testing procedures have been recommended for or developed to delineate specific areas and subareas of functioning and malfunctioning in perception, intellective performance, communication, etc. (Frostig, Lefever, and Whittlesey, 1961; McCarthy and Kirk, 1961; Ayres, 1962; Money, 1962; Silver and Hagin, 1964; Beck, Rubin, Llorens, Beall, and Mottley, 1965). Special approaches have been programed to develop potentialities and remediate inadequacies therein (Frostig and Horne, 1964; Llorens, Rubin, Braun, Beck, Mottley, and Beall, 1964; Silver and Hagin, 1965).

Such fractional approaches are indeed laudable in their attempts to provide greater structure and specificity to the sprawling field of special education practice. They hold, however, some disturbing portents for special education: in their often facile extrapolation of unsettled and controversial experimental and theoretical issues into educational and clinical dicta and practice; in their establishment of techniques of uncertain and, at best, limited validity, as prime diagnostic and treatment instruments; in their seeming disregard of the handicapped child as a unitary, though complex, organism; in their approach to him as a collection of discrete and isolated functions.

The writers hope that an overview of this new wave in special education, and a critical assessment of it, may be useful as a corrective to the enthusiastic endorsements which are presently appearing in many quarters (Bateman, 1964; Gallagher, 1964; Stevens, 1965).

OVERVIEW

In attempting to obtain historical perspective of the present fractional trend in special education, one is impressed firstly by the fact that attempts to

* From *Exceptional Children* 1967, *33*, pp. 311–317. Reprinted by permission of the senior author and the publisher.

fractionate behavior, whether under the rubric of soul, or psyche, or other hypothetical constructs, appear to characterize man's efforts to understand man, from the four element theory of Empedocles and Anaxagoras through Guilford's (1956b) multidimensional conceptualization of intelligence.

Special education has its unique history of fractional practices. Indeed, much of what has been termed its clinical approach and what the writers less euphemistically assess as fractional appear as revivals and occasionally as transmogrifications of very old techniques, indeed. The work of such pioneers as Itard, Seguin, and Decroly, whose training approaches emphasized sensory and motor training, appears in many instances to have been directly, if not literally, translated into modern day special education practice.

In attempting to understand the current appeal of fractional approaches to special education, it becomes apparent that they are very much an expression of the present day scientific zeitgeist, with its emphasis upon discrimination and manipulation of precisely delineated variables. They represent an extension of modern behavioral and educational sciences which have been increasingly emphatic in recent years in their attempts to dissect behavior, stimulated by sophisticated multivariate approaches, by new developments in experimental manipulanda, and by computer accommodation. They are a reflection of the labors of the test makers of our day who increasingly work toward differential evaluation of abilities and achievement in testing programs. They express, additionally, the growing interest and participation of the physician in special education with his tradition of differential diagnosis, and of the clinical psychologist with his orientation towards test analysis.

Finally, the very real, cogent, and compelling realities of helping the handicapped child appear to have directed special education's present orientation to fractional practices. It has become increasingly clear that classification of handicapped children according to diagnosis provides insufficient and inadequate guidelines for educational and remedial practices. It has become additionally clear that there are vast areas of communality and similarity in the needs, problems, and dysfunctioning of handicapped children with diverse diagnoses (Bryant, 1964; Gallagher, 1964). As a consequence, attention has quite necessarily been directed to the "dysfunctions" themselves and to the diagnostic and educational techniques that might be used in their remediation. The new fractional approaches appear to offer manifest answers in these respects. It is for this reason, lest special education overcommit itself, that a critical examination of fractional diagnosis and training is needed.

The present criticisms of the fractional approaches are promulgated on both epistemological and empirical grounds. They are not intended to be fully exhaustive but rather to highlight certain significant issues. A number of these are inextricably entwined and must be considered as but different facets of the same problem. However, they will be categorized under different headings for convenience of exposition.

ASSESSMENT OF SPECIFIC ABILITIES

The basic assumption underlying the development and utilization of fractional approaches is that human behavior may be successfully separated, as it were, into specific entities, units, or functions, these being essentially independent and capable of being individually evaluated and/or exercised. Advocates of fractional approaches appear to be proceeding as if this assumption were a fully demonstrated and effective operational viability (Bateman, 1964; Lindsley, 1965).

The evidence to date hardly justifies their position. The writers do not question the possibilities of effective delineation through conceptual and experimental operations, or statistical manipulation of certain behavioral specificities. We may accept on conceptual and heuristic grounds that separation of hue from intensity, pitch from loudness, pain from heat, sweet from sour—these representing fractional separations of the more molar behaviors of sight, hearing, touch, and taste. Within limitations, such fractional behaviors may be precisely and operationally anchored in objective realities. They are associated, in reasonably veridical fashion, with concrete environmental events. Their variations can be validated through the latter.

However, the picture is not as sanguine when we turn to the higher or more complex functions such as are subsumed under perception, intelligence, language—behaviors with which the special education fractionator is specifically concerned. While certain gross and general ability areas can be differentiated and assessed effectively (McNemar, 1942; Cropley, 1964; McNemar, 1964), one finds but little convincing empirical substantiation for the claimed specificities of such widely heralded tests as the ITPA or Frostig approaches.

It is important to note that the failure of special educators to clearly and effectively establish useful specificities through their assessment techniques is by no means unique to them. It is a continuing and pervasive problem for psychological and educational measurement (Guilford, 1956a). This is dramatically apparent when we examine the areas of intelligence and achievement assessments, ones with long histories of assiduous endeavor in respect to fractionation practices. It is in these areas, where voluminous research has been carried out, that we might most likely expect to find breakthroughs. The practical consequences of such endeavors, however, have been surprisingly limited. Despite repeated efforts to establish "primary mental abilities" and subareas of achievement functioning, measures of intelligence tapping g rather than s still remain the most meaningful assessors and predictors of performance.

In respect to school achievement, for example, a survey of efforts with the DAT, a possessor of 4096 validity coefficients, leads to the conclusion that "better predictions are possible via old fashioned general intelligence tests than through multi-test batteries" (McNemar, 1964, p. 875). And in this context, it is worth remembering that initial attempts at intellectual and performance mensuration through fractional methods, such as those of Cattell, Jastrow, and Galton, were without useful consequence (Terman, 1916). It remained for Binet, with his global appreciation of man's functioning capacities, to shotgun a test approach that, with all its failings, remains the "standard" of intellectual assessment.

If the above is the case for sophisticated measurement approaches in areas which provide reasonably clearcut opportunities to establish criteria and carry out normative, validation, and predictive studies, it behooves the special educator, who is proceeding on far more uncertain ground, to tread lightly in his assumptions of specificity. While human behavior appears complex indeed, recognition of that complexity does not represent a solution to its measurement. The day when abilities may be precisely articulated is still not with us. Certainly not in special education. For the latter, the concept of general ability may well be a myth (Lindsley, 1965), but it has proven to be a most serviceable one. In assessing and predicting behavior, the small g stands for goodness.

RELATION OF FRACTIONAL TESTS TO RESPONSE VARIABLES

The special education fractionator appears to presume that the behaviors he assesses through his tests and other procedures are related directly to basic events, processes, variables in the individuals being assessed; that in fact their tests and measures tap and mensurate these processes, and that the results obtained can be used to effectively order individuals ipsatively or normatively in accordance to the quality, effectiveness, or amount possessed of the latter. Thus, one child is tested and found to be better in establishing object constancy than another; another individual is better in auding than he is in encoding; one child has more firmly established laterality.

How does the special education fractionator know what his tests are measuring, assuming for the time being that the latter are capable of the fractional analyses he claims for them. Unless he wishes to resort to an outmoded and sterile operationism, he will have to take the arduous route of construct validity (Cronbach and Meehl, 1955; Campbell and Fiske, 1959) to legitimately presume that auditory decoding, spatial ability, figure ground perception, or what have you, are properly being assessed by his techniques. This the special education fractionator does not appear to have effectively done. Retitling standard types of intelligence test items as has been done in the ITPA does not constitute construct validation, nor does Frostig's quasiscientific utilization of constructs from areas of experimental psychology or the extrapolation of labels assigned to the factor analyst's products as we find in Ayres' tests.

Many fractionators appear to have made the stimulus error, in their proceedings, of directly identifying test responses and the processes they putatively represent with the names of the tests which elicit and supposedly measure them—an exercise in tautology, not scientific procedure. They have proceeded still further along the path of error by implicitly reifying the response variables associated with their tests into separate abilities and functions in ways unfortunately reminiscent of faculty psychology. The consequences of reification are all too blatantly on view in such concretizations as the IQ to encourage their multiplication in fractional test practices.

TRAINING OF SPECIFIC FUNCTIONS

Special education, being a training oriented discipline, is concerned first and foremost with programs of teaching and management. It is because of this that the fractional practices have been so well received in special education. Rather than diffuse, ill defined programs of general teaching, the fractionators offer techniques to specifically train and remediate areas of weakness and impairment (Bateman, 1964).

Unfortunately, the overwhelming bulk of evidence from investigations in learning and transfer of training does not support the effectiveness of training procedures directed towards the formal training of abilities in the ways intended by many of the fractional approaches. Specific skills may certainly be trained and are, continually, in a vast variety of educational endeavors. It would be entirely inappropriate to equate success of this variety with the ancient and once discredited faculty psychology that appears to be renascent in many of the recent fractional approaches. Shape constancy, for example, is a multiple problem (Epstein and Park, 1963), not a specific mental process to be exercised as Frostig might suggest.

Much of the research in child development contraindicates the value of the vertical, incremental building block type of training recommended by fractionators. Behavior apparently develops from diffuse states to those of articulation and delineation (Gibson, 1963). Its development may also be discontinuous (Piaget and Inhelder, 1956). It is certainly hierarchical from many standpoints (Haynes and Sells, 1963) and a dynamic interactional process (Klapper, 1965). Most fractional training approaches appear far too simple in conception and execution to do justice to its complexity.

EVIDENCE FOR FRACTIONAL APPROACHES

It would be unfair and inaccurate to give the impression that proponents of the fractional approaches have not marshaled evidence to support their positions. Considerable effort has been devoted to substantiating and validating such techniques. Can it be sustained upon critical examination?

Factor Analysis. Factor analysis appears to have been one of the major impetuses to fractional practices, and a bulwark of support (Guilford, 1961). However, it would be incorrect to presume that factor analysis of and by itself can prove anything (McNemar, 1964), or that its methods and implications and values have been firmly established and agreed upon by behavioral scientists (Horst, 1950; Riegel and Riegel, 1962; Thompson, 1962; Coan, 1964; Overall, 1964; Smedslund, 1964; Vernon, 1965). Factors are statistical artifacts which may or may not manifest relevant relationships to significant behavioral variables. Such relationships have not been satisfactorily demonstrated in special education for such procedures as the Ayres Space Test.

Validity Studies. Proponents of fractional measurement can point out legitimately that their techniques have been demonstrated to differentiate different types of handicaps one from the other and in comparison with normal groups (Sievers, McCarthy, Olson, Bateman, and Kass, 1963). However, their validation efforts are typically of the concurrent validity variety, the limitations of which are well discussed by Yates (1966). They appear to have disregarded the problem of base rates (Meehl and Rosen, 1955). And in any case it must be questioned whether their techniques improve in the diagnoses of such groups over and above the results of many other tests of such conditions (Safrin, 1964; Holroyd and Wright, 1965); this they have not demonstrated.

However, the special education fractionator also professes to differentially assess functions and dysfunctions. Our critique has already found their efforts insufficient and unconvincing. Several additional points can be made in respect to this particular and most important issue. Firstly, it would be in error to assume that differential patterns revealed through the fractional tests can be regarded as veridically representative of variations in organismic functioning. It has been demonstrated (Haynes and Sells, 1963) that the properties of the tests, rather than the properties of the individual, may be responsible for such patterns. It would be equally in error to assume that the latter are, in any case, more significant than a variety of others that could be established if testing of a different sort were carried out (Graham and Berman, 1961; Safrin, 1964). If the aphasic child, for example, is found lacking in one or several areas of the ITPA, ipsatively opposed to other areas or normatively compared to a normal child's performance, further study may show that this malfunctioning extends into many areas other than those assessed by the ITPA (Jenkins and Schuell, 1964). The brain injured child generally manifests problems in gait, gripping of pencil, visual scanning, etc., as well as in the specific areas assessed by perceptual tests (Holroyd and Wright, 1965). In short, handicapped individuals show problems in a great number of ways and through a variety of assessment approaches. And it is quite possible to conceptualize their varied problems in terms of general molar abilities and disabilities differentially reflected in varied types of test situations. It behooves the special education fractionator to demonstrate otherwise, and, if able to do so, why the areas he has chosen to assess are more important than others he might choose from, either diagnostically or therapeutically.

Finally, let us consider the claims for therapeutic efficacy of fractional instruments. The most immediate and glaring error is seen in attempts to demonstrate their value through tests that have a close facsimilitude to the training devices themselves. The Frostig tests, for one, and the Frostig training techniques appear quite similar, and it seems to these writers entirely inappropriate to assess the efficacy of one through the other. We would appear to be merely assessing a sustained practice effect by so doing.

It is unfortunate, additionally, that the efficacy of an instrument cannot be simply assessed on the basis of success with it. The entire problem of Hawthorne and placebo effects is at issue here, which inevitably affect all attempts to remedially or therapeutically influence people (Rosenthal and Frank, 1956). In medical efforts placebo effects are reported to account for from one-fourth to two-thirds of therapeutic successes. Recent investigations into drug effects, wherein such effects may be more efficaciously controlled than in education, have revealed surprising complications and interactions between patient expectancies and drug action (Kurland, 1960; Ross and Cole, 1960; Conners, Eisenberg, and Sharp, 1964). The situation in education, where double blind procedures and other precautions are not possible, is considerably more involved. Much of any improvement that we see in special education may be due to novelty effects, enthusiasm, teacher expectancies (Rosenthal and Jacobson, 1966), and a vast variety of other motivational variables. The well known therapeutic fallacy of medicine applies with a vengeance in special education.

At a time when special education has not been found to be special in its successes (Johnson, 1962), and when specific programs have been demonstrated in the past to be less successful than general ones (Sparks and Blackman, 1965), claims of therapeutic success through fractional approaches should be accepted with caution.

CONCLUSIONS

Special education, like nature, abhors a vacuum. Faced with a multitude of perplexing problems, and a rather impoverished armamentarium to utilize in helping the handicapped child, the special educator finds the charisma of the new fractional approaches dazzling indeed. With them he is now able to program remedial approaches to a variety of problems. There is, additionally, an air of space age sophistication and novelty accompanying these new approaches. Like others in the field, the writers are fascinated by their brave new world. However, they are also disturbed by the hard sell accompanying a number of them that appears to have precipitated programs of evaluation and training on the basis of unsubstantial evidence.

The writers' exposition, by this time, may well appear to the reader to be a calculated exercise in critical nihilism. But they have attempted, rather, to place the fractional approaches in better perspective. This with the hope that the latter will continue to be welcomed as new and challenging approaches to the problems of the handicapped, but only tentatively and cautiously until they have appropriately proven their worth. Till then, the special educator might well consider continuing in large with perhaps dull and unromantic but reasonably productive techniques of assessment via traditional psychometric approaches, and the education of handicapped children with modified curricular approaches.

Pavlov, the great pioneer in modern day fractional methodology was nevertheless, reports Razran, a steadfast votary of interdependent and holistic interaction. He once explained that "of course a behavior is not just a sum of reflexes, a sort of sack filled pell-mell with potatoes, apples, cucumbers. . ." (Razran, 1965). It is to the child and his behavior as a total organism, rather than the "potatoes, apples, cucumbers" of fractional practices that the special educator, at least for the present, can most effectively direct his efforts.

REFERENCES

Ayres, A. J. *The Ayres space test*. Los Angeles: Western Psychological Services, 1962.

Bateman, Barbara. Learning disabilities—yesterday, today, and tomorrow. *Exceptional Children*, 1964, 31, 167–177.

Beck, G. R., Rubin, Jean B., Llorens, Lela A., Beall, C. D., and Mottley, N. Educational aspects of cognitive-perceptual-motor deficits in emotionally disturbed children. *Psychology in Schools* 1965, 2, 233–238.

Bryant, N. D. Characteristics of dyslexia and their remedial implication. *Exceptional Children*, 1964, 31, 195–199.

Campbell, D. T., and Fiske, D. W. Convergent and discriminant validation by the multitrait-multimethod matrix. *Psychological Bulletin*, 1959, 56, 81–105.

Coan, R. W. Facts, factors, and artifacts: the quest for psychological meaning. *Psychological Review*, 1964, 71, 123–140.

Conners, C. K., Eisenberg, L., and Sharp, L. Effects of Methylphenidate (Ritalin) on paired-associate learning and Porteus Maze performance in emotionally disturbed children. *Journal of Consulting Psychology*, 1964, 28, 14–22.

Cronbach, L. J., and Meehl, P. E. Construct validity in psychological tests. *Psychological Bulletin*, 1955, 52, 281–302.

Cropley, A. J. Differentiation of abilities, socio-economic status, and the WISC. *Journal of Consulting Psychology*, 1964, 28, 512–517.

Epstein, W., and Park, J. N. Shape constancy: functional relationships and theoretical formulations. *Psychological Bulletin*, 1963, 60, 265–288.

Frostig, Marianne, and Horne, D. The Frostig program for the development of visual perception. Chicago: Follett Publishing Company, 1964.

Frostig, Marianne, Lefever, D. W., and Whittlesey, J. R. B. A developmental test of visual perception evaluating normal and neurologically handicapped children. *Perceptual Motor Skills*, 1961, 12, 383–394.

Gallagher, J. J. Learning disabilities: an introduction to selected papers. *Exceptional Children*, 1964, 31, 165–166.

Gibson, Eleanor J. Perceptual development. In H. W. Stevenson, J. Kagan, and C. Spiker

(Editors), *Child psychology, part 1*. Chicago: University of Chicago Press, 1963. Pp. 144–195.

Graham, F. K., and Berman, P. W. Current status of behavior tests for brain damage in infants and preschool children. *American Journal of Orthopsychiatry*, 1961, 31, 713–728.

Guilford, J. P. *Fundamental statistics in psychology and education*. (Third edition) New York: McGraw-Hill, 1956. (a)

Guilford, J. P. The structure of intellect. *Psychological Bulletin*, 1956, 53, 257–293. (b)

Guilford, J. P. Factorial angles to psychology, *Psychological Review*, 1961, 68, 1–19.

Haynes, J. R., and Sells, S. B. Assessment of organic brain damage by psychological tests. *Psychological Bulletin*, 1963, 60, 316–325.

Holroyd, Jean, and Wright, F. Neurological implications of WISC verbal performance discrepancies in a psychiatric setting. *Journal of Consulting Psychology*, 1965, 29, 206–212.

Horst, P. Uses and limitations of factor analysis in psychological research. In *Proceedings, 1949 invitational conference on testing problems*. Princeton, New Jersey: Educational Testing Service, 1950. Pp. 50–56.

Jenkins, J. J., and Schuell, H. Further work on language deficit in aphasia. *Psychological Review*, 1964, 71, 87–93.

Johnson, G. Special education for the mentally handicapped—a paradox. *Exceptional Children*, 1962, 29, 62–69.

Klapper, Zelda. Perception and cerebral palsy. *Rehabilitation Literature*, 1965, 26, 370–372.

Kurland, A. A. Placebo effect. In L. Uhr and J. G. Miller (Editors), *Drugs and behavior*. New York: Wiley, 1960. Pp. 156–165.

Lindsley, O. R. Can deficiency produce specific superiority—the challenge of the idiot savant. *Exceptional Children*, 1965, 31, 225–232.

Llorens, Lela A., Rubin, E. Z., Braun, Jean, Beck, Gayle R., Mottley, N., and Beall, D. Training in cognitive-perceptual-motor functions: a preliminary report. *American Journal of Occupational Therapy*, 1964, 17, 5.

McCarthy, J. J., and Kirk, S. A. *Illinois Test of Psycholinguistic Abilities: experimental edition*. Urbana: University of Illinois, 1961.

McNemar, Q. *The revision of the Stanford-Binet scale*. Boston: Houghton Mifflin, 1942.

McNemar, Q. Lost: our intelligence? why? *American Psychologist*, 1964, 19, 871–882.

Meehl, P. E., and Rosen, A. Antecedent probability and the efficiency of psychometric signs, patterns, or cutting scores. *Psychological Bulletin*, 1955, 52, 194–216.

Money, J. (Editor). *Reading disability: progress in research needs in dyslexia*. Baltimore: Johns Hopkins Press, 1962.

Overall, J. E. Note on the scientific status of factors. *Psychological Bulletin*, 1964, 61, 270–276.

Piaget, J., and Inhelder, B. *The child's conception of space*. London: Routledge, 1956.

Razran, G. Russian physiologists' psychology and American experimental psychology: a historical and a systematic collation and a look into the future. *Psychological Bulletin*, 1965, 63, 42–64.

Riegel, Ruth M., and Riegel, K. F. A. A comparative reinterpretation of factor structures of the W-B, the WAIS, and the HAWIE on aged persons. *Journal of Consulting Psychology*, 1962, 26, 31–37.

Rosenthal, D., and Frank, J. D. Psychotherapy and the placebo effect. *Psychological Bulletin*, 1956, 53, 294–302.

Rosenthal, R., and Jacobson, Lenore. Teachers' expectancies: determinants of pupils' IQ gains. *Psychological Reports*, 1966, 19, 115–118.

Ross, S., and Cole, J. O. Psychopharmacology. *Annual Review of Psychology*, 1960, 11, 415–438.

Safrin, R. K. Differences in visual perception and in visual-motor functioning between psychotic and nonpsychotic children. *Journal of Consulting Psychology*, 1964, 28, 41–45.

Sievers, Dorothy J., McCarthy, J. J., Olson, J. L., Bateman, Barbara, and Kass, Corrine E. *Selected studies on the Illinois Test of Psycholinguistic Abilities*. Madison, Wisconsin: Photo Press, Inc., 1963.

Silver, A., and Hagin, Rosa A. Specific reading disability: follow-up studies. *American Journal of Orthopsychiatry*, 1964, 34, 95–102.

Silver, A. A., and Hagin, Rosa A. Specific reading disability: teaching through stimulation of deficit perceptual areas. *American Journal of Orthopsychiatry*, 1965, 65, 350–351.

Smedslund, J. Educational psychology. In P. Farnsworth, Olga McNemar, and Q. McNemar (Editors), *Annual review of psychology*. Palo Alto, California: Annual Reviews, Inc., 1964. Pp. 251–276.

Sparks, H. L., and Blackman, L. S. What is special about special education revisited: the mentally retarded. *Exceptional Children*, 1965, 31, 242–249.

Stevens, H. A. ". . . The field is rich . . . and ready for harvest. . . ." *American Journal of Mental Deficiency*, 1965, 70, 4–15.

Terman, L. M. *The measurement of intelligence*. Boston: Houghton Mifflin, 1916.

Thompson, J. W. Meaningful and unmeaningful rotation of factors. *Psychological Bulletin*, 1962, 59, 221–223.

Vernon, P. E. Ability factors and environmental influence. *American Psychologist*, 1965, 20, 723–733.

Yates, A. J. Psychological deficit. In P. R. Farnsworth, Olga McNemar, and Q. McNemar (Editors), *Annual review of psychology*. Palo Alto, California: Annual Reviews, Inc., 1966. Pp. 111–144.

A Reaction

MAYNARD C. REYNOLDS

I have been asked to react to the paper by Mann and Phillips and am glad to do so because I believe they deal thoughtfully with some important and timely issues. Although these brief comments may appear to be nega-

∗ From *Exceptional Children* 1967, *33*, pp. 317–318. Reprinted by permission of the author and the publisher.

tive in tone, let me record here that I read the paper with much interest and profit.

In one fundamental way Mann and Phillips mislead us, I believe, and to that extent fail in their mission to "place fractional approaches in better perspective." It appears that they think of tests mainly as devices for quantifying attributes (assessment) and making predictions. Furthermore, if several tests of presumably independent attributes can be shown to collapse into a single dimension (in a Guttman type analysis, for example) or to produce high communality (as in factor analyses) they say that we had better put our marbles on the more general variable. They are not alone in thinking this way; it is highly reminiscent of views expressed by Terman, McNemar, many of the British psychologists, and others.

The trouble is, I think, that this line of thinking takes us to the wrong ball park as far as the practical matters of instruction are concerned. Teachers are involved mainly in choices between curricula, teaching methods, special placements, and materials—with the aim of influencing achievement—not in making grand, long range predictions. A key point, as noted by Cronbach, is that ". . . since the general test predicts grades in every curriculum to about the same degree, it sheds no light on the decision"(s) the teachers must make (1965, p. 141). The Mann and Phillips discussion develops mainly from the framework of classical measurement theory; I'm proposing that a decision theory framework is much more relevant. In the latter frame what is required of a test is that it produce significant interaction effects with "methods," not high zero order predictions.

Highly g saturated tests have dominated the schools for years, and they have served quite well in making certain kinds of predictions. But precisely because they predict so much within methods, they are not very useful in choosing between methods, and it is the latter that must occupy teachers. Simple predictions might be of interest to psychometricians and to employment counselors, but are of minor import to teachers. Let it be clear that teachers must fractionate, to use the Mann-Phillips terminology. One cannot deal with the universe and teachers cannot teach all and everything at once. They are constantly called upon to make judgments about specifics and they will seek whatever minor helps test makers can give them. Everyone recognizes, I hope, that isolating any aspect of behavior is delusional if it fails to recognize the larger interactions and wholeness of behavior.

In a practical sense, I agree with Mann and Phillips that there are many problems in some of the newer approaches in special education. Sometimes excesses in diagnostics merely cover ignorance in methodology. Some techniques are sold before they meet any decent test. On the other hand, we should honor the people, such as those who have produced the ITPA, who carry through the very difficult work of evaluation.

Finally, it appears that Mann and Phillips posit general versus fractional approaches as competitive. I think this fails to see that the problems of general assessment and prediction may be quite distinct from problems of instruction. I have long believed that we can have our cake and yet eat it in this sphere of things; just as it is possible and useful to look carefully at highly specific language abilities and at the same time to look at a general language ability measure which might be generated at some second order level. It doesn't seem terribly important to me whether one considers the general factor to be primary or of a second order nature, so long as we test carefully for usefulness of each variable entered into the total system.

REFERENCE

Cronbach, L. J., and Gleser, G. C. *Psychological tests and personnel decisions.* Urbana: University of Illinois Press, 1965.

A Reply to Reynolds

LESTER MANN AND WILLIAM A. PHILLIPS

Dr. Reynolds' critical review of *our* critical review is a tempered and scholarly one that helps to clarify some of the issues with which our original paper is concerned.

We believe he errs, however, in attempting to reduce, or perhaps to banish, a number of our criticisms to the status of a psychometric tempest in a teapot.

Our criticisms of fractional practices in special education hang but little on any particular psychometric position regarding the nature of man's abilities. Whether Dr. Reynolds, or others, or we ourselves prefer simple multidimensional models, hierarchical models, the matrix model that is presently so influential, or what have you—this really is not the primary issue in our critique. What are at issue are (a) the practical value of tests which, with but limited empirical substantiation, are being applied with unwarranted diagnostic panache in special education and (b) the type of faculty training that is their consequence.

We propose, too, that the use of tests to assess and guide educational

* From *Exceptional Children* 1967, 33, pp. 318–319. Reprinted by permission of the senior author and the publisher.

practice is not really at issue, either, in our critique. There are reasonable consensuses as to what constitutes achievement in one or another academic area (though arguments can certainly be raised against the improper use of tests in this respect as well). Can the same be said for the delineations of subareas in perception, language, and other behaviors that the fractionators decide can be isolated, measured, and used to develop educational prescriptions? The list of potential human functions that one can choose to measure is infinite. How and why do we decide which ones to select from, measure, and promulgate on in our increasing involvement with psychometric phrenology? The writers are disturbed over the proliferation of activities in fractional behavior charting and the training anodynes developed along similar lines. One does not have to be a measurement troglodyte to recommend, with Gerard, that "measurement can be helpful only when the proper things have been found to measure" (Gerard, 1961, p. 204) and to suggest that you can't treat specifics specifically if they cannot be specified.

We wish to make clear that we, as well as the fractionators, recognize that human behavior is complex and variable; we heartily recommend the continued search for pure narrow instruments of assessment (Fiske, 1963). We believe, as well, that training programs should be differentiated for different types of problems. It is the hows and the whys, the heuristics and the philosophies that guide us which are at stake here.

We salute with admiration Frostig's achievement in bringing perception so clearly to the fore in special education, the developers of the ITPA for their efforts in focusing attention upon language functions in a theory guided fashion, and the efforts of other pioneers in differential assessment and training. We continue to be dismayed at many of the consequences of their work.

REFERENCES

Fiske, D. W. Homogeneity and variation in measuring personality. *American Psychologist*, 1963, 18, 643–652.

Gerard, R. W. Quantification in biology. In H. Woolf (Editor), *Quantification: a history of the meaning of measurement in the natural and social sciences.* New York: Bobbs-Merrill, 1961. Pp. 204–222.

** 41 **

Special Education and the Inner City: A Challenge for the Future or Another Means for Cooling the Mark Out?

JOHN L. JOHNSON

The recent call by the National Advisory Committee on Handicapped Children for "Program Development for Handicapped Children in Inner City Areas" represents, on the surface, a new challenge—an invitation for special education to become involved in the solution of one of the major crises facing America in the next decade. Education in the inner city is now in a state of crisis and will not improve unless massive changes are brought about in a creative fashion. The Committee's stated need for "special studies" and for "identification and determination of needed diagnostic and remedial services" (p. 37–9) challenges every specialized segment of our profession. Certainly, a problem orientation comes to the fore when "inner city" is suggested as the geographic designation for any professional intervention.

Equality of educational opportunity is a pressing problem in all metropolitan areas, and recent legal decisions have amplified the problem all the more. Specialized and segregated tracking systems and discriminatory intelligence tests can no longer be justified when the basic rights of the individual are at stake. Because of the issue of equality of educational opportunity, an extremely serious problem has developed within the American educational establishment. It has to do with the role to be taken by special education within the total revitalization of education in metropolitan areas. Lloyd Dunn's (1968) condemnation of the practices and procedures of special education has essentially gone unanswered and Donahue & Nichtern's (1965) findings that teacher-moms can help public school disturbed children have been scoffed at and ignored by special educators.

The general body of special education is proceeding along the course of

* From *The Journal of Special Education* 1969, 3, pp. 241–251. Reprinted by permission of the author and the publisher.

"special education and programs for disadvantaged children and youth" (Tanenbaum, 1968) with assistance from 15 percent of Titles I and III, all of Title VI, P.L. 88–164, and more recently from EPDA. These efforts have the clear support of the special education establishment.

⌐ In spite of research and clinical evidence which show that current models of general education are less than successful, efforts continue to be directed toward the establishment of a parallel and separate school structure called special education. The indictment against the general educational enterprise includes special education, for it is both passive and active in perpetuating the present conditions of inequality, failure, and the rendering of impotence, especially in the inner city.

The inner city itself is a problem which is deeply imbedded in America, but for no one is the problem more severe than for professional educators. Education, and special education in particular, faces a major challenge in the coming decade. Whether to take up the challenge or to continue business as usual is the major question to be considered in this paper. This question has political, social, psychological and educational ramifications.

Who and What are We Talking About?

When we speak of inner city, or ghetto, or core area, and when we use euphemisms such as educationally disadvantaged, culturally deprived, and poverty-ridden, we are really talking about Black people or Afro-Americans. While Puerto Ricans, Indians, and poor whites may be included, at the heart of the matter is the fact that inner city means Black. Based upon 1965 estimates (Clark, 1968, p. 119) Black Americans constitute 66 percent of the total population in Washington, D.C.; 44 percent in Atlanta; 34 percent in Detroit; 31 percent in Philadelphia; and 22 percent in Kansas City. The school-age populations for these cities—which are among the 15 having the largest percentages of Blacks—are even larger: for instance, the school population in Washington, D.C., is more than 90 percent Black and in Chicago it is more than 70 percent Black. This is mainly because of one pervasive reason: Blacks are forced to live in the inner city, mainly in depressed, ghetto conditions. The Kerner Report (1968) has clearly cited the cause for this condition:

> What white Americans have never fully understood—but what the Negro can never forget—is that white society is deeply implicated in the ghetto. White institutions created it, white institutions maintain it, and white society condones it (p. 2).

What is most distressing is that in spite of what is termed a massive effort to improve the conditions under which Black Americans live, they appear to be worsening in both intensity and extent. Clark's chapter, "The Negro and the Urban Crisis," in the Brookings Institutions Papers (1968) amply documents the problem. He stated:

The fact of the ghetto—the involuntary restriction of the masses of Negroes to a particular geographic area of the city—underlies every other aspect of the problem. The ghetto results in de facto school segregation, which affects middle and low-income Negroes alike, and the inferiority in education that is invariably related to it. Inferior education, in turn, reinforces the overriding economic fact of disproportionate Negro unemployment and underemployment (p. 119–20).

America's history of slavery, segregation, discrimination, and bigotry against Blacks comes to focus in the inner city, and in particular in its inferior education. The Kerner Report (1968) cites the role of the school as an institution:

The bleak record of public education for ghetto children is growing worse. In the critical skills—verbal and reading ability—Negro students are falling further behind whites with each year of school completed. The high unemployment and underemployment rate for Negro youth is evidence, in part, of the growing educational crisis.

One can conclude that public education bears a large share of the responsibility for the miserable condition of the Black, inner city resident. There are two pathologically symbiotic reasons for the conclusion, one having to do with the overall values of education in America and the other having to do with education for Blacks.

First, as a transmitter of culture and a force which liberates men by providing them with truth, American education has failed. It has offered only a form of technological mind-shaping which permits its products to understand and to develop the great theories of nuclear fission, to recite the philosophies of Hume and Locke, and to master economics and business, while remaining almost totally unable to comprehend and act upon the simple words of 20,000,000 men, women and children who are saying:

I want to be free; I want equal opportunity in a country which was founded upon this very premise; I want to determine the course of my own future; I am human.

Thus, we find all around us liberal intellectuals who can eloquently articulate the concepts of democracy and equality, but who have little commitment to carrying out these ideals. In essence, our schools have transmitted to an entire generation values of passivity, acquiescence, exploitation and omission, instead of integrity and social responsibility.

The schools have also produced an increasingly vocal group of bigots who would systematically relegate entire segments of this society to lower status position, largely on the basis of color, although differences in physique, economic status, and religious preference are also favorite targets for their seething prejudice. The large majority of our schools avoid teaching truth and sensitivity about race, physique, economic status and culture, instead fostering a system in which an increasing number of students learn bigotry, discrimination and segregation. The root cause of America's major social problem is the value system which permits racism and exploitation to exist, which in turn is the result of the educational establishment's failure to transmit concepts of human dignity, brotherhood, equality and democracy to its charges.

Secondly, the educational system's overt practices of segregation and discrimination, feckless fostering of programs upon entire populations without so much as a cursory consideration of their culture, values and heritage, and its dehumanization of students through corporal punishment and rejection simply because they do not present themselves as "ideal clients" (Becker, 1952) have resulted in oppression of its Black students. This results in large numbers of young people who, until recently, had no other method of gaining success and attention than through such self-defeating mechanisms as sex, violent confrontation with the images and agents of white society, or narcotics.

The increased racial hostility and the rising suicide rate in the ghettos are, to a great extent, the consequences of the white educational establishment's failure to provide viable programs which make social, educational and economic opportunity a reality for Blacks. Instead, a set of panaceas has been offered which represent a commitment to system maintenance rather than to the clientele the system purports to serve. As long as there is not too much threat to the model which has precipitated the failure, then attempts to find causes for the obvious facts are encouraged. A number of the panaceas, for instance, involve the assumption that quantitative inputs will effect qualitative outputs. Thus, one finds sincere attempts to fight cancer with corn plasters. The proponents of this view hold that we must sensitize the teachers, inject Negro history, reduce class size, and add some new services (but only when substantial outside pressure to do so is exerted). Where these initial attempts to patch up the system fail, schools can always fall back upon the processes of labeling and stigmatizing inner-city children as deviants either culturally, socially or emotionally, and thus placing them in "special" or "compensatory" programs. Then, the children can be blamed, rather than the racism which permeates our educational institutions.

What Role Has Special Education Played?

It must be crystal clear by now that I am suggesting that the educational system has failed in its responsibilities to Black Americans. What, then, about special education, which has long been involved in educational endeavors in inner cities?

Its Black clientele has been labeled delinquent and retarded, thus helping the general educational enterprise to avoid some of the responsibility for its failure to adapt to individual and collective needs. Basically, this labeling process imputes a lack of ability or a lack of values and behavior which are acceptable to the school. Recent sophistication in labeling has added such terms as learning disability, slow learner, learning and adjustment problem, and conduct disorder to the more shop-worn phrases such as mentally retarded and emotionally disturbed. The rule of thumb for Black children is: IQ below 75 = learning problem or stupidity; and IQ above 75 = behavior problem or crazy.

The latest attempt at system maintenance is the generation of data to show that Blacks may actually be genetically less intelligent and therefore less able to learn. Most of this psychometric data rests upon classical controlled variable research but has absolutely no ecological validity. Special education is implicated, for it has cheerfully accepted the charge with little or no scrutiny of either the faulty concept upon which IQ is grounded or the socio-cultural environment of its clientele. Special education has continued blithely initiating special classes, work-study programs, resource rooms, and other stigmatizing innovations which blame the poor, Black child for the failure of the dominant educational system. Are we to assume that the new challenge for special education will be handled differently? The research evidence from within the field suggests that current efforts in special education are "obsolete and unjustifiable from the point of view of the pupils so placed" (Dunn, 1968, p. 6). We must, also, consider that the efficacy research on special classes for the retarded shows that children who are placed in special classes achieve no better than those who remain in regular classes, and that those who remain in regular classes learn more social skills than special class children (Goldstein, Moss & Jordan, 1964). Research evidence on therapeutic educational provisions for behavior problem children has not been productive, and research on special class achievement is also sparse and conflicting (Glavin & Quay, 1969). Where evidence is available, it has been obtained largely from white-majority populations. Thus, we must pose the question: If special education placement, as currently operating, is questionable for white children, what makes it any more valid for Blacks? There is direct evidence to document its ineffectiveness (Clark, 1965; Schulz, 1969; Tyler, 1968), on top of the fact that placement out of the mainstream of education and other forms of tracking are illegal and racist-motivated. Thus, if special education becomes involved in this new effort in the inner city, then we will be operationalizing bigotry, discrimination and segregation.

How Did All This Come About?

The current plight of the Black is, in fact, a direct result of the regular school's failure to cope with individual and collective differences in learning and conduct of an increasing number of pupils. Regular schools have been the major force for accommodation of the "regular" Blacks and special education receives the "hard to break" Blacks. It is an unwritten pact between the two.

Goffman's (1952) concept of "cooling the mark out" is relevant to Blacks when consideration is given to the relationship between special education and the general educational system. Goffman has analyzed adaptation to failure and the methods by which one individual can aid another who has failed by helping him to build a new framework for judging himself. This process is called cooling the mark out.

General education, by definition, is supposed to be capable of teaching all children, but when confronted with inner-city Black children, it has failed. Given traditional methodology and most crash programs, both white and Afro-American teachers have found themselves impotent when it comes to educating increasing numbers of Black children. One method by which these individuals and the school can preserve their identities is by cooling the child out. Special programs are mandated on the basis that the new placement is helping the child. In essence, he is given a seemingly better provision in hopes that he will stop putting up a fuss. It is easier for all to cool out the child and to find him a new place than it is to change the system for his benefit.

Special education is part of the arrangement for cooling out students. It has helped to erect a parallel system which permits relief of institutional guilt and humiliation stemming from the failure to achieve competence and effectiveness in the task given to it by society. Special education is helping the regular school maintain its spoiled identity when it creates special programs (whether psycho-dynamic or behavioral modification) for the "disruptive child" and the "slow learner," many of whom, for some strange reason, happen to be Black and poor and live in the inner city.

Some systems are already involved in programs for the "emotionally disturbed" and "socially maladjusted," which are no more than euphemisms for aggressive, Black, male children.[1] For instance, a past issue of *Instructor Magazine*, a classroom teachers' periodical, featured an article on a "special education program for emotionally disturbed children" in a city where more than 75 percent of the school-age population is Black and resides in massive ghetto areas. An extensive "therapeutic program" including entire schools for "disturbed" children is described. There is a subtle connotation of sickness or craziness. The schools involved are able to co-opt not only special education, but psychiatry, psychology and social work (including indigenous para-professionals) in a direct fashion, and to effectively invalidate the cultural experiences of a select group of Black children (Laing, 1969). The perpetrators of this type of cultural invalidation are products of the white racist value system spoken of earlier.

What are the Social-political Implications?

It is obvious that Black people cannot sit idly by and watch white conceptions of normality and abnormality, or appropriateness and inappropriateness of school behavior, foisted upon their children. Black professionals are, of course, implicated in this insidious practice by virtue of their white

[1] When Black "deviant" children are rated by white teachers, there is a tendency for their behavior to be classified more often as aggressive and acting out (cf. Quay, 1966; Rich, 1969).

educations and ideologies, but a growing number have "come home" and are helping to formulate a challenge to the system of racist values which now permeates our schools.

This is the heart of the inner-city problem for special education. Left to whites and to special education, Blacks have a choice: be labeled crazy or unable to learn and get cooled out, or submit to a far worse plight—loss of their own Black identity and integrity by permitting themselves to be integrated and thus convinced that the white man's values are the ones which must be adopted—the very values which created the condition in the first place.

What Is To Be Done?

I have grave doubts that anything can be done within the present system. I reject the assumption that the basic model of age-graded education as we know it must be preserved, even in view of the patching that is being attempted. It is not a model for Blacks, it has failed Blacks, and it is dominated by white values and methods. It is incompatible, even in its special forms, with Black culture.

The first step toward solution is straightforward: *Black Self-Determination.* Blacks, as a people, must define themselves in a way that is meaningful to them. We will determine our identity, not as culturally-deprived or Negro, but as Black and Afro-American, if we so choose. We will determine what is in our best interests in this country, culturally, socially, economically, politically and educationally. We will develop ourselves through institutions which support feelings of self-pride and attitudes of racial dignity, social responsibility, and human dignity.

The essence of this social-political implication lies in the *power* to carry out the task in the inner city. There is no doubt that it is the Black American who has the most stake in the inner cities and their institutions. Blacks *are* the inner city and therefore they must determine its course. Institutions which serve Blacks must become accountable first to Blacks and then to the rest of society.

The new spirit of the inner city reflects this ideology. Black self-determination, Black pride, and Black consciousness are the values which inner-city schools must teach. The new way of "taking care of business" involves Black people from all walks and persuasions coming together to decide what is in their best interests; this necessitates a temporary withdrawal until we know our brothers and until we awaken all of them to the need for enhancing Afro-American culture in this country—not a culture that is physically separate, but one that is of our collective mind and one in which we can determine the course of our existence without white interference, domination, exploitation or classification. Certainly, whites must be involved, but only at the operational level. The planning and leadership levels will be for Blacks. Whites may be consulted, but decisions about Blacks cannot be made by whites and then followed by Blacks.

Most of all, we have to preserve the integrity of our culture. Cultural preservation is our goal, not integration toward whites. The achievement of soul is important, soul being the "conscious release from white values determined without Black participation. It is a freedom from shame imposed from without" (Scott, 1969, p. 19).

In our minds, the preservation of Saturday night, CPT, Sounding, our emotional styles, our free sharing, our natural hair styles, telling it like it is, the way we listen, our postural gestures, and the noise we make are important. Integrated education which would make us "copies" of the quiet, white, racist middle class, therefore, from our point of view, would really mean cultural deprivation. There is a definite, traceable and positive Afro-American culture which contains its own products and reflects certain psychological processes. This culture must be reflected in schooling and education in the inner city.

A first operational step is the process of social regeneration for Blacks by Blacks. The recognition of a positive heritage, the building of community, and the defining of goals by Blacks are the initial steps for destigmatization and for the building of positive self-identity. Education is a central force in any movement for cultural preservation, and this force must be directed toward goals determined by Black communities. It is obvious, then, that such concepts as cultural deprivation, mental retardation, and emotional disturbance are bankrupt, and have little place in the new schema for building viable educational programs to serve Afro-Americans.

What are the Psychological and Educational Implications?

Political and philosophical rationales based upon Black self-determination and Black pride must determine the goals of child-rearing and socialization, within which education has a role. What becomes "special" about education is the manner and force with which it understands the saliencies of Afro-American culture and *then* seeks to serve that culture rather than to accommodate it.

One of the most critical areas of concern is child development and the need for the establishment of a positive pedagogy for Afro-American children. Considerable attention is now being given to "cognitive development" and "socialization" for inner-city children, based upon the presumed effects of social deprivation. There is in this, first, a tacit assumption that most, if not all, of the early experiences and later development of Black children is negative and deprived. Secondly, there is an assumption of Black-inferiority/white-superiority typical of the subtle supremacy argument: "What you need is to be like us because white is right!" In essence, Afro-American children can then be subjected to "cognitive stimulation," "language development," and "behavior modification" programs, all based on the assumption that they have neither a unique cognitive style nor a language which is expressive and communicative, and that their behavior is obnoxious. The extensions of this inferiority argument reach into other domains, including the imputation of family instability and the application of Victorian views of sexual behavior, to name two.

The fact of the matter is that there is little precise ecological data about child-rearing practices and socialization processes for any cultural group, and the little that is available for Afro-Americans was generated from a social order which perpetuated unconscious racism and a purposively negative view of the Afro-American experience in this country. Essentially, the pedagogical descriptions of Black children have been negative, emphasizing intellectual retardation, maladaptive and delinquent behavior, self-derogation, and hopelessness. What have been systematically ignored are: (1) the spontaneity, problem-solving ability, and creativity which exist and grow even under severe environmental limitations, (2) the nature and effect of peer collectives, which are the major socializing agent for the urban Black child, and (3) the development of acute social perceptiveness, particularly the cognitive and affective styles which permit the development of extensive non-verbal communication processes (Johnson & Wilderson, 1969).

There is mounting evidence that the Afro-American child develops normally and positively within the dimensions of his own cultural and social environment. What must first be ascertained is, just what is the environment in which many Black children live?

Living conditions for many Black children are such that their primary referents are Black and all other persons are intruders into the values and culture of the ghetto and thus are viewed as hostile agents of the other (white) America. To Blacks, the other America is all that is not within the Black community. There *is* an especial "Black norm" of life that must be understood (Grier & Cobbs, 1968, p. 149). We need to devote attention to understanding the socialization of the Black child in his Black community. We need to understand and remove the Black norm from any thoughts of treatment for so-called psychopathology or determination of behavioral disorders. We need to explicate their unique cognitive styles before we dare classify Black children's "learning disorders." We need to build and support models of the non-verbal and verbal communications which exist in the Black community.

An important task within the next few years becomes clear: *Time and knowledge must be turned toward understanding the course of socialization and affective development of Afro-American children, with Black self-perceptions being the dominant focus.* The time has ended for describing Afro-American children as deviant, deficient, deprived, retarded or disadvantaged. The development of a positive pedagogy, in terms of Black self-determination, is the pressing order of business, rather than more regular and special education. Until the establishment adopts a positive perspective of Blacks and builds educational programs which are special for Blacks, determined by Blacks, then Blacks have little alternative except to reject what is offered as racist, stigmatizing, and helping to maintain a vast number of children in good and bad "nigger roles." Education must support our culture as we determine it, as it can do in a multi-social, pleuralistic, technological and humanistic society.

Education: Special or Regular in the New Conception of Urban America?

There is little doubt that the role and process of education in the cities must be based upon conceptions which are acceptable to Blacks. The new environment for man in the metropolitan areas of America cannot permit conceptions which label and stigmatize its children or condone an extensive and separate educational system for special, compensatory or supplementary concerns. The main concern of the new education must be in the form of Haworth's (1963) *The Good City:* It must include power, freedom and community, with community being the main force for creating independence and a nexus of voluntary associations. In this conception, education must be the central force. Its goals for Blacks at all levels must include more than the learning of basic subjects and the development of social and vocational skills. Education must emphasize the development of knowledge, cooperative attitudes, positive Black self-identity, and an ideology of Black self-determination.

What is in order is a careful determination of goals and objectives of community development for the future. We will have to develop new institutions to support these goals. One of them will be the education-centered community (Melby, 1959), in which all the forces of voluntary associations and extensive peer collectives will be directed toward education. In this institution, community involvement, leadership development, and civic participation are needed. All other structures—newspapers, radio and TV, churches, etc.—have a role to carry out, as has the school. As Melby (1959) has stated:

> At the education-centered-community level of development, schools are not only doing things for people; they are involving people in the process of building both themselves and their communities and thus adding a new dimension of power to their activities (p. 49).

Another institution of the future might well be the child care community, suggested by John R. Platt (1969). He has proposed a new "self-maintaining social institution" based upon the functions of child rearing and child care. The basic model is of a group collective or self-help organization in the form of an entire neighborhood or large apartment building:

> Such a child care community might be organized with as few as 10 to 20 families, or 50 to 100 adults and children. Larger communities, with 50 to 100 families, or a total of 200 to 500 persons, would probably be able to afford more professional managerial services and a better teaching staff, with separate teachers for different age groups; the quality and efficiency of the dining services would probably be better as well (Platt, 1969, p. 18).

We will have to look also at changed conceptions of schooling and the concepts and roles which will be required for the future. Head Start, store-front schools, individualized instruction, and team teaching are well-known and certainly must continue. However, in the Black community, the development of preventive educational planning may also be a necessity. Such preventive planning would include teams of educators and social scientists, contracted by a community, who would move into that community and begin to develop educational programs for students who are not yet born and for those who are about to make a transition to a new level of schooling. Once their target population becomes available, the team would carry out the schooling and a new team would began planning for a new population. The demands of decentralization, pedagogical integrity, and accountability could thus be met. Schooling would remain flexible and person-centered, yet achieve the goals of community development.

New structural arrangements may have to be developed, but within a set of non-materialistic values that will not permit large, expensive physical structures to determine the course of education. Schooling might take place in school-homes for children from the ages of three to six, the school being essentially an extension of the child's home and neighborhood. These units could be established in available but especially designed spaces, including learning laboratories and other environments which evoke explorative responses and provide immediate feedback of results. The next stage might be school-units organized upon principles of group development rather than by grades. Such a unit would provide for continuous progress and task-oriented group work. A no-retention policy would be in effect. Another structure might be the satellite school, attached to a central core. There might be a number of satellite units and one technologically advanced core. The satellite school would house 300 to 500 pupils, while the core would contain services shared by a number of satellites, including computer-assisted instruction, instructional modulation centers, closed circuit TV production capacity, and electronic information retrieval, all formulated into an individually prescribed instructional format.

New roles, obviously, will be required. Child development specialists who have been trained in ways of managing the child's milieu, and in the techniques of causal teaching, psycho-educational assessment, and life space interviewing will be essential. Prescription teachers with competency in criterion-referenced assessment, the specification of behavioral objectives, and programmed learning will also be required. Finally, group inter-action teachers, who possess the ability to mobilize group forces and whose everyday content will be the teaching of emotional skills and strengths, will be necessary.

Above all, the new roles in this conception of education must include a commitment to the goals of the Afro-American community and attention to administrative and instructional behavior which will respect the right of self-determination. The new education must create a force for learning in which form and function are congruent.

SUMMARY AND CONCLUSIONS

One might ask, How does special education fit into all this? How will "deviant" children be dealt with? Better questions might be: Will there be a need for special education? Will there be special classes in education-centered communities? Will child-rearing communities produce disturbed children? Will any satellite school child who can achieve 90 percent success on all educational tasks be disruptive? Will any Black child who is taught by persons committed to the goals of his community suffer racial dis-identity? The problem at hand is neither the reshaping of what is now called special education nor a thrust into the gradual changing of a failing, racist institution. The goal must be the establishment of a revolutionary process of education, in which no child is labeled special, in which self-enhancement, not mental health, is an objective, and in which community is the force for learning. Where "special education" fits into this revolutionary process is up to special education.

The message is clear: Special education in our inner cities suffers from obsolete, racist conceptions of deviance and unjustifiable ways of cooling out children. If special education as a way of producing self-enhancement can agree to the new Black ideology and work within it, then it has a place in the new conception of education.

If not, then it falls to special education and those of us in the field to answer the question: Special education and the inner city; a challenge for the future or another means for cooling the mark out? Black Americans are not to be cooled out any longer.

REFERENCES

Becker, H. S. Social class variations in the teacher-pupil relationship. *Journal of Educational Sociology*, 1952, **25**, 451–65.

Clark, K. B. *Dark ghetto*. New York: Harper, 1965. Chap. 6.

Clark, K. B. The negro and the urban crisis. In K. Gordon, (Ed.)., *Agenda for the Nation*. Garden City, N.J.: Doubleday, 1968.

Donahue, G. T. & Nichtern, S. *Teaching the troubled child*. New York: Free Press, 1965.

Dunn, L. M. Special education for the mildly retarded—is much of it justifiable? *Exceptional Children*, 1968, **35**, 5–24.

———. Emotionally disturbed children: Whose Fault? Whose responsibility? *Instructor Magazine*, August/September, 1967.

Glavin, J. P. & Quay, H. C. Behavior problems. *Review of Educational Research*, 1969, **39**, 83–102.

Goffman, E. On cooling the mark out: Some aspects of adaptation to failure. *Psychiatry*, 1952, **15**, 451–63.

Goldstein, H., Moss, J. W. & Jordan, Laura J. The efficacy of special class training on the development of mentally retarded children. Cooperative Research Project 619, U.S. Dept. HEW, Office of Education, 1964.

Grier, W. H. & Cobbs, P. H. *Black rage.* New York: Bantam, 1968.

Haworth, L. *The good city.* Bloomington: University of Indiana Press, 1963.

Johnson, J. L. & Wilderson, F. B. The Institute for Research on the Social and Emotional Development of Afro-American Children. Manuscript-proposal, Syracuse, N.Y., March 2, 1969.

Kerner, O., et al. Report of the National Advisory Commission on Civil Disorders. New York: *Bantam,* 1968.

Laing, R. D. *The politics of experience.* New York: Balantine, 1969.

Melby, E. O. *Education for renewed faith in freedom.* Columbus: Ohio State University Press, 1959.

Platt, J. R. Child care communities: Units for better urban living. *Urban Review,* 1969, 3, 17–8.

Quay, H. C., et al. Some correlates of personality disorder and conduct disorder in a child guidance clinic sample. *Psychology in the Schools,* 1966, 1, 44–57.

Rich, H. L. An investigation of the social-emotional climate in a class of disturbed children. Unpublished doctoral dissertation, Syracuse University, 1969.

Schulz, D. A. *Coming up black.* Englewood Cliffs, N.J.: Prentice-Hall, 1969. Pp. 158–161.

Scott, B. *The coming of the black man.* Boston, Mass.: Beacon Press, 1969.

Tanenbaum, A. J. (Ed.) *Special education and the programs for disadvantaged children and youth.* Washington, D.C.: Council for Exceptional Children, 1968.

Tyler, R. W. Investing in better schools. In K. Gordon, (Ed.), *Agenda for the Nation.* Garden City, N.J.: Doubleday, 1968.

** 42 **

Special Education for the Mildly Retarded— Is Much of It Justifiable?

LLOYD M. DUNN

A better education than special class placement is needed for socioculturally deprived children with mild learning problems who have been labeled educable mentally retarded. Over the years, the status of these pupils who come from poverty, broken and inadequate homes, and low status ethnic groups has been a checkered one. In the early days, these children were simply excluded from school. Then, as Hollingworth (1923)

* From *Exceptional Children* 1968, 34, pp. 5–22. Reprinted by permission of the author and the publisher.

pointed out, with the advent of compulsory attendance laws, the schools and these children "were forced into a reluctant mutual recognition of each other." This resulted in the establishment of self contained special schools and classes as a method of transferring these "misfits" out of the regular grades. This practice continues to this day and, unless counter-forces are set in motion now, it will probably become even more prevalent in the immediate future due in large measure to increased racial integration and militant teacher organizations. For example, a local affiliate of the National Education Association demanded of a local school board recently that more special classes be provided for disruptive and slow learning children (Nashville *Tennessean,* December 18, 1967).

The number of special day classes for the retarded has been increasing by leaps and bounds. The most recent 1967–1968 statistics compiled by the US Office of Education now indicate that there are approximately 32,000 teachers of the retarded employed by local school systems—over one-third of all special educators in the nation. In my best judgment, about 60 to 80 percent of the pupils taught by these teachers are children from low status backgrounds—including Afro-Americans, American Indians, Mexicans, and Puerto Rican Americans; those from nonstandard English speaking, broken, disorganized, and inadequate homes; and children from other nonmiddle class environments. This expensive proliferation of self contained special schools and classes raises serious educational and civil rights issues which must be squarely faced. It is my thesis that we must stop labeling these deprived children as mentally retarded. Furthermore we must stop segregating them by placing them into our allegedly special programs.

The purpose of this article is twofold: first, to provide reasons for taking the position that a large proportion of this so called special education in its present form is obsolete and unjustifiable from the point of view of the pupils so placed; and second, to outline a blueprint for changing this major segment of education for exceptional children to make it more acceptable. We are not arguing that we do away with our special education programs for the moderately and severely retarded, for other types of more handicapped children, or for the multiply handicapped. The emphasis is on doing something better for slow learning children who live in slum conditions, although much of what is said should also have relevance for those children we are labeling emotionally disturbed, perceptually impaired, brain injured, and learning disordered. Furthermore, the emphasis of the article is on children, in that no attempt is made to suggest an adequate high school environment for adolescents still functioning as slow learners.

REASONS FOR CHANGE

Regular teachers and administrators have sincerely felt they were doing these pupils a favor by removing them from the pressures of an unrealistic and inappropriate program of studies. Special educators have also fully believed that the children involved would make greater progress in special schools and classes. However, the overwhelming evidence is that our present and past practices have their major justification in removing pressures on regular teachers and pupils, at the expense of the socio-culturally deprived slow learning pupils themselves. Some major arguments for this position are outlined below.

Homogeneous Grouping

Homogeneous groupings tend to work to the disadvantage of the slow learners and underprivileged. Apparently such pupils learn much from being in the same class with children from white middle class homes. Also, teachers seem to concentrate on the slower children to bring them up to standard. This principle was dramatically applied in the Judge J. Skelly Wright decision in the District of Columbia concerning the track system. Judge Wright ordered that tracks be abolished, contending they discriminated against the racially and/or economically disadvantaged and therefore were in violation of the Fifth Amendment of the Constitution of the United States. One may object to the Judge's making educational decisions based on legal considerations. However, Passow (1967), upon the completion of a study of the same school system, reached the same conclusion concerning tracking. The recent national study by Coleman, et al. (1966), provides supporting evidence in finding that academically disadvantaged Negro children in racially segregated schools made less progress than those of comparable ability in integrated schools. Further-more, racial integration appeared to deter school progress very little for Caucasian and more academically able students.

What are the implications of Judge Wright's rulings for special education? Clearly special schools and classes are a form of homogeneous grouping and tracking. This fact was demonstrated in September, 1967, when the District of Columbia (as a result of the Wright decision) abolished Track 5, into which had been routed the slowest learning pupils in the District of Columbia schools. These pupils and their teachers were returned to the regular classrooms. Complaints followed from the regular teachers that these children were taking an inordinate amount of their time. A few parents observed that their slow learning children were frustrated by the other students. Thus, there are efforts afoot to develop a special education program in D.C. which cannot be labeled a track. Self contained special classes will probably not be tolerated under the present court ruling but perhaps itinerant and resource room programs would be. What if the Supreme Court ruled against tracks, and all self contained special classes across the nation which serve primarily ethically and/or economically disadvantaged children were forced to close down? Make no mistake— this could happen! If I were a Negro from the slums or a disadvantaged parent who had heard of the Judge Wright decision and knew what I know now about special classes for the educable mentally retarded, other things being equal, I would then go to court before allowing the schools to label my child as "mentally retarded" and place him in a "self contained special school or class." Thus there is the real possibility that additional court actions will be forthcoming.*

Efficacy Studies

The findings of studies on the efficacy of special classes for the educable mentally retarded constitute another argument for change. These results are well known (Kirk, 1964) and suggest consistently that retarded pupils make as much or more progress in the regular grades as they do in special education. Recent studies such as those by Hoelke (1966) and Smith and Kennedy (1967) continue to provide similar evidence. Johnson (1962) has summarized the situation well:

> It is indeed paradoxical that mentally handicapped children having teachers especially trained, having more money (per capita) spent on their education, and being designed to provide for their unique needs, should be accomplishing the objectives of their education at the same or at a lower level than similar mentally handicapped children who have not had these advantages and have been forced to remain in the regular grades [p. 66].

Efficacy studies on special day classes for other mildly handicapped children, including the emotionally handicapped, reveal the same results. For example, Rubin, Senison, and Betwee (1966) found that disturbed children did as well in the regular grades as in special classes, concluding that there is little or no evidence that special class programing is generally beneficial to emotionally disturbed children as a specific method of intervention and correction. Evidence such as this is another reason to find better ways of serving children with mild learning disorders than placing them in self contained special schools and classes.

Labeling Processes

Our past and present diagnostic procedures comprise another reason for change. These procedures have probably been doing more harm than good in that they have resulted in disability labels and in that they have grouped children homogeneously in school on the basis of these labels. Generally,

* Litigation has now occurred. According to an item in a June 8, 1968, issue of the *Los Angeles Times* received after this article was sent to the printer, the attorneys in the national office for the rights of the indigent filed a suit in behalf of the Mexican-American parents of the Santa Ana Unified School District asking for an injunction against the District's classes for the educable mentally retarded because the psychological examinations required prior to placement are unconstitutional since they have failed to use adequate evaluation techniques for children from different language and cultural backgrounds, and because parents have been denied the right of hearing to refute evidence for placement. Futhermore, the suit seeks to force the district to grant hearings on all children currently in such special classes to allow for the chance to remove the stigma of the label "mentally retarded" from school records of such pupils.

these diagnostic practices have been conducted by one of two procedures. In rare cases, the workup has been provided by a multidisciplinary team, usually consisting of physicians, social workers, psychologists, speech and hearing specialists, and occasionally educators. The avowed goal of this approach has been to look at the complete child, but the outcome has been merely to label him mentally retarded, perceptually impaired, emotionally disturbed, minimally brain injured, or some other such term depending on the predispositions, idiosyncracies, and backgrounds of the team members. Too, the team usually has looked for causation, and diagnosis tends to stop when something has been found wrong with the child, when the why has either been found or conjectured, and when some justification has been found for recommending placement in a special education class.

In the second and more common case, the assessment of educational potential has been left to the school psychologist who generally administers —in an hour or so—a psychometric battery, at best consisting of individual tests of intelligence, achievement, and social and personal adjustment. Again the purpose has been to find out what is wrong with the child in order to label him and thus make him eligible for special education services. In large measure this has resulted in digging the educational graves of many racially and/or economically disadvantage children by using a WISC or Binet IQ score to justify the label "mentally retarded." This term then becomes a destructive, self fulfilling prophecy.

What is the evidence against the continued use of these diagnostic practices and disability labels?

First, we must examine the effects of these disability labels on the attitudes and expectancies of teachers. Here we can extrapolate from studies by Rosenthal and Jacobson (1966) who set out to determine whether or not the expectancies of teachers influenced pupil progress. Working with elementary school teachers across the first six grades, they obtained pretest measures on pupils by using intelligence and achievement tests. A sample of pupils was randomly drawn and labeled "rapid learners" with hidden potential. Teachers were told that these children would show unusual intellectual gains and school progress during the year. All pupils were retested late in the school year. Not all differences were statistically significant, but the gains of the children who had been arbitrarily labeled rapid learners were generally significantly greater than those of the other pupils, with especially dramatic changes in the first and second grades. To extrapolate from this study, we must expect that labeling a child "handicapped" reduces the teacher's expectancy for him to succeed.

Second, we must examine the effects of these disability labels on the pupils themselves. Certainly none of these labels are badges of distinction. Separating a child from other children in his neighborhood—or removing him from the regular classroom for therapy or special class placement— probably has a serious debilitating effect upon his self image. Here again our research is limited but supportive of this contention. Goffman (1961) has described the stripping and mortification process that takes place when an individual is placed in a residential facility. Meyerowitz (1965) demonstrated that a group of educable mentally retarded pupils increased in feelings of self derogation after one year in special classes. More recent results indicate that special class placement, instead of helping such a pupil adjust to his neighborhood peers, actually hinders him (Meyerowitz, 1967). While much more research is needed, we cannot ignore the evidence that removing a handicapped child from the regular grades for special education probably contributes significantly to his feelings of inferiority and problems of acceptance.

Improvements in General Education

Another reason self contained special classes are less justifiable today than in the past is that regular school programs are now better able to deal with individual differences in pupils. No longer is the choice just between a self contained special class and a self contained regular elementary classroom. Although the impact of the American Revolution in Education is just beginning to be felt and is still more an ideal than a reality, special education should begin moving now to fit into a changing general education program and to assist in achieving the program's goals. Because of increased support at the local, state, and federal levels, four powerful forces are at work:

CHANGES IN SCHOOL ORGANIZATION. In place of self contained regular classrooms, there is increasingly more team teaching, ungraded primary departments, and flexible groupings. Radical departures in school organization are projected—educational parks in place of neighborhood schools, metropolitan school districts cutting across our inner cities and wealthy suburbs, and, perhaps most revolutionary of all, competing public school systems. Furthermore, and of great significance to those of us who have focused our careers on slow learning children, public kindergartens and nurseries are becoming more available for children of the poor.

CURRICULAR CHANGES. Instead of the standard diet of Look and Say readers, many new and exciting options for teaching reading are evolving. Contemporary mathematics programs teach in the primary grades concepts formerly reserved for high school. More programed textbooks and other materials are finding their way into the classroom. Ingenious procedures, such as those by Bereiter and Engelman (1966), are being developed to teach oral language and reasoning to preschool disadvantaged children.

CHANGES IN PROFESSIONAL PUBLIC SCHOOL PERSONNEL. More ancillary personnel are now employed by the schools—i.e., psychologists, guidance workers, physical educators, remedial educators, teacher aides, and technicians. Furthermore, some teachers are functioning in different ways, serving as teacher coordinators, or cluster teachers who provide released time for other teachers to prepare lessons, etc. Too, regular classroom teachers are increasingly better trained to deal with individual differences —although much still remains to be done.

HARDWARE CHANGES. Computerized teaching, teaching machines, feedback typewriters, ETV, videotapes, and other materials are making autoinstruction possible, as never before.

We must ask what the implications of this American Revolution in Education are for special educators. Mackie (1967), formerly of the US Office of Education, addressed herself to the question: "Is the modern school changing sufficiently to provide [adequate services in general education] for large numbers of pupils who have functional mental retardation due to environmental factors [p. 5]?" In her view, hundreds—perhaps even thousands—of so called retarded pupils may make satisfactory progress in schools with diversified programs of instruction and thus will never need placement in self contained special classes. With earlier, better, and more flexible regular school programs many of the children should not need to be relegated to the type of special education we have so often provided.

In my view, the above four reasons for change are cogent ones. Much of special education for the mildly retarded is becoming obsolete. Never in our history has there been a greater urgency to take stock and to search out new roles for a large number of today's special educators.

A BLUEPRINT FOR CHANGE

Two major suggestions which constitute my attempt at a blueprint for change are developed below. First, a fairly radical departure from conventional methods will be proposed in procedures for diagnosing, placing, and teaching children with mild learning difficulties. Second, a proposal for curriculum revision will be sketched out. These are intended as proposals which should be examined, studied, and tested. What is needed are programs based on scientific evidence of worth and not more of those founded on philosophy, tradition, and expediency.

A THOUGHT

There is an important difference between regular educators talking us into trying to remediate or live with the learning difficulties of pupils with which they haven't been able to deal; versus striving to evolve a special education program that is either developmental in nature, wherein we assume responsibility for the total education of more severely handicapped children from an early age, or is supportive in nature, wherein general education would continue to have central responsibility for the vast majority of the children with mild learning disabilities—with us serving as resource teachers in devising effective prescriptions and in tutoring such pupils.

A Clinical Approach

Existing diagnostic procedures should be replaced by expecting special educators, in large measure, to be responsible for their own diagnostic teaching and their clinical teaching. In this regard, it is suggested that we do away with many existing disability labels and the present practice of grouping children homogeneously by these labels into special classes. Instead, we should try keeping slow learning children more in the mainstream of education, with special educators serving as diagnostic, clinical, remedial, resource room, itinerant and/or team teachers, consultants, and developers of instructional materials and prescriptions for effective teaching.

The accomplishment of the above *modus operandi* will require a revolution in much of special education. A moratorium needs to be placed on the proliferation (if not continuance) of self contained special classes which enroll primarily the ethnically and/or economically disadvantaged children we have been labeling educable mentally retarded. Such pupils should be left in (or returned to) the regular elementary grades until we are "tooled up" to do something better for them.

PRESCRIPTIVE TEACHING. In diagnosis one needs to know how much a child can learn, under what circumstances, and with what materials. To accomplish this, there are three administrative procedures possible. One would be for each large school system—or two or more small districts—to establish a "Special Education Diagnostic and Prescription Generating Center." Pupils with school learning problems would be enrolled in this center on a day and/or boarding school basis for a period of time— probably up to a month and hopefully until a successful prescription for effective teaching had been evolved. The core of the staff would be a variety of master teachers with different specialties—such as in motor development, perceptual training, language development, social and personality development, remedial education, and so forth. Noneducators such as physicians, psychologists, and social workers would be retained in a consultative role, or pupils would be referred out to such paraeducational professionals, as needed. A second procedure, in lieu of such centers with their cadres of educational specialists, would be for one generalist in diagnostic teaching to perform the diagnostic and prescription devising functions on her own. A third and even less desirable procedure would be for one person to combine the roles of prescriptive and clinical teacher which will be presented next. It is suggested that 15 to 20 percent of the most insightful special educators be prepared for and/or assigned to prescriptive teaching. One clear virtue of the center is that a skilled director could coordinate an inservice training program and the staff could learn through, and be stimulated by, one another. In fact, many special educators could rotate through this program.

Under any of these procedures, educators would be responsible for the administration and interpretation of individual and group psychoeducational tests on cognitive development (such as the WISC and Binet), on language development (such as the ITPA), and on social maturity (such as the Vineland Social Maturity Scale). However, these instruments —with the exception of the ITPA which yields a profile of abilities and disabilities—will be of little use except in providing baseline data on the level at which a child is functioning. In place of these psychometric tests which usually yield only global scores, diagnostic educators would need to rely heavily on a combination of the various tools of behavior shapers and clinical teachers. The first step would be to make a study of the child to find what behaviors he has acquired along the dimension being considered. Next, samples of a sequential program would be designed to move him forward from that point. In presenting the program, the utility of different reinforcers, administered under various conditions, would be investigated. Also, the method by which he can best be taught the material should be determined. Different modalities for reaching the child would also be tried. Thus, since the instructional program itself becomes the diagnostic device, this procedure can be called diagnostic teaching. Failures are program and instructor failures, not pupil failures. In large measure, we would be guided by Bruner's dictum (1967) that almost any child can be taught almost anything if it is programed correctly.*

This diagnostic procedure is viewed as the best available since it enables us to assess continuously the problem points of the instructional program against the assets of the child. After a successful and appropriate prescription has been devised, it would be communicated to the teachers in the pupil's home school and they would continue the procedure as long as it is necessary and brings results. From time to time, the child may need to return to the center for reappraisal and redirection.

Clearly the above approach to special education diagnosis and treatment is highly clinical and intuitive. In fact, it is analogous to the rural doctor of the past who depended on his insights and a few diagnostic and treatment devices carried in his small, black bag. It may remain with us for some time to come. However, it will be improved upon by more standardized procedures. Perhaps the two most outstanding, pioneering efforts in this regard are now being made by Feuerstein (1968) in Israel, and by Kirk (1966) in the United States. Feuerstein has devised a *Learning Potential Assessment Device* for determining the degree of modifiability of

---

* By ignoring genetic influences on the behavioral characteristics of children with learning difficulties, we place responsibility on an inadequate society, inadequate parents, unmotivated pupils, and/or in this case inadequate teachers. Taking this extreme environmental approach could result in placing too much blame for failure on the teacher and too much pressure of the child. While we could set our level of aspiration too high, this has hardly been the direction of our error to date in special education of the handicapped. Perhaps the sustained push proposed in this paper may not succeed, but we will not know until we try it. Insightful teachers should be able to determine when the pressures on the pupil and system are too great.

the behavior of an individual pupil, the level at which he is functioning, the strategies by which he can best learn, and the areas in which he needs to be taught. Also, he is developing a variety of exercises for teaching children with specific learning difficulties. Kirk and his associates have not only given us the ITPA which yields a profile of abilities and disabilities in the psycholinguistic area, but they have also devised exercises for re-mediating specific psycholinguistic disabilities reflected by particular types of profiles (Kirk, 1966). Both of these scientists are structuring the assess-ment and remediation procedures to reduce clinical judgment, although it would be undesirable to formalize to too great a degree. Like the country doctor versus modern medicine, special education in the next fifty years will move from clinical intuition to a more precise science of clinical in-struction based on diagnostic instruments which yield a profile of abilities and disabilities about a specific facet of behavior and which have incorpo-rated within them measures of a child's ability to learn samples or units of materials at each of the points on the profile. If psychoeducational tests had these two characteristics, they would accomplish essentially the same thing as does the diagnostic approach described above—only under more standardized conditions.

ITINERANT AND RESOURCE ROOM TEACHING. It is proposed that a second eche-lon of special educators be itinerant or resource teachers. One or more resource teachers might be available to each sizable school, while an itinerant teacher would serve two or more smaller schools. General edu-cators would refer their children with learning difficulties to these teachers. If possible, the clinical teacher would evolve an effective prescription for remediating the problem. If this is not possible, she would refer the child to the Special Education Diagnostic and Prescription Generating Center or to the more specialized prescriptive teacher who would study the child and work out an appropriate regimen of instruction for him. In either event, the key role of the resource room and itinerant clinical educators would be to develop instructional materials and lessons for implementing the prescription found effective for the child, and to consult and work with the other educators who serve the child. Thus, the job of special educators would be to work as members of the schools' instructional teams and to focus on children with mild to moderate school learning problems. Special educators would be available to all children in trouble (except the severely handicapped) regardless of whether they had, in the past, been labeled educable mentally retarded, minimally brain injured, educationally handi-capped, or emotionally disturbed. Children would be regrouped con-tinually throughout the school day. For specific help these children who had a learning problem might need to work with the itinerant or resource room special educator. But, for the remainder of the day, the special educator would probably be more effective in developing specific exercises which could be taught by others in consultation with her. Thus, the special educator would begin to function as a part of, and not apart from, general education. Clearly this proposed approach recognizes that all children have assets and deficits, not all of which are permanent. When a child was having trouble in one or more areas of learning, special educators would be available to devise a successful teaching approach for him and to tutor him when necessary. Perhaps as many as 20 to 35 percent of our present special educators are or could be prepared for this vital role.

TWO OTHER OBSERVATIONS. First, it is recognized that some of today's special educators—especially of the educable mentally retarded—are not prepared to serve the functions discussed. These teachers would need to either withdraw from special education or develop the needed competencies. Assuming an open door policy and playing the role of the expert educational diagnostician and the prescriptive and clinical educator would place us in the limelight. Only the best will succeed. But surely this is a responsibility we will not shirk. Our avowed *raison d'etre* has been to provide special education for children unable to make adequate progress in the regular grades. More would be lost than gained by assigning less than master teachers from self contained classes to the diagnostic and clinical educator roles. Ainsworth (1959) has already compared the relative effectiveness of the special class versus itinerant special educators of the retarded and found that neither group accomplished much in pupil progress. A virtue of these new roles for special education is that they are high status positions which should appeal to the best and therefore enhance the recruitment of master regular teachers who should be outstanding in these positions after having obtained specialized graduate training in behavior shaping, psychoeducational diagnostics, remedial education, and so forth.

Second, if one accepts these procedures for special education, the need for disability labels is reduced. In their stead we may need to substitute labels which describe the educational intervention needed. We would thus talk of pupils who need special instruction in language or cognitive development, in sensory training, in personality development, in vocational training, and other areas. However, some labels may be needed for administrative reasons. If so, we need to find broad generic terms such as "school learning disorders."

New Curricular Approaches

Master teachers are at the heart of an effective school program for children with mild to moderate learning difficulties—master teachers skilled at educational diagnosis and creative in designing and carrying out interventions to remediate the problems that exist. But what should they teach? In my view, there has been too great an emphasis in special classes on practical arts and practical academics, to the exclusion of other ingredients. Let us be honest with ourselves. Our courses of study have tended to be watered down regular curriculum. If we are to move from the clinical stage to a science of instruction, we will need a rich array of validated prescriptive programs of instruction at our disposal. To assemble these programs will take time, talent, and money; teams of specialists including creative teachers, curriculum specialists, programers, and theoreticians will be needed to do the job.

What is proposed is a chain of Special Education Curriculum Development Centers across the nation. Perhaps these could best be affiliated with colleges and universities, but could also be attached to state and local school systems. For these centers to be successful, creative educators must be found. Only a few teachers are remarkably able to develop new materials. An analogy is that some people can play music adequately, if not brilliantly, but only a few people can compose it. Therefore, to move special education forward, some 15 to 20 percent of our most creative special educators need to be identified, freed from routine classroom instruction, and placed in a stimulating setting where they can be maximally productive in curriculum development. These creative teachers and their associates would concentrate on developing, field testing, and modifying programs of systematic sequences of exercises for developing specific facets of human endeavor. As never before, funds are now available from the US Office of Education under Titles III and VI of PL 89-10 to embark upon at least one such venture in each state. In fact, Title III was designed to support innovations in education and 15 percent of the funds were earmarked for special education. Furthermore, most of the money is now to be administered through state departments of education which could build these curriculum centers into their state plans.

The first step in establishing specialized programs of study would be to evolve conceptual models upon which to build our treatments. In this regard the creative teachers would need to join with the theoreticians, curriculum specialists, and other behavioral scientists. Even the identification of the broad areas will take time, effort, and thought. Each would require many subdivisions and extensive internal model building. A beginning taxonomy might include the following eight broad areas: (a) environmental modifications, (b) motor development, (c) sensory and perceptual training, (d) cognitive and language development including academic instruction, (e) speech and communication training, (f) connative (or personality) development, (g) social interaction training, and (h) vocational training. (Of course, under cognitive development alone we might evolve a model of intellect with some ninety plus facets such as that of Guilford [1967], and as many training programs.)

In the area of motor development we might, for example, involve creative special and physical educators, occupational and physical therapists, and experts in recreation and physical medicine, while in the area of language development a team of speech and hearing specialists, special educators, psychologists, linguists, and others would need to come together to evolve a conceptual model, to identify the parameters, and to develop the specialized programs of exercises. No attempt is made in this article to do more than provide an overview of the problem and the approach. Conceptualizing the specific working models would be the responsibility of cadres of experts in the various specialties.

ENVIRONMENTAL MODIFICATIONS. It would seem futile and rather unrealistic to believe we will be able to remediate the learning difficulties of children from ethnically and/or economically disadvantaged backgrounds when the schools are operating in a vacuum even though top flight special education instructional programs are used. Perhaps, if intensive around the clock and full calendar year instruction were provided beginning at the nursery school level, we might be able to counter appreciably the physiological weaknesses and inadequate home and community conditions of the child. However, the field of education would be enhanced in its chances of success if it became a part of a total ecological approach to improve the environments of these children. Thus special educators need to collaborate with others—social workers, public health officials, and other community specialists. Interventions in this category might include (a) foster home placement, (b) improved community conditions and out of school activities, (c) parent education, (d) public education, and (e) improved cultural exposures. For optimal pupil development, we should see that children are placed in a setting that is both supportive and stimulating. Therefore, we must participate in environmental manipulations and test their efficacy. We have made a slight beginning in measuring the effects of foster home placement and there is evidence that working with parents of the disadvantaged has paid off. The model cities programs would also seem to have promise. But much more human and financial effort must be invested in this area.

MOTOR DEVELOPMENT. Initial work has been done with psychomotor training programs by a number of persons including Delacato (1966), Oliver (1958), Cratty (1967), Lillie (1967), and others. But we still need sets of sequential daily activities built around an inclusive model. Under this category, we need to move from the early stages of psychomotor development to the development of fine and large movements required as vocational skills. Programs to develop improved motor skills are important for a variety of children with learning problems. In fact, one could argue that adequate psychomotor skills constitute the first link in the chain of learning.

SENSORY AND PERCEPTUAL TRAINING. Much of our early efforts in special education consisted of sensory and perceptual training applied to severe handicapping conditions such as blindness, deafness, and mental deficiency. Consequently, we have made a good beginning in outlining programs of instruction in the areas of auditory, visual, and tactual training. Now we must apply our emerging technology to work out the step by step sequence of activities needed for children with mild to moderate learning difficulties. In this regard, visual perceptual training has received growing emphasis, pioneered by Frostig (1964), but auditory perceptual training has been neglected. The latter is more important for school instruction than the visual channel. Much attention needs to be given to this second link in the chain of learning. Children with learning problems need to be systematically taught the perceptual processes: they need to be able to organize and convert bits of input from the various sense modalities into units of awareness which have meaning.

COGNITIVE AND LANGUAGE DEVELOPMENT INCLUDING ACADEMIC INSTRUCTION. This is the heart of special education for slow learning children. Our business is to facilitate their thinking processes. We should help them not only to acquire and store knowledge, but also to generate and evaluate it. Language development could largely be included under this caption— especially the integrative components—since there is much overlap between the development of oral language and verbal intelligence. However, much of receptive language training might be considered under sensory and perceptual training, while expressive language will be considered in the next topic.

A major fault of our present courses of study is failure to focus on the third link in the chain of learning—that of teaching our children systematically in the areas of cognitive development and concept formation. A major goal of our school program should be to increase the intellectual functioning of children we are now classifying as socioculturally retarded. For such children, perhaps as much as 25 percent of the school day in the early years should be devoted to this topic. Yet the author has not seen one curriculum guide for these children with a major emphasis on cognitive development—which is a sad state of affairs indeed!

Basic psychological research by Guilford (1959) has provided us with a useful model of intellect. However, little is yet known about the trainability of the various cognitive processes. Actually, Thurstone (1948) has contributed the one established set of materials for training primary mental abilities. Thus, much work lies ahead in developing programs of instruction for the training of intellect.

We are seeing more and more sets of programed materials in the academic areas, most of which have been designed for average children. The most exciting examples today are in the computer assisted instruction studies. Our major problem is to determine how these programed exercises need to be modified to be maximally effective for children with specific learning problems. Work will be especially needed in the classical areas of instruction including written language and mathematics. Hopefully, however, regular teachers will handle much of the instruction in science and social studies, while specialists would instruct in such areas as music and the fine arts. This will free special educators to focus on better ways of teaching the basic 3 Rs, especially written language.

SPEECH AND COMMUNICATION TRAINING. This area has received much attention, particularly from speech correctionists and teachers of the deaf. Corrective techniques for specific speech problems are probably more advanced than for any other area, yet essentially no carefully controlled research has been done on the efficacy of these programs. Speech correctionists have tended to be clinicians, not applied behavioral scientists. They often create the details of their corrective exercises while working with their clients in a one to one relationship. Thus, the programs have often been intuitive. Furthermore, public school speech therapists have been spread very thin, usually working with 75 to 100 children. Many have been convinced that only *they* could be effective in this work. But remarkable changes have recently occurred in the thinking of speech therapists; they are recognizing that total programs of oral language development go far beyond correcting articulation defects. Furthermore, some speech therapists believe they could be more productive in working with only the more severe speech handicaps and devoting much attention to the development and field testing of systematic exercises to stimulate overall language and to improve articulation, pitch, loudness, quality, duration, and other speech disorders of a mild to moderate nature. These exercises need to be programed to the point at which teachers, technicians, and perhaps teacher aides can use them. Goldman (1968) is now developing such a program of exercises to correct articulation defects. This seems to be a pioneering and heartening first step.

CONNATIVE (OR PERSONALITY) DEVELOPMENT. This emerging area requires careful attention. We must accept the position that much of a person's behavior is shaped by his environment. This applies to all aspects of human thought, including attitudes, beliefs, and mores. Research oriented clinical psychologists are providing useful information on motivation and personality development and before long we will see reports of research in shaping insights into self, the effects of others on self, and one's effects on others. It is not too early for teams of clinical psychologists, psychiatric social workers, creative special educators (especially for the so called emotionally disturbed), and others to begin developing programs of instruction in this complex field.

SOCIAL INTERACTION TRAINING. Again we have an emerging area which overlaps considerably with some of those already presented, particularly connative development. Special educators have long recognized that the ability of a handicapped individual to succeed in society depends, in large measure, on his skill to get along with his fellow man. Yet we have done little to develop his social living skills, a complex area of paramount importance. Training programs should be developed to facilitate development in this area of human behavior.

VOCATIONAL TRAINING. Closely tied to social interaction training is vocational training. Success on the job for persons that we have labeled educable mentally retarded has depended on good independent work habits, reliability, and social skills, rather than on academic skills. Consequently, early and continuing emphasis on developing these traits is necessary. In fact, it is likely to be even more important in the years ahead with fewer job opportunities and increasing family disintegration providing less shelter and support for the so called retarded. Therefore sophisticated programs of instruction are especially needed in this area. Even with our best efforts in this regard, it is likely that our pupils, upon reaching adolescence, will continue to need a variety of vocational services, including trade and technical schools, work study programs, and vocational training.

ANOTHER OBSERVATION. It seems to me to be a red herring to predict that special educators will use these hundreds of specialized instructional programs indiscriminately as cookbooks. Perhaps a few of the poor teachers will. But, the clinical teachers proposed in this article would be too sophisticated and competent to do this. They would use them as points of departure, modifying the lessons so that each child would make optimal progress. Therefore, it seems to me that this library of curriculum materials is necessary to move us from a clinical and intuitive approach to a more scientific basis for special education.

AN EPILOGUE

The conscience of special educators needs to rub up against morality. In large measure we have been at the mercy of the general education establishment in that we accept problem pupils who have been referred out of the regular grades. In this way, we contribute to the delinquency of the general educations since we remove the pupils that are problems for them and thus reduce their need to deal with individual differences. The *entente* of mutual delusion between general and special education that special class placement will be advantageous to slow learning children of poor parents can no longer be tolerated. We must face the reality—we are asked to take children others cannot teach, and a large percentage of these are from ethnically and/or economically disadvantaged backgrounds. Thus much of special education will continue to be a sham of dreams unless we immerse ourselves into the total environment of our children from inadequate homes and backgrounds and insist on a comprehensive ecological push—with a quality educational program as part of it. This is hardly compatible with our prevalent practice of expediency in which we employ many untrained and less than master teachers to increase the number of special day classes in response to the pressures of waiting lists. Because of these pressures from the school system, we have been guilty of fostering quantity with little regard for quality of special education instruction. Our first responsibility is to have an abiding commitment to the less fortunate children we aim to serve. Our honor, integrity, and honesty should no longer be subverted and rationalized by what we hope and may believe we are doing for these children—hopes and beliefs which have little basis in reality.

Embarking on an American Revolution in Special Education will require strength of purpose. It is recognized that the structure of most, if not all, school programs becomes self perpetuating. Teachers and state and local directors and supervisors of special education have much at stake in terms of their jobs, their security, and their programs which they have built up over the years. But can we keep our self respect and continue to increase the numbers of these self contained special classes for the educable mentally retarded which are of questionable value for many of the children they are intended to serve? As Ray Graham said in his last article in 1960: [p. 4.]

We can look at our accomplishments and be proud of the progress we have made; but satisfaction with the past does not assure progress in the future. New developments, ideas, and facts may show us that our past practices have become out-moded. A growing child cannot remain static— he either grows or dies. We cannot become satisfied with a job one-third done. We have a long way to go before we can rest assured that the desires of the parents and the educational needs of handicapped children are being fulfilled [p. 4].

REFERENCES

Ainsworth, S. H. *An exploratory study of educational, social and emotional factors in the education of mentally retarded children in Georgia public schools.* US Office of Education Cooperative Research Project Report No. 171(6470). Athens, Ga.: University of Georgia, 1959.

Bereiter, C., & Englemann, S. *Teaching disadvantaged children in the preschool.* Englewood Cliffs, N.J.: Prentice-Hall, 1966.

Bruner, J. S., Olver, R. R., & Greenfield, P. M. *Studies in cognitive growth.* New York: Wiley, 1967.

Coleman, J. S., et al. *Equality of educational opportunity.* Washington, D.C.: USGPO, 1966.

Cratty, P. J. *Developmental sequences of perceptual motor tasks.* Freeport, Long Island, N.Y.: Educational Activities, 1967.

Delacato, C. H. (Ed.) *Neurological organization and reading problems.* Springfield, Ill.: Charles C Thomas, 1966.

Feuerstein, R. *The Learning Potential Assessment Device* Jerusalem, Israel: Haddassa Wizo Canada Child Guidance Clinic and Research Unit, 1968.

Frostig, M., & Horne, D. *The Frostig program for the development of visual perception.* Chicago: Follett, 1964.

Graham, R. Special education for the sixties. *Illinois Educational Association Study Unit,* 1960, 23, 1–4.

Goffman, E. *Asylums: Essays on the social situation of mental patients and other inmates.* Garden City, N.Y.: Anchor, 1961.

Goldman, R. *The phonemic-visual-oral association technique for modifying articulation disorders in young children.* Nashville, Tenn.: Bill Wilkerson Hearing and Speech Center, 1968.

Guilford, J. P. *The nature of human intelligence.* New York: McGraw-Hill, 1967.

Hoelke, G. M. *Effectiveness of special class placement for educable mentally retarded children.* Lincoln, Neb.: University of Nebraska, 1966.

Hollingworth, L. S. *The psychology of subnormal children.* New York: MacMillan, 1923.

Johnson, G. O. Special education for mentally handicapped—a paradox. *Exceptional Children,* 1962, **19,** 62–69.

Kirk, S. A. Research in education. In H. A. Stevens & R. Heber (Eds.), *Mental retardation.* Chicago, Ill.: University of Chicago Press, 1964.

Kirk, S. A. *The diagnosis and remediation of psycholinguistic disabilities.* Urbana, Ill.: University of Illinois Press, 1966.

Lillie, D. L. The development of motor proficiency of educable mentally retarded children. *Education and Training of the Mentally Retarded,* 1967, **2,** 29–32.

Mackie, R. P. *Functional handicaps among school children due to cultural or economic deprivation.* Paper presented at the First Congress of the International Association for the Scientific Study of Mental Deficiency, Montpellier, France, September, 1967.

Meyerowitz, J. H. Family background of educable mentally retarded children. In H. Goldstein, J. W. Moss & L. J. Jordan. *The efficacy of special education training on the development of mentally retarded children.* Urbana, Ill.: University of Illinois Institute for Research on Exceptional Children, 1965. Pp. 152–182.

Meyerowitz, J. H. Peer groups and special classes. *Mental Retardation,* 1967, **5,** 23–26.

Oliver, J. N. The effects of physical conditioning exercises and activities on the mental characteristics of educationally sub-normal boys. *British Journal of Educational Psychology,* 1958, **28,** 155–165.

Passow, A. H. *A Summary of findings and recommendations of a study of the Washington, D.C. schools.* New York: Teachers College, Columbia University, 1967.

Rosenthal, R., & Jacobson, L. Teachers' expectancies: Determinants of pupils' IQ gains. *Psychological Reports,* 1966, **19,** 115–118.

Rubin, E. Z., Senison, C. B., & Betwee, M. C. *Emotionally handicapped children in the elementary school.* Detroit: Wayne State University Press, 1966

Smith, H. W., & Kennedy, W. A. Effects of three educational programs on mentally retarded children. *Perceptual and Motor Skills,* 1967, **24,** 174.

Thurstone, T. G. *Learning to think series.* Chicago, Ill.: Science Research Associates, 1948.

Wright, Judge J. S. *Hobson vs. Hansen: U.S. Court of Appeals decision on the District of Columbia's track system. Civil Action No. 82–66.* Washington, D.C.: US Court of Appeals, 1967.

Special Education for the Mildly Retarded: Servant or Savant

DONALD L. MACMILLAN

Seldom, if ever, has one single article had an impact on the field of special education comparable to that of Professor Dunn's (1968) regarding special education for minority children labelled as educable mentally retarded (EMR). The debate stimulated by that article has been extensive. Some school districts have whole-heartedly endorsed what they perceive Dunn's position to be, and have moved toward total integration of EMR-labelled children into regular classes. In addition, state departments of education have made policy decision designed to prevent misidentification of minority children as EMR. Clearly, Dunn has been an important influence in reversing a trend toward the proliferation of self-contained special classes for the EMR, which he sensed and spoke out against.

For years preceding the publication of the Dunn article, concern was expressed by many special educators as well as increasingly militant minority groups about the overrepresentation of minority children in special classes for the EMR. However, it took someone of Dunn's stature to stimulate the field into action by recommending a plan for change in an attempt to ameliorate this social problem.

I do not agree with some professionals who apparently interpret Dunn's article as "proof" that EMR classes should be totally abolished—though admittedly nowhere does Dunn himself call for such a move. Certainly, some special educators have seen EMR classes as *the* way to educate children with IQs from 50–70, and this restrictive view has proven stifling (see Macmillan, 1969). Nevertheless, total abolition of these classes seems to me premature. For these reasons it seems time for the issues regarding special class placement to be clarified and for someone to re-evaluate the evidence on which the case was made by Dunn (1968).

In stating the reasons for a change, Professor Dunn presents *evidence* which supports his contention that special classes have proven a disservice to the mildly retarded. In the course of this paper, that evidence will be re-examined and other evidence, of which Dr. Dunn was either unaware

* From *Focus On Exceptional Children* (in press). Reprinted by permission of the author and the publisher.

or chose to ignore will be presented. Hopefully, the discussion can bring to light the complexity of the issues presented which must be considered in deciding the most efficacious administrative arrangement for a particular child. Finally, an attempt is made to restate the problem as I see it and make recommendations regarding it. Specifically, the issues raised, and the bases on which my case is built, are:

1) Though self-contained classes fail to promote academic and personal growth of the dimensions originally expected, such classes are still useful for some low IQ children.

2) The method of identifying children as mentally retarded described by Dunn (1968), reflects a strict psychometric definition of mental retardation and thereby ignores the consensus AAMD definition.

3) Evidence on the effects of placement and labelling is sorely lacking; hence these effects must not be considered as a sole *cause* of achievement and adjustment problems.

4) Adjustments in the environment which are strictly cognitive in nature are unlikely to aid learning in low-IQ children whose problems are emotional or motivational—a description which probably fits many minority children of low IQ.

5) The real issue is not whether special classes or regular classes are better for the mildly retarded, but rather—the extent to which a wider range of individual differences can be accomodated in the regular class.

One point must be clarified before moving on. In no way am I arguing that homogeneous classes for children of IQs ranging between 50–70 or 75 are the best arrangement. Rather, on the basis of the evidence uncovered so far, I would contend that a self-contained special class may well be the best placement for certain low IQ children.

SELF-CONTAINED SPECIAL CLASSES

A given administrative arrangement is neither good nor bad. As Goldberg *et al.* (1961) pointed out with regard to the gifted, what really counts is what is done with the group once it is established. The argument applies equally well when applied to the lower end of the intellectual distribution; hence, poor implementation should not be interpreted to invalidate the administrative organization. Indeed, a debate over which administrative arrangement, special class or regular class, for low-IQ children categorically degenerates into an academic exercise with no meaning for the real world.

For any given case, the better placement depends on a whole host of variables unspecified in the question of the efficacy of special or regular classes for low IQ children. Among the questions which must be raised are the following: (a) How competent are the teachers in each setting for dealing with the specific characteristics of the child in question? (b) To what extent has the child developed prerequisite readiness skills in the regular class? (c) How does the child respond to the consequences likely to be used in the regular class? (d) What is the general level of functioning of other children in the regular class, or to what degree will that child deviate from the other children? (e) Does the regular class teacher have the time needed to accommodate this child? Therefore, what is needed is an interaction model which includes, at least:

ADMINISTRATIVE ARRANGEMENT × CHILD × TEACHER
                    ×   CHILDREN IN ALTERNATE PLACEMENTS

maybe the least important of which is the administrative arrangement.

EFFICACY STUDIES

As Dunn suggests (1968, p. 8), an examination of studies on the efficacy of special classes is in order. Such an examination should, however, begin with the methodology utilized, not with the results. With few exceptions (e.g., Goldstein, Moss, and Jordan, 1965) these studies could be described as poorly designed, replete with sampling biases which render the results uninterpretable. For example, in both the Cassidy and Stanton (1959) and Thurstone (1960) studies, the investigators failed to randomly assign subjects to the self-contained and regular class placements. Therefore, the finding that EMR children in the regular classes exceeded the EMR children in the self-contained classes on some achievement measures is difficult, if not impossible, to interpret. More specifically, were those EMR children allowed to remain in the regular class left there *because* they were, in fact, academically advanced by comparison?

At the same time, the means of assessing "adjustment" in these two studies are questionable. Cassidy and Stanton (1959) used teacher ratings as one measure, while the Thurstone (1960) study used a sociometric device. In the former case, the validity of the teachers' ratings is questionable due to variable frames of reference while the latter procedure makes the results difficult to compare, since acceptance within a special class is hardly comparable to acceptance in a class with higher ability children.

In the one study where EMR subjects were randomly assigned to the treatments (Goldstein, Moss, and Jordan, 1965), EMRs in the regular class were found to achieve significantly better in reading at the end of a two-year period. However, by the end of four years, the EMR children in the self-contained classes had caught up to the former group. Post hoc comparisons of low-IQ children within each group revealed this subsample achieved significantly better on certain achievement measures than did the low-IQ subsample placed in regular classes.

Hence, the best controlled of the studies concerned with efficacy of special classes does little to undermine Dunn's contention that special classes have failed to live up to original expectancies. Raised as an empirical question, the fact that such classes have not been found to result in superior achievement or adjustment *must not* be interpreted to mean that there are no differences in the two placements. In the cases where significantly superior performance was found for the regular class placement (Cassidy and Stanton, 1959; Thurstone, 1960), the sampling bias renders the results questionable.

Using different criteria (i.e., social competence and economic efficiency) than typical achievement and adjustment measures, Porter and Milazzo (1958) concluded that the post–school adjustment of children who had been enrolled in special classes was markedly superior to that of equally retarded children who had remained in regular classes. Again, the small sample size (twelve in each group) and the sampling procedures render definite conclusions hazardous.

While Dunn (1968) cites Kirk's (1964) review as supportive of his contention that retarded pupils make as much or more progress in regular grades as they do in special education, he fails to include Kirk's (1964) mention of the pitfalls inherent in the studies which deal with the special versus regular class debate:

1) Problems in sampling—taking *in situ* groups to compare.

2) No control over the length of time spent in special classes prior to the evaluation.

3) Lack of a delineation of a special class, the curriculum, or the teacher qualifications.

4) Measurement instruments used in the studies were often improvised, and therefore of questionable validity and reliability.

Kirk goes on to conclude that "until we obtain well-controlled studies of a longitudinal nature, our opinions about the benefits or detriments of special classes will remain partly in the realm of conjecture." (Kirk, 1964, p. 63)

The teacher variable has defied educational researchers in evaluating curricula and administrative arrangements since the beginning of educational research. Likewise, the failure to control this variable has plagued the attempts at evaluating special classes. Any particular low-IQ child placed with the "right" teacher, regardless of the administrative arrangement, is likely to benefit. Unfortunately the reverse is just as true. In a recent article, Davis (1970) argues that because of the demand for more and more teachers in classes for the mentally retarded, specified requirements for credentialling are frequently modified or postponed. While one *would not* consider being operated on by a surgeon operating on a "postponement of requirements" or being defended in a court of law by a lawyer operating on a "partial fulfillment of requirements," we seem satisfied to allow children identified as needing special teaching skills to learn under a teacher's direction whose preparation fails to meet *minimal* standards as set by a particular state. Is it any wonder, then, that the children assigned to such a setting have not progressed at a rate considered appropriate? To what extent are the "failures" of special classes attributable to the administrative arrangement, *per se,* and to what extent [are they] attributable to the teacher's inadequacies?

Related to the above discussion is the possibility that teachers of the mentally retarded enjoy little status in the schools. A study by Jones and

Gottfried (1966) had teachers rate the prestige of teachers of various exceptionalities (e.g., severely retarded, blind, gifted, orthopedically handicapped). They found that teachers of the EMR enjoy little status among colleagues and individuals in teacher training. The most dramatic finding, however, was that the teachers of the EMR rated themselves lower than they were rated by regular classroom teachers. Hence, not only are they assigned little prestige in the schools, but they appear to accept the lack of prestige as being justified. If the above findings are taken at face value they well might support Dunn; however, they may also reflect a phenomenon related to the *type* of teacher attracted to this phase of special education. If we attract those threatened by regular classes, or those who are not as capable, then the failure of special classes must not be interpreted as a failure of the administrative arrangement *per se*, but rather a failure of implementation. If we cannot determine how to individualize in a setting where there is one teacher for 15–18 students, are we ready to advise on how individualization can occur in a setting with 30 children and one teacher?

IDENTIFICATION PROCESS

On the point that numerous minority children are inappropriately labelled as EMR, I find myself in complete agreement with Professor Dunn. The stigma attached to this label very probably operates in direct opposition to the potential advantages accrued to reduced pupil/teacher ratio. Of course, special educators tend not to participate in the identification procedure often deferring judgment instead to the psychologist, psychometrist, or physician—and in most cases it is the latter upon whom the focus of this criticism should probably be directed.

The precise reason so much consideration went into the development of a flexible definition of mental retardation by the American Association on Mental Deficiency with the support of the National Institute of Mental Health was to deal with the borderline cases (Heber, 1959; revised, 1961). Severely and profoundly retarded individuals are identified with a minimum of difficulty, but borderline cases require careful attention. The definition agreed upon was, "Mental retardation refers to subaverage general intellectual functioning which originates during the developmental period and is associated with impairment in adaptive behavior." (Heber, 1961, p. 3).

Clearly, three specific criteria must be met before an individual is to be considered retarded: (1) IQ at least one standard deviation below the population mean, (2) mental retardation must occur prior to age 16, and (3) there must be evidence indicating impaired adjustment. The absence of any one of the three criteria should preclude placement in a special class. In practice, an intelligence test may be used on occasion to "justify the label 'mentally retarded'" (Dunn, 1968, p. 9); however, such a practice goes on in violation of criteria constituted to determine the presence of the condition or state labelled as mentally retarded.

Most professionals in the field of mental retardation feel somewhat uneasy about the reliance upon IQ in diagnosing retardation, particularly when dealing with borderline cases involving minority children from culturally different backgrounds. Clausen (1967) stated what many others have come to realize when attempting to use the AAMD classification system; namely, that there are few guidelines for determining an impairment in adaptive behavior. As a result, one makes extremely subjective evaluations of "social adequacy"; hence, clinicians ignore social adequacy and make the diagnosis on the basis of general intellectual functioning alone.

Alternative tacks may be taken in atempts to deal with the above problem. Clausen (1967) suggests the cut-off be dropped from one standard deviation below the mean (i.e., IQ = 84 or 85) to two standard deviations (i.e., IQ = 68–70) for evidence of subaverage intellectual functioning. He contends that below IQ = 70 or 75 individuals tend to show evidence of impaired social adaptive behavior caused by the low level of intellectual functioning (Clausen, 1967, p. 743). This would appear to be Dunn's preference. In his recent address, Dunn (1970) set the following IQ cut-offs for EMR placement: Anglo children—IQ = 70; American Indian children—IQ = 65; and inner-city black children—IQ = 55. Such limits are arbitrary and still reflect a psychometric definition of retardation of which Dunn (1968) was. critical.

Another approach would be to develop more objective means of assessing adaptive behavior which would be valid for use with borderline children of minority status. Such an attempt has been made by Mercer (1970) on an experimental basis. Her adaptive behavior scales and pluralistic norms provide an interesting and promising alternative to the strict psychometric classification system used by some.

It has been my experience that committees charged with considering EMR placement for a child approach the task with far more consideration than was implied by Dunn. Before such a conference is called, two bits of information are already available. First, the child's performance in the regular class has been poor enough, by comparison to the class as a whole, to attract the teacher's attention. Second, an individual intelligence test (usually supplemented by an entire battery of tests) has been administered on which the child scores below the district cut-off for EMR (usually IQ of 70).

At this point, I must agree that minority children are at a particular disadvantage when it comes to taking an intelligence test. Specifically, I suspect emotional and motivational variables prevent many such children from performing near the level of which they are capable. Riessman (1962) refers to this as the issue of the relation of examiner to examined. When examiners who differ from the children on the basis of social class and ethnic origin see the child briefly, it is difficult to establish the type of rapport conducive to best functioning of the child (Pasamanick and Knobloch, 1955). Performance, then, becomes difficult to evaluate since it could reflect the effects of poor relations between the examiner and the examined or a true measure of a child's abilities and achievements. Psychologists and psychometrists charged with evaluating children from different social and/or ethnic backgrounds might find the procedures reported in Hertzig et al. (1968) or the "optimizing" test conditions used by Zigler and Butterfield (1968) as helpful in countering this source of bias.

One may argue that tests of intelligence in use are culturally biased and thereby discriminate against the minority child. However, they are biased in the same direction as are the schools. As a result, these instruments do have rather good predictive validity on a short term basis. Taken in combination (regular class problems plus low IQ), these bits of evidence tells us that this child is likely to continue encountering problems if he is left in the regular classroom and presented with a standard curriculum. In other words, this child needs something "special." In this context, special education is not synonymous with self-contained class.

Among minority children meeting the two criteria specified above, there are at least several *types* of children.

1) Bilingual children (e.g., Chicano, Puerto Rican) in need of accommodation in the area of language, but who, genotypically speaking, are not defective or retarded.

2) Children from environments described as impoverished, in that they are lacking in materials or experiences considered beneficial to a child in adjusting to the school. Again, these children are not genotypically retarded.

3) Children who have developed failure sets—i.e., who have poor self-concepts and expect to fail before they even attempt a task.

4) Children of dull–normal ability with so much emotional overlay that their performance in school and on the intelligence test is depressed below the district cut-off.

5) Children who simply received a poor genetic pool or suffered prenatal, paranatal, or post-natal damage resulting in lowered cognitive capacity. These children are genotypically retarded.

Obviously, one could go on to specify greater numbers of types and any typology suffers from ignoring within-type variance. However, the point to be made concerns the nature of the "something special" needed by each of the types of minority children of low IQ described. In what kind of administrative arrangement can an individual child maximally benefit? In some cases (such as those described in 2 and 3 above) a resource specialist, as described by Dunn, may be sufficient. In others (such as 1, 4, and 5) a more intensive program may be needed. Some, in fact, may be best off in a self-contained special class! In none of the cases should the child be allowed to flounder in a regular class with no ancillary services.

Before leaving the topic of placement, I should mention the fact that many minority children whose IQs alone would warrant EMR placement remain in regular classes. In her demographic study, Mercer (in press) identified a group of children she labelled as *eligibles*—IQ below 75 but for a variety of reasons not placed in EMR classes. Most of these eligibles were functioning adequately in the regular program. It should be noted, however, that IQ alone did not appear to automatically result in EMR placement. Rather, other variables in addition to IQ were considered, and those with low IQ but adequate functioning remained in regular classes.

EFFECTS OF PLACEMENT

While my suspicion coincides with Dunn's with respect to the operation of a self-fulfilling prophecy, the dynamics underlying such a phenomenon are complex and far from fully understood. Could one extrapolate so easily from the Rosenthal and Jacobsen (1968) work as is implied by Dunn, the problem could be solved immediately by simply labelling the children under consideration "gifted" and thereby increase the teachers' expectancy for them to succeed. Secondly, the methodology underlying research on expectancy appears to affect the results considerably (see Barber and Silver, 1968a, 1968b; Rosenthal's response, 1968), and the hypothesis testing utilized is often inappropriate. Thirdly, using the Rosenthal and Jacobsen (1968) work to any extent as support for the operation of a self-fulfilling prophecy is hazardous in light of the telling critique of Thorndike (1968). In discussing the study he states:

> Alas, it is so defective technically that one can only regret that it ever got beyond the eyes of the original investigators! Though the volume may be an effective addition to educational propagandizing, it does nothing to raise the standards of educational research. (1968, p. 708)

In addition to the self-fulfilling prophecy, the principal objection raised by Dunn concerns the effects of labels upon the child. Granted, the label "mentally retarded" is not a badge of distinction. Neither, however, is being called "dummy" by higher ability children in the regular class typically prescribed for such children. Again, the effects of such a label are likely to be varied. In discussing the concern over the negative effects of such labels, Goldstein (1963) writes:

> There are those who wish to avoid the false positives inherent in early placement. They express the very reasonable fear that some children will be tainted unjustifiably with the label "retarded" if they are admitted to a special class at age six and later gain intellectually beyond the upper limits for such classes. However, we must not overlook the fact that such a child, through his adequate achievement in an appropriate regular class placement, stands an excellent chance of erasing the label.
> Instead of becoming preoccupied solely with labels and stigma, we might do well to look at the other side of the coin and ask what effects delayed placement has on the personality development of the child, the status he acquires among his regular class peers, and the pressures placed on the family. In all justice, we cannot close our eyes to the fact that the retarded child in the

regular class can be and frequently is labelled by his peers in much the same way as children in special classes. (1963, pp. 12, 52)

Some empirical evidence is available on the last point made by Goldstein. Johnson (1950) and Johnson and Kirk (1950) studied the social position of retarded children in regular classes. Unfortunately, the sampling problems discussed earlier regarding efficacy studies contaminates the findings of these studies as well. A type of psychological segregation was found typical for retardates in regular class placements in both studies. Johnson (1950) did, however, find approximately 5 percent of the retardates identified as "stars" on a sociometric device. It would be interesting to have descriptions of these children, in that it might indicate characteristics associated with high social standing in a regular class which could aid us in determining which EMR children might profit from such placements.

The evidence cited by Dunn as supportive of the negative impact of such labels warrants a closer look. Goffman (1961) does, in fact, discuss the stripping and mortification of the self—important concepts indeed in understanding the careers of inmates of institutions such as monasteries, military camps, prisons, and mental hospitals. Note, however, that the institutions mentioned do not even include institutions for the mentally retarded. Among the degrading experiences described (Goffman, 1957) are the removal of personal clothing and possessions, the restrictions on privacy, the reduction of independence of movement and decision, the restriction of communication with the outside world. These experiences are hardly typical in a special class for the EMR. Hence, extrapolation of findings from these settings to a setting (i.e., self-contained EMR class) which is not an institution and contains individuals who are labelled in an altogether different manner from the above groups seems risky at best. At the same time, Dunn failed to mention the work of Edgerton and Sabagh (1962) which did apply Goffman's constructs to patients in an institution for the mentally retarded. These investigators studied stripping and mortification as they applied to the careers of the mentally retarded and their findings were not consistent with those of Goffman (1961).

Edgerton and Sabagh (1962) suggest that the mortifications of the self may be fewer within institutions for the high-grade retardate than is the case on the outside. In fact, for the high-grade retardate there may be certain *aggrandizements* of the self accrued as a result of having low-grade retardates with which to compare himself for greater social success within the institution, the support and approval from ward personnel, and the opportunity for validation of his normality provided by his peers. As noted by Cromwell (1963), these arguments are reminiscent of the rationale presented by Johnson and Kirk (1950) with regard to the EMR in special classes. That is, the social position of the EMR is improved when placed in a setting where the mean IQ is reduced.

The effect a label, such as mentally retarded, has on a given child depends on a whole host of variables. To begin with it is necessary to examine his pre-identification career. To what extent has the child been labelled "dumb" or "stupid" by peers or others (e.g., parents, teachers, and other adults)? To what extent has he been isolated or rejected socially in the regular class and in other social situations? Answers to these questions provide clues to the extent to which the self has suffered mortifications *before* he has been formally labelled and placed.

Secondly, one must assess whether or not the child accepts or rejects these external evaluations. If he rejects them, he is also likely to reject the "mentally retarded" label when the educators try to attach that to him. Edgerton and Sabagh (1962) describe children coming from minority families of low socioeconomic status as follows:

> This nonacceptance may have been facilitated by several circumstances. For instance, the entire family of the retarded person may have been rejected and mortified by the community at large and feel the need to protect its members against the onslaught of "authorities." Many of the mentally retarded come from families of low ethnic or socioeconomic status, and the family members may have had humiliating experiences with law enforcement or welfare agencies. Such a family will protect its members against those who 'accuse' them of mental retardation, and may not even believe that the accused actually is retarded, since his intellectual level may not be much below that of his relatives. To them, this may simply be another instance of discrimination against the whole family. (1962, pp. 265–266)

In such an instance, that child may be immunized against mortifications of the self, in which case the label may have far less effect than would be the case where the child accepts the label as accurate.

Once a child is identified, labelled, and placed in a special class, it would again be helpful to understand whether he accepts the label as accurate or whether he denies the accuracy of such a label. Should a child reject the label and find himself in a class with children of clearly inferior status, he is able to derive certain aggrandizements by means of comparison. Hence, he renews his attempt to define the self as adequate and rejects those things that challenge such a positive self perception. It may be that for some low IQ children the special class provides a haven which supports his denial of retardation, whereas a regular class would confront him with evidence and confirmation of his retardation in that his peers would be clearly superior academically. Such a situation would confirm the accuracy of such derogatory labels and disarm the child of his defense mechanisms.

Meyerowitz (1962, 1967) did study the effects of placement on personality characteristics of the mentally retarded, and it was done within the context of a study in which the subjects were randomly assigned to classes (i.e., Goldstein, Moss, and Jordan, 1965). He did find more self-derogation in children placed in special classes; however, the findings are based on an instrument (Illinois Index of Self Derogation) of unknown validity and reliability.

In conclusion, we do not yet understand the effects of placement on personality. On the one hand we find evidence (Meyerowitz, 1962) indicating that the child suffers in a special class, while on the other the evidence indicates that he suffers in a regular class (Johnson, 1950; Johnson and Kirk, 1950). In other words according to the evidence the child can't win—but all of the evidence is of questionable validity in terms of sampling bias, lack of control of pre-placement experience, and the questionable nature of the criterion instruments.

COGNITIVE ADJUSTMENTS

Any discussion of grouping, of which special classes are one form, must ultimately consider the flexibility, or inflexibility, of a particular grouping arrangement. Special classes for low IQ children came to be considered *the best way* to educate such children. Paradoxically, a field committed to individual differences appears to have assumed a homogeneity within the group labelled "mental retarded." Despite the failure of evidence to conclusively support the special class arrangement, children achieving IQs in the EMR range have been placed in such classes and taught "the EMR curriculum," since it was assumed that they share common characteristics. About the only characteristic on which there is any commonality is on IQ (see Berkson, 1966), while on virtually every other characteristic there is as great, if not greater, intragroup variability as among nonretarded children. Yet the adaptations which occurred have been principally cognitive adaptations of the environment.

In an earlier article, MacMillan (in press) argued that attempts to adapt the environment in special classes for low IQ children have been basically cognitive adaptations. It is as if the line of reasoning went as follows: Since these children are *mentally* retarded, remediation must be designed that will ameliorate their *mental* deficits. Yet the literature abounds with evidence which indicates that for a high proportion of low socioeconomic status, low IQ children, the problems in learning (or more accurately performance) originate in the *motivational* sphere rather than in the *cognitive* sphere (see Zigler and Butterfield, 1968; MacMillan, in press). Hence, one of the reasons special classes have failed to achieve the degree of success hoped for may lie in the fact that these environments have tried to treat problems originating in the motivational sphere by apapting the environment to treat cognitive deficits. Such a lack of balanced emphasis would seem to doom a program to failure.

Zigler (1966) has summarized extensive evidence which indicates that motivational and emotional variables depress the performance of retardates below the level indicated on the basis of their cognitive development. In his American Educational Research Association address (Zigler, 1968), many of the findings with institutionalized patients were generalized to disadvantaged children. While space does not permit a comprehensive review of motivationally-related variables which probably effect academic performance (see MacMillan, in press), three variables have been selected in order to show how such phenomena depress performance levels of disadvantaged children below what would be expected. The three variables are: expectancy for failure, positive and negative reaction tendencies, and outerdirectedness.

Expectancy of failure

As a result of personal academic failure and social "histories of failure" many children develop problem-solving approaches characterized by the primary motivation to avoid failure rather than to achieve success. Failure occurs so often in their life space that such children approach a new task with an expectancy to fail before they even attempt the task (MacMillan and Keogh, in press). The development of a failure set often results in a lowered level of aspiration, which prevents the child from attempting tasks slightly beyond their present level of achievement.

Clearly, teachers must reverse this failure set if the child is to progress at the rate of which he is capable. Teachers cannot allow the child to avoid tasks which are slightly beyond him; yet, at the same time must protect the child from experiencing unnecessary additional failure. Techniques such as prompting, as opposed to confirmation, may provide a means to guarantee success while still "challenging" him with tasks which are not trivial and for which successful completion represents mastery.

Positive and Negative Reaction Tendencies

Zigler (1966) labelled the desire to interact with an approving adult as the "positive reaction tendency," and the wariness of adults as the "negative reaction tendency." Children who have experienced social deprivation desire to interact with an approving adult and at the same time are hesitant to do so due to their many negative encounters with adults (e.g., teachers). These two phenomena are thought to be positively related to the amount of social deprivation experienced and the amount of negative interaction with adults. In describing the operation of these two variables with disadvantaged children, Zigler writes:

> Children who do not receive enough affection and attention from the important adults in their life space, suffer in later years from an atypically high need for attention and affection. We find that such children, when faced with cognitive tasks, are not particularly motivated to solve the intellectual problems confronting them. Rather, those children employ their interactions with adults to satisfy their hunger for attention, affection, and yes, as unscientific as it may be, their need for love. (Zigler, 1968, p. 21)

As the child expends energy protecting the self, less energy is available for solving cognitive or academic tasks. Hence, the teacher must cope with these motivational variables before the child can devote his energies toward the solution of academic tasks.

Related to the above discussion is the child's reinforcer hierarchy; a construct unique for each individual. Zigler (1968) contends that being correct is not as high on the hierarchy for disadvantaged and retarded children as it is on the hierarchy of a middle-class nonretarded child. Therefore, one cannot assume that lower-class EMRs are putting forth a maximum effort in order to be correct. In fact, there is evidence to the effect that such children perform significantly better under extrinsic reward conditions than under intrinsic reward conditions (Keogh and MacMillan, in press; Terrell, Durkin, and Wiesley, 1959). Hence, it is essential that incentives be found on an individual basis which serve as reinforcers and which do result in maximum effort on the part of the child.

Outerdirectedness

Repeated failure can also result in a problem-solving style characterized as outerdirected. Zigler described it as follows: ". . . the retarded child comes to distrust his own solutions to problems and therefore seeks guides to action in the immediate environment" (1966, p. 99). As a result, the child comes to over-rely on external cues; a tendency which runs counter to a normal developmental trend in which children become more inner-directed as cognitive development releases the child from his dependence on external cues.

MacMillan (in press) describes and suggests techniques for dealing with children exhibiting these motivational characteristics. As Dunn (1968) describes the role of the resource teacher, the adaptations of the environment are still primarily cognitive in nature. As such, the resource teacher arrangement for serving those low IQ children whose performance deficits originate in the motivational sphere would seem as inappropriate as have those self-contained classes wherein the environmental adaptation have been cognitive in nature. Regardless of the administrative arrangement into which these children are placed, such children, in substantial numbers, are likely to manifest a high expectancy for failure, positive and negative reaction tendencies, and outer-directedness. Unless these motivational variables are dealt with by teachers, children of this type are unlikely to succeed in an integrated situation to any greater extent than they have in the special class.

RESTATEMENT OF THE PROBLEM

Special educators must not allow the present issues to become one of special classes versus regular class placement lest they find themselves in a quagmire analogous to that which resulted from the nature–nurture debates over intelligence. Yet, that is precisely what seems to be developing; polarization in which one group condemns special classes while others feel compelled to defend them. Implicit in the title of Dunn's (1968) article is the notion that special education and self-contained classes are synonymous; a notion which must be rejected.

The larger issue, and one which if debated and researched could prove fruitful is: *To what extent, and under what circumstances, can a wider range of individual differences be accommodated in the regular class than is presently the case?*

Attempts to answer this question would, first of all, have to determine the extent to which regular class teachers are accommodating the range of individual differences represented in their classes at present. Despite the new developments cited by Dunn, the evidence indicates that regular class teachers are unable to cope with the range of abilities they are presently faced with, hence the introduction of children who deviate more markedly would seem inadvisable. While the list of characteristics (i.e., individual differences) related to success in school is long (e.g., achievement, behavior, language abilities, motivational characteristics), the IQ will be used for illustrative purposes, because it is the one common variable on which EMR children differ from *most* children in the regular classes.

■ *FIGURE 1*

TMR Class	EMR Class	Regular Class	Gifted Class

IQ = 25	IQ = 50	IQ = 75	IQ = 100	IQ = 125	IQ = 150

At present, a regular class typically contains children with IQs between 75 and 125. Those children whose IQs fall below 75 or above 125 or 130 are thought to require "special" adaptations in order that they can maximally benefit from the educational experience. After all, that's virtually the definition of the exceptional child. Now the question becomes, how can we modify the regular class in such a way as to enable the child with IQ below 75 to benefit maximally from that setting?

Hopefully, in attempts to modify the regular class in order to accommodate those children with IQ below 75, a variety of educational models will be developed, implemented, and evaluated. Dunn (1968) outlines one such model in his article; that is, the resource teacher to supplement the regular teacher. This model must not, however, come to be accepted as *the best* way to educate low IQ children any more than the self-contained class has in the past been thought to be *the best* way. There should not be a proliferation of resource teachers, but rather a proliferation of different models all designed to provide for the accommodation of a wider range of individual differences in the regular class.

No one to date has advocated the integration of TMR children into regular classes. Obviously, they deviate too markedly on too many variables to make that arrangement feasible. So, however, will many EMR children; among their number will be some borderline cases of minority status. In the immediate future, the removal of large numbers of EMRs from special classes and replacement into regular classes would seem inadvisable in that the regular classes do not appear capable of handling them. For the time being, then, it seems desirable to focus our energies and resources on three fronts:

1) *Preventative Programs.* Rather than constantly focusing our resources on the remediation of problems once they exist, we might focus on the prediction and prevention of learning problems. For instance, one might look to the possibility that certain learning problems occur because of the unfortunate environmental demands which the student cannot meet. One might be able to identify certain skills (e.g., high verbal ability, docile classroom behavior) which are essential if a child is to be successful in a given teacher's class. If a child does not possess these skills, he becomes a likely candidate for failure in that teacher's class. Hence, it may be possible to prevent failure (and subsequent EMR referral) for some children by matching their abilities with a teacher in whose class these abilities enhance the possibility for success.

2) *Transitional Programs.* Assuming that the misidentified children in special classes for the EMR can be identified, the next concern is how does one enable them to move back into the regular program. Clearly, if such children are thrust back unaided, the likelihood for success is minimal. Even though such children may warrant reassignment on the basis of IQ and social adjustment, most curricula for EMR classes lag behind in the presentation of tool subjects. Therefore, intensive acceleration in tool subjects is essential if these children are to be placed in regular classes with their peers. How can transition be facilitated? A variety of transitional programs should be designed, implemented, and evaluated in attempts to answer the above question.

3) *Model Regular Programs.* At present, regular class teachers are unable to cope with the range of individual differences they find in their classes. Therefore, without rather radical modifications in the classroom organization and the development of teacher competences not presently possessed, the feasibility of inserting children who deviate more markedly is questionable. The resource specialist described by Dunn (1968) may provide one model. Competence based models, in which skills teachers must possess are specified, must be developed and evaluated. Subsequently, regular class teachers are going to have to be retrained or replaced. The former alternative will require inservice training of teachers, and this will require follow-up procedures to insure the competencies taught are being developed and employed.

The innovations mentioned above will require development of many educational models, implementation of these models, and their evaluation. This means cooperation between researchers and school personnel. Without such cooperation, the results of such studies are likely to be invalidated by the lack of controls described earlier with regard to the special versus regular class studies. Unless the quality of the research is high, it will not provide us with the necessary information on which we must make educational decisions regarding children. School personnel will have to endure some inconveniences in order that variables known to affect dependent measures can be controlled (e.g., sampling, teacher variable). Conversely, researchers must involve school personnel from the earliest stages in order that they can provide input on concerns of teachers and constraints operating in the school setting. By working in concert, researchers might control independent variables sufficiently to make for tight research, and at the same time research questions that will be seen as important by public school personnel.

REFERENCES

Barber, T. X. and M. J. Silver, "Fact, fiction, and the experimenter bias effect," *Psychological Bulletin Monograph* (1968), 70, 1–29 (No. 6, pt. 2).

Barber, T. X. and M. J. Silver, "Pitfalls in data analysis and interpretation: A reply to Rosenthal," *Psychological Bulletin Monograph* (1968), 70, 48–62.

Berkson, G. "When exceptions obscure the rule," *Mental Retardation* (1966), 24–27.

Cassidy, V. and J. Stanton, "An investigation of factors in the educational placement of mentally retarded children: A study of differences between children in special and regular classes in Ohio," U.S. Office of Educational Cooperative Research Programs, Project No. 043. Columbus, Ohio: Ohio State University, 1959.

Clausen, J., "Mental deficiency: Development of a concept," *American Journal of Mental Deficiency* (1967), 71, 727–745.

Cromwell, R. L., "A social learning approach to mental retardation," in N. R. Ellis (ed.), *Handbook of mental deficiency*. New York: McGraw-Hill (1963), 41–91.

Davis, F. R., "Demand-degradable teacher standards: Expediency and professional thantos," *Mental Retardation* (1970), 8, 37–40.

Dunn, L. M. "Special education for the mildly retarded—Is much of it justifiable?" *Exceptional Children* (1968), 5–22.

Dunn, L. M., "The 70's: A decade of restitution from special miseducation for the retarded," AAMD Region II Annual Fall Conference, Los Angeles, California, Nov. 14, 1970.

Edgerton, R. B. and G. Sabagh, "From mortification to aggrandizement: Changing self-conceptions in the careers of the mentally retarded," *Psychiatry* (1962), 25, 263–272.

Goffman, E., "Characteristics of total institutions," *Symposium on Preventative and Social Psychiatry*. Washington, D.C.: U.S. Government Printing Office, 1957.

Goffman, E., *Asylums: Essays on the social situation of mental patients and other inmates*. Garden City, N.Y.: Anchor, 1961.

Goldberg, M., J. Justman, A. H. Parson, and J. Hage, "The effects of ability grouping: A comparative study of broad, medium, and narrow-range classes in the elementary school," Horace-Mann-Lincoln Inst. Interim Report. New York: Teachers College, Columbia University, 1961.

Goldstein, H., "Issues in the education of the educable mentally retarded," *Mental Retardation* (1963), 1, 10–12, 52–53.

Goldstein, H., J. W. Moss, and L. J. Jordan, "The efficacy of special class training on the development of mentally retarded children," U.S. Department of Health, Education and Welfare, Office of Education, Cooperative Research Project No. 619, Urbana, Ill.: Institute for Research on Exceptional Children, University of Illinois, 1965.

Herber, R. F., "A manual on terminology and classification in mental retardation," *American Journal of Mental Deficiency*, Monograph Supplement (Rev. ed. 1961), *64*, 1959.

Hertzig, M. E., H. G. Birch, A. Thomas and O. A. Mendez, "Class and ethnic differences in the responsiveness of preschool children to cognitive demands," *Monographs of the Society for Research in Child Development* (1968), *33*, No. 1, Serial No. 117.

Johnson, G. O., "A study of the social position of mentally handicapped children in regular grades," *American Journal of Mental Deficiency* (1950), *55*, 60–89.

Johnson, G. O. and S. A. Kirk, "Are mentally handicapped children segregated in the regular grades?" *Journal of Exceptional Children* (1950), *17*, 65–68.

Jones, R. L. and N. W. Gottfried, "The prestige of special education teaching," *Exceptional Children* (1966), *32*, 465–468.

Keogh, B. K. and D. L. MacMillan, "Effects of motivational and presentation conditions on digit recall of children of differing socioeconomic, racial, and intelligence groups," *American Educational Research Journal* (in press).

Kirk, S. A., "Research in education," in H. A. Stevens and R. Heber (eds.), *Mental retardation: A review of research*. Chicago: The University of Chicago Press (1964), 57–99.

MacMillan, D. L., "An examination of developmental assumptions underlying special classes for educable retardates," *California Journal for Instructional Improvement* (1969), *12*, 165–173.

MacMillan, D. L., "The problem of motivation in the education of the mentally retarded," *Exceptional Children* (in press).

MacMillan, D. L. and B. K. Keogh, "Normal and retarded children's expectancy for failure," *Developmental Psychology* (in press).

Mercer, J. R., "The meaning of mental retardation," in R. Koch and J. Dobson (eds.), *The Mentally retarded living in the community*. Seattle, Wash.: Special Child Publishing Company, 1970.

Meyerowitz, J. H., "Peer groups and special classes," *Mental Retardation* (1967), *5*, 23–26.

Meyerowitz, J. H., "Self derogation in young retardates and special class placement," *Child Development* (1962), *33*, 443–451.

Pasamanick, B. and H. Knobloch, "Early language behavior in Negro children and the testing of intelligence," *Journal of Abnormal and Social Psychology* (1955), *50*, 401–402.

Porter, R. B. and T. C. Milazzo, "A comparison of mentally retarded adults who attended a special class with those who attended regular school classes," *Exceptional Children* (1958), *24*, 410–412.

Riessman, F., *The culturally deprived child*. New York: Harper, 1962.

Rosenthal, R., "Experimenter expectancy and the reassuring nature of the null hypothesis decision procedure," *Psychological Bulletin Monograph* (1968), *70*, 30–47.

Rosenthal, R. and L. Jacobsen, *Pygmalion in the classroom*. New York: Holt, Rinehart and Winston, 1968.

Terrell, G., Jr., Durkin and M. Wiesley, "Social class and the nature of the incentive in discrimination learning," *Journal of Abnormal and Social Psychology* (1959), *59*, 270–272.

Thorndike, R. L., "Review of Rosenthal, R. and L. Jacobsen, *Pygmalion in the classroom*," *American Educational Research Journal* (1968), *5*, 708–711.

Thurstone, T. G., "An evaluation of educating mentally handicapped children in special classes and in regular grades," U.S. Office of Education Cooperative Research Program, Project No. OE-SAE-6452. Chapel Hill, N.C.: University of North Carolina, 1960.

Zigler, E., "Research on personality structure in the retardate," in N. R. Ellis (ed.), *International review of research in mental retardation*, Vol. I. New York: Academic Press, 1966.

Zigler, E. and E. Butterfield, "Motivational Aspects of Changes in IQ Test Performance of Culturally Deprived Nursery School Children," *Child Development* (1968), 39, 1–14.

INDEX

ABCDEFGHIJ- KP -7654321